Napoleon's Russian Campaign

Napoleon's Russian Campaign
The Invasion, Battles and Retreat
by an Aide-de-Camp on
the Emperor's Staff

Both Volumes in a
Single Edition

Philippe Henri de Segur

*Napoleon's Russian Campaign: the Invasion, Battles and Retreat
by an Aide-de-Camp on the Emperor's Staff
Both Volumes in a Single Edition*
by Philippe Henri de Segur

Published by Leonaur Ltd in 2007

Originally published 1825 under the title:

*History of the Expedition to Russia Undertaken by
the Emperor Napoleon in the Year 1812*

Text in this form and material original to this edition
copyright © 2007 Leonaur Ltd

ISBN: 978-1-84677-340-2 (hardcover)
ISBN: 978-1-84677-339-6 (softcover)

http://www.leonaur.com

Publisher's Notes

In the interests of authenticity, the spellings, grammar and place names
used have been retained from the original edition.

The opinions expressed in this book are those of the author
and are not necessarily those of the publisher.

Contents

To the Veterans of the Grand Army	9
Napoleon Turns to Russia	11
Prussia	14
Turkey	21
Sweden	29
Opposition to Napoleon's Plans	38
Support from Poniatowski	43
Josephine	50
The Peninsula	55
Talleyrand	58
A Gathering of Princes	62
Davoust	69
The Russian Frontier	74
Five Armies	80
Crossing the Niemen	84
Lithuania	90
The Centre Column	97
Wilna	101
Bagration	106
Murat Charges	112
Lancers!	119
The Düna	125
The Generals	132
Defeat at Inkowo	139
Consolation	143
Krasnoë	146

Smolensk	149
Smolensk Occupied	154
Reconnoissance	158
The Army Sickens	163
The Battle of Valoutina	167
The Russian People	173
Petersburgh Rejected	178
Polotsk	181
Provisions	187
Murat & Davoust	191
Gjatz	196
Kutusoff	200
Impending Battle	203
Napoleon's Strategy	208
Orders	212
We Have Them at Last!	216
The Battle of Borodino	220
Exhaustion	223
Caulaincourt	228
The Imperfect Victory	233
The Russians Retreat	238
Moscow	243
The City Abandoned	248
Fili	254
Moscow Entered	259
The Kremlin	263
Fire!	266
Napoleon Leaves Moscow	272
Moscow Destroyed	276
'I Must Have Peace'	281
Cossacks	288

Stay or Go?	294
The Retreat Begins	301
Malo-Yaroslawetz	304
The Emperor Draws His Sword	310
The Road to Kalouga	314
Wilson—the Englishman	317
A Land in Flames	322
The Field of Borodino Again	327
Burning Wagons	330
Wiazma	333
Hard Pressed	336
The Snow Falls	340
Ney at Bay	344
Disaster at the Wop	348
No Respite in Smolensk	353
Saint Cyr	358
Winter	363
The Road to Europe Closed	371
Deception	375
Stachowa	380
Minsk Falls	387
The Berezina	392
The Bravest of the Brave	398
'I Have Saved My Eagles'	405
The Dnieper	410
Towards the Berezina	415
The Crossing Opposed	419
The Bridge	422
The Emperor Crosses the River	425
Errors!	428
A Division Surrenders	431

Russia Attacks	434
Carnage in the River	438
Brilowa	442
Napoleon Leaves the Army	445
The Weather Worsens	448
Murat Takes Command	451
Every Man for Himself	454
The Last Days of the Grand Army	459
Wilna!	464
The Rear Guard	470
Konigsberg	475
Riga	478
Macdonald	481
The Russian Desert	484
The Defection of Allies	488
The Austrians	491
The Vistula	494
Conclusion	497

To the Veterans of the Grand Army

Comrades,

I have undertaken the task of tracing the History of the Grand Army and its Leader during the year 1812. I address it to such of you as the ices of the North have disarmed, and who can no longer serve their country, but by the recollections of their misfortunes and their glory. Stopped short in your noble career, your existence is much more in the past than in the present; but when the recollections are so great, it is allowable to live solely on them. I am not afraid, therefore, of troubling that repose which you have so dearly purchased, by placing before you the most fatal of your deeds of arms. Who is there of us but knows, that from the depth of his obscurity the looks of the fallen man are involuntarily directed towards the splendour of his past existence—even when its light illuminates the shoal on which the bark of his fortune struck, and when it displays the fragments of the greatest of shipwrecks?

****

For myself, I will own, that an irresistible feeling carries me back incessantly to that disastrous epoch of our public and private calamities. My memory feels a sort of melancholy pleasure in contemplating and renewing the painful traces which so many horrors have left in it. Is the soul, also, proud of her deep and numerous wounds? Does she delight in displaying them? Are they a property of which she has reason to be proud? Is it rather, that after the desire of knowing them, her first wish is to impart her sensations? To feel, and to excite feeling, are not these the most powerful springs of our soul?

****

But in short, whatever may be the cause of the sentiment which actuates me, I have yielded to the desire of retracing the various sensations which I experienced during that fatal war. I have employed my leisure hours in separating, arranging, and combining with method my scattered and confused recollections. Comrades! I also invoke yours! Suffer not such great remembrances, which have been so dearly purchased, to be lost; for us they are the only property which the past leaves to the future. Single, against so many enemies, ye fell with greater glory than they rose. Learn, then, that there was no shame in being vanquished! Raise once more those noble fronts, which have been furrowed with all the thunders of Europe! Cast not down those eyes, which have seen so many subject capitals, so many vanquished kings! Fortune, doubtless, owed you a more glorious repose; but, such as it is, it depends on yourselves to make a noble use of it. Let history inscribe your recollections. The solitude and silence of misfortune are propitious to her labours; and let truth, which is always present in the long nights of adversity, at last enlighten labours that may not prove unproductive.

As for me, I will avail myself of the privilege, sometimes painful, sometimes glorious, of telling what I have seen, and of retracing, perhaps with too scrupulous attention, its most minute details; feeling that nothing was too minute in that prodigious Genius and those gigantic feats, without which we should never have known the extent to which human strength, glory, and misfortune, may be carried.

Chapter 1

Napoleon Turns to Russia

Ever since 1807, when the space between the Rhine and the Niemen had been overrun, the two great empires of which these rivers were the boundaries had become rivals. By his concessions at Tilsit, at the expense of Prussia, Sweden, and Turkey, Napoleon had only satisfied Alexander. That treaty was the result of the defeat of Russia, and the date of her submission to the continental system. Among the Russians, it was regarded by some as attacking their honour; and by all it was felt to be ruinous to their interests.

By the continental system Napoleon had declared eternal war against the English; to that system he attached his honour, his political existence, and that of the nation under his sway. That system banished from the Continent all merchandise which was English, or had paid duty in any shape to England. He could not succeed in establishing it but by the unanimous consent of the continental nations, and that consent could not be hoped for but under a single and universal dominion.

France had besides alienated the nations of Europe from her by her conquests, and the monarchs by her revolution and her new dynasty. Henceforward she could no longer look forward to have either friends or rivals, but merely subjects; for the first would have been false, and the second implacable: it followed that all must be subject to her, or she to all.

With feelings of this kind, her leader, influenced by his position, and urged on by his enterprising character, filled his imagination with the vast project of becoming the sole master of Europe, by overwhelming Russia, and wresting Poland from her dominion. He had so much difficulty in concealing this project, that hints of it began to escape him in all directions. The immense preparations which so distant an enterprise required, the enormous quantities of provisions and ammunition collecting, the noise of arms, of carriages, and the march of such numbers of soldiers—the universal movement the majestic and terrible course of all the forces of the West against the East—every thing announced to Europe that her two colossuses were about to measure their strength with each other.

But, to get within reach of Russia, it was necessary to go beyond Austria, to cross Prussia, and to march between Sweden and Turkey; an offensive alliance with these four powers was therefore indispensable. Austria was as much subject to the influence of Napoleon as Prussia was to his arms: to them he had only to declare his intentions; Austria voluntarily and eagerly entered into his plans, and Prussia he easily prevailed on to join him.

Austria, however, did not act blindly. Situated between the two great colossuses of the North and the West, she was not displeased to see them at war: she looked to their mutually weakening each other, and to the increase of her own strength by their exhaustion. On the 14th of March, 1812, she promised France 30,000 men; but she prepared prudent secret instructions for them. She obtained a vague promise of an increase of territory, as an indemnity for her share of the expenses of the war, and the possession of Gallicia was guaranteed to her. She admitted, however, the future possibility of a cession of part of that province to the kingdom of Poland; but in exchange for that she would have received the Illyrian provinces. The sixth article of the secret treaty establishes that fact.

The success of the war, therefore, in no degree depended on the cession of Gallicia, or the difficulties arising from the Austrian jealousy of that possession. Napoleon, consequently, might on his entrance into Wilna, have publicly proclaimed the liberation of the whole of Poland, instead of betraying the expectations of her people, astonishing and rendering them indifferent by expressions of wavering import.

This, however, was one of those prominent points, which in politics as well as in war are decisive, with which every thing is connected, and from which nothing ought to have made him swerve. But whether it was that Napoleon reckoned too much on the ascendancy of his genius, or the strength of his army, and the weakness of Alexander; or that, considering what he left behind him, he felt it too dangerous to carry on so distant a war slowly and methodically; or whether, as we shall presently be told by himself, he had doubts of the success of his undertaking; certain it is, that he either neglected, or could not yet determine to proclaim the liberation of that country whose freedom he had come to restore.

And yet he had sent an ambassador to her Diet. When this inconsistency was remarked to him, he replied, that "that nomination was an act of war, which only bound him during the war, while by his words he would be bound both in war and peace." Thus it was, that he made no other reply to the enthusiasm of the Lithuanians than evasive expressions, at the very time he was following up his attack on Alexander to the very capital of his empire.

He even neglected to clear the southern Polish provinces of the feeble hostile armies which kept the patriotism of their inhabitants in check, and to secure, by strongly organizing their insurrection, a solid basis of operation. Accustomed to short methods, and to rapid attacks, he wished to imitate himself, in spite of the difference of places and circumstances; for such is the weakness of man, that he is always led by imitation, either of others, or of himself, which in the latter case, that of great men, is habit; for habit is nothing more than the imitation of one's self. So true it is, that by their strongest side these extraordinary men are undone!

The one in question committed himself to the fortune of battles. Having prepared an army of six hundred and fifty thousand men, he fancied that that was doing sufficient to secure victory, from which he expected every thing. Instead of sacrificing every thing to obtain victory, it was by that he looked to obtain every thing; he made use of it as a *means*, when it ought to have been his *end*. In this manner he made it too necessary; it was already rather too much so. But he confided so much of futurity to it, he overloaded it with so much responsibility, that it became urgent and indispensable to him. Hence his precipitation to get within reach of it, in order to extricate himself from so critical a position.

But we must not be too hasty in condemning a genius so great and universal; we shall shortly hear from himself by what urgent necessity he was hurried on; and even admitting that the rapidity of his expedition was only equalled by its rashness, success would have probably crowned it, if the premature decline of his health had left the physical constitution of this great man all the vigour which his mind still retained.

Chapter 2

Prussia

As to Prussia, of which Napoleon was completely master, it is not known whether it was from his uncertainty as to the fate which he reserved for her, or as to the period at which he should commence the war, that he refused, in 1811, to contract the alliance which she herself proposed to him, and of which he dictated the conditions, in 1812.

His aversion to Frederick William was remarkable. Napoleon had been frequently heard to speak reproachfully of the cabinet of Prussia for its treaties with the French republic. He said, "It was a desertion of the cause of kings; that the negotiations of the court of Berlin with the Directory displayed a timid, selfish, and ignoble policy, which sacrificed its dignity, and the general cause of monarchs, to petty aggrandizements." Whenever he followed with his finger the traces of the Prussian frontiers upon the map, he seemed to be angry at seeing them still so extensive, and exclaimed, "Is it possible that I have left this man so large a territory?"

This dislike to a mild and pacific monarch was surprising. As there is nothing in the character of Napoleon unworthy of historical remembrance, it is worth while to examine the cause of it. Some persons trace back the origin of it to the rejection which he experienced, when First Consul, from Louis XVIII. of the propositions which he made to him through the medium of the king of Prussia; and they suppose that Napoleon laid the blame of this refusal upon the mediator. Others attribute it to the seizure of Rumbold, the English agent at Hamburgh, by the orders of Napoleon, and to his being compelled to give him up by Frederick, as protector of the neutrality of the north of Germany. Before that time, Frederick and Napoleon had carried on a secret correspondence, which was of so intimate a nature, that they used to confide to each other even the details of their household; that circumstance, it is said, put an end to it.

At the beginning of 1805, however, Russia, Austria, and England, made ineffectual attempts to engage Frederick in their third coalition against France. The court of Berlin, the queen, the princes, the minister Hardenberg, and all the young Prussian military, excited by the ardour of displaying the inheritance of glory which had been left them by the great Frederick, or by the wish of blotting out the disgrace of the campaign of 1792, entered heartily into the views of the allied powers; but the pacific policy of the king, and of his minister Haugwitz, resisted them, until the violation of the Prussian territory, near Anspach, by the march of a corps of French troops, exasperated the passions of the Prussians to such a degree, that their cry for immediate war prevailed.

Alexander was then in Poland; he was invited to Potsdam, and repaired thither immediately; and on the 3rd of November, 1805, he engaged Frederick in the third coalition. The Prussian array was immediately withdrawn from the Russian frontiers, and M. de Haugwitz repaired to Brünn to threaten Napoleon with it. But the battle of Austerlitz shut his mouth; and within a fortnight after, the wily minister, having quickly turned round to the side of the conqueror, signed with him the participation of the fruits of victory.

Napoleon, however, dissembled his displeasure; for he had his army to re-organize, to give the grand duchy of Berg to Murat, his brother-in-law, Neufchatel to Berthier, to conquer Naples for his brother Joseph, to mediatize Switzerland, to dissolve the Germanic body, and to create the Rhenish confederation, of which he declared himself protector; to change the republic of Holland into a kingdom, and to give it to his brother Louis. These were the reasons which induced him, on the 15th of December, to cede Hanover to Prussia, in exchange for Anspach, Cleves, and Neufchatel.

The possession of Hanover at first tempted Frederick, but when the treaty was to be signed, he appeared to feel ashamed, and to hesitate; he wished only to accept it by halves, and to retain it merely as a deposit. Napoleon had no idea of such timid policy. "What!" said he, "does this monarch dare neither to make peace nor war? Does he prefer the English to me? Is there another coalition preparing? Does he despise my alliance?" Indignant at the idea, by a fresh treaty, on the 8th of March, 1806, he compelled Frederick to declare war against England, to take possession of Hanover, and to admit French garrisons into Wesel and Hameln.

The king of Prussia alone submitted; his court and his subjects were exasperated; they reproached him with allowing himself to be vanquished without attempting to fight; and elevating themselves on the remembrance of their past glory, they fancied that for them alone was reserved the honour of triumphing over the conqueror of Europe. In their impatience they insulted the minister of Napoleon; they sharpened their swords on the threshold of his gate. Napoleon himself they loaded with abuse. Even the queen, so distinguished by her graces and attractions, put on a warlike attitude. Their princes, one of them particularly (whose carriage and features, spirit and intrepidity, seemed to promise them a hero), offered to be their leaders. A chivalrous ardour and fury animated the minds of all.

It is asserted, that at the same time there were persons, either treacherous or deceived, who persuaded Frederick that Napoleon was obliged to show himself pacific, that that warrior was averse to war; they added, that he was perfidiously treating for peace with England, on the terms of restoring Hanover, which he was to take back from Prussia. Drawn in at last by the general feeling, the king allowed all these passions to burst forth. His army advanced, and threatened Napoleon; fifteen days afterwards he had neither army nor kingdom; he fled alone; and Napoleon dated from Berlin his decrees against England.

Humbled and conquered as Prussia thus was, it was impossible for Napoleon to abandon his hold of her; she would have immediately rallied, under the cannon of the Russians. Finding it impossible to gain her to his interests, like Saxony, by a great act of generosity, the next plan was to divide her; and yet, either from compassion, or the effect of Alexander's presence, he could not resolve to dismember her. This was a mistaken policy, like most of those where we stop half-way; and Napoleon was not long before he became sensible of it. When he exclaimed, therefore, "Is it possible that I have left this man so large a territory?" it is probable that he did not forgive Prussia the protection of Alexander; he hated her, because he felt that she hated him.

In fact, the sparks of a jealous and impatient hatred escaped from the youth of Prussia, whose ideas were exalted by a system of education, national, liberal, and mystical. It was among them that a formidable power arose in opposition to that of Napoleon. It included all whom his victories had humbled or offended; it had all the strength of the weak and the oppressed, the law of nature, mystery, fanaticism, and revenge! Wanting support on earth, it looked up for aid to Heaven, and its moral forces were wholly out of the reach of the material power of Napoleon. Animated by the devoted and indefatigable spirit of an ardent sect, it watched the slightest movements and weakest points of its enemy, insinuated itself into all the interstices of his power, and holding itself ready to strike at every opportunity, it waited quietly with the patience and phlegm which are the peculiar characteristics of the Germans, which were the causes of their defeat, and against which our victory wore itself out.

This vast conspiracy was that of the *Tugendbund*[1], or *Friends of Virtue*. Its head, in other words, the person who first gave a precise and definite direction to its views, was Stein. Napoleon perhaps might have gained him over to his interests, but preferred punishing him. His plan happened to be discovered by one of those chances to which the police owes the best part of its miracles; but when conspiracies enter into the interests, passions, and even the consciences of men, it is impossible to seize their ramifications: every one understands without communicating; or rather, all is communication—a general and simultaneous sympathy.

This focus spread its fires and gained new partisans every day; it attacked the power of Napoleon in the opinion of all Germany, extended itself into Italy, and threatened its complete overthrow. It was already easy to see that, if circumstances became unfavourable to us, there would be no want of men to take advantage of them. In 1809,

---

1: In 1808, several literary men at Königsberg, afflicted with the evils which desolated their country, ascribed it to the general corruption of manners. According to these philosophers, it had stifled true patriotism in the citizens, discipline in the army, and courage in the people. Good men therefore were bound to unite to regenerate the nation, by setting the example of every sacrifice. An association was in consequence formed by them, which took the title of *Moral and Scientific Union*. The government approved of it, merely interdicting it from political discussions. This resolution, noble as it was, would probably have been lost, like many others, in the vagueness of German metaphysics; but about that time William, Duke of Brunswick, who had been stripped of his duchy, had retired to his principality of Oels in Silesia. In the bosom of this retreat he is said to have observed the first progress of the *Moral Union* among the Prussians. He became a member of it; and his heart swelling with hatred and revenge, he formed the idea of another association, which was to consist of men resolved to overthrow the confederation of the Rhine, and to drive the French entirely out of Germany. This society, whose object was more real and positive than that of the first, soon swallowed up the other; and from these two was formed that of the *Tugendbund*, or *Friends of Virtue*. About the end of May, 1809, three enterprises—those of Katt, Dörnberg, and Schill—had already given proofs of its existence. That of Duke William began on the 14th of May. He was at first supported by the Austrians. After a variety of adventures, this leader, abandoned to his own resources in the midst of subjugated Europe, and left with only 2000 men to combat with the whole power of Napoleon, refused to yield: he stood his ground, and threw himself into Saxony and Hanover; but finding it impossible to raise them into insurrection, he cut his way through several French corps, which he defeated, to Elsfleth, where he found an English vessel waiting to receive and to convey him to England, with the laurels he had acquired.

even before the disaster of Esslingen, the first who had ventured to raise the standard of independence against Napoleon were Prussians. He sent them to the galleys; so important did he feel it to smother that cry of revolt, which seemed to echo that of the Spaniards, and might become general.

Independently of all these causes of hatred, the position of Prussia, between France and Russia, compelled Napoleon to remain her master; he could not reign there but by force—he could not be strong there but by her weakness.

He ruined the country, although he must have known well that poverty creates audacity; that the hope of gain becomes the moving principle of those who have nothing more to lose; and finally, that in leaving them nothing but the sword, he in a manner obliged them to turn it against himself. In consequence, on the approach of the year 1812, and of the terrible struggle which it was to produce, Frederick, uneasy and tired of his subservient position, was determined to extricate himself from it, either by an alliance or by war. In March, 1811, he offered himself to Napoleon as an auxiliary in the expedition which he was preparing. In the month of May, and again in the month of August, he repeated that offer; and as he received no satisfactory answer, he declared, that as the great military movements which surrounded, crossed, or drained his kingdom, were such as to excite his apprehension that his entire destruction was meditated, "he took up arms, because circumstances imperiously called upon him to do so, deeming it far preferable to die sword in hand than to fall with disgrace."

It was said at the same time, that Frederick secretly offered to Alexander to give him possession of Graudentz, and his magazines, and to put himself at the head of his insurgent subjects, if the Russian army should advance into Silesia. If the same authorities are to be believed, Alexander received this proposition, very favourably. He immediately sent to Bagration and Wittgenstein sealed marching orders. They were instructed not to open them until they received another letter from their sovereign, which he never wrote, having changed his resolution. A variety of causes might have dictated that change; 1st, a wish not to be the first to commence so great a war, and his anxiety to have divine justice and the opinion of mankind on his side, by not appearing the aggressor; 2nd, that Frederick, becoming less uneasy as to the plans of Napoleon, had resolved to follow his fortunes. It is probable, after all, that the noble sentiments which Alexander expressed in his reply to the king were his only motives: we are assured that he wrote to him, "That in a war which might begin by reverses, and in which perseverance was required, he only felt courageous for himself, and that the misfortunes of an ally might shake his resolution; that it would grieve him to chain Prussia to his fortune if it was bad; that if it was good he should always be ready to share it with her, whatever line of conduct necessity might oblige her to pursue."

These details have been certified to us by a witness, although an inferior one. However, whether this counsel proceeded from the generosity or the policy of Alexander, or Frederick was determined solely by the necessity of the case, it is certain that it was high time for him to come to a decision; for in February, 1812, these communications with Alexander, *if there were such*, or the hope of obtaining better terms from France having made him hesitate in replying to the definitive propositions of Napoleon, the latter, becoming impatient, sent additional forces to Dantzic, and made Davoust enter Pomerania. His orders for this invasion of a Swedish province were repeated and pressing; they were grounded on the illicit commerce carried on by the Pomeranians with the English, and subsequently on the necessity of compelling Prussia to accede to his terms. The Prince of Eckmühl even received orders to hold himself in readiness to take immediate possession of that kingdom, and to seize the person of her sovereign, if within eight days from the date of these orders the latter had not concluded the offensive alliance dictated to him by France; but while the marshal was tracing the few marches necessary for this operation, he received intelligence that the treaty of the 21st of February, 1812, had been ratified.

This submission did not altogether satisfy Napoleon. To his strength he added artifice; his suspicions still led him to covet the occupation of the fortresses, which he was ashamed not to leave in Frederick's hands; he required the king to keep only 50 or 80 invalids in some, and desired that some French officers should be admitted into others; all of whom were to send their reports to him, and to follow his orders. His solicitude extended to every thing. "Spandau," said he, in his letters to Davoust, "is the citadel of Berlin, as Pillau is that of Königsberg;" and French troops had orders to be ready to introduce themselves at the first signal: the manner he himself pointed out. At Potsdam, which the king had reserved for himself, and which our troops were interdicted from entering, his orders were, that the French officers should frequently show themselves, in order to observe, and to accustom the people to the sight of them. He recommended every degree of respect to be shown, both to the king and his subjects; but at the same time he required that every sort of arms should be taken from the latter, which might be of use to them in an insurrection; and he pointed out every thing of the kind, even to the smallest weapon. Anticipating the possibility of the loss of a battle, and the chances of Prussian *vespers*, he ordered that his troops should be either put into barracks or encampments, with a thousand other precautions of the minutest description. As a final security, in case of the English making a descent between the Elbe and the Vistula, although Victor, and subsequently Augereau, were to occupy Prussia with 50,000 men, he engaged by treaty the assistance of 10,000 Danes.

All these precautions were still insufficient to remove his distrust; when the Prince of Hatzfeld came to require of him a subsidy of 25 millions of francs to meet the expenses of the war which was preparing, his reply to Daru was, "that he would take especial care not to furnish an enemy with arms against himself." In this manner did Frederick, entangled as it were in a net of iron, which surrounded and held him tight in every part, put between 20 and 30,000 of his troops, and his principal fortresses and magazines, at the disposal of Napoleon[2].

2: By this treaty, Prussia agreed to furnish two hundred thousand quintals of rye, twenty-four thousand of rice, two million bottles of beer, four hundred thousand quintals of wheat, six hundred and fifty thousand of straw, three hundred and fifty thousand of hay, six million bushels of oats, forty-four thousand oxen, fifteen thousand horses, three thousand six hundred wagons, with harness and drivers, each carrying a load of fifteen hundred weight; and finally, hospitals provided with every thing necessary for twenty thousand sick. It is true, that all these supplies were to be allowed in deduction of the remainder of the taxes imposed by the conquest.

CHAPTER 3

Turkey

These two treaties opened the road to Russia to Napoleon; but in order to penetrate into the interior of that empire, it was necessary to make sure of Sweden and Turkey.

Military combinations were then so much aggrandized, that in order to sketch a plan of warfare, it was no longer necessary to study the configuration of a province, or of a chain of mountains, or the course of a river. When monarchs, such as Alexander and Napoleon, were contending for the dominion of Europe, it was necessary to regard the general and relative position of every state with a universal *coup d'oeil*; it was no longer on single maps, but on that of the whole globe, that their policy had to trace its plans of hostility.

Russia is mistress of the heights of Europe; her flanks are supported by the seas of the north and south. Her government can only with great difficulty be driven into a straight, and forced to submit, in a space almost beyond the imagination to conceive: the conquest of which would require long campaigns, to which her climate is completely opposed. From this, it follows, that without the concurrence of Turkey and Sweden, Russia is less vulnerable. The assistance of these two powers was therefore requisite in order to surprise her, to strike her to the heart in her modern capital, and to turn at a distance, in the rear of its left, her grand army of the Niemen,—and not merely to precipitate attacks on a part of her front, in plains where the extent of space prevented confusion, and left a thousand roads open to the retreat of that army.

The meanest soldier in our ranks, therefore, expected to hear of the combined march of the Grand Vizier towards Kief, and of Bernadotte against Finland. Eight sovereigns were already enlisted under the banners of Napoleon; but the two who had the greatest interest in the quarrel were still deaf to his call. It was an idea worthy of the great emperor to put all the governments and all the religions of Europe in motion for the accomplishment of his great designs: their triumph would have been then secured; and if the voice of another Homer had been wanting to this king of so many kings, the voice of the nineteenth century, the great century, would have supplied it; and the cry of astonishment of a whole age, penetrating and piercing through futurity, would have echoed from generation to generation, to the latest posterity!

So much glory was not in reserve for us.

Which of us, in the French army, can ever forget his astonishment, in the midst of the Russian plains, on hearing the news of the fatal treaties of the Turks and Swedes with Alexander; and how anxiously our looks were turned towards our right uncovered, towards our left enfeebled, and upon our retreat menaced? *Then* we only looked at the fatal effects of the peace between our allies and our enemy; *now* we feel desirous of knowing the causes of it.

The treaties concluded about the end of the last century, had subjected the weak sultan of the Turks to Russia; the Egyptian expedition had armed him against us. But ever since Napoleon had assumed the reins of power, a well-understood common interest, and the intimacy of a mysterious correspondence, had reconciled Selim with the first consul: a close connexion was established between these two princes, and they had exchanged portraits with each other. Selim attempted to effect a great revolution in the Turkish customs. Napoleon encouraged him, and was assisting him in introducing the European discipline into the Ottoman army, when the victory of Jena, the war of Poland, and the influence of Sebastiani, determined the sultan to throw off the yoke of Alexander. The English made hasty attempts to oppose this, but they were driven from the sea of Constantinople. Then it was that Napoleon wrote the following letter to Selim.

Osterode, April 3, 1807.

My ambassador informs me of the bravery and good conduct of the Mussulmans against our common enemies. Thou hast shown thyself the worthy descendant of the Selims and the Solimans. Thou hast asked me for some officers; I send them to thee. I regretted that thou hadst not required of me some thousand men,—thou hast only asked for five hundred; I have given orders for their immediate departure. It is my intention that they shall be paid and clothed at my expense, and that thou shalt be reimbursed the expenses which they may occasion thee. I have given orders to the commander of my troops in Dalmatia to send thee the arms, ammunition, and every thing thou shalt require of me. I have given the same orders at Naples; and artillery has been already placed at the disposal of the pasha of Janina. Generals, officers, arms of every description, even money—I place all at thy disposal. Thou hast only to ask: do so in a distinct manner, and all which thou shalt require I will send thee on the instant. Arrange matters with the shah of Persia, who is also the enemy of the Russians; encourage him to stand fast, and to attack warmly the common enemy. I have beaten the Russians in a great battle; I have taken from them seventy-five pieces of cannon, sixteen standards, and a great number of prisoners. I am at the distance of eighty leagues beyond Warsaw, and am about to take advantage of the fifteen days' repose which I have given to my army, to repair thither, and there to receive thy ambassador. I am sensible of the want thou hast of artillerymen and troops; I have offered both to thy ambassador; but he has declined them, from a fear of alarming the delicacy of the Mussulmans. Confide to me all thy wants; I am sufficiently powerful, and sufficiently interested in thy prosperity, both from friendship and policy, to have nothing to refuse thee. Peace has been proposed to me here. I have been offered all the advantages which I could desire; but they wished that I should ratify the state of things established between the Porte and Russia by the treaty of Sistowa, and I refused. My answer was, *that it was necessary that the Porte should be secured in complete independence; and that all the treaties extorted from her, during the time that France was asleep, should be revoked.*

This letter of Napoleon had been preceded and followed by verbal but formal assurances, that he would not sheath the sword, until the Crimea was restored to the dominion of the crescent. He had even authorized Sebastiani to give the divan a copy of his instructions, which contained these promises.

Such were his words, with which his actions at first corresponded. Sebastiani demanded a passage through Turkey for an army of 25,000 French, which he was to command, and which was to join the Ottoman army. An unforeseen circumstance, it is true, deranged this plan; but Napoleon then made Selim the promise of an auxiliary force of 9000 French, including 5000 artillerymen, who were to be conveyed in eleven vessels of the line to Constantinople. The Turkish ambassador was at the same time treated with the greatest distinction in the French camp; he accompanied Napoleon in all his reviews: the most flattering attentions were paid to him, and the grand-equerry (Caulaincourt,) was already treating with him for an alliance, offensive and defensive, when a sudden attack by the Russians interrupted the negotiation.

The ambassador returned to Warsaw, where the same respect continued to be shown him, up to the day of the decisive victory of Friedland. But on the following day his illusion was dissipated; he saw himself neglected; for it was no longer Selim whom he represented. A revolution had just hurled from the throne the monarch who had been the friend of Napoleon, and with him all hope of giving the Turks a regular army, upon which he could depend. Napoleon, therefore, judging that he could no longer reckon upon the assistance of these barbarians, changed his system. Henceforward it was Alexander whom he wished to gain; and as his was a genius which never hesitated, he was already prepared to abandon the empire of the East to that monarch, in order that he might be left at liberty to possess himself of that of the West.

As his great object was the extension of the continental system, and to make it surround Europe, the co-operation of Russia would complete its development. Alexander would shut out the English from the North, and compel Sweden to go to war with them; the French would expel them from the centre, from the south, and from the west of Europe. Napoleon was already meditating the expedition to Portugal, if that kingdom would not join his coalition. With these ideas floating in his brain, Turkey was now only an accessory in his plans, and he agreed to the armistice, and to the conferences at Tilsit.

But a deputation had just come from Wilna, soliciting the restoration of their national independence, and professing the same devotion to his cause as had been shown by Warsaw; Berthier, whose ambition was satisfied, and who began to be tired of war, dismissed these envoys rudely, styling them traitors to their sovereign. The Prince of Eckmühl, on the contrary, favoured their object, and presented them to Napoleon, who was irritated with Berthier for his treatment of these Lithuanians, and received them graciously, without, however, promising them his support. In vain did Davoust represent to him that the opportunity was favourable, owing to the destruction of the Russian army; Napoleon's reply was, "that Sweden had just declared her armistice to him; that Austria offered her mediation between France and Russia, which he looked upon as a hostile step; that the Prussians, seeing him at such a distance from France, might recover from their intimidation; and finally, that Selim, his faithful ally, had just been dethroned, and his place filled by Mustapha IV., of whose dispositions he knew nothing."

The emperor of France continued, therefore, to negotiate with Russia; and the Turkish ambassador, neglected and forgotten, wandered about our camp, without being summoned to take any part in the negotiations which terminated the war; he returned to Constantinople soon after, in great displeasure. Neither the Crimea, nor even Moldavia and Wallachia, were restored to that barbarous court by the treaty of Tilsit; the restitution of the two latter provinces was only stipulated by an armistice, the conditions of which were never meant to be executed. But as Napoleon professed to be the mediator between Mustapha and Alexander, the ministers of the two powers repaired to Paris. But there, during the long continuance of that feigned mediation, the Turkish plenipotentiaries were never admitted to his presence.

If we must even tell the whole truth, it is asserted, that at the interview at Tilsit, and subsequently, a treaty for the partition of Turkey was under discussion. It was proposed to Russia to take possession of Wallachia, Moldavia, Bulgaria, and a part of Mount Hemus. Austria was to have Serbia and a part of Bosnia; France the other part of that province, Albania, Macedonia, and all Greece as far as Thessalonica: Constantinople, Adrianople, and Thrace, were to be left to the Turks.

Whether the conferences respecting this partition were really of a serious nature, or merely the communication of a great idea, is uncertain; so much is certain, that shortly after the interview at Tilsit, Alexander's ambition was very sensibly moderated. The suggestions of prudence had shown him the danger of substituting for the ignorant, infatuated, and feeble Turkey, an active, powerful, and unaccommodating neighbour. In his conversations on the subject at that time, he remarked, "that he had already too much desert country; that he knew too well, by the occupation of the Crimea, which was still depopulated, the value of conquest over foreign and hostile religions and manners; that besides, France and Russia were too strong to become such near neighbours; that two such powerful bodies coming into immediate contact, would be sure to jostle; and that it was much better to leave intermediate powers between them."

On the other side, the French emperor urged the matter no further; the Spanish insurrection diverted his attention, and imperiously required his presence with all his forces. Even previous to the interview at Erfurt, after Sebastiani's return from Constantinople, although Napoleon still seemed to adhere to the idea of dismembering Turkey in Europe, he had admitted the correctness of his ambassador's reasoning: "That in this partition, the advantages would be all against him; that Russia and Austria would acquire contiguous provinces, which would make their dominions more complete, while we should be obliged to keep 80,000 men continually in Greece to retain it in subjection; that such an army, from the distance and losses it would sustain from long marches, and the novelty and unhealthiness of the climate, would require 30,000 recruits annually, a number which would quite drain France: that a line of operation extending from Athens to Paris, was out of all proportion; that besides, it was strangled in its passage at Trieste, at which point only two marches would enable the Austrians to place themselves across it, and thereby cut off our army of observation in Greece from all communication with Italy and France."

Here Napoleon exclaimed, "that Austria certainly complicated every thing; that she was there like a dead weight; that she must be got rid off; and Europe must be divided into two empires: that the Danube, from the Black Sea to Passau, the mountains of Bohemia to Königsgratz, and the Elbe to the Baltic, should be their lines of demarcation. Alexander should become the emperor of the north, and he of the south of Europe." Abandoning, subsequently, these lofty ideas, and reverting to Sebastiani's observations on the partition of European Turkey, he terminated the conferences, which had lasted three days, with these words: "You are right, and no answer can be given to that! I give it up. Besides, that accords with my views on Spain, which I am going to unite to France."—"What do I hear?" exclaimed Sebastiani, astonished, "unite it! And your brother!"—"What signifies my brother?" retorted Napoleon; "does one give away a kingdom like Spain? I am determined to unite it to France. I will give that nation a great national representation. I will make the emperor Alexander consent to it, by allowing him to take possession of Turkey to the Danube, and I will evacuate Berlin. As to Joseph, I will indemnify him."

The congress at Erfurt took place just after this. He could have no motive at that time for supporting the rights of the Turks. The French army, which had advanced imprudently into the very heart of Spain, had met with reverses. The presence of its leader, and that of his armies of the Rhine and the Elbe, became there every day more and more necessary, and Austria had availed herself of the opportunity to take up arms. Uneasy respecting the state of Germany, Napoleon was therefore anxious to make sure of the dispositions of Alexander, to conclude an alliance offensive and defensive with him, and even to engage him in a war. Such were the reasons which induced him to abandon Turkey as far as the Danube to that emperor.

The Porte therefore had very soon reason to reproach us for the war which was renewed between it and Russia. Notwithstanding, in July, 1808, when Mustapha was dethroned, and succeeded by Mahmoud, the latter announced his accession to the French emperor; but Napoleon had then to keep upon terms with Alexander, and felt too much regret at the death of Selim, detestation of the barbarity of the Mussulmans, and contempt for their unstable government, to allow him to notice the communication. For three years he had returned no reply to the sultan, and his silence might be interpreted into a refusal to acknowledge him.

He was in this ambiguous position with the Turks, when all of a sudden, on the 21st of March, 1812, only six weeks before the war with Russia commenced, he solicited an alliance with Mahmoud: he demanded that, within five days from the period of the communication, all negotiation between the Turks and Russians should be broken off; and that an army of 100,000 men, commanded by the sultan himself, should march to the Danube within nine days. The return which he proposed to make for this assistance was, to put the Porte in possession of the very same Moldavia and Wallachia, which, under the circumstances, the Russians were but too happy to restore as the price of a speedy peace; and the promise of procuring the restoration of the Crimea, which he had made six years before to Selim, was again renewed.

We know not whether the time which this despatch would take to arrive at Constantinople had been badly calculated, whether Napoleon believed the Turkish army to be stronger than it really was, or whether he had flattered himself with surprising and captivating the determination of the divan by so sudden and advantageous a proposition. It can hardly be supposed that he was ignorant of the long invariable custom of the Mussulmans, which prevented the grand signor from ever appearing in person at the head of his army.

It appears as if the genius of Napoleon could not stoop so low as to impute to the divan the brutish ignorance which it exhibited of its real interests. After the manner in which he had abandoned the interests of Turkey in 1807, perhaps he did not make sufficient allowance for the distrust which the Mussulmans were likely to entertain of his new promises; he forgot that they were too ignorant to appreciate the change which recent circumstances had effected in his political views; and that barbarians like them could still less comprehend the feelings of dislike with which they had inspired him, by their deposition and murder of Selim, to whom he was attached, and in conjunction with whom he had hoped to make European Turkey a military power capable of coping with Russia.

Perhaps he might still have gained over Mahmoud to his cause, if he had sooner made use of more potent arguments; but, as he has since expressed himself, it revolted his pride to make use of corruption. We shall besides shortly see him hesitating about beginning a war with Alexander, or laying too much stress on the alarm with which his immense preparations would inspire that monarch. It is also possible, that the last propositions which he made to the Turks, being tantamount to a declaration of war against the Russians, were delayed for the express purpose of deceiving the Czar as to the period of his invasion. Finally, whether it was from all these causes, from a confidence founded on the mutual hatred of the two nations, and on his treaty of alliance with Austria, which had just guaranteed Moldavia and Wallachia to the Turks, he detained the ambassador whom he sent to them on his road, and waited, as we have just seen, to the very last moment.

But the divan was surrounded by the Russian, English, Austrian, and Swedish envoys, who with one voice represented to it, "that the Turks were indebted for their existence in Europe solely to the divisions which existed among the Christian monarchs; that the moment these were united under one influence, the Mohammedans in Europe would be overwhelmed; and that as the French emperor was advancing rapidly to the attainment of universal empire, it was him whom the Turks had most reason to dread."

To these representations were added the intrigues of the two Greek princes Morozi. They were of the same religion with Alexander, and they looked to him for the possession of Moldavia and Wallachia. Grown rich by his favours and by the gold of England, these dragomans enlightened the unsuspecting ignorance of the Turks, as to the occupation and military surveys of the Ottoman frontiers by the French. They did a great deal more; the first of them influenced the dispositions of the divan and the capital, and the second those of the Grand Vizier and the army; and as the proud Mahmoud resisted, and would only accept an honourable peace, these treacherous Greeks contrived to disband his army, and compelled him, by insurrections, to sign the degrading treaty of Bucharest with the Russians.

Such is the power of intrigue in the seraglio; two Greeks whom the Turks despised, there decided the fate of Turkey, in spite of the sultan himself. As the latter depended for his existence on the intrigues of his palace, he was, like all despots who shut themselves up in them, obliged to yield: the Morozi carried the day; but afterwards he had them both beheaded.

Chapter 4
Sweden

In this manner did we lose the support of Turkey; but Sweden still remained to us; her monarch had sprung from our ranks; a soldier of our army, it was to that he owed his glory and his throne: was it likely that he would desert our cause on the first opportunity he had of showing his gratitude? It was impossible to anticipate such ingratitude; still less, that he would sacrifice the real and permanent interests of Sweden to his former jealousy of Napoleon, and perhaps to a weakness too common among the upstart favourites of fortune; unless it be that the submission of men who have newly attained to greatness to those who boast of a transmitted rank, is a necessity of their position rather than an error of their self-love.

In this great contest between aristocracy and democracy, the ranks of the former had been joined by one of its most determined enemies. Bernadotte being thrown almost singly among the ancient courts and nobility, did every thing to merit his adoption by them, and succeeded. But his success must have cost him dear, as in order to obtain it, he was first obliged to abandon his old companions, and the authors of his glory, in the hour of peril. At a later period he did more; he was seen marching over their bleeding corpses, joining with all their, and formerly his, enemies, to overwhelm the country of his birth, and thereby lay that of his adoption at the mercy of the first czar who should be ambitious of reigning over the Baltic.

On the other hand, it would appear that the character of Bernadotte, and the importance of Sweden in the decisive struggle which was about to commence, were not sufficiently weighed in the political balance of Napoleon. His ardent and exclusive genius hazarded too much; he overloaded a solid foundation so much that he sank it. Thus it was, that after justly appreciating the Swedish interests as naturally bound up with his, the moment he wished to weaken the power of Russia, he fancied that he could exact every thing from the Swedes without promising them any thing in return: his pride did not make any allowance for theirs, judging that they were too much interested in the success of his cause, for them ever to think of separating themselves from it.

We must, however, take up the history a little earlier; facts will prove that the defection of Sweden was as much attributable to the jealous ambition of Bernadotte as to the unbending pride of Napoleon. It will be seen that her new monarch assumed to himself a great part of the responsibility of the rupture, by offering his alliance at the price of an act of treachery.

When Napoleon returned from Egypt, he did not become the chief of his equals with all their concurrence. Such of them as were already jealous of his glory then became still more envious of his power. As they could not dispute the first, they attempted to refuse obedience to the second. Moreau, and several other generals, either by persuasion or surprise, had co-operated in the revolution of the 18th Brumaire: they afterwards repented having done so. Bernadotte had refused all participation in it. Alone, during the night, in Napoleon's own residence, amidst a thousand devoted officers, waiting only for the conqueror's orders, Bernadotte, then a strenuous republican, was daring enough to oppose his arguments, to refuse the second place in the republic, and to retort upon his anger by threats. Napoleon saw him depart, bearing himself proudly, and pass through the midst of his partisans, carrying with him his secrets, and declaring himself his enemy, and even his denouncer. Either from respect to his brother, to whom Bernadotte was allied by marriage, from moderation, the usual companion of strength, or from astonishment, he suffered him to depart quietly.

In the course of the same night, a conventicle, consisting of ten deputies of the Council of Five Hundred, met at the house of S——; thither Bernadotte repaired. They settled, that at nine o'clock next morning the Council should hold a sitting, to which those only should be invited who were of the same way of thinking; that there a decree should be passed, that in imitation of the Council of Ancients, which had prudently named Bonaparte general of its guard, the Council of Five Hundred had appointed Bernadotte to command theirs; and that the latter, properly armed, should be in readiness to be summoned to it. It was at S——'s house that this plan was formed. S—— himself immediately afterwards ran to Napoleon, and disclosed the whole to him. A threat from the latter was quite sufficient to keep the conspirators in order; not one of them dared show his face at the Council, and the next day the revolution of the 18th Brumaire was completed.

Bernadotte was prudent enough afterwards to feign submission, but Napoleon had not forgotten his opposition. He kept a watchful eye on all his movements. Not long after, he suspected his being at the head of a republican conspiracy which had been forming against him in the west. A premature proclamation discovered it; an officer who had been arrested for other causes, and an accomplice of Bernadotte, denounced the authors. On that occasion Bernadotte's ruin would have been sealed, if Napoleon had been able to convict him of it.

He was satisfied with banishing him to America, under the title of minister of the Republic. But fortune favoured Bernadotte, who was already at Rochefort, by delaying his embarkation until the war with England was renewed. He then refused to go, and Napoleon could no longer compel him.

All the relations between them had thus been those of hatred; and this check only served to aggravate them. Soon after, Napoleon was heard reproaching Bernadotte with his envious and treacherous inaction during the battle of Auerstadt, and his order of the day at Wagram, in which he had assumed the honour of that victory. He also spoke reproachfully of his character, as being much more ambitious than patriotic; and perhaps of the fascination of his manners,—all of them things considered dangerous to a recently established government; and yet he had showered rank, titles, and distinctions upon him, while Bernadotte, always ungrateful, seemed to accept them merely as in justice due to his merits, or to the want which was felt of him. These complaints of Napoleon were not without foundation.

Bernadotte, on his side, abusing the emperor's moderation and desire to keep on terms with him, gradually incurred an increase of his displeasure, which his ambition was pleased to call enmity. He demanded why Napoleon had placed him in such a dangerous and false position at Wagram? why the report of that victory had been so unfavourable to him? to what was he to attribute the jealous anxiety to weaken his eulogium in the journals by artful notes? Up to that time, however, the obscure and underhand opposition of this general to his emperor had been of no importance; but a much wider field was then opened to their misunderstanding.

By the treaty of Tilsit, Sweden, as well as Turkey, had been sacrificed to Russia and the continental system. The mistaken or mad politics of Gustavus IV. had been the cause of this. Ever since 1804 that monarch appeared to have enlisted himself in the pay of England; it was he also who had been the first to break the ancient alliance between France and Sweden. He had obstinately persevered in that false policy to such an extent at first, as to contend against France when she was victorious over Russia, and afterwards with Russia and France united. The loss of Pomerania, in 1807, and even that of Finland and the islands of Aland, which were united to Russia in 1808, were not sufficient to shake his obstinacy.

It was then that his irritated subjects resumed that power which had been wrested from them, in 1772 and 1788, by Gustavus III., and of which his successor made so bad a use. Gustavus Adolphus IV. was imprisoned and dethroned; his lineal descendants were excluded from the throne; his uncle was put in his place, and the prince of Holstein-Augustenburg elected hereditary prince of Sweden. As the war had been the cause of this revolution peace was the result of it; it was concluded with Russia in 1809; but the newly-elected hereditary prince then died suddenly.

In the beginning of 1810, France restored Pomerania and the Island of Rugen to Sweden, as the price of her accession to the continental system. The Swedes, worn out, impoverished, and become almost islanders, in consequence of the loss of Finland, were very loath to break with England, and yet they had no remedy; on the other side they stood in awe of the neighbouring and powerful government of Russia. Finding themselves weak and isolated, they looked round for support.

Bernadotte had just been appointed to the command of the French army which took possession of Pomerania; his military reputation, and still more that of his nation and its sovereign, his fascinating mildness, his generosity, and his flattering attentions to the Swedes, with whom he had to treat, induced several of them to cast their eyes upon him. They appeared to know nothing of the misunderstanding between this marshal and the emperor; they fancied that by electing him for their prince, they should not only obtain an able and experienced general, but also a powerful mediator between France and Sweden, and a certain protector in the emperor: it happened quite the contrary.

During the intrigues to which this circumstance gave rise, Bernadotte fancied that to his previous complaints against Napoleon he had to add others. When, in opposition to the king, and the majority of the members of the diet, he was proposed as successor to the crown of Sweden; when his pretensions were supported by Charles's prime minister, (a man of no family, who owed, like him, all his illustration to himself,) and the count de Wrede, the only member of the diet who had reserved his vote for him; when he came to solicit Napoleon's interference, why did he, when Charles XIII. desired to know his wishes, exhibit so much indifference? Why did he prefer the union of the three northern crowns on the head of a prince of Denmark? If he, Bernadotte, succeeded in the enterprise, he was not at all indebted for it to the emperor of France; he owed it to the pretensions of the king of Denmark, which counteracted those of the duke of Augustenburg[3], his most dangerous rival; to the grateful audacity of the baron de Moerner, who was the first to come to him, and offer to put him on the lists, and to the aversion of the Swedes to the Danes; above all he owed it to a passport which had been adroitly obtained by his agent from Napoleon's minister. It was said that this document was audaciously produced by Bernadotte's secret emissary, as a proof of an autograph mission with which he pretended to be charged, and of the formal desire of the French emperor to see one of his lieutenants, and the relation of his brother, placed upon the throne of Sweden.

Bernadotte also felt that he owed this crown to the chance, which brought him in communication with the Swedes, and made them acquainted with his characteristic qualities; to the birth of his son, which secured the heredity succession; to the address of his agents, who, either with or without his authority, dazzled the poverty of the Scandinavians with the promise of fourteen millions with which his election was to enrich their treasury; and finally to his flattering attentions, which had gained him the voices of several Swedish officers who had been his prisoners. But as to Napoleon, what did he owe to him? What was his reply to the news of the offer of several Swedes, when he himself waited upon him to inform him of it? "I am at too great a distance from Sweden, to mix myself up in her affairs. You must not reckon upon my support." At the same time it is true, that either from necessity, from his dreading the election of the duke of Oldenburg; or finally from respect for the wishes of fortune, Napoleon declared that he would leave it to her to decide: and Bernadotte was in consequence elected crown prince of Sweden.

The newly-elected prince immediately paid his respects to the emperor, who received him frankly. "As you are offered the crown of Sweden, I permit you to accept it. I had another wish, as you know; but, in short, it is your sword which has made you a king, and you are sensible that it is not for me to stand in the way of your good fortune." He then entered very fully with him into the whole plan of his policy, in which Bernadotte appeared entirely to concur; every day he attended the emperor's levee together with his son, mixing with the other courtiers. By such marks of deference, he completely gained the

---

3: Brother of the deceased prince of that name.

heart of Napoleon. He was about to depart, poor. Unwilling that he should present himself to the Swedish throne in that necessitous state, like a mere adventurer, the emperor generously gave him two millions out of his own treasury; he even granted to his family the donations which as a foreign prince he could no longer retain himself; and they parted on apparent terms of mutual satisfaction.

It was natural that the expectations of Napoleon as to the alliance with Sweden should be heightened by this election, and by the favours which he had bestowed. At first Bernadotte's correspondence with him was that of a grateful inferior, but the very moment he was fairly out of France, feeling himself as it were relieved from a state of long and painful constraint, it is said that his hatred to Napoleon vented itself in threatening expressions, which, whether true or false, were reported to the emperor.

On his side, that monarch, forced to be absolute in his continental system, cramped the commerce of Sweden; he wished her even to exclude American vessels from her ports; and at last he declared that he would only regard as friends the enemies of Great Britain. Bernadotte was obliged to make his election; the winter and the sea separated him from the assistance, or protected him from the attacks, of the English; the French were close to his ports; a war with France therefore would be real and effective; a war with England would be merely on paper. The prince of Sweden adopted the latter alternative.

Napoleon, however, being as much a conqueror in peace as in war, and suspecting the intentions of Bernadotte, had demanded from Sweden several supplies of rigging for his Brest fleet, and the despatch of a body of troops, which were to be in his pay; in this manner weakening his allies to subdue his enemies, so as to allow him to be the master of both. He also required that colonial produce should be subjected in Sweden, the same as in France, to a duty of five per cent. It is even affirmed that he applied to Bernadotte to allow French custom-house officers to be placed at Gottenburg. These demands were eluded.

Soon after, Napoleon proposed an alliance between Sweden, Denmark, and the grand duchy of Warsaw; a northern confederation, of which he would have declared himself protector, like that of the Rhine. The answer of Bernadotte, without being absolutely negative, had the same effect; it was the same with the offensive and defensive treaty which Napoleon again proposed to him. Bernadotte has since declared, that in four successive letters written with his own hand, he had frankly stated the impossibility he was under of complying with his wishes, and repeated his protestations of attachment to his former sovereign, but that the latter never deigned to give him any reply. This impolitic silence (if the fact be true,) can only be attributed to the pride of Napoleon, which was piqued at Bernadotte's refusals. No doubt he considered his protestations as too false to deserve any answer.

The irritation increased; the communications became disagreeable; they were interrupted by the recall of Alquier, the French minister in Sweden. As the pretended declaration of war by Bernadotte against England remained a dead letter, Napoleon, who was not to be denied or deceived with impunity, carried on a sharp war against the Swedish commerce by means of his privateers. By them, and the invasion of Swedish Pomerania on the 27th of January, 1812, he punished Bernadotte for his deviations from the continental system, and obtained as prisoners several thousand Swedish soldiers and sailors, whom he had in vain demanded as auxiliaries.

Then also our communications with Russia were broken off. Napoleon immediately addressed himself to the prince of Sweden; his notes were couched in the style of a lord paramount who fancies he speaks in the interest of his vassal, who feels the claims he has upon his gratitude or submission, and who calculates upon his obedience. He demanded that Bernadotte should declare a real war against England, shut her out from the Baltic, and send an army of 40,000 Swedes against Russia. In return for this, he promised him his protection, the restoration of Finland, and twenty millions, in return for an equal amount of colonial produce, which the Swedes were first to deliver. Austria undertook to support this proposition; but Bernadotte, already feeling himself settled on the throne, answered like an independent monarch. Ostensibly he declared himself neutral, opened his ports to all nations, proclaimed his rights and his grievances, appealed to humanity, recommended peace, and offered himself as a mediator; secretly, he offered himself to Napoleon at the price of Norway, Finland, and a subsidy.

At the reading of a letter conceived in this new and unexpected style, Bonaparte was seized with rage and astonishment. He saw in it, and not without reason, a premeditated defection on the part of Bernadotte, a secret agreement with his enemies! He was filled with indignation; he exclaimed, striking violently on the letter, and the table on which it lay open: "He! the rascal! he presume to give me advice! to dictate the law to me! to dare propose such an infamous act[4] to me! And this from a man who owes every thing to my bounty! What ingratitude!" Then,

---

4: Napoleon no doubt spoke of the proposal which Bernadotte made to him to take Norway from Denmark, his faithful ally, in order by this act of treachery to purchase the assistance of Sweden.

pacing the room with rapid strides, at intervals he gave vent to such expressions as these: "I ought to have expected it! he has always sacrificed every thing to his interests! This is the same man, who, during his short ministry, attempted the resurrection of the infamous Jacobins! When he looked only to gain by disorder, he opposed the 18th Brumaire! He it was who was conspiring in the west against the re-establishment of law and religion! Has not his envious and perfidious inaction already betrayed the French army at Auerstadt? How many times, from regard to Joseph, have I pardoned his intrigues and concealed his faults! And yet I have made him general-in-chief, marshal, duke, prince, and finally king! But see how all these favours and the pardon of so many injuries, are thrown away on a man like this! If Sweden, half devoured by Russia, for a century past, has retained her independence, she owes it to the support of France. But it matters not; Bernadotte requires the baptism of the ancient aristocracy! a baptism of blood, and of French blood! and you will soon see, that to satisfy his envy and ambition, he will betray both his native and adopted country."

In vain did they attempt to calm him. They represented the difficulties which Bernadotte's new situation had imposed on him; that the cession of Finland to Russia had separated Sweden from the continent, almost made an island of that country, and thereby enlisted her in the English system.—In such critical circumstances, all the need which he had of this ally was unable to vanquish his pride, which revolted at a proposition which he regarded as insulting; perhaps also in the new prince of Sweden he still saw the same Bernadotte who was lately his subject, and his military inferior, and who at last affected to have cut out for himself a destiny independent of his. From that moment his instructions to his minister bore the impress of that disposition; the latter, it is true, softened the bitterness of them, but a rupture became inevitable.

It is uncertain which contributed most to it, the pride of Napoleon, or the ancient jealousy of Bernadotte; it is certain that on the part of the former the motives of it were honourable. "Denmark" he said, "was his most faithful ally; her attachment to France had cost her the loss of her fleet and the burning of her capital. Must he repay a fidelity which had been so cruelly tried, by an act of treachery such as that of taking Norway from her to give to Sweden?"

As to the subsidy which Sweden required of him, he answered, as he had done to Turkey, "that if the war was to be carried on with money, England would always be sure to outbid him;" and above all, "that there was weakness and baseness in triumphing by corruption." Reverting by this to his wounded pride, he terminated the conference by exclaiming, "Bernadotte impose conditions on me! Does he fancy then that I have need of him? I will soon bind him to my victorious career, and compel him to follow my sovereign impulse."

But the active and speculative English, who were out of his reach, made a judicious estimate of the weak points of his system, and found the Russians ready to act upon their suggestions. They it was who had been endeavouring for the last three years to draw the forces of Napoleon into the defiles of Spain, and to exhaust them; it was they also who were on the watch to take advantage of the vindictive enmity of the prince of Sweden.

Knowing that the active and restless vanity of men newly risen from obscurity is always uneasy and susceptible, in the presence of ancient *parvenus*, George and Alexander were lavish of their promises and flattery, in order to cajole Bernadotte. It was thus that they caressed him, at the time that the irritated Napoleon was threatening him; they promised him Norway and a subsidy, when the other, forced to refuse him that province of a faithful ally, took possession of Pomerania. While Napoleon, a monarch deriving his elevation from himself, relying on the faith of treaties, on the remembrance of past benefits, and on the real interests of Sweden, required succours from Bernadotte, the hereditary monarchs of London and Petersburgh required his opinion with deference, and submitted themselves by anticipation to the counsels of his experience. Finally, while the genius of Napoleon, the grandeur of his elevation, the importance of his enterprise, and the habit of their former relations, still classed Bernadotte as his lieutenant, these monarchs appeared already to treat him as their general. How was it possible for him not to seek to escape on the one hand from this sense of inferiority, and on the other to resist a mode of treatment, and promises so seductive? Thus the future prospects of Sweden were sacrificed, and her independence for ever laid at the mercy of Russian faith by the treaty of Petersburgh, which Bernadotte signed on the 24th of March, 1812. That of Bucharest, between Alexander and Mahmoud, was concluded on the 28th of May.—Thus did we lose the support of our two wings.

Nevertheless, the emperor of the French, at the head of more than six hundred thousand men, and already too far advanced to think of retreating, flattered himself that his strength would decide every thing; that a victory on the Niemen would cut the knot of all these diplomatic difficulties, which he despised, probably too much; that then all the monarchs of Europe, compelled to acknowledge his ascendancy, would be eager to return into his system, and that all those satellites would be drawn into its vortex.

CHAPTER 5

Opposition to Napoleon's Plans

Napoleon meanwhile was still at Paris, in the midst of his great officers, who were alarmed by the terrible encounter which was preparing. The latter had nothing more to acquire, but much to preserve; their personal interest, therefore, was united with the general desire of nations, which were fatigued with war; and without disputing the utility of this expedition, they dreaded its approach. But they only confessed this to each other in secret, either from fear of giving umbrage, of impairing the confidence of nations, or of being proved wrong by the result. For that reason, in Napoleon's presence they remained silent, and even appeared to be uninformed as to a war, which for a considerable time had furnished a subject of conversation to the whole of Europe.

But at length this respectful taciturnity, which he himself had taken pains to impose, became disagreeable; he suspected that it proceeded more from disapprobation than reserve. Obedience was not sufficient for him; it was his wish to combine it with conviction: that was like another conquest. Besides, no one was more convinced than himself of the power of public opinion, which, according to him, *created or destroyed sovereigns*. In short, whether through policy or self-love, it was his desire to persuade.

Such were the dispositions of Napoleon and of the grandees who surrounded him, when the veil being about to be rent, and war evident, their silence towards him assumed a greater appearance of indiscretion than hazarding a few timely words. Some of them, therefore, commenced the task, and the emperor anticipated the others.

A show was made[5] at first of comprehending all the emergencies of his position. "It was necessary to complete what had been begun; it

---

5: The arch-chancellor.

was impossible to stop in the midst of so rapid an acclivity, and so near the summit. The empire of Europe was adapted to his genius; France would become its centre and its base; great and entire, she would perceive around her none but states so feeble and so divided, that all coalition among them would become contemptible or impossible; but with such an object why did he not commence the task by subjecting and partitioning the states immediately around him?"

To this objection Napoleon replied, "That such had been his project in 1809, in the war with Austria, but that the misfortune of Esslingen had deranged his plan; that that event, and the doubtful dispositions which Russia had since exhibited, had led him to marry an Austrian princess, and strengthen himself by an alliance with the Austrian against the Russian emperor.

"That he did not create circumstances, but that he would not allow them to escape him; that he comprehended them all, and held himself in as much readiness as possible for their appearance; that in order to accomplish his designs, he was fully aware that twelve years were necessary, but that he could not afford to wait so long.

"That besides, he had not provoked this war; that he had been faithful to his engagements with Alexander; proofs of which were to be found in the coldness of his relations with Turkey and Sweden, which had been delivered up to Russia, one almost entirely, the other shorn of Finland, and even of the Isle of Aland, which was so near Stockholm. That he had only replied to the distressed appeal of the Swedes, by advising them to make the cession.

"That, nevertheless, since 1809, the Russian army destined to act in concert with Poniatowski in Austrian Gallicia had come forward too late, was too weak, and had acted perfidiously; that since that time, Alexander, by his ukase of the 31st of December, 1810, had abandoned the continental system, and by his prohibitions declared an actual war against French commerce; that he was quite aware that the interest and national spirit of the Russians might have compelled him to that, but that he had then communicated to their emperor that he was aware of his position, and would enter into every kind of arrangement which his repose required; in spite of which, Alexander, instead of modifying his ukase, had assembled 80,000 men, under pretence of supporting his custom-house officers; that he had suffered himself to be seduced by England; that, lastly, he even now refused to recognize the thirty-second military division, and demanded the evacuation of Prussia by the French; which was equivalent to a declaration of war."

Through all these complaints, some persons thought they perceived that the pride of Napoleon was wounded by the independent attitude which Russia was daily resuming. The dispossession of the Russian Princess of Oldenburg of her duchy led to other conjectures; it was said that hints had been given both at Tilsit and Erfurt about a divorce, after which a closer alliance might be contracted with Russia; that these hints had not been encouraged, and that Napoleon retained a resentful remembrance of it. This fact is affirmed by some, and denied by others.

But all those passions which so despotically govern other men, possessed but a feeble influence over a genius so firm and vast as his: at the utmost, they may have imparted the first momentum which impelled him into action earlier than he would have wished; but without penetrating so deeply beneath the folds of his great mind, a single idea, an obvious fact, was enough to hurry him, sooner or later, into that decisive struggle,—that was, the existence of an empire, which rivalled his own in greatness, but was still young, like its prince, and growing every day; while the French empire, already mature, like its emperor, could scarcely anticipate any thing but its decrease.

Whatever was the height to which Napoleon had raised the throne of the south and west of Europe, he perceived the northern throne of Alexander ever ready to overshadow him by its eternally menacing position. On those icy summits of Europe, whence, in former times, so many floods of barbarians had rushed forth, he perceived all the elements of a new inundation collecting and maturing. Till then, Austria and Prussia had opposed sufficient barriers; but these he himself had humbled and overthrown: he stood, therefore, single, front to front with what he feared; he alone remained the champion of the civilization, the riches, and the enjoyments of the nations of the south, against the rude ignorance, and the fierce cupidity, of the poorer people of the north, and against the ambition of their emperor and his nobility.

It was obvious, that war alone could decide this great arbitrament,—this great and eternal struggle between the poor and the rich; and, nevertheless, this war, with reference to us, was neither European, nor even national. Europe entered into it against her inclination, because the object of the expedition was to add to the strength of her conqueror. France was exhausted, and anxious for repose; her grandees, who formed the court of Napoleon, were alarmed at the double-headed character of the war, at the dispersion of our armies from Cadiz to Moscow; and even when admitting the *eventual* necessity of the struggle, its *immediate* urgency did not appear to them so legitimately proved.

They knew that it was more especially by an appeal to his political interest that they had any chance of shaking the resolution of a prince, whose principle was, "that there exist individuals whose conduct can but rarely be regulated by their private sentiments, but always by surrounding circumstances." In this persuasion, one of his ministers[6] said to him, "that his finances required tranquillity;" but he replied, "On the contrary, they are embarrassed, and require war." Another[7] added, "that the state of his revenues never, in fact, had been more flourishing; that, independent of a furnished account of from three to four millions, it was really wonderful to find France unencumbered with any urgent debts; but that this prosperous condition was approaching its termination, since it appeared that with the year 1812 a ruinous campaign was to commence; that hitherto, war had been made to support the expense of war; that we had every where found the table laid out; but that, in future, we could no longer live at the expense of Germany, since she had become our ally; but, on the contrary, it would be necessary to support her contingents, and that without any hope of remuneration, whatever the result might be; that we should have to pay at Paris for every ration of bread which would be consumed at Moscow, as the new scenes of action offered us no harvest to reap, independent of glory, but cordage, pitch, and shipping-tackle, which would certainly go but a small way towards the discharge of the expenses of a continental war. That France was not in a condition to subsidize all Europe in this manner, especially at a moment when her resources were drained by the war in Spain; that it was like lighting a fire at both ends at once, which, gaining ground upon the centre, exhausted by so many efforts,—would probably end in consuming ourselves."

This minister was listened to; the emperor surveyed him with a smiling air, accompanied with one of his familiar caresses. He imagined that he had secured conviction, but Napoleon said to him,—"So you think that I shall not be able to find a paymaster to discharge the expenses of the war?" The duke endeavoured to learn upon whom the burden was to fall, when the emperor, by a single word, disclosing all the grandeur of his designs, closed the lips of his astonished minister.

He estimated, however, but too accurately all the difficulties of his enterprise. It was that, perhaps, which drew upon him the reproach of availing himself of a method which he had rejected in the Austrian war, and of which the celebrated Pitt had set the example in 1793.

6: Count Mollien.
7: The Duke of Gaeta.

Towards the end of 1811, the prefect of police at Paris learnt, it was said, that a printer was secretly counterfeiting Russian bank-bills; he ordered him to be arrested; the printer resisted; but in the result his house was broken into, and himself taken before the magistrate, whom he astonished by his assurance, and still more by his appeal from the minister of police. This printer was instantly released: it has even been added, that he continued his counterfeiting employment; and that, from the moment of our first advance into Lithuania, we propagated the report that we had gained possession at Wilna of several millions of Russian bank-bills in the military chests of the hostile army.

Whatever may have been the origin of this counterfeit money, Napoleon contemplated it with extreme repugnance; it is even unknown whether he resolved on making any use of it; at least, it is certain that during the period of our retreat, and when we abandoned Wilna, the greater part of these bills were found there untouched, and burnt by his orders.

CHAPTER 6

Support from Poniatowski

Prince Poniatowski, however, to whom this expedition appeared to hold out the prospect of a throne, generously united his exertions with those of the emperor's ministers in the attempt to demonstrate its danger. Love of country was in this Polish prince a great and noble passion; his life and death have proved it; but it never infatuated him. He depicted Lithuania as an impracticable desert; its nobility as already become half Russian; the character of its inhabitants as cold and backward: but the impatient emperor interrupted him; he required information for the sake of conducting the enterprise, and not to be deterred from it.

It is true that the greater part of these objections were but a feeble repetition of all those which, for a long time past, had presented themselves to his own mind. People were not aware of the extent to which he had appreciated the danger; of his multiplied exertions, from the 30th of December 1810, to ascertain the nature of the territory which, sooner or later, was destined to become the theatre of a decisive war; how many emissaries he had despatched for the purpose of survey; the multitude of memorials which he caused to be prepared for him respecting the roads to Petersburgh and Moscow; respecting the dispositions of the inhabitants, especially of the mercantile class; and, finally, the resources of every kind which the country was enabled to supply. If he persevered, it was because, far from deceiving himself as to the extent of his force, he did not share in that confidence which, perhaps, precluded others from perceiving of how much consequence the humiliation of Russia was to the future existence of the great French empire.

In this spirit, he once more addressed himself to three[8] of his great officers, whose well-known services and attachment authorized a tone

---

8: The Duke of Frioul, the Count de Segur, (the author's father,) the Duke of Vicenza.

of frankness. All three, in the capacity of ministers, envoys, and ambassadors, had become acquainted with Russia at different epochs. He exerted himself to convince them of the utility, justice, and necessity of this war; but one[9] of them, in particular, often interrupted him with impatience; for when a discussion had once commenced, Napoleon submitted to all its little breaches of decorum.

That great officer, yielding to the inflexible and impetuous frankness which he derived from his character, from his military education, and, perhaps, from the province which gave him birth, exclaimed, "That it was useless to deceive himself, or pretend to deceive others; that after possessing himself of the Continent, and even of the states belonging to the family of his ally, that ally could not be accused of abandoning the continental system. While the French armies covered all Europe, how could the Russians be reproached for increasing their army? Did it become the ambition of Napoleon to denounce the ambition of Alexander?

"That, in addition to this, the determination of that prince was made up; that, Russia once invaded, no peace could be expected, while a single Frenchman remained upon her soil; that, in that respect, the national and obstinate pride of the Russians was in perfect harmony with that of their emperor.

"That, it was true, his subjects accused Alexander of weakness, but very erroneously; that he was not to be judged of by the complacency which, at Tilsit and at Erfurt, his admiration, his inexperience, and some tincture of ambition, had extorted from him. That this prince loved justice; that he was anxious to have right on his side, and he might, indeed, hesitate till he thought it was so, but then he became inflexible; that, finally, looking to his position with reference to his subjects, he incurred more danger by making a disgraceful peace, than by sustaining an unfortunate war.

"How was it possible, moreover, to avoid seeing that in this war every thing was to be feared, even our allies? Did not Napoleon hear their discontented kings murmuring that they were only his prefects? When they, all of them, only waited a suitable occasion in order to turn against him, why run the risk of giving that occasion birth?"

At the same time, supported by his two colleagues, the duke added, "that since 1805 a system of war which compelled the most disciplined soldier to plunder, had sown the seeds of hatred throughout the whole of that Germany, which the emperor now designed to traverse.

9: The Duke of Vicenza.

Was he then going to precipitate himself and his army beyond all those nations whose wounds, for which they were indebted to us, were not yet healed? What an accumulation of enmity and revenge would he not, by so doing, interpose between himself and France!

"And upon whom did he call, to be his *points d'appui?*—on Prussia, whom for five years we had been devouring, and whose alliance was hollow and compulsive? He was about, therefore, to trace the longest line of military operations ever drawn, through countries whose fear was taciturn, supple, and perfidious, and which, like the ashes of volcanoes, hid terrific flames, the eruption of which might be provoked by the smallest collision[10].

"To sum up all[11], what would be the result of so many conquests? To substitute lieutenants for kings, who, more ambitious than those of Alexander, would, perhaps, imitate their example, without, like them, waiting for the death of their sovereign,—a death, moreover, which he would inevitably meet among so many fields of battle; and that, before the consolidation of his labours, each war reviving in the interior of France the hopes of all kinds of parties, and reviving discussions which had been regarded as at an end.

"Did he wish to know the opinion of the army? That opinion pronounced that his best soldiers were then in Spain; that the regiments, being too often recruited, wanted unity; that they were not reciprocally acquainted; that each was uncertain whether, in case of danger, it could depend upon the other; that the front rank vainly concealed the weakness of the two others; that already, from youth and weakness, many of them sank in their first march beneath the single burden of their knapsacks and their arms.

"And, nevertheless, in this expedition, it was not so much the war which was disliked, as the country where it was to be carried on[12]. The Lithuanians, it was said, desired our presence; but on what a soil? in what a climate? in the midst of what peculiar manners? The campaign of 1806 had made those circumstances too well known! Where could they ever halt, in the midst of these level plains, divested of every species of position fortified by nature or by art?

"Was it not notorious, that all the elements protected these countries from the first of October to the first of June? that, at any other time than the short interval comprised between these two epochs,

---

10: The Duke of Vicenza, the Count de Segur.
11: The Count de Segur.
12: The Duke of Frioul, the Count de Segur, the Duke of Vicenza.

an army engaged in those deserts of mud and ice might perish there entirely, and ingloriously?" And, they added, "that Lithuania was much more Asiatic than Spain was African; and that the French army, already all but banished from France by a perpetual war, wished at least to preserve its European character.

"Finally, when face to face with the enemy in these deserts, what different motives must actuate the different armies! On the side of the Russians were country, independence, every description of interest, private and public, even to the secret good wishes of our allies! On our side, and in the teeth of so many obstacles, glory alone, unassociated even with that desire of gain, to which the frightful poverty of these countries offered no attraction.

"And what is the end of so many exertions? The French already no longer recognized each other, in the midst of a country now uncircumscribed by any natural frontier; and in which the diversity was so great in manners, persons, and languages." On this particular point, the eldest[13] of these great officers added, "That such an extension was never made without proportionate exhaustion; that it was blotting out France to merge it in Europe; for, in fact, when France should become Europe, it would be France no longer. Would not the meditated departure leave her solitary, deserted, without a ruler, without an army, accessible to every diversion? Who then was there to defend her?" "*My renown!*" exclaimed the emperor: "*I leave my name behind me, and the fear inspired by a nation in arms.*"

And, without appearing in the least shaken by so many objections, he announced "that he was about to organize the empire into cohorts of *Ban* and *Arrière Ban*; and without mistrust to leave to Frenchmen the protection of France, of his crown, and of his glory.

"That as to Prussia, he had secured her tranquillity by the impossibility in which he had placed her of moving, even in case of his defeat, or of a descent of the English on the coasts of the North Sea, and in our rear; that he held in his hands the civil and military power of that kingdom; that he was master of Stettin, Custrin, Glogau, Torgau, Spandau, and Magdeburg; that he would post some clear-sighted officers at Colberg, and an army at Berlin; and that with these means, and supported by the fidelity of Saxony, he had nothing to fear from Prussian hatred.

"That as for the rest of Germany, an ancient system of policy, as well as the recent intermarriages with Baden, Bavaria, and Austria, attached her to the interest of France; that he made sure of such of her kings as

---

13: M. de Segur.

were indebted to him for their new titles: that after having suppressed anarchy, and ranged himself on the side of kings, strong as he was, the latter could not attack him without inciting their people by the principles of democracy; but that it was scarcely probable that sovereigns would ally themselves with that natural enemy of thrones—an enemy, which, had it not been for him, would have overthrown them, and against which he alone was capable of defending them.

"That, besides, the Germans were a tardy and methodical people, and that in dealing with them he should always have time on his side; that he commanded all the fortresses of Prussia; that Dantzic was a second Gibraltar." This was incorrect, especially in winter. "That Russia ought to excite the apprehension of all Europe, by her military and conquering government, as well as by her savage population, already so numerous, and which augmented annually in the proportion of half a million. Had not her armies been seen in all parts of Italy, in Germany, and even on the Rhine? That by demanding the evacuation of Prussia, she required an impossible concession; since to abandon Prussia, morally ulcerated as she was, was to surrender her into the hands of Russia, in order to be turned against ourselves."

Proceeding afterwards with more animation, he exclaimed, "Why menace my absence with the different parties still alleged to exist in the interior of the empire? Where are they? I see but a single one against me; that of a few royalists, the principal part of the ancient *noblesse*, superannuated and inexperienced. But they dread my downfall more than they desire it. This is what I told them in Normandy. I am cried up as a great captain, as an able politician, but I am scarcely mentioned as an administrator: that which I have, however, accomplished, of the most difficult and most beneficial description, is the stemming the revolutionary torrent; it would have swallowed up every thing, Europe and yourselves. I have united the most opposite parties, amalgamated rival classes, and yet there exist among you some obstinate nobles who resist; they refuse my places! Very well! what is that to me? It is for your advantage, for your security, that I offer them to you. What would you do singly by yourselves, and without me? You are a mere handful opposed to masses. Do you not see that it is necessary to put an end to the struggle between the *tiers-état* and the *noblesse*, by a complete fusion of all that is best worth preservation in the two classes? I offer you the hand of amity, and you reject it! but what need have I of you? While I support you, I do myself an injury in the eyes of the people; for what am I but the king of the *tiers-état*: is not that sufficient?"

Passing more calmly to another question: "He was quite aware," he said, "of the ambition of his generals; but it was diverted by war, and would never be sanctioned in its excesses by French soldiers, who were too proud of, and too much attached to their country. That if war was dangerous, peace had also its dangers: that in bringing back his armies into the interior, it would enclose and concentrate there too many daring interests and passions, which repose and their association would tend to ferment, and which he should no longer be able to keep within bounds: that it was necessary to give free vent to all such aspirations; and that, after all, he dreaded them less without the empire than within it."

He concluded thus: "Do you dread the war, as endangering my life? It was thus that, in the times of conspiracy, attempts were made to frighten me about Georges; he was said to be every where upon my track: that wretched being was to fire at me. Well! suppose he had! He would at the utmost have killed my aide-de-camp: but to kill me was impossible! Had I at that time accomplished the decrees of fate? I feel myself impelled towards a goal of which I am ignorant. As soon as I shall have reached it, so soon shall I no longer be of service,—an atom will then suffice to put me down; but till then, all human efforts can avail nothing against me. Whether I am in Paris, or with the army, is, therefore, quite indifferent. When my hour comes, a fever, or a fall from my horse in hunting, will kill me as effectually as a bullet: our days are numbered."

This opinion, useful as it may be in the moment of danger, is too apt to blind conquerors to the price at which the great results which they obtain are purchased. They indulge a belief in pre-destination, either because they have experienced, more than other men, whatever is most unexpected in human destiny, or because it relieves their consciences of too heavy a load of responsibility. It was like a return to the times of the crusades, when these words, *it is the will of God*, were considered a sufficient answer to all the objections of a prudent and pacific policy.

Indeed, the expedition of Napoleon into Russia bears a mournful resemblance to that of St. Louis into Egypt and Africa. These invasions, the one undertaken for the interests of Heaven, the other for those of the earth, terminated in a similar manner; and these two great examples admonish the world, that the vast and profound calculations of this age of intelligence may be followed by the same results as the irregular impulses of religious frenzy in ages of ignorance and superstition.

In these two expeditions, however, there can be no comparison between their opportunities or their chances of success. The last was indispensable to the completion of a great design on the point of being accomplished: its object was not out of reach; the means for reaching it were not inadequate. It may be, that the moment for its execution was ill chosen; that the progress of it was sometimes too precipitate, at other times unsteady; but on these points facts will speak sufficiently: it is for them to decide.

Chapter 7
Josephine

In this manner did Napoleon reply to all objections. His skilful hand was able to comprehend and turn to his purpose every disposition; and, in fact, when he wanted to persuade, there was a kind of charm in his deportment which it was impossible to resist. One felt overpowered by his superior strength, and compelled, as it were, to submit to his influence. It was, if it may be so expressed, a kind of magnetic influence; for his ardent and variable genius infused itself entirely into all his desires, the least as well as the greatest: whatever he willed, all his energies and all his faculties united to effect: they appeared at his beck; they hastened forward; and, obedient to his dictation, simultaneously assumed the forms which he desired.

It was thus that the greater part of those whom he wished to gain over found themselves, as it were, fascinated by him in spite of themselves. It was flattering to your vanity to see the master of Europe appearing to have no other ambition, no other desire than that of convincing you; to behold those features, so formidable to multitudes, expressing towards you no other feeling but a mild and affecting benevolence; to hear that mysterious man, whose every word was historical, yielding, as if for your sake alone, to the irresistible impulse of the most frank and confiding disclosure; and that voice, so caressing while it addressed you, was it not the same, whose lowest whisper rang throughout all Europe, announced wars, decided battles, settled the fate of empires, raised or destroyed reputations? What vanity could resist a charm of so great potency? Any defensive position was forced on all points; his eloquence was so much more persuasive, as he himself appeared to be persuaded.

On this occasion, there was no variety of tints with which his brilliant and fertile imagination did not adorn his project, in order to convince and allure. The same text supplied him with a thousand different commentaries, with which the character and position of each of his interlocutors inspired him; he enlisted each in his undertaking, by presenting it to him under the form and colour, and point of view, most likely to gratify him.

We have just seen in what way he silenced the one who felt alarmed at the expenses of the conquest of Russia, which he wished him to approve, by holding out the perspective, that another would be made to defray them.

He told the military man, who was astonished by the hazard of the expedition, but likely to be easily seduced by the grandeur of ambitious ideas, that peace was to be conquered at Constantinople; that is to say, at the extremity of Europe; the individual was thus free to anticipate, that it was not merely to the staff of a marshal, but to a royal sceptre, that he might elevate his pretensions.

To a minister[14] of high rank under the ancient regime, whom the idea of shedding so much blood, to gratify ambition, filled with dismay, he declared "that it was a war of policy exclusively; that it was the English alone whom he meant to attack through Russia; that the campaign would be short; that afterwards France would be at rest; that it was the fifth act of the drama—the *dénouement*."

To others, he pleaded the ambition of Russia, and the force of circumstances, which dragged him into the war in spite of himself. With superficial and inexperienced individuals, to whom he neither wished to explain nor dissemble, he cut matters short, by saying, "You understand nothing of all this; you are ignorant of its antecedents and its consequents."

But to the princes of his own family he had long revealed the state of his thoughts; he complained that they did not sufficiently appreciate his position. "Can you not see," said he to them, "that as I was not born upon a throne, I must support myself on it, as I ascended it, by my renown? that it is necessary for it to go on increasing; that a private individual, become a sovereign like myself, can no longer stop; that he must be continually ascending, and that to remain stationary will be his ruin?"

He then depicted to them all the ancient dynasties armed against his, devising plots, preparing wars, and seeking to destroy, in his person, the dangerous example of a *roi parvenu*. It was on that account that every peace appeared in his eyes a conspiracy of the weak against the strong, of the vanquished against the victor; and especially of the great

---

14: Count Molé.

by birth against the great by their own exertions. So many successive coalitions had confirmed him in that apprehension! Indeed, he often thought of no longer tolerating an ancient power in Europe, of constituting himself into an epoch, of becoming a new era for thrones; in short, of making every thing take its date from him.

It was in this manner that he disclosed his inmost thoughts to his family by those vivid pictures of his political position, which, at the present day, will probably appear neither false nor over-coloured: and yet the gentle Josephine, always occupied with the task of restraining and calming him, often gave him to understand "that, along with the consciousness of his superior genius, he never seemed to possess sufficient consciousness of his own power: that, like all jealous characters, he incessantly required fresh proofs of its existence. How came it, amidst the noisy acclamations of Europe, that his anxious ear could hear the few solitary voices which disputed his legitimacy? that in this manner his troubled spirit was always seeking agitation as its element: that strong as he was to desire, but feeble to enjoy, he himself, therefore, would be the only one whom he could never conquer."

But in 1811 Josephine was separated from Napoleon, and although he still continued to visit her in her seclusion, the voice of that empress had lost the influence which continual intercourse, familiar habits of affection, and the desire of mutual confidence, impart.

Meanwhile, fresh disagreements with the pope complicated the relations of France. Napoleon then addressed himself to cardinal Fesch. Fesch was a zealous churchman, and overflowing with Italian vivacity: he defended the papal pretensions with obstinate ardour; and such was the warmth of his discussions with the emperor, on a former occasion, that the latter got into a passion, and told him, "that he would compel him to obey." "And who contests your power?" returned the cardinal: "but force is not argument; for if I am right, not all your power can make me wrong. Besides, your majesty knows that I do not fear martyrdom."—"Martyrdom!" replied Buonaparte, with a transition from violence to laughter; "do not reckon on that, I beseech you, M. le Cardinal: martyrdom is an affair in which there must be two persons concerned; and as to myself, I have no desire to make a martyr of any individual."

It is said that these discussions assumed a more serious character towards the end of 1811. An eye-witness asserts that the cardinal, till that time a stranger to politics, then began to mix them up with his religious controversies; that he conjured Napoleon not thus to fly in the face of men, the elements, religion, earth and heaven, at the same time; and that, at last, he expressed his apprehension of seeing him sink under such a weight of enmity.

The only reply which the emperor made to this vehement attack was to take him by the hand, and leading him to the window, to open it, and inquire, "Do you see that star above us?"—"No, sire."—"Look again."—"Sire, I do not see it."—"Very well! *I* see it!" replied Napoleon. The cardinal, seized with astonishment, remained silent, concluding that there was no human voice sufficiently loud to make itself heard by an ambition so gigantic, that it already reached the heavens.

As to the witness of this singular scene, he understood in quite a different sense these words of his sovereign. They did not appear to him like the expression of an overweening confidence in his destiny, but rather of the great distinction which Napoleon meant to infer as existing between the grasp of his genius and that of the cardinal's policy.

But granting even that Napoleon's soul was not exempt from a tendency to superstition, his intellect was both too strong and too enlightened to permit such vast events to depend upon a weakness. One great inquietude possessed him; it was the idea of that same death, which he appeared so much to brave. He felt his strength decaying; and he dreaded that when he should be no more, the French empire, that sublime trophy of so many labours and victories, would fall a prey to dismemberment.

"The Russian emperor," he said, "was the only sovereign who pressed upon the summit of that colossal edifice. Replete with youth and animation, the strength of his rival was constantly augmenting, while his was already on the decline." It seemed to him that Alexander, on the banks of the Niemen, only waited the intelligence of his death, to possess himself of the sceptre of Europe, and snatch it from the hands of his feeble successor. "While all Italy, Switzerland, Austria, Prussia, and the whole of Germany, were marching under his banners, why should he delay to anticipate the danger, and consolidate the fabric of the great empire, by driving back Alexander and the Russian power, enfeebled as they would be by the loss of all Poland, beyond the Boristhenes?"

Such were his sentiments, pronounced in secret confidence; they, doubtless, comprised the true motives of that terrible war. As to his precipitation in commencing it, he was, it would seem, hurried on by the instinct of his approaching death. An acrid humour diffused through his blood, and to which he imputed his irascibility, ("but without which," added he, "battles are not to be gained,") undermined his constitution.

A profound knowledge of the organization and mysteries of the human frame would probably enable us to decide whether this concealed malady was not one of the causes of that restless activity which hurried on the course of events, and in which originated both his elevation and his fall.

This internal enemy testified its presence, more and more, by an internal pain, and by the violent spasms of the stomach which it inflicted. Even in 1806, at Warsaw, during one of its agonizing crises, Napoleon was[15] heard to exclaim, "that he carried about with him the germ of premature dissolution; and that he should die of the same malady as his father."

Short rides in hunting, even the most gentle gallop of his horse, already began to fatigue him: how then was he to support the long journeys, and the rapid and violent movements preparatory to battles? Thus it was, that while the greater part of those who surrounded him concluded him to be impelled into Russia by his vast ambition, by his restless spirit and his love of war, he in solitude, and almost unobserved, was poising the fearful responsibilities of the enterprise, and urged by necessity, he only made up his mind to it after a course of painful hesitation.

At length, on the 3rd of August, 1811, at an audience in the midst of all the ambassadors of Europe, he declared himself; but the burst of indignation which was the presage of war, was an additional proof of his repugnance to commence it. It might be that the defeat which the Russians had just sustained at Routschouk had inflated his hopes; perhaps he imagined that he might, by menace, arrest the preparations of Alexander.

It was prince Kourakin whom he addressed. That ambassador having just made protestations of the pacific intentions of his master, he interrupted him: "No," exclaimed he, "your master desires war; I know, through my generals, that the Russian army is hurrying towards the Niemen! The emperor Alexander deludes, and gains all my envoys!" Then, perceiving Caulaincourt, he rapidly traversed the hall, and violently appealing to him, said: "Yes, and you too have become a Russian: you have been seduced by the emperor Alexander." The duke firmly replied, "Yes, sire; because, in this question, I consider him to be a Frenchman." Napoleon was silent; but from that moment, he treated that great dignitary coldly, without, however, absolutely repelling him: several times he even essayed, by fresh arguments, intermixed with familiar caresses, to win him over to his opinion, but ineffectually; he always found him inflexible; ready to serve him, but without approving the nature of the service.

15: By the count Lobau.

Chapter 8
The Peninsula

While Napoleon, prompted by his natural character, by his position, and by circumstances, thus appeared to wish for, and to accelerate the period of conflict, he preserved the secret of his embarrassment. The year 1811 was wasted in parleys about peace, and preparations for war. 1812 had just begun, and the horizon was already obscured. Our armies in Spain had given way; Ciudad Rodrigo was taken by the English (on the 19th of January, 1812); the discussions of Napoleon with the Pope increased in bitterness; Kutusoff had destroyed the Turkish army on the Danube (on the 8th of December, 1811); France even became alarmed about her means of subsistence; every thing, in short, appeared to divert the attention of Napoleon from Russia; to recall it to France, and fix it there; while he, far from blinding his judgment, recognized in these contrarieties the indications of his ever-faithful fortune.

It was, especially in the midst of those long winter nights, when individuals are left more than usually to their own reflections, that his star seemed to enlighten him with its most brilliant illumination: it exhibited to him the different ruling genii of the vanquished nations, in silence awaiting the moment for avenging their wrongs; the dangers which he was about to confront, those which he left behind him, even in his own family: it showed him, that like the returns of his army, the census of the population of his empire was delusive, not so much in respect to its numerical as to its real strength; scarcely any men were included in it but those who were old in years, or worn out in the service, and children—few men in the prime of life. Where were they? The tears of wives, the cries of mothers answered! bowed in sadness to the earth, which, but for them, would remain uncultivated, they cursed the scourge of war as identified in his person.

Nevertheless, he was about to attack Russia, without having subjected Spain; forgetting the principle of which he himself so often supplied both the precept and example, "never to strike at two points at once; but on one only, and always in mass." Wherefore, in fact, should he abandon a brilliant, though uncertain position, in order to throw himself into so critical a situation, that the slightest check might ruin every thing; and where every reverse would be decisive?

At that moment, no necessity of position, no sentiment of self-love, could prompt Napoleon to combat his own arguments, and prevent him from listening to himself. Hence he became thoughtful and agitated. He collected accounts of the actual condition of the different powers of Europe; he ordered an exact and complete summary of them to be made; and buried himself in the perusal: his anxiety increased; to him of all men, irresolution was a punishment.

Frequently was he discovered half reclined on a sofa, where he remained for hours, plunged in profound meditation; then he would start up, convulsively, and with an ejaculation, fancying he heard his name, he would exclaim, "Who calls me?" Then rising, and walking about with hurried steps, he at length added, "No! beyond a doubt, nothing is yet sufficiently matured round me, even in my own family, to admit of so distant a war. It must be delayed for three years!" And he gave orders that the summary which reminded him of the dangers of his position should be constantly left on his table. It was his frequent subject of consultation, and every time he did so, he approved and repeated his first conclusions.

It is not known what dictated so salutary an inspiration; but it is certain, that about that epoch (the 25th of March, 1812), Czernicheff was the bearer of new proposals to his sovereign. Napoleon offered to make a declaration that he would contribute, neither directly nor indirectly, to the re-establishment of the kingdom of Poland; and to come to an understanding about the other subjects in dispute.

At a later period, (on the 17th of April,) the Duke of Bassano proposed to Lord Castlereagh an arrangement relative to the Peninsula, and the kingdom of the Two Sicilies; and in other respects offered to negotiate on the basis, that each of the two powers should keep all that war could not wrest from it. But Castlereagh replied, that the engagements of good faith would not permit England to treat without making the recognition of Ferdinand VII. as king of Spain a preliminary of the negotiation.

On the 25th of April, Maret, in apprising Count Romanzoff of this communication, recapitulated a portion of the complaints which Napoleon made against Russia;—firstly, the ukase of the 31st of December, 1810, which prohibited the entry into Russia of the greater part of French productions, and destroyed the continental system; secondly, the protest of Alexander against the union of the duchy of Oldenburg; and thirdly, the armaments of Russia.

This minister referred to the fact of Napoleon having offered to grant an indemnity to the Duke of Oldenburg, and to enter into a formal engagement not to concur in any undertaking for the re-establishment of Poland; that, in 1811, he had proposed to Alexander, to give Prince Kourakin the requisite powers to treat with the duke of Bassano respecting all matters in dispute; but that the Russian emperor had eluded the overture, by promising to send Nesselrode to Paris; a promise which was never fulfilled.

The Russian ambassador, almost at the same time, transmitted the emperor Alexander's ultimatum, which required the entire evacuation of Prussia; that of Swedish Pomerania; a reduction of the garrison of Dantzic. On the other hand, he offered to accept an indemnity for the duchy of Oldenburg; he was willing to enter into commercial arrangements with France; and finally promised empty modifications of the ukase of the 31st December, 1810.

But it was too late: besides, at the point to which both parties were now arrived, that ultimatum necessarily led to war. Napoleon was too proud, both of himself and of France, he was too much overruled by his position, to yield to a menacing negotiator, to leave Prussia at liberty to throw herself into the open arms of Russia, and thus to abandon Poland. He was too far advanced; he would be obliged to retrograde, in order to find a resting point; and in his situation, Napoleon considered every retrograde step as the incipient point of a complete downfall.

CHAPTER 9

Talleyrand

His wishes for delay being thus frustrated, he surveyed the enormous volume of his military strength; the recollections of Tilsit and Erfurt were revived; he received with complacency delusive information respecting the character of his rival. At one time, he hoped that Alexander would give way at the approach of so menacing an invasion; at another, he gave the reins to his conquering imagination; he indulgently allowed it to deploy its masses from Cadiz to Cazan, and to cover the whole of Europe. In the next moment his fancy rioted in the pleasure of being at Moscow. That city was eight hundred leagues from him, and already he was collecting information with respect to it, as if he was on the eve of occupying it. A French physician having recently arrived from that capital, he sent for, and interrogated him as to the diseases there prevalent; he even went back to the plague which had formerly desolated it; he was anxious to learn its origin, progress, and termination. The answers of this physician were so satisfactory, that he immediately attached him to his service.

Fully impressed, however, with a sense of the peril in which he was about to embark, he sought to surround himself with all his friends. Even Talleyrand was recalled; he was to have been sent to Warsaw, but the jealousy of a rival and an intrigue again involved him in disgrace; Napoleon, deluded by a calumny, adroitly circulated, believed that he had been betrayed by him. His anger was extreme; its expression terrible. Savary made vain efforts to undeceive him, which were prolonged up to the epoch of our entry into Wilna; there that minister again sent a letter of Talleyrand to the emperor; it depicted the influence of Turkey and Sweden on the Russian war, and made an offer of employing his most zealous efforts in negotiating with those two powers.

But Napoleon only replied to it by an exclamation of contempt: "Does that man believe himself to be so necessary? Does he expect to teach me?" He then compelled his secretary to send that letter to the very minister who stood most in dread of Talleyrand's influence.

It would not be correct to say, that all those about Napoleon beheld the war with an anxious eye. Inside the palace, as well as without it, many military men were found who entered with ardour into the policy of their chief. The greater part agreed as to the possibility of the conquest of Russia, either because their hopes discerned in it a means of acquiring something, according to their position, from the lowest distinction up to a throne; or that they suffered themselves to participate in the enthusiasm of the Poles; or that the expedition, if conducted with prudence, might fairly look to success; or, to sum up all, because they conceived every thing possible to Napoleon.

Among the ministers of the emperor, several disapproved it; the greater number preserved silence: one alone was accused of flattery, and that without any ground. It is true he was heard to repeat, "That the emperor was not sufficiently great; that it was necessary for him to become greater still, in order to be able to stop." But that minister was, in reality, what so many courtiers wished to appear; he had a real and absolute faith in the genius and fortune of his sovereign.

In other respects, it is wrong to impute to his counsels a large portion of our misfortunes. Napoleon was not a man to be influenced. So soon as his object was marked out, and he had made advances towards its acquisition, he admitted of no farther contradiction. He then appeared as if he would hear nothing but what flattered his determination; he repelled with ill-humour, and even with apparent incredulity, all disagreeable intelligence, as if he feared to be shaken by it. This mode of acting changed its name according to his fortune; when fortunate, it was called force of character; when unfortunate, it was designated as infatuation.

The knowledge of such a disposition induced some subalterns to make false reports to him. Even a minister himself felt occasionally compelled to maintain a dangerous silence. The former inflated his hopes of success, in order to imitate the proud confidence of their chief, and in order, by their countenance, to stamp upon his mind the impression of a happy omen; the second sometimes declined communicating bad news, in order, as he said, to avoid the harsh rebuffs which he had then to encounter.

But this fear, which did not restrain Caulaincourt and several others, had as little influence upon Duroc, Daru, Lobau, Rapp, Lauriston, and sometimes even Berthier. These ministers and generals, each in his sphere, did not spare the emperor when the truth was to be told. If it so happened that he was enraged by it, Duroc, without yielding, assumed an air of indifference; Lobau resisted with roughness; Berthier sighed, and retired with tears in his eyes; Caulaincourt and Daru, the one turning pale, the other reddening with anger, repelled the vehement contradictions of the emperor; the first with impetuous obstinacy, and the second with short and dry determination.

It should, however, be added here, that these warm discussions were never productive of bad consequences; good temper was restored immediately after, apparently without leaving any other impression than redoubled esteem on the part of Napoleon, for the noble frankness which they had displayed.

I have entered into these details, because they are either not known, or imperfectly known; because Napoleon in his closet was quite different from the emperor in public; and because this portion of the palace has hitherto remained secret; for, in that new and serious court, there was little conversation: all were rigorously classed, so that one *salon* knew not what passed in another; finally, because it is difficult to comprehend the great events of history, without a perfect knowledge of the character and manners of the principal personages.

Meantime a famine threatened France. The universal panic quickly aggravated the evil, by the precautions which it suggested. Avarice, always prompt in seizing the means of enriching itself, monopolized the corn while at a low price, and waited till hunger should repurchase it at an exorbitant rate. The alarm then became general. Napoleon was compelled to suspend his departure; he impatiently urged his council; but the steps to be taken were important, his presence necessary; and that war, in which the loss of every hour was irreparable, was delayed for two months longer.

The emperor did not give way to this obstacle; the delay, besides, gave the new harvests of the Russians time to grow. These would supply his cavalry; his army would require fewer transports in its train: its progress being lightened, would be more rapid; he would sooner reach the enemy; and this great expedition, like so many others, would be terminated by a battle.

Such were his anticipations; for, without deceiving himself as to his good fortune, he reckoned on its influence upon others; it entered into his estimate of his forces. It was for this reason that he always pushed it forward where other things failed, making up by that whatever was deficient in his means, without fearing to wear it out by constant use, in the conviction that his enemies would place even more faith in it than himself. However, it will be seen in the sequel of this expedition, that he placed too much reliance on its power, and that Alexander was able to evade it.

Such was Napoleon! Superior to the passions of men by his native greatness, and also by the circumstance of being controlled by a still greater passion! for when, indeed, are these masters of the world ever entirely masters of themselves? Meantime blood was again about to flow; and thus, in their great career, the founders of empires press forward to their object, like Fate, whose ministers they seem, (and whose march neither wars nor earthquakes, nor all the scourges which Providence permits, ever arrest,) without deigning to make the utility of their purposes comprehensible to their victims.

Chapter 10
A Gathering of Princes

The time for deliberation had passed, and that for action at last arrived. On the 9th of May, 1812, Napoleon, hitherto always triumphant, quitted a palace which he was destined never again to enter victorious.

From Paris to Dresden his march was a continued triumph. The east of France, which he first traversed, was a part of the empire entirely devoted to him; very different from the west and the south, she was only acquainted with him by means of benefits and victories. Numerous and brilliant armies, attracted by the fertility of Germany, and which imagined themselves marching to a prompt and certain glory, proudly traversed those countries, scattering their money among them, and consuming their productions. War, in that quarter, always bore the semblance of justice.

At a later period, when our victorious bulletins reached them, the imagination, astonished to see itself surpassed by the reality, caught fire; enthusiasm possessed these people, as in the times of Austerlitz and Jena; numerous groups collected round the couriers, whose tidings were listened to with avidity; and the inhabitants, in a transport of joy, never separated without exclamations of "Long live the emperor! Long live our brave army!"

It is, besides, well known, that this portion of France has been warlike from time immemorial. It is frontier ground; its inhabitants are nursed amidst the din of arms; and arms are, consequently, held there in honour. It was the common conversation in that quarter, that this war would liberate Poland, so much attached to France; that the barbarians of Asia, with whom Europe was threatened, would be driven back into their native deserts; that Napoleon would once more return, loaded with all the fruits of victory. Would not the eastern departments profit most by that event? Up to that time, were they not indebted for their wealth to war, which caused all the commerce of

France with Europe to pass through their hands? Blockaded, in fact, in every other quarter, the empire only breathed and received its supplies through its eastern provinces.

For ten years, their roads had been covered with travellers of all ranks, hastening to admire the great nation, its daily embellished metropolis, the *chefs-d'oeuvre* of all the arts, and of all ages, which victory had there assembled; and especially that extraordinary man who seemed destined to carry the national glory beyond every degree of glory hitherto known. Gratified in their interests, flattered in their vanity, the people of the east of France owed every thing to victory. Neither were they ungrateful; they followed the emperor with their warmest wishes: on all sides were acclamations and triumphal arches; on all sides the same intensity of devotion.

In Germany, there was less affection, but, perhaps, more homage. Conquered and subjected, the Germans, either as soothing to their vanity, or from habitual inclination for the marvellous, were tempted to consider Napoleon as a supernatural being. Astonished, beside themselves, and carried along by the universal impulse, these worthy people exerted themselves to *be*, sincerely, all that it was requisite to *seem*.

They hurried forward to line both sides of the long road by which the emperor passed. Their princes quitted their capitals, and thronged the towns, where the great arbiter of their destiny was to pass a few short moments of his journey. The empress, and a numerous court, followed Napoleon; he proceeded to confront the terrible risks of a distant and perilous war, as if he were returning victorious and triumphant. This was not the mode in which he was formerly accustomed to meet a conflict.

He had expressed a wish that the Emperor of Austria, several kings, and a crowd of princes, should meet him at Dresden on his way: his desire was fulfilled; all thronged to meet him—some led by hope, others prompted by fear: for himself, his motives were to make sure of his power, to exhibit and to enjoy it.

In this approximation with the ancient house of Austria, his ambition delighted in exhibiting to Germany a family meeting. He imagined that so brilliant an assemblage of sovereigns would advantageously contrast with the isolated state of the Russian monarch; and that he would probably be alarmed by so general a desertion. In fact, this assembly of coalesced monarchs seemed to announce that this war with Russia was European.

He was then in the centre of Germany, exhibiting to it his consort, the daughter of its emperors, sitting by his side. Whole nations had quitted their homes to throng his path; rich and poor, nobles and plebeians, friends and enemies, all hurried to the scene. Their curious and anxious groups were seen crowding together in the streets, the roads, and the public places; they passed whole days and nights with their eyes fixed on the door and windows of his palace. It was not his crown, his rank, the luxury of his court, but him only, on whom they desired to feast their eyes; it was a memento of his features which they were anxious to obtain: they wished to be able to tell their less fortunate countrymen and posterity, that they had seen Napoleon.

On the stage, poets so far degraded themselves as to make him a divinity. It was in this manner that whole nations became his flatterers.

There was, in fact, little difference between kings and people in the homage of admiration; no one waited for the example of imitation; the agreement was unanimous. Nevertheless, the inward sentiments were very different.

At this important interview, we were attentive in observing the different degrees of zeal which these princes exhibited, and the various shades of our chieftain's pride. We had hoped that his prudence, or the worn-out feeling of displaying his power, would prevent him from abusing it; but was it to be expected that he, who, while yet an inferior, never spoke, even to his superiors, but in the language of command, now that he was the conqueror and master of them all, could submit to tedious and minute details of ceremony? He, however, displayed moderation, and even tried to make himself agreeable; but it was obviously an effort, and not without allowing the fatigue it gave him to be perceived. Among these princes, he had rather the air of receiving them, than of being by them received.

As to them, it might be said, that, knowing his pride, and become hopeless of subduing him, except by means of himself, these monarchs and their people only humbled themselves before him, in order to aggravate the disproportion of his elevation, and by so doing, to dazzle his moral vision. In their assemblies, their attitude, their words, even the tone of their voice, attested his ascendancy over them. All were assembled there for his sake alone! They scarcely hazarded an objection, so impressed were they with the full conviction of that superiority, of which he was himself too well aware. A feudal lord could not have exacted more of his vassal chiefs.

His levee presented a still more remarkable spectacle! Sovereign princes came to it in order to wait for an audience of the conqueror of Europe. They were so intermingled with his officers, that the latter were frequently warning each other to take care, and not to crowd upon these new courtiers, who were confounded with them. It was thus that the presence of Napoleon made distinctions disappear; he was as much their chief as ours. This common dependency appeared to put all around him on a level. It is probable that, even then, the ill-disguised military pride of several French generals gave offence to these princes, with whom they conceived themselves raised to an equality; and, in fact, whatever may be the noble blood and rank of the vanquished, his victor becomes his equal.

The more prudent among us, however, began to be alarmed; they said, but in an under-tone, that a man must fancy himself more than human to denaturalize and displace every thing in this manner, without fearing to involve himself in the universal confusion. They saw these monarchs quitting the palace of Napoleon with their eyes inflamed, and their bosoms swollen with the most poignant resentment. They pictured them, during the night, when alone with their ministers, giving vent to the heartfelt chagrin by which they were devoured. Every thing was calculated to render their suffering more acute! How importunate was the crowd which it was necessary to pass through, in order to reach the gate of their proud master, while their own remained deserted! Indeed, all things, even their own people, appeared to betray them. While boasting of his good fortune, was it not evident that he was insulting their misfortunes? They had, therefore, come to Dresden in order to swell the pomp of Napoleon's triumph—for it was over them that he thus triumphed: each cry of admiration offered to him was a cry of reproach to them; his grandeur was their humiliation, his victory their defeat.

Doubtless they, in this manner, gave vent to their bitter feelings; and hatred, day after day, sank more deeply into their hearts. One prince was first observed to withdraw precipitately from this painful position. The Empress of Austria, whose ancestors General Buonaparte had dispossessed in Italy, made herself remarked by her aversion, which she vainly endeavoured to disguise; it escaped from her by an involuntary impulse, which Napoleon instantly detected, and subdued by a smile: but she employed her understanding and attraction in gently winning hearts to her opinion, in order to sow them afterwards with the seeds of her hatred.

The Empress of France unintentionally aggravated this fatal disposition. She was observed to eclipse her mother-in-law by the superior magnificence of her costume: if Napoleon required more reserve, she resisted, and even wept, till the emperor, either through affection, fatigue, or absence of mind, was induced to give way. It is also asserted that notwithstanding her origin, remarks calculated to wound German pride escaped that princess, in extravagant comparisons between her native and her adopted country. Napoleon rebuked her for this, but gently; he was pleased with a patriotism which he had himself inspired; and he fancied he repaired her imprudent language by the munificence of his presents.

This assemblage, therefore, could not fail of irritating a variety of feelings: the vanity of many was wounded by the collision. Napoleon, however, having exerted himself to please, thought that he had given general satisfaction: while waiting at Dresden the result of the marches of his army, the numerous columns of which were still traversing the territories of his allies, he more especially occupied himself with his political arrangements.

General Lauriston, ambassador from France at Petersburgh, received orders to apply for the Russian emperor's permission to proceed to Wilna, in order to communicate definitive proposals to him. General Narbonne, aid-de-camp of Napoleon, departed for the imperial head-quarters of Alexander, in order to assure that prince of the pacific intentions of France, and to invite him to Dresden. The archbishop of Malines was despatched in order to direct the impulses of Polish patriotism. The King of Saxony made up his mind to the loss of the grand duchy; but he was flattered with the hope of a more substantial indemnity.

Meantime, ever since the first days of meeting, surprise was expressed at the absence of the King of Prussia from the imperial court; but it was soon understood that he was prohibited from coming. This prince was the more alarmed in proportion as he had less deserved such treatment. His presence would have been embarrassing. Nevertheless, encouraged by Narbonne, he resolved on making his appearance. When his arrival was announced to the emperor, the latter grew angry, and at first refused to see him:—"What did this prince want of him? Was not the constant importunity of his letters, and his continual solicitations sufficient? Why did he come again to persecute him with his presence? What need had he of him?" But Duroc insisted; he reminded Napoleon of the want that he would experience of Prussia, in a war with Russia; and the doors of the emperor were opened to the monarch. He was received with the respect due to his superior rank. His renewed assurances of fidelity, of which he gave numerous proofs, were accepted.

It was reported at that time, that this monarch was led to expect the possession of the Russo-German provinces, which his troops were to be commissioned to invade. It is even affirmed that, after their conquest, he demanded their investiture from Napoleon. It has been added, but in vague terms, that Napoleon allowed the Prince-Royal of Prussia to aspire to the hand of one of his nieces. This was to be the remuneration for the services which Prussia was to render him in this new war. He promised, so he expressed himself, that he would go and sound her. It was thus that Frederick, by becoming the relation of Napoleon, would be enabled to preserve his diminished power; but proofs are wanting, to show that the idea of this marriage seduced the King of Prussia, as the hope of a similar alliance had seduced the Prince of Spain.

Such at that time was the submission of sovereigns to the power of Napoleon. It offers a striking example of the empire of necessity over all persons, and shows to what lengths the prospect of gain and the fear of loss will lead princes as well as private persons.

Meanwhile, Napoleon still waited the result of the negotiations of Lauriston and of Narbonne. He hoped to vanquish Alexander by the mere aspect of his united army, and, above all, by the menacing splendour of his residence at Dresden. He himself expressed this opinion, when, some days after, at Posen, he said to General Dessolles, "The assemblage at Dresden not having persuaded Alexander to make peace, it was now solely to be expected from war."

On that day he talked of nothing but his former victories. It seemed as if, doubtful of the future, he recurred to the past, and that he found it necessary to arm himself with all his most glorious recollections, in order to confront a peril of so great a magnitude. In fact, then, as since, he felt the necessity of deluding himself with the alleged weakness of his rival's character. As the period of so great an invasion approached, he hesitated in considering it as certain; for he no longer possessed the consciousness of his infallibility, nor that warlike assurance which the fire and energy of youth impart, nor that feeling of success which makes it certain.

In other respects, these parleys were not only attempts to preserve peace, but an additional *ruse de guerre*. By them he hoped to render the Russians either sufficiently negligent, to let themselves be surprised, dispersed, or, if united, sufficiently presumptuous to venture to wait his approach. In either case, the war would be finished by a *coup-de-main*, or by a victory. But Lauriston was not received. Narbonne, when he returned, stated, "that he had found the Russians in a state of mind as remote from dejection as from boasting. From their emperor's reply to him, it appeared that they preferred war to a dishonourable peace;

that they would take care not to expose themselves to the hazards of a battle against too formidable an enemy; and that, in short, they were resolved on making every sacrifice, in order to spin out the war, and to baffle Napoleon."

This answer, which reached the emperor in the midst of the greatest display of his glory, was treated with contempt. To say the truth, I must add, that a great Russian nobleman had contributed to deceive him: either from mistaken views, or from artifice, this Muscovite had persuaded him, that his own sovereign would recede at the sight of difficulties, and be easily discouraged by reverses. Unfortunately, the remembrance of Alexander's obsequiousness to him at Tilsit and at Erfurt confirmed the French emperor in that fallacious opinion.

He remained till the 29th of May at Dresden, proud of the homage which he knew how to appreciate, exhibiting to Europe princes and kings, sprung from the most ancient families of Germany, forming a numerous court round a prince deriving all distinction from himself. He appeared to take a pleasure in multiplying the chances of the great game of fortune, as if to encircle with them, and render less extraordinary, that which placed him on the throne, and thus to accustom others as well as himself to them.

Chapter 11
Davoust

At length, impatient to conquer the Russians, and escape from the homage of the Germans, Napoleon quitted Dresden. He only remained at Posen long enough to satisfy the Poles. He neglected Warsaw, whither the war did not imperiously call him, and where he would have again been involved in politics. He stopped at Thorn, in order to inspect his fortifications, his magazines, and his troops. There the complaints of the Poles, whom our allies pillaged without mercy, and insulted, reached him. Napoleon addressed severe reproaches, and even threats, to the King of Westphalia: but it is well known that these were thrown away; that their effect was lost in the midst of too rapid a movement; that, besides, his fits of anger, like all other fits, were followed by exhaustion; that then, with the return of his natural good humour, he regretted, and frequently tried, to soften the pain he had occasioned; that, finally, he might reproach himself as the cause of the disorders which provoked him; for, from the Oder to the Vistula, and even to the Niemen, if provisions were abundant and properly stationed, the less portable foraging supplies were deficient. Our cavalry were already forced to cut the green rye, and to strip the houses of their thatch, in order to feed their horses. It is true, that all did not stop at that; but when one disorder is authorized, how can others be forbidden?

The evil augmented on the other side of the Niemen. The emperor had calculated upon a multitude of light cars and heavy wagons, each destined to carry several thousand pounds weight, through a sandy region, which carts, with no greater weight than some quintals, with difficulty traversed. These conveyances were organized in battalions and squadrons. Each battalion of light cars, called *comtoises*, consisted of six hundred, and might carry six thousand quintals of flour. The battalion of heavy vehicles, drawn by oxen, carried four thousand eight hundred quintals. There were besides twenty-six squadrons of wagons, loaded with military equipages; a great quantity of wagons with tools of all kinds, as well as thousands of artillery and hospital wagons, one siege and six bridge equipages.

The provision-wagons were to take in their loading at the magazines established on the Vistula. When the army passed that river, it was ordered to provide itself, without halting, with provisions for twenty-five days, but not to use them till they were beyond the Niemen. In conclusion, the greater part of these means of transport failed, either because the organization of soldiers, to act as conductors of military convoys, was essentially vicious, the motives of honour and ambition not being called into action to maintain proper discipline; or chiefly because these vehicles were too heavy for the soil, the distances too considerable, and the privations and fatigues too great; certain it is that the greater number of them scarcely reached the Vistula.

The army, therefore, provisioned itself on its match. The country being fertile, wagons, cattle, and provisions of all kinds, were swept off; every thing was taken, even to such of the inhabitants as were necessary to conduct these convoys. Some days after, at the Niemen, the embarrassment of the passage, and the celerity of the first hostile marches, caused all the fruits of these requisitions to be abandoned with an indifference only equalled by the violence with which they had been seized.

The importance of the object, however, was such as might excuse the irregularity of these proceedings. That object was to surprise the Russian army, either collected or dispersed; in short, to make a *coup-de-main* with 400,000 men. War, the worst of all scourges, would thus have been shortened in its duration. Our long and heavy baggage-wagons would have encumbered our march. It was much more convenient to live on the supplies of the country, as we should be able to indemnify the loss afterwards. But superfluous wrong was committed as well as necessary wrong, for who can stop midway in the commission of evil? What chief could be responsible for the crowd of officers and soldiers who were scattered through the country in order to collect its resources? To whom were complaints to be addressed? Who was to punish? All was done in the course of a rapid march; there was neither time to try, nor even to find out the guilty. Between the affair of the day before, and that of the following day, how many others had sprung up! for at that time the business of a month was crowded into a single day.

Moreover, some of the leaders set the example; there was a positive emulation in evil. In that respect, many of our allies surpassed the French. We were their teachers in every thing; but in copying our qualities, they caricatured our defects. Their gross and brutal plunder was perfectly revolting.

But the emperor was desirous to have order kept in the middle of disorder. Pressed by the accusing reproaches of two allied nations, two names were more especially distinguished by his indignation. In his letters are found these words; "I have suspended generals —— and ——. I have suppressed the brigade ——; I have cashiered it in the face of the army, that is to say, of Europe.—I have written to ——, informing him that he ran great risks of being broke, if he did not take care." Some days after he met this ——, at the head of his troops, and still indignant, he called to him, "You disgrace yourself; you set the example of plunder. Be silent, or go back to your father; I do not want your services any further."

From Thorn, Napoleon descended the Vistula. Graudentz belonged to Prussia; he avoided passing it; but as that fortress was important to the safety of the army, an officer of artillery and some fireworkers were sent thither, with the ostensible motive of making cartridges; the real motive remained a secret; the Prussian garrison, however, was numerous, and stood on its guard, and the emperor, who had proceeded onward, thought no more of it.

It was at Marienburg that the emperor again met Davoust. That marshal, whether through pride, natural or acquired, was not well pleased to recognize as his leader any other individual than the master of Europe. His character, besides, was despotic, obstinate, and tenacious; and as little inclined to yield to circumstances as to men. In 1809, Berthier was his commander for some days, during which Davoust gained a battle, and saved the army, by disobeying him. Hence arose a terrible hatred between them: during the peace it augmented, but secretly; for they lived at a wide distance from each other, Berthier at Paris, Davoust at Hamburgh; but this Russian war again brought them together.

Berthier was getting enfeebled. Ever since 1805, war had become completely odious to him. His talent especially lay in his activity and his memory. He could receive and transmit, at all hours of the day and night, the most multiplied intelligence and orders; but on this occasion he had conceived himself entitled to give orders himself. These orders displeased Davoust. Their first interview was a scene of violent altercation; it occurred at Marienburg, where the emperor had just arrived, and in his presence.

Davoust expressed himself harshly, and even went so far as to accuse Berthier of incapacity or treachery. They both threatened each other, and when Berthier was gone, Napoleon, influenced by the naturally suspicious character of the marshal, exclaimed, "It sometimes happens that I entertain doubts of the fidelity of my oldest companions in arms; but at such times my head turns round with chagrin, and I do my utmost to banish so heart-rending a suspicion."

While Davoust was probably enjoying the dangerous pleasure of having humbled his enemy, the emperor proceeded to Dantzic, and Berthier, stung by resentment, followed him there. From that time, the zeal, the glory of Davoust, the exertions he had made for this new expedition, all that ought to have availed him, began to be looked upon unfavourably. The emperor had written to him "that as the war was about to be carried into a barren territory, where the enemy would destroy every thing, it was requisite to prepare for such a state of things, by providing every thing within ourselves:" Davoust had replied to this by an enumeration of his preparations—"He had 70,000 men, who were completely organized; they carried with them twenty-five days' provisions. Each company comprised swimmers, masons, bakers, tailors, shoemakers, armourers, and workmen of every class. They carried every thing they required with them; his army was like a colony; hand-mills followed. He had anticipated every want; all means of supplying them were ready."

Such great exertions ought to have pleased; they, however, displeased; they were misrepresented. Insidious observations were overheard by the emperor. "This marshal," said they to him, "wishes to have it thought that he has foreseen, arranged, and executed every thing. Is the emperor, then, to be no more than a spectator of this expedition? Must the glory of it devolve on Davoust?"—"In fact," exclaimed the emperor, "one would think it was he that commanded the army."

They even went further, and awakened some of his dormant fears: "Was it not Davoust who, after the victory of Jena, drew the emperor into Poland? Is it not he who is now anxious for this new Polish war?—He who already possesses such large property in that country, whose accurate and severe probity has won over the Poles, and who is suspected of aspiring to their throne?"

It is not easy to say whether the pride of Napoleon was shocked by seeing that of his lieutenants encroaching so much on his own; or whether, in the course of this irregular war, he felt himself thwarted more and more by the methodical genius of Davoust; certain it is, the unfavourable impression against him struck deeper; it was productive of fatal consequences; it removed from his confidence a bold, tenacious and prudent warrior, and favoured his predilection for Murat, whose rashness was much more flattering to his ambitious hopes. In other respects, these dissensions between his great officers did not displease Napoleon; they gave him information; their harmony would have made him uneasy.

From Dantzic the emperor proceeded, on the 12th of June, to Königsberg. At that place ended the inspection of his immense magazines, and of the second resting-point and pivot of his line of operations. Immense quantities of provisions, adequate to the immensity of the undertaking, were there accumulated. No detail had been neglected. The active and impassioned genius of Napoleon was then entirely directed towards that most important and difficult department of his expedition. In that he was profuse of exhortations, orders, and even money, of which his letters are a proof. His days were occupied in dictating instructions on that subject; at night he frequently rose to repeat them again. One general received, on a single day, six despatches from him, all distinguished by the same solicitude.

In one, these words were remarked, "For masses like these, if precautions be not taken, the grain of no country can suffice." In another, "It will be requisite for all the provision-wagons to be loaded with flour, bread, rice, vegetables, and brandy, besides what is necessary for the hospital service. The result of all my movements will assemble 400,000 men on a single point. There will be nothing then to expect from the country, and it will be necessary to have every thing within ourselves." But, on the one hand, the means of transport were badly calculated; and, on the other, he allowed himself to be hurried on as soon as he was put in motion.

CHAPTER 12

The Russian Frontier

From Königsberg to Gumbinnen, he reviewed several of his armies; conversing with the soldiers in a gay, frank, and often abrupt style; well aware that, with such unsophisticated and hardy characters, abruptness is looked upon as frankness, rudeness as force, haughtiness as true nobility; and that the delicacy and graces which some officers bring with them from the salons are in their eyes no better than weakness and pusillanimity; that these appear to them like a foreign language, which they do not understand, and the accents of which strike them as ridiculous.

According to his usual custom, he promenaded before the ranks. Knowing in which of his wars each regiment had been with him, at the sight of the oldest soldiers he occasionally halted; to one he recalled the battle of the Pyramids; another he reminded of Marengo, Austerlitz, Jena, or Friedland, and always by a single word, accompanied by a familiar caress. The veteran who believed himself personally recognized by his emperor, rose in consequence in the estimation of his junior companions, who regarded him as an object of envy.

Napoleon, in this manner, continued his inspection; he overlooked not even the youngest soldiers: it seemed as if every thing which concerned them was to him matter of deep interest; their least wants seemed known to him. He interrogated them: Did their captains take care of them? had they received their pay? were they in want of any requisite? he wished to see their knapsacks.

At length he stopped at the centre of the regiment; there being apprised of the places that were vacant, he required aloud the names of the most meritorious in the ranks; he called those who were so designated before him, and questioned them. How many years' service? how many campaigns? what wounds? what exploits? He then appointed them officers, and caused them to be immediately installed, himself prescribing the forms;—all particularities which delighted the soldier! They told each other how this great emperor, the judge of nations in the mass, occupied himself with them in their minutest details; that they composed his oldest and his real family! Thus it was that he instilled into them the love of war, of glory and himself.

The army, meantime, marched from the Vistula to the Niemen. This last river, from Grodno as far as Kowno, runs parallel with the Vistula. The river Pregel, which unites the two, was loaded with provisions: 220,000 men repaired thither from four different points; there they found bread and some foraging provisions. These provisions ascended that river with them, as far as its direction would allow.

When the army was obliged to quit the flotilla, its select corps took with them sufficient provisions to reach and cross the Niemen, to prepare for a victory, and to arrive at Wilna. There, the emperor calculated on the magazines of the inhabitants, on those of the enemy and on his own, which he had ordered to be brought from Dantzic, by the Frischhaff, the Pregel, the Deine, the canal Frederic, and the Vilia.

We were upon the verge of the Russian frontier; from right to left, or from south to north, the army was disposed in the following manner, in front of the Niemen. In the first place, on the extreme right, and issuing from Gallicia, on Drogiczin, Prince Schwartzenberg and 34,000 Austrians; on their left, coming from Warsaw, and marching on Bialystok and Grodno, the King of Westphalia, at the head of 79,200 Westphalians, Saxons, and Poles; by the side of them was the Viceroy of Italy, who had just effected the junction, near Marienpol and Pilony, of 79,500 Bavarians, Italians and French; next, the emperor, with 220,000 men, commanded by the King of Naples, the Prince of Eckmühl, the Dukes of Dantzic, Istria, Reggio, and Elchingen. They advanced from Thorn, Marienwerder, and Elbing, and, on the 23rd of June, had assembled in a single mass near Nogarisky, a league above Kowno. Finally, in front of Tilsit, was Macdonald, and 32,500 Prussians, Bavarians, and Poles, composing the extreme left of the grand army.

Every thing was now ready. From the banks of the Guadalquivir, and the shores of the Calabrian sea, to the Vistula, were assembled 617,000 men, of whom 480,000 were already present; one siege and six bridge equipages, thousands of provision-wagons, innumerable herds of oxen, 1372 pieces of cannon, and thousands of artillery and hospital-wagons, had been directed, assembled, and stationed at a short distance from the Russian frontier river. The greatest part of the provision-wagons were alone behind.

Sixty thousand Austrians, Prussians, and Spaniards, were preparing to shed their blood for the conqueror of Wagram, of Jena, and of Madrid; for the man who had four times beaten down the power of Austria, who had humbled Prussia, and invaded Spain. And yet all were faithful to him. When it was considered that one-third of the army of Napoleon was either foreign to him or hostile, one hardly knew at which most to be astonished,—the audacity of one party, or the resignation of the other. It was in this manner that Rome made her conquests contribute to her future means for conquering.

As to us Frenchmen, he found us all full of ardour. Habit, curiosity, and the pleasure of exhibiting themselves in the character of masters in new countries, actuated the soldiers; vanity was the great stimulant of the younger ones, who thirsted to acquire some glory which they might recount, with the attractive quackery peculiar to soldiers; these inflated and pompous narratives of their exploits being moreover indispensable to their relaxation when no longer under arms. To this must certainly be added, the hope of plunder; for the exacting ambition of Napoleon had as often disgusted his soldiers, as the disorders of the latter tarnished his glory. A compromise was necessary: ever since 1805, there was a sort of mutual understanding, on his part to wink at their plunder—on theirs, to suffer his ambition.

This plunder, however, or rather, this marauding system, was generally confined to provisions, which, in default of supplies, were exacted of the inhabitants, but often too extravagantly. The most culpable plunderers were the stragglers, who are always numerous in frequent forced marches. These disorders, indeed, were never tolerated. In order to repress them, Napoleon left *gendarmes* and flying columns on the track of the army; and when these stragglers subsequently rejoined their corps, their knapsacks were examined by their officers; or, as was the case at Austerlitz, by their comrades; and strict justice was then executed among themselves.

The last levies were certainly too young and too feeble; but the army had still a stock of brave and experienced men, used to critical situations, and whom nothing could intimidate. They were recognizable at the first glance by their martial countenances, and by their conversation; they had no other past nor future but war; and they could talk of nothing else. Their officers were worthy of them, or at least were becoming so; for, in order to preserve the due authority of their rank over such men, it was necessary for them to have wounds to show, and to be able to appeal to their own exploits.

Such was, at that period, the life of those men; all was action within its sphere, even to words. They often boasted too much, but even that had its advantage; for as they were incessantly put to the proof, it was then necessary for them to be what they wished to appear. Such especially is the character of the Poles; they boast in the first instance of being more than they have been, but not more than they are capable of being. Poland in fact is a nation of heroes! pawning their words for exploits beyond the truth, but subsequently redeeming them with honour, in order to verify what at first was neither true nor even probable.

As to the old generals, some of them were no longer the hardy and simple warriors of the republic; honours, hard service, age, and the emperor particularly, had contributed to soften many of them down. Napoleon compelled them to adopt a luxurious style of living by his example and his orders; according to him, it was a means of influencing the multitude. It might be also, that such habits prevented them from accumulating property, which might have made them independent; for, being himself the source of riches, he was glad to keep up the necessity of repairing to it, and in this manner to bring them back within his influence. He had, therefore, pushed his generals into a circle from which it was difficult to escape; forcing them to pass incessantly from want to prodigality, and from prodigality to want, which he alone was able to relieve.

Several had nothing but their appointments, which accustomed them to an ease of living with which they could no longer dispense. If he made them grants of land, it was out of his conquests, which were exposed to insecurity by war, and which war only could preserve.

But in order to retain them in dependence, glory, which with some was a habit, with others a passion, with all a want, was the all-sufficient stimulant; and Napoleon, absolute master as he was of his own century, and even dictating to history, was the distributor of that glory. Though he fixed it at a high price, there was no rejecting his conditions; one would have felt ashamed to confess one's weakness in presence of his strength, and to stop short before a man whose ambition was still mounting, great as was the elevation which he had already attained.

Besides, the renown of so great an expedition was full of charm; its success seemed certain; it promised to be nothing but a military march to Petersburgh and Moscow. With this last effort his wars would probably be terminated. It was a last opportunity, which one would repent to have let escape; one would be annoyed by the glorious narratives which others would give of it. The victory of to-day would make that of yesterday so old! And who would wish to grow old with it?

And then, when war was kindled in all quarters, how was it possible to avoid it? The scenes of action were not indifferent; here Napoleon would command in person; elsewhere, though the cause might be the same, the contest would be carried on under a different commander. The renown shared with the latter would be foreign to Napoleon, on whom, nevertheless, depended glory, fortune, every thing; and it was well known, whether from preference or policy, that he was only profuse in his favours to those whose glory was identified with his glory; and that he rewarded less generously such exploits as were not his. It was requisite, therefore, to serve in the army which he commanded; hence the anxiety of young and old to fill its ranks. What chief had ever before so many means of power? There was no hope which he could not flatter, excite, or satiate.

Finally, we loved him as the companion of our labours; as the chief who had conducted us to renown. The astonishment and admiration which he inspired flattered our self-love; for all these we shared in common with him.

With respect to that youthful elite, which in those times of glory filled our camps, its enthusiasm was natural. Who is there amongst us who, in his early years, has not been fired by the perusal of the warlike exploits of the ancients and of our ancestors? Should we not have all desired, at that time, to be the heroes whose real or fictitious history we were perusing? During that state of enthusiasm, if those recollections had been suddenly realized before us; if our eyes, instead of reading, had witnessed the performance of those wonders; if we had felt their sphere of action within our reach, and if employments had been offered to us by the side of those brave paladins, whose adventurous lives and brilliant renown our young and vivid imaginations had so much envied; which of us would have hesitated? Who is there that would not have rushed forward, replete with joy and hope, and disdaining an odious and scandalous repose?

Such were the rising generations of that day. At that period every one was free to be ambitious! a period of intoxication and prosperity, during which the French soldier, lord of all things by victory, considered himself greater than the nobleman, or even the sovereign, whose states he traversed! To him it appeared as if the kings of Europe only reigned by permission of his chief and of his arms.

Thus it was that habit attracted some, disgust at camp service others; novelty prompted the greater part, and especially the thirst of glory: but all were stimulated by emulation. In fine, confidence in a chief who had been always fortunate, and hope of an early victory, which would terminate the war at a blow, and restore us to our firesides; for a war, to the entire army of Napoleon (as it was to some volunteers of the court of Louis XIV.) was often no more than a single battle, or a short and brilliant journey.

We were now about to reach the extremity of Europe, where never European army had been before! We were about to erect new columns of Hercules. The grandeur of the enterprise; the agitation of co-operating Europe; the imposing spectacle of an army of 400,000 foot and 80,000 horse: so many warlike reports and martial clamours, kindled the minds of veterans themselves. It was impossible for the coldest to remain unmoved amid the general impulse; to escape from the universal attraction.

In conclusion;—independent of all these motives for animation, the composition of the army was good, and every good army is desirous of war.

Chapter 13
Five Armies

Napoleon, satisfied with his preparations, at length declared himself. "Soldiers," said he, "the second Polish war is commenced. The first was concluded at Friedland and at Tilsit. At Tilsit, Russia swore eternal alliance with France, and war with England. She now violates her oaths. She will give no explanation of her capricious conduct, until the French eagles have repassed the Rhine; by that means leaving our allies at her mercy. Russia is hurried away by fatality; her destiny must be accomplished. Does she then believe us to be degenerated? Are we not still the soldiers of Austerlitz? She places us between war and dishonour; the choice cannot be doubtful. Let us advance, then; let us pass the Niemen, and carry the war into her territory! The second Polish war will be as glorious for the French arms as the first; but the peace we shall this time conclude will carry with it its own guarantee; it will put an end to the fatal influence which Russia for the last fifty years has exercised over the affairs of Europe."

This tone, which was at that time deemed prophetic, befitted an expedition of an almost fabulous character. It was quite necessary to invoke Destiny, and give credit to its empire, when the fate of so many human beings, and so much glory, were about to be consigned to its mercy.

The Emperor Alexander also harangued his army, but in a very different manner. The difference between the two nations, the two sovereigns, and their reciprocal position, were remarked in these proclamations. In fact, the one which was defensive was unadorned and moderate; the other, offensive, was replete with audacity and the confidence of victory. The first sought support in religion, the other in fatality; the one in love of country, the other in love of glory; but neither of them referred to the liberation of Poland, which was the real cause of contention.

We marched towards the east, with our left towards the north, and our right towards the south. On our right, Volhynia invoked us with all her prayers; in the centre, were Wilna, Minsk, and the whole of Lithuania, and Samogitia; in front of our left, Courland and Livonia awaited their fate in silence.

The army of Alexander, composed of 300,000 men, kept those provinces in awe. From the banks of the Vistula, from Dresden, from Paris itself, Napoleon had critically surveyed it. He had ascertained that its centre, commanded by Barclay, extended from Wilna and Kowno to Lida and Grodno, resting its right on Vilia, and its left on the Niemen.

That river protected the Russian front by the deviation which it makes from Grodno to Kowno; for it was only in the interval between these two cities, that the Niemen, running toward the north, intersected the line of our attack, and served as a frontier to Lithuania. Before reaching Grodno, and on quitting Kowno, it flows westward.

To the south of Grodno was Bagration, with 65,000 men, in the direction of Wolkowisk; to the north of Kowno, at Rossiana and Keydani, Wittgenstein, with 26,000 men, substituted their bayonets for that natural frontier.

At the same time, another army of 50,000 men, called the reserve, was assembled at Lutsk, in Volhynia, in order to keep that province in check, and observe Schwartzenberg; it was confided to Tormasof, till the treaty about to be signed at Bucharest permitted Tchitchakof, and the greater part of the army in Moldavia, to unite with it.

Alexander, and, under him, his minister of war, Barclay de Tolly, directed all these forces. They were divided into three armies, called, the first western army, under Barclay; the second western army, under Bagration; and the army of reserve, under Tormasof. Two other corps were forming; one at Mozyr, in the environs of Bobruisk; and the other at Riga and Dünabourg. The reserves were at Wilna and Swentziany. In conclusion, a vast entrenched camp was erected before Drissa, within an elbow of the Düna.

The French emperor's opinion was, that this position behind the Niemen was neither offensive nor defensive, and that the Russian army was no better off for the purpose of effecting a retreat; that this army, being so much scattered over a line of sixty leagues, might be surprised and dispersed, as actually happened to it; that, with still more certainty, the left of Barclay, and the entire army of Bagration, being stationed at Lida and at Wolkowisk, in front of the marshes of the Berezina, which they covered, instead of being covered by them, might be thrown back on them and taken; or, at least, that an abrupt and direct attack on Kowno and Wilna would cut them off from their line of operation, indicated by Swentziany and the entrenched camp at Drissa.

In fact, Doctorof and Bagration were already separated from that line; for, instead of remaining in mass with Alexander, in front of the roads leading to the Düna, to defend them and profit by them, they were stationed forty leagues to the right.

For this reason it was that Napoleon separated his forces into five armies. While Schwartzenberg, advancing from Gallicia with his 30,000 Austrians, (whose numbers he had orders to exaggerate,) would keep Tormasof in check, and draw the attention of Bagration towards the south; while the King of Westphalia, with his 80,000 men, would employ that general in front, towards Grodno, without pressing him too vehemently at first; and while the Viceroy of Italy, in the direction of Pilony, would be in readiness to interpose between the same Bagration and Barclay; in fine, while at the extreme left, Macdonald, debouching from Tilsit, would invade the north of Lithuania, and fall on the right of Wittgenstein; Napoleon himself, with his 200,000 men, was to precipitate himself on Kowno, on Wilna, and on his rival, and destroy him at the first shock.

Should the Emperor of Russia give way, he would press him hard, and throw him back upon Drissa, and as far as the commencement of his line of operations; then, all at once, propelling his detachments to the right, he would surround Bagration, and the whole of the corps of the Russian left, which, by this rapid irruption, would be separated from their right.

I will shortly sketch a brief and rapid summary of the history of our two wings, being anxious to return to the centre, and to be enabled uninterruptedly to exhibit the great scenes which were enacted there. Macdonald commanded the left wing; his invasion, supported by the Baltic, overcame the right wing of the Russians; it threatened Revel first, next Riga, and even Petersburgh. He soon reached Riga. The war became stationary under its walls; although of little importance, it was conducted by Macdonald with prudence, science, and glory, even in his retreat, to which he was neither compelled by the winter nor by the enemy, but solely by Napoleon's orders.

With regard to his right wing, the emperor had counted on the support of Turkey, which failed him. He had inferred that the Russian army of Volhynia would follow the general movement of Alexander's retreat; but, on the contrary, Tormasof advanced upon our rear. The

French army was thus uncovered, and menaced with being turned on those vast plains. Nature not supplying it in that quarter with any support, as she did on the left wing, it was necessarily compelled to rely entirely on itself. Forty thousand Saxons, Austrians, and Poles, remained there in observation.

Tormasof was beaten; but another army, rendered available by the treaty of Bucharest, arrived and formed a junction with the remnant of the first. From that moment, the war upon that point became defensive. It was carried on feebly, as was to be expected, notwithstanding some Polish troops and a French general were left with the Austrian army. That general had been long and strenuously cried up for ability, although he had met with reverses, and his reputation was not undeserved.

No decisive advantage was gained on either side. But the position of this corps, almost entirely Austrian, became more and more important, as the grand army retreated upon it. It will be seen whether Schwartzenberg deceived its confidence,—whether he left us to be surrounded on the Berezina,—and whether it be true, that he seemed on that occasion to aspire to no other character than that of an armed witness to the great dispute.

Chapter 14
Crossing the Niemen

Between these two wings, the grand army marched to the Niemen, in three separate masses. The king of Westphalia, with 80,000 men, moved upon Grodno; the viceroy of Italy, with 75,000 men, upon Pilony; Napoleon, with 220,000 men, upon Nogaraiski, a farm situated three leagues beyond Kowno. The 23rd of June, before daylight, the imperial column reached the Niemen, but without seeing it. The borders of the great Prussian forest of Pilwisky, and the hills which line the river, concealed the great army, which was about to cross it.

Napoleon, who had travelled in a carriage as far as that, mounted his horse at two o'clock in the morning. He reconnoitred the Russian river, without disguising himself, as has been falsely asserted, but under cover of the night crossing this frontier, which five months afterwards he was only enabled to repass under cover of the same obscurity. When he came up to the bank, his horse suddenly stumbled, and threw him on the sand. A voice exclaimed, "This is a bad omen; a Roman would recoil!" It is not known whether it was himself, or one of his retinue, who pronounced these words.

His task of reconnoitring concluded, he gave orders that, at the close of the following day, three bridges should be thrown over the river, near the village of Poniémen; he then retired to his head-quarters, where he passed the whole day, sometimes in his tent, sometimes in a Polish house, listlessly reclined, in the midst of a breathless atmosphere, and a suffocating heat, vainly courting repose.

On the return of night, he again made his approaches to the river. The first who crossed it were a few sappers in a small boat. They approached the Russian side with some degree of apprehension, but found no obstacle to oppose their landing. There they found peace; the war was entirely on their own side; all was tranquil on that foreign soil, which had been described to them as so menacing. A single officer of

Cossacks, however, on patrol, presented himself to their view. He was alone, and appeared to consider himself in full peace, and to be ignorant that the whole of Europe in arms was at hand. He inquired of the strangers who they were?—"Frenchmen!" they replied.—"What do you want?" rejoined the officer; "and wherefore do you come into Russia?"—A sapper briskly replied, "To make war upon you; to take Wilna; to deliver Poland."—The Cossack then withdrew; he disappeared in the woods, into which three of our soldiers, giving vent to their ardour, and with a view to sound the forest, discharged their fire-arms.

Thus it was, that the feeble report of three muskets, to which there was no reply, apprised us of the opening of a new campaign, and the commencement of a great invasion.

Either from a feeling of prudence, or from presentiment, this first signal of war threw the emperor into a state of violent irritation. Three hundred voltigeurs immediately passed the river, in order to cover the erection of the bridges.

The whole of the French columns then began to issue from the valleys and the forest. They advanced in silence to the river, under cover of thick darkness. It was necessary to touch them in order to recognize their presence. Fires, even to sparks, were forbidden; they slept with arms in their hands, as if in the presence of an enemy. The crops of green rye, moistened with a profuse dew, served as beds to the men, and provender to the horses.

The night, its coolness preventing sleep, its obscurity prolonging the hours, and augmenting wants; finally, the dangers of the following day, every thing combined to give solemnity to this position. But the expectation of a great battle supported our spirits. The proclamation of Napoleon had just been read; the most remarkable passages of it were repeated in a whisper, and the genius of conquest kindled our imagination.

Before us was the Russian frontier. Our ardent gaze already sought to invade the promised land of our glory athwart the shades of night. We seemed to hear the joyful acclamations of the Lithuanians, at the approach of their deliverers. We pictured to ourselves the banks of the river lined with their supplicating hands. Here, we were in want of every thing; there, every thing would be lavished upon us! The Lithuanians would hasten to supply our wants; we were about to be encircled by love and gratitude. What signified one unpleasant night? The day would shortly appear, and with it its warmth and all its illusions. The day did appear! and it revealed to us dry and desert sands, and dark and gloomy forests. Our eyes then reverted sadly upon ourselves, and we were again inspired by pride and hope, on observing the imposing spectacle of our united army.

Three hundred yards from the river, on the most elevated height, the tent of the emperor was visible. Around it the hills, their slopes, and the subjacent valleys, were covered with men and horses. As soon as the earth exhibited to the sun those moving masses, clothed with glittering arms, the signal was given, and instantly the multitude began to defile off in three columns, towards the three bridges. They were observed to take a winding direction, as they descended the narrow plain which separated them from the Niemen, to approach it, to reach the three passages, to compress and prolong their columns, in order to traverse them, and at last reach that foreign soil, which they were about to devastate, and which they were soon destined to cover with their own enormous fragments.

So great was their ardour, that two divisions of the advanced guard disputed for the honour of being the first to pass, and were near coming to blows; and some exertions were necessary to quiet them. Napoleon hastened to plant his foot on the Russian territory. He took this first step towards his ruin without hesitation. At first, he stationed himself near the bridge, encouraging the soldiers with his looks. The latter all saluted him with their accustomed acclamations. They appeared, indeed, more animated than he was; whether it was that he felt oppressed by the weight of so great an aggression, or that his enfeebled frame could not support the effect of the excessive heat, or that he was already intimidated by finding nothing to conquer.

At length he became impatient; all at once he dashed across the country into the forest which girt the sides of the river. He put his horse to the extremity of his speed; he appeared on fire to come singly in contact with the enemy. He rode more than a league in the same direction, surrounded throughout by the same solitude; upon which he found it necessary to return in the vicinity of the bridges, whence he re-descended the river with his guard towards Kowno.

Some thought they heard the distant report of cannon. As we marched, we endeavoured to distinguish on which side the battle was going on. But, with the exception of some troops of Cossacks on that, as well as the ensuing days, the atmosphere alone displayed itself in the character of an enemy. In fact, the emperor had scarcely passed the river, when a rumbling sound began to agitate the air. In a short time the day became overcast, the wind rose, and brought with it the inauspicious mutterings of a thunder-storm. That menacing sky and unsheltered country filled us with melancholy impressions. There were even some amongst us, who, enthusiastic as they had lately been, were terrified at what they conceived to be a fatal presage. To them it appeared that those combustible vapours were collecting over our heads, and that they would descend upon the territory we approached, in order to prevent us from entering it.

It is quite certain, that the storm in question was as great as the enterprise in which we were engaged. During several hours, its black and heavy masses accumulated and hung upon the whole army: from right to left, over a space of fifty leagues, it was completely threatened by its lightnings, and overwhelmed by its torrents: the roads and fields were inundated; the insupportable heat of the atmosphere was suddenly changed to a disagreeable chillness. Ten thousand horses perished on the march, and more especially in the bivouacs which followed. A large quantity of equipages remained abandoned on the sands; and great numbers of men subsequently died.

A convent served to shelter the emperor against the first fury of the tempest. From hence he shortly departed for Kowno, where the greatest disorder prevailed. The claps of thunder were no longer noticed; those menacing reports, which still murmured over our heads, appeared forgotten. For, though this common phenomenon of the season might have shaken the firmness of some few minds, with the majority the time of omens had passed away. A scepticism, ingenious on the part of some, thoughtless or coarse on the part of others, earth-born passions and imperious wants, have diverted the souls of men from that heaven whence they are derived, and to which they should return. The army, therefore, recognized nothing but a natural and unseasonable accident in this disaster; and far from interpreting it as the voice of reprobation against so great an aggression, for which, moreover, it was not responsible, found in it nothing but a motive of indignation against fortune or the skies, which whether by chance, or otherwise, offered it so terrible a presage.

That very day, a particular calamity was added to this general disaster. At Kowno, Napoleon was exasperated, because the bridge over the Vilia had been thrown down by the Cossacks, and opposed the passage of Oudinot. He affected to despise it, like every thing else that opposed him, and ordered a squadron of his Polish guard to swim the river. These fine fellows threw themselves into it without hesitation. At first, they proceeded in good order, and when out of their depth redoubled their exertions. They soon reached the middle of the river by swimming. But there, the increased rapidity of the current broke their order. Their horses then became frightened, quitted their ranks, and were carried away by the violence of the waves. They no longer swam, but floated about in scattered groups. Their riders struggled, and made vain efforts; their strength gave way, and they, at last, resigned themselves to their fate. Their destruction was certain; but it was for their country; it was in her presence, and for the sake of their deliverer, that they had devoted themselves; and even when on the point of being engulfed for ever, they suspended their unavailing struggles, turned their faces toward Napoleon, and exclaimed, *"Vive l'Empereur!"* Three of them were especially remarked, who, with their heads still above the billows, repeated this cry and perished instantly. The army was struck with mingled horror and admiration.

As to Napoleon, he prescribed with anxiety and precision the measures necessary to save the greater number, but without appearing affected: either from the habit of subduing his feelings; from considering the ordinary emotions of the heart as weaknesses in times of war, of which it was not for him to set the example, and therefore necessary to suppress; or finally, that he anticipated much greater misfortunes, compared with which the present was a mere trifle.

A bridge thrown over this river conveyed Marshal Oudinot and the second corps to Keydani. During that time, the rest of the army was still passing the Niemen. The passage took up three entire days. The army of Italy did not pass it till the 29th, in front of Pilony. The army of the king of Westphalia did not enter Grodno till the 30th.

From Kowno Napoleon proceeded in two days as far as the defiles which defend the plain of Wilna. He waited, in order to make his appearance there, for news from his advanced posts. He was in hopes that Alexander would contest with him the possession of that capital. The report, indeed, of some musketry, encouraged him in that hope; when intelligence was brought him that the city was undefended. Thither he advanced, ruminating and dissatisfied. He accused his generals of the advanced guard of suffering the Russian army to escape. It was the most active of them, Montbrun, whom he reproached, and against whom his anger rose to the point of menace. A menace without effect, a violence without result! and less blameable than remarkable, in a warrior, because they contributed to prove all the importance which he attached to an immediate victory.

In the midst of his anger, he displayed address in his dispositions for entering Wilna. He caused himself to be preceded and followed by Polish regiments. But more occupied by the retreat of the Russians than the grateful and admiring acclamations of the Lithuanians, he rapidly passed through the city, and hurried to the advanced posts.

Several of the best hussars of the 8th, having ventured themselves in a wood, without proper support, had just perished in an action with the Russian guard; Segur[16], who commanded them, after a desperate defence, had fallen, covered with wounds.

The enemy had burnt his bridges and his magazines, and was flying by different roads, but all in the direction of Drissa. Napoleon ordered all which the fire had spared to be collected, and restored the communications. He sent forward Murat and his cavalry, to follow the track of Alexander: and after throwing Ney upon his left, in order to support Oudinot, who had that day driven back the lines of Wittgenstein, from Deweltowo as far as Wilkomir, he returned to occupy the place of Alexander at Wilna. There, his unfolded maps, military reports, and a crowd of officers requiring his orders, awaited his arrival. He was now on the theatre of war, and at the moment of its most animated operations; he had prompt and urgent decisions to make; orders of march to give; hospitals, magazines, and lines of operations, to establish.

It was necessary to interrogate, to read, and then compare; and at last to discover and grasp the truth, which always appeared to fly and conceal itself in the midst of a thousand contradictory answers and reports.

This was not all: Napoleon, at Wilna, had a new empire to organize; the politics of Europe, the war of Spain, and the government of France, to direct. His political, military, and administrative correspondence, which he had suffered to accumulate for some days, imperiously demanded his attention. Such, indeed, was his custom, on the eve of a great event, as that would necessarily decide the character of many of his replies, and impart a colouring to all. He therefore established himself at his quarters, and in the first instance threw himself on a bed, less for the sake of sleep than of quiet meditation; whence, abruptly starting up shortly after, he rapidly dictated the orders which he had conceived.

Intelligence was just then brought him from Warsaw and the Austrian army. The discourse at the opening of the Polish diet displeased the emperor; and he exclaimed, as he threw it from him, "This is French! It ought to be Polish!" As to the Austrians, it was never dissembled to him that, in their whole army, there was no one on whom he could depend but its commander. The certainty of that seemed sufficient for him.

16: Brother of the Author.

CHAPTER 15
Lithuania

Meantime, every thing was rekindling at the bottom of the hearts of the Lithuanians a patriotism which was still burning, though almost extinguished. On one side, the precipitate retreat of the Russians, and the presence of Napoleon; on the other, the cry of independence emitted by Warsaw, and more especially the sight of those Polish heroes, who returned with liberty to the soil whence they had been expelled along with her. The first days, therefore, were entirely devoted to joy: the happiness appeared general—the display of feeling universal.

The same sentiments were thought to be traceable everywhere; in the interior of the houses, as well as at the windows, and in the public places. The people congratulated and embraced each other on the high-roads; the old men once more resumed their ancient costume, reviving ideas of glory and independence. They wept with joy at the sight of the national banners which had been just re-erected; an immense crowd followed them, rending the air with their acclamations. But this enthusiasm, unreflecting in some, and the mere effect of excitement in others, was but of short duration.

On their side, the Poles of the grand duchy were always animated by the noblest enthusiasm: they were worthy of liberty, and sacrificed to it that property for which liberty is sacrificed by the greater part of mankind. Nor did they belie themselves on this occasion: the diet of Warsaw constituted itself into a general confederation, and declared the kingdom of Poland restored; it convened the dietins; invited all Poland to unite; summoned all the Poles in the Russian army to quit Russia; caused itself to be represented by a general council; maintained the established order; and, finally, sent a deputation to the king of Saxony, and an address to Napoleon.

The senator Wibicki presented this address to him at Wilna. He told him "that the Poles had neither been subjected by peace nor by war, but by treason; that they were therefore free *de jure*, before God and man; that being so now *de facto*, that right became a duty; that they claimed the independence of their brethren, the Lithuanians, who were still slaves; that they offered themselves to the entire Polish nation as the centre of a general union; but that it was to him who dictated his history to the age, in whom resided the force of Providence, they looked to support the efforts which he could not but approve; that on that account they came to solicit Napoleon the Great to pronounce these few words, *"Let the kingdom of Poland exist!"* and that it then would exist; that all the Poles would devote themselves to the orders of the founder of the fourth French dynasty, to whom ages were but as a moment, and space no more than a point."

Napoleon replied: "Gentlemen deputies of the confederation of Poland, I have listened with deep interest to what you have just told me. Were I a Pole, I should think and act like you; I should have voted with you in the assembly of Warsaw: the love of his country is the first duty of civilized man.

"In my position, I have many interests to reconcile, and many duties to fulfil. Had I reigned during the first, second, or third partition of Poland, I would have armed my people in her defence. When victory supplied me with the means of re-establishing your ancient laws, in your capital, and a portion of your provinces, I did so without seeking to prolong the war, which might have continued to waste the blood of my subjects.

"I love your nation! For sixteen years I have found your soldiers by my side on the plains of Italy and Spain. I applaud what you have done; I authorize your future efforts; I will do all which depends on me to second your resolutions. If your efforts be unanimous, you may cherish the hope of compelling your enemies to recognize your rights; but in countries so distant and extensive, it must be entirely on the exertions of the population which inhabits them, that you can justly ground hopes of success.

"From the first moment of my entering Poland, I have used the same language to you. To this it is my duty to add, that I have guaranteed to the emperor of Austria the integrity of his dominions, and that I cannot sanction any manoeuvre, or the least movement, tending to disturb the peaceable possession of what remains to him of the Polish provinces.

"Only provide that Lithuania, Samogitia, Witepsk, Polotsk, Mohilef, Volhynia, the Ukraine, Podolia, be animated by the same spirit which I have witnessed in the Greater Poland; and Providence will crown your good cause with success. I will recompense that devotion of your provinces which renders you so interesting, and has acquired you so many claims to my esteem and protection, by every means that can, under the circumstances, depend upon me."

The Poles had imagined that they were addressing the sovereign arbiter of the world, whose every word was a law, and whom no political compromise was capable of arresting. They were unable to comprehend the cause of the circumspection of this reply. They began to doubt the intentions of Napoleon; the zeal of some was cooled; the luke-warmness of others confirmed; all were intimidated. Even those around him asked each other what could be the motives of a prudence which appeared so unseasonable, and with him so unusual. "What, then, was the object of this war? Was he afraid of Austria? Had the retreat of the Russians disconcerted him? Did he doubt his good fortune, or was he unwilling to contract, in the face of Europe, engagements which he was not sure of being able to fulfil?

"Had the coldness of the Lithuanians infected him? or rather, did he dread the explosion of a patriotism which he might not be able to master? Was he still undecided as to the destiny he should bestow upon them?"

Whatever were his motives, it was obviously his wish that the Lithuanians should appear to liberate themselves; but as, at the same time, he created a government for them, and gave a direction to their public feeling, that circumstance placed him, as well as them, in a false position, wherein every thing terminated in errors, contradictions, and half measures. There was no reciprocal understanding between the parties; a mutual distrust was the result. The Poles desired some positive guarantees in return for the many sacrifices they were called upon to make. But their union in a single kingdom not having been pronounced, the alarm which is common at the moment of great decisions increased, and the confidence which they had just lost in him, they also lost in themselves. It was then that he nominated seven Lithuanians to the task of composing the new government. This choice was unlucky in some points; it displeased the jealous pride of an aristocracy at all times difficult to satisfy.

The four Lithuanian provinces of Wilna, Minsk, Grodno, and Bialystok, had each a government commission and national sub-prefects. Each commune was to have its municipality; but Lithuania was, in reality, governed by an imperial commissioner, and by four French auditors, with the title of intendants.

In short, from these, perhaps inevitable, faults, and from the disorders of an army placed between the alternative of famishing, or plundering its allies, there resulted a universal coolness. The emperor could not remain blind to it; he had calculated on four millions of Lithuanians; a few thousands were all that joined him! Their pospolite, which he had estimated at more than 100,000 men, had decreed him a guard of honour; only three horsemen attended him! The population of Volhynia remained immoveable, and Napoleon again appealed from them to victory. When fortunate, this coolness did not disturb him sufficiently; when unfortunate, whether through pride or justice, he did not complain of it.

As for us, ever confident in him and in ourselves, the disposition of the Lithuanians at first affected us very little; but when our forces diminished, we looked about us, and our attention was awakened by our danger. Three Lithuanian generals, distinguished by their names, their property, and their sentiments, followed the emperor. The French generals at last reproached them with the coolness of their countrymen. The ardour of the people of Warsaw, in 1806, was held out to them as an example. The warm discussion which ensued, passed, like several others similar, which it is necessary to record, at Napoleon's quarters, near the spot where he was employed; and as there was truth on both sides; as, in these conversations, the opposite allegations contended without destroying each other; and as the first and last causes of the coolness of the Lithuanians were therein revealed, it is impossible to omit them.

These generals then replied, "That they considered they had received becomingly the liberty which we brought them; that, moreover, every one expressed regard according to his habitual character; that the Lithuanians were more cold in their manner than the Poles, and consequently less communicative; that, after all, the sentiment might be the same, though the expression was different.

"That, besides, there was no similarity in the cases; that in 1806, it was after having conquered the Prussians, that the French had delivered Poland; that now, on the contrary, if they delivered Lithuania from the Russian yoke, it was before they had subjugated Russia. That, in this manner, it was natural for the first to receive a victorious and certain freedom with transport; and equally natural for the last to receive an uncertain and dangerous liberty with gravity; that a benefit was not purchased with the same air as if it were gratuitously accepted; that six years back, at Warsaw, there was nothing to be done but to prepare festivals; while at Wilna, where the whole power of Russia had just been exhibited, where its army was known to be untouched, and the motives of its retreat understood, it was for battles that preparation was to be made.

"And with what means? Why was not that liberty offered to them in 1807? Lithuania was then rich and populous. Since that time the continental system, by sealing up the only vent for its productions, had impoverished it, while Russian foresight had depopulated it of recruits, and more recently of a multitude of nobles, peasants, wagons, and cattle, which the Russian army had carried away with it."

To these causes they added "the famine resulting from the severity of the season in 1811, and the damage to which the over-rich wheats of those countries are subject. But why not make an appeal to the provinces of the south? In that quarter there were men, horses, and provisions of all kinds. They had nothing to do but to drive away Tormasof and his army from them. Schwartzenberg was, perhaps, marching in that direction; but was it to the Austrians, the uneasy usurpers of Gallicia, that they ought to confide the liberation of Volhynia? Would they station liberty so near slavery? Why did not they send Frenchmen and Poles there? But then it would be necessary to halt, to carry on a more methodical war, and allow time for organization; while Napoleon, doubtless urged by his distance from his own territory, by the daily expense of provisioning his immense army, depending on that alone, and hurrying after victory, sacrificed every thing to the hope of finishing the war at a single blow."

Here the speakers were interrupted: these reasons, though true, appeared insufficient excuses. "They concealed the most powerful cause of the immobility of their countrymen; it was to be discovered in the interested attachment of their grandees to the crafty policy of Russia, which flattered their self-love, respected their customs, and secured their right over the peasants, whom the French came to set free. Doubtless, national independence appeared too dear a purchase at such a price."

This reproach was well founded, and although it was not personal, the Lithuanian generals became irritated at it. One of them exclaimed, "You talk of our independence; but it must be in great peril, since you, at the head of 400,000 men, are afraid to commit yourselves by its recognition; indeed, you have not recognized it either by your words or actions. You have placed auditors, men quite new, at the head of an administration equally new, to govern our provinces. They levy heavy contributions, but they forget to inform us for whom it is that we make such sacrifices, as are only made for our country. They exhibit to us the emperor everywhere, but the republic hitherto nowhere. You have held out no object to set us in motion, and you complain of our being unsteady. Persons whom we do not respect as our countrymen, you set over us as our chiefs. Notwithstanding our entreaties, Wilna remains separated from Warsaw; disunited as we thus are, you require of us that confidence in our strength which union alone can give. The soldiers you expect from us are offered you; 30,000 would be now ready; but you have refused them arms, clothing, and the money in which we are deficient."

All these imputations might still have been combated; but he added: "True, we do not market for liberty, but we find that in fact it is not disinterestedly offered. Wherever you go, the report of your disorders precedes your march; nor are they partial, since your army marches upon a line of fifty leagues in front. Even at Wilna, notwithstanding the multiplied orders of your emperor, the suburbs have been pillaged, and it is natural that a liberty which brings such licence with it should be mistrusted.

"What then do you expect from our zeal? A happy countenance, acclamations of joy, accents of gratitude?—when every day each of us is apprised that his villages and granaries are devastated; for the little which the Russians did not carry away with them, your famishing columns have devoured. In their rapid marches, a multitude of marauders of all nations, against whom it is necessary to keep on the watch, detach themselves from their wings.

"What do you require more? that our countrymen should throng your passage; bring you their grain and cattle; that they should offer themselves completely armed and ready to follow you? Alas! what have they to give you? Your pillagers take all; there is not even time for them to make you the offer. Turn your eyes round towards the entrance of the imperial head-quarters. Do you see that man? He is all but naked; he groans and extends towards you a hand of supplication. That unhappy man who excites your pity, is one of those very nobles whose assistance you look for: yesterday, he was hurrying to meet you, full of ardour, with his daughter, his vassals, and his wealth; he was coming to present himself to your emperor; but he met with some Wurtemberg pillagers on his way, and was robbed of every thing; he is no longer a father,—he is scarcely a man."

Every one shuddered, and hurried to assist him; Frenchmen, Germans, Lithuanians, all agreed in deploring those disorders, for which no one could suggest a remedy. How, in fact, was it possible to restore discipline among such immense masses, so precipitately propelled, conducted by so many leaders of different manners, characters, and countries, and forced to resort to plunder for subsistence?

In Prussia, the emperor had only caused the army to supply itself with provisions for twenty days. This was as much as was necessary for the purpose of gaining Wilna by a battle. Victory was to have done the rest, but that victory was postponed by the retreat of the enemy. The emperor might have waited for his convoys; but as by surprising the Russians he had separated them, he did not wish to forego his grasp and lose his advantage. He, therefore, pushed forward on their track 400,000 men, with twenty days' provisions, into a country which was incapable of feeding the 20,000 Swedes of Charles XII.

It was not for want of foresight; for immense convoys of oxen followed the army, either in herds, or attached to the provision cars. Their drivers had been organized into battalions. It is true that the latter, wearied with the slow pace of these heavy animals, either slaughtered them, or suffered them to die of want. A great number, however, got as far as Wilna and Minsk; some reached Smolensk, but too late; they could only be of service to the recruits and reinforcements which followed us.

On the other hand, Dantzic contained so much corn, that she alone might have fed the whole army; she also supplied Königsberg. Its provisions had ascended the Pregel in large barges up to Vehlau, and in lighter craft as far as Insterburg. The other convoys went by land-carriage from Königsberg to Labiau, and from thence, by means of the Niemen and the Vilia, to Kowno and Wilna. But the water of the Vilia having shrunk so much through drought as to be incapable of floating these transports, it became necessary to find other means of conveyance.

Napoleon hated jobbers. It was his wish that the administration of the army should organize the Lithuanian wagons; 500 were assembled, but the appearance of them disgusted him. He then permitted contracts to be made with the Jews, who are the only traders in the country; and the provisions stopped at Kowno at last arrived at Wilna, but the army had already left it.

CHAPTER 16

The Centre Column

It was the largest column, that of the centre, which suffered most; it followed the road which the Russians had ruined, and of which the French advanced guard had just completed the spoliation. The columns which proceeded by lateral routes found necessaries there, but were not sufficiently careful in collecting and in economizing them.

The responsibility of the calamities which this rapid march occasioned ought not, therefore, to be laid entirely on Napoleon, for order and discipline were maintained in the army of Davoust; it suffered less from dearth: it was nearly the same with that of Prince Eugene. When pillage was resorted to in these two corps, it was always with method, and nothing but necessary injury was inflicted; the soldiers were obliged to carry several days' provisions, and prevented from wasting them. The same precautions should have been taken elsewhere; but, whether it was owing to the habit of making war in fertile countries, or to habitual ardour of constitution, many of the other chiefs thought much less of administering than of fighting.

On that account, Napoleon was frequently compelled to shut his eyes to a system of plunder which he vainly prohibited: too well aware, also, of the attraction which that mode of subsistence had for the soldier; that it made him love war, because it enriched him; that it pleased him, in consequence of the authority which it frequently gave him over classes superior to his own; that in his eyes it had all the charm of a war of the poor against the rich; finally, that the pleasure of being, and proving that he was the strongest, was under such circumstances incessantly repeated and brought home to him.

Napoleon, however, grew indignant at the intelligence of these excesses. He issued a threatening proclamation, and he directed moveable columns of French and Lithuanians to see to its execution. We, who were irritated at the sight of the pillagers, were eager to pursue and punish them; but when we had stripped them of the bread, or of the cattle which they had been robbing, and when we saw them, slowly retiring, sometimes eyeing us with a look of condensed despair, sometimes bursting into tears; and when we heard them murmuring, that, "not content with giving them nothing, we wrested every thing from them, and that, consequently, our intention must be to let them perish of hunger;" We, then, in our turn, accusing ourselves of barbarity to our own people, called them back, and restored their prey to them. Indeed, it was imperious necessity which impelled to plunder. The officers themselves had no other means of subsistence than the share which the soldiers allowed them.

A position of so much excess engendered fresh excesses. These rude men, with arms in their hands, when assailed by so many immoderate wants, could not remain moderate. When they arrived near any habitations, they were famished; at first they asked, but, either for want of being understood, or from the refusal or impossibility of the inhabitants to satisfy their demands, and of their inability to wait, altercations generally arose; then, as they became more and more exasperated with hunger, they became furious, and after tumbling either cottage or palace topsy-turvy, without finding the subsistence they were in quest of, they, in the violence of their despair, accused the inhabitants of being their enemies, and revenged themselves on the proprietors by destroying their property.

There were some who actually destroyed themselves, rather than proceed to such extremities; others did the same after having done so: these were the youngest. They placed their foreheads on their muskets, and blew out their brains in the middle of the high-road. But many became hardened; one excess led them to another, as people often grow angry with the blows which they inflict. Among the latter, some vagabonds took vengeance of their distresses upon persons; in the midst of so inauspicious an aspect of nature, they became denaturalized; abandoned to themselves at so great a distance from home, they imagined that every thing was allowed them, and that their own sufferings authorized them in making others suffer.

In an army so numerous, and composed of so many nations, it was natural also to find more malefactors than in smaller ones: the causes of so many evils induced fresh ones; already enfeebled by famine, it was necessary to make forced marches in order to escape from it, and to reach the enemy. At night when they halted, the soldiers thronged into the houses; there, worn out with fatigue and want, they threw themselves upon the first dirty straw they met with.

The most robust had barely spirits left to knead the flour which they found, and to light the ovens with which all those wooden houses were supplied; others had scarcely strength to go a few paces in order to make the fires necessary to cook some food; their officers, exhausted like themselves, feebly gave orders to take more care, and neglected to see that their orders were obeyed. A piece of burnt wood, at such times escaping from an oven, or a spark from the fire of the bivouacs, was sufficient to set fire to a castle or a whole village, and to cause the deaths of many unfortunate soldiers who had taken refuge in them. In other respects, these disorders were very rare in Lithuania.

The emperor was not ignorant of these details, but he had committed himself too far. Even at Wilna, all these disorders had taken place; the Duke of Treviso, among others, informed him, "that he had seen, from the Niemen to the Vilia, nothing but ruined habitations, and baggage and provision-wagons abandoned; they were found dispersed on the highways and in the fields, overturned, broke open, and their contents scattered here and there, and pillaged, as if they had been taken by the enemy: he should have imagined himself following a defeated army. Ten thousand horses had been killed by the cold rains of the great storm, and by the unripe rye, which had become their new and only food. Their carcases were lying encumbering the road: they sent forth a mephitic smell impossible to breathe: it was a new scourge, which some compared to famine, but much more terrible: several soldiers of the young guard had already perished of hunger."

Up to that point Napoleon listened with calmness, but here he abruptly interrupted the speaker. Wishing to escape from distress by incredulity, he exclaimed, "It is impossible! where are their twenty days' provisions? Soldiers well commanded never die of hunger."

A general, the author of this last report, was present. Napoleon turned towards him; appealed to him, and pressed him with questions; and that general, either from weakness or uncertainty, replied, "that the individuals referred to had not died of hunger, but of intoxication."

The emperor then remained convinced that the privations of the soldiers had been exaggerated to him. As to the rest, he exclaimed, "The loss of the horses must be borne with; of some equipages, and even some habitations; it was a torrent that rolled away: it was the worst side of the picture of war; an evil exchanged for a good; to misery her share must be given; his treasures, his benefits would repair the loss: one great result would make amends for all; he only required a single victory; if sufficient means remained for accomplishing that, he should be satisfied."

The duke remarked, that a victory might be overtaken by a more methodical march, followed by the magazines; but he was not listened to. Those to whom this marshal (who had just returned from Spain,) complained, replied to him, "That, in fact the emperor grew angry at the account of evils, which he considered irremediable, his policy imposing on him the necessity of a prompt and decisive victory."

They added, "that they saw too clearly that the health of their leader was impaired; and that being compelled, notwithstanding, to throw himself into positions more and more critical, he could not survey, without ill temper, the difficulties which he passed by, and suffered to accumulate behind him; difficulties which he then affected to treat with contempt, in order to disguise their importance, and preserve the energy of mind which he himself required to surmount them. This was the reason that, being already disturbed and fatigued by the new and critical situation into which he had thrown himself, and impatient to escape from it, he kept marching on, always pushing his army forward, in order to bring matters sooner to a termination."

Thus it was that Napoleon was constrained to shut his eyes to facts. It is well known that the greater part of his ministers were not flatterers. Both facts and men spoke sufficiently; but what could they teach him? Of what was he ignorant? Had not all his preparations been dictated by the most clear-sighted foresight? What could be said to him, which he had not himself said and written a hundred times? It was after having anticipated the minutest details; having prepared for every inconvenience, having provided every thing for a slow and methodical war, that he divested himself of all these precautions, that he abandoned all these preparations, and suffered himself to be hurried away by habit, by the necessity of short wars, of rapid victories, and sudden treaties of peace.

CHAPTER 17
Wilna

It was in the midst of these grave circumstances that Balachoff, a minister of the Russian emperor, presented himself with a flag of truce at the French advanced posts. He was received, and the army, now become less ardent, indulged anticipations of peace.

He brought this message from Alexander to Napoleon, "That it was not yet too late to negotiate; a war which the soil, the climate, and the character of Russia, rendered interminable, was begun; but all reconciliation was not become impossible, and from one bank of the Niemen to the other they might yet come to an understanding." He, moreover, added, "that his master declared, in the face of Europe, that he was not the aggressor; that his ambassador at Paris, in demanding his passports, did not consider himself as having broken the peace; that thus, the French had entered Russia without a declaration of war." There were, however, no fresh overtures, either verbal or written, presented by Balachoff.

The choice of this flag of truce had been remarked; he was the minister of the Russian police; that office required an observant spirit, and it was thought that he was sent to exercise it amongst us. What rendered us more mistrustful of the character of the negotiator was, that the negotiation appeared to have no character, unless it were that of great moderation, which, under the actual circumstances, was taken for weakness.

Napoleon did not hesitate. He would not stop at Paris; how could he then retreat at Wilna? What would Europe think? What result could he exhibit to the French and allied armies as a motive for so many fatigues; for such vast movements; for such enormous individual and national expenditure: it would be confessing himself vanquished. Besides, his language before so many princes, since his departure from Paris, had pledged him as much as his actions; so that, in fact, he found himself as much compromised on the score of his allies as of his enemies. Even then, it is said, the warmth of conversation with Balachoff hurried him away. "What had brought him to Wilna? What did the Emperor of Russia want with him? Did he pretend to resist him? He was only a parade general. As to himself, his head was his counsellor; from that every thing proceeded. But as to Alexander,—who was there to counsel him? Whom had he to oppose to him? He had only three generals,—Kutusoff, whom he did not like, because he was a Russian; Beningsen, superannuated six years ago, and now in his second childhood; and Barclay: the last could certainly manoeuvre; he was brave; he understood war; but he was a general only good for a retreat." And he added, "You all believe yourselves to understand the art of war, because you have read Jomini; but if his book could have taught it you, do you think that I should have allowed it to be published?" In this conversation, of which the above is the Russian version, it is certain that he added, "that, however, the Emperor Alexander had friends even in the imperial head-quarters." Then, pointing out Caulaincourt to the Russian minister, "There," said he, "is a knight of your emperor; he is a Russian in the French camp."

Probably Caulaincourt did not sufficiently comprehend, that by that expression Napoleon only wished to point him out as a negotiator who would be agreeable to Alexander; for as soon as Balachoff was gone, he advanced towards the emperor, and in an angry tone, asked him why he had insulted him? exclaiming, "that he was a Frenchman! a true Frenchman! that he had proved it already; and would prove it again by repeating, that this war was impolitic and dangerous; that it would destroy his army, France, and himself. That, as to the rest, as he had just insulted him, he should quit him; that all that he asked of him was a division in Spain, where nobody wished to serve, and the furthest from his presence possible." The emperor attempted to appease him; but not being able to obtain a hearing, he withdrew, Caulaincourt still pursuing him with his reproaches. Berthier, who was present at this scene, interposed without effect. Bessières, more in the back-ground, had vainly tried to detain Caulaincourt by holding him by the coat.

The next day, Napoleon was unable to bring his grand equerry into his presence, without formal and repeated orders. At length he appeased him by caresses, and by the expression of an esteem and attachment which Caulaincourt well deserved. But he dismissed Balachoff with verbal and inadmissible proposals.

Alexander made no reply to them; the full importance of the step he had just taken was not at the time properly comprehended. It was his determination neither to address nor even answer Napoleon any more. It was a last word before an irreparable breach; and that circumstance rendered it remarkable.

Meantime, Murat pursued the flying steps of that victory which was so much coveted; he commanded the cavalry of the advanced guard; he at last reached the enemy on the road to Swentziani, and drove him in the direction of Druïa. Every morning, the Russian rear-guard appeared to have escaped him; every evening he overtook it again, and attacked it, but always in a strong position, after a long march, too late, and before his men had taken any refreshment; there were, consequently, every day fresh combats, producing no important results.

Other chiefs, by other routes, followed the same direction. Oudinot had passed the Vilia beyond Kowno, and already in Samogitia, to the north of Wilna, at Deweltowo, and at Vilkomir, had fallen in with the enemy, whom he drove before him towards Dünabourg. In this manner he marched on, to the left of Ney and the King of Naples, whose right was flanked by Nansouty. From the 15th of July, the river Düna, from Disna to Dünabourg, had been approached by Murat, Montbrun, Sebastiani, and Nansouty, by Oudinot and Ney, and by three divisions of the 1st corps, placed under the orders of the Count de Lobau.

It was Oudinot who presented himself before Dünabourg: he made an attempt on that town, which the Russians had vainly attempted to fortify. This too eccentric march of Oudinot displeased Napoleon. The river separated the two armies. Oudinot re-ascended it in order to put himself in communication with Murat; and Wittgenstein, in order to form a junction with Barclay. Dünabourg remained without assailants and without defenders.

On his march, Wittgenstein had a view, from the right bank, of Druïa, and a vanguard of French cavalry, which occupied that town with too negligent a security. Encouraged by the approach of night, he made one of his corps pass the river, and on the 15th, in the morning, the advanced posts of one of our brigades were surprised, sabred, and carried off. After this, Wittgenstein recalled his people to the right bank, and pursued his way with his prisoners, among whom was a French general. This *coup-de-main* gave Napoleon reason to hope for a battle: believing that Barclay was resuming the offensive, he suspended, for a short time, his march upon Witepsk, in order to concentrate his troops and direct them according to circumstances. This hope, however, was of short duration.

During these events, Davoust, at Osmiana, to the south of Wilna, had got sight of some scouts of Bagration, who was already anxiously seeking an outlet towards the north. Up to that time, short of a victory, the plan of the campaign adopted at Paris had completely succeeded. Aware that the enemy was extended over too long a defensive line, Napoleon had broken it by briskly attacking it in one direction, and by so doing had thrown it back and pursued its largest mass upon the Düna; while Bagration, whom he had not brought into contact till five days later, was still upon the Niemen. During an interval of several days, and over a front of eighty leagues, the manoeuvre was the same as that which Frederic the Second had often employed upon a line of two leagues, and during an interval of some few hours.

Already Doctorof, and several scattered divisions of each of these two separated masses had only escaped by favour of the extent of the country, of chance, and of the usual causes of that ignorance, which always exists during war, as to what passes close at hand in the ranks of an enemy.

Several persons have pretended that there was too much circumspection or too much negligence in the first operations of the invasion; that from the Vistula, the assailing army had received orders to march with all the precaution of one attacked; that the aggression once commenced, and Alexander having fled, the advanced guard of Napoleon ought to have re-ascended the two banks of the Vilia with more celerity and more in advance, and that the army of Italy should have followed this movement more closely. Perhaps Doctorof, who commanded the left wing of Barclay, being forced to cross our line of attack, in order to fly from Lida toward Swentziany, might then have been made prisoner. Pajol repulsed him at Osmiana; but he escaped by Smorgony. Nothing but his baggage was taken; and Napoleon laid the blame of his escape on Prince Eugene, although he had himself prescribed to him every one of his movements.

But the army of Italy, the Bavarian army, the 1st corps and the guard, very soon occupied and surrounded Wilna. There it was that, stretched out over his maps (which he was obliged to examine in that manner, on account of his short sight, which he shared with Alexander the Great and Frederic the Second), Napoleon followed the course of the Russian army; it was divided into two unequal masses: one with its emperor towards Drissa, the other with Bagration, who was still in the direction of Myr.

Eighty leagues in front of Wilna, the Düna and the Borishenes separate Lithuania from old Russia. At first, these two rivers run parallel to each other from east to west, leaving between them an interval of about twenty-five leagues of an unequal, woody, and marshy soil. They arrive in that manner from the interior of Russia, on its frontiers; at this point, at the same time, and as if in concert, they turn off; the one abruptly at Orcha towards the south; the other, near Witepsk, towards the north-west. It is in that new direction that their course traces the frontiers of Lithuania and old Russia.

The narrow space which these two rivers leave between them before taking this opposite direction seems to constitute the entrance, and as it were the gates of Muscovy. It is the focus of the roads which lead to the two capitals of that empire.

Napoleon's whole attention was directed to that point. By the retreat of Alexander upon Drissa, he foresaw that which Bagration would attempt to make from Grodno towards Witepsk, through Osmiana, Minsk, and Docktzitzy, or by Borizof; he determined to prevent it, and instantly pushed forward Davoust towards Minsk, between these two hostile bodies, with two divisions of infantry, the cuirassiers of Valence, and several brigades of light cavalry.

On his right, the king of Westphalia was to drive Bagration on Davoust, who would cut off his communication with Alexander, make him surrender, and get possession of the course of the Boristhenes; on his left, Murat, Oudinot, and Ney, already before Drissa, were directed to keep Barclay and his emperor in their front; he himself with the elite of his army, the army of Italy, the Bavarian army, and three divisions detached from Davoust, was to march upon Witepsk between Davoust and Murat, ready to join one or the other of them; in this manner penetrating and interposing between the two hostile armies, forcing himself between them and beyond them; finally, keeping them separate, not only by that central position, but by the uncertainty which it would create in Alexander as to which of his two capitals it would be requisite for him to defend. Circumstances would decide the rest.

Such was Napoleon's plan on the 10th of July at Wilna; it was written in this form on that very day under his dictation, and corrected by his own hand, for one of his chiefs, the individual who was most concerned in its execution. Immediately, the movement, which was already begun, became general.

Chapter 18
Bagration

The king of Westphalia then went along the Niemen at Grodno, with a view to repass it at Bielitza, to overpower the right of Bagration, put it to the rout, and pursue it.

This Saxon, Westphalian, and Polish army had in front of it a general and a country both difficult to conquer. It fell to its lot to invade the elevated plain of Lithuania: there are the sources of the rivers which empty their waters into the Black and Baltic seas. But the soil there is slow in determining their inclination and their current, so that the waters stagnate and overflow the country to a great extent. Some narrow causeways had been thrown over those woody and marshy plains; they formed there long defiles, which Bagration was easily enabled to defend against the king of Westphalia. The latter attacked him carelessly; his advanced guard only three times encountered the enemy, at Nowogrodeck, at Myr, and at Romanof. The first rencontre was entirely to the advantage of the Russians; in the two others, Latour-Maubourg remained master of a sanguinary and contested field of battle.

At the same time, Davoust, proceeding from Osmiana, extended his force towards Minsk and Ygumen, behind the Russian general, and made himself master of the outlet of the defiles, in which the king of Westphalia was compelling Bagration to engage himself.

Between this general and his retreat was a river which takes its source in an infectious marsh; its uncertain, slow, and languid current, across a rotten soil, does not belie its origin; its muddy waters flow towards the south-east; its name possesses a fatal celebrity, for which it is indebted to our misfortunes.

The wooden bridges, and long causeways, which, in order to approach it, had been thrown over the adjacent marshes, abut upon a town named Borizof, situated on its left bank, on the Russian side.

This bank is generally higher than the right; a remark applicable to all the rivers which in this country run in the direction of one pole to the other, their eastern bank commanding their western bank, as Asia does Europe.

This passage was important; Davoust anticipated Bagration there by taking possession of Minsk on the 8th of July, as well as the entire country from the Vilia to the Berezina; accordingly when the Russian prince and his army, summoned by Alexander, to the north, pushed forward their piquets, in the first instance upon Lida, and afterwards successively upon Olzania, Vieznowo, Troki, Bolzoï, and Sobsnicki, they came in contact with Davoust, and were forced to fall back upon their main body. They then bent their course a little more in the rear and to the right, and made a new attempt on Minsk, but there again they found Davoust. A scanty platoon of that marshal's vanguard was entering by one gate, when the advanced guard of Bagration presented itself at another; on which, the Russian retreated once more into his marshes, towards the south.

At this intelligence, observing Bagration and 40,000 Russians cut off from the army of Alexander, and enveloped by two rivers and two armies, Napoleon exclaimed, "I have them!" In fact, it only required three marches more to have hemmed in Bagration completely. But Napoleon, who since accused Davoust of suffering the escape of the left wing of the Russians by remaining four days in Minsk, and afterwards, with more justice, the king of Westphalia, had just then placed that monarch under the orders of the marshal. It was this change, which was made too late, and in the midst of an operation, which destroyed the unity of it.

This order arrived at the very moment when Bagration, repulsed from Minsk, had no other retreat open to him than a long and narrow causeway. It occurs on the marshes of Nieswig, Shlutz, Glusck, and Bobruisk. Davoust wrote to the king to push the Russians briskly into this defile, the outlet of which at Glusck he was about to occupy. Bagration would never have been able to get out of it. But the king, already irritated by the reproaches which the uncertainty and dilatoriness of his first operations had brought upon him, could not suffer a subject to be his commander; he quitted his army, without leaving any one to replace him, or without even communicating, if we are to credit Davoust, to any of his generals, the order which he had just received. He was permitted to retire into Westphalia without his guard; which he accordingly did.

Meanwhile Davoust vainly waited for Bagration at Glusck. That general, not being sufficiently pressed by the Westphalian army, had the option of making a new detour towards the south, to get to Bobruisk, and there cross the Berezina, and reach the Boristhenes near Bickof. There again, if the Westphalian army had had a commander, if that commander had pressed the Russian leader more closely, if he had replaced him at Bickof, when he came in collision with Davoust at Mohilef, it is certain that in that case Bagration, enclosed between the Westphalians, Davoust, the Boristhenes, and the Berezina, would have been compelled to conquer or to surrender We have seen that the Russian prince could not pass the Berezina but at Bobruisk, nor reach the Boristhenes, except in the direction of Novoï-Bikof, forty leagues to the south of Orcha, and sixty leagues from Witepsk, which it was his object to reach.

Finding himself driven so far out of his track, he hastened to regain it by re-ascending the Boristhenes, to Mohilef. But there again he found Davoust, who had anticipated him at Lida by passing the Berezina at the very point at which Charles XII. had formerly done so.

This marshal, however, had not expected to find the Russian prince on the road to Mohilef. He believed him to be already on the left bank of the Boristhenes. Their mutual surprise turned in the first instance to the advantage of Bagration, who cut off a whole regiment of his light cavalry. At that time Bagration had with him 35,000 men, Davoust 12,000. On the 23rd of July, the latter chose an elevated ground, defended by a ravine, and flanked by two woods. The Russians had no means of extending themselves on this field of battle; they, nevertheless, accepted the challenge. Their numbers were there useless; they attacked like men sure of victory; they did not even think of profiting by the woods, in order to turn Davoust's right.

The Muscovites say that, in the middle of the contest they were seized with a panic at the idea of finding themselves in the presence of Napoleon; for each of the enemy's generals imagined him to be opposed to them, Bagration at Mohilef; and Barclay at Drissa. He was believed to be in all places at once: so greatly does renown magnify the man of genius! so strangely does it fill the world with its fame! and convert him into an omnipresent and supernatural being!

The attack was violent and obstinate on the part of the Russians, but without scientific combination. Bagration was roughly repulsed, and again compelled to retrace his steps. He finally crossed the Boristhenes at Novoï-Bikof, where he re-entered the Russian interior, in order finally to unite with Barclay, beyond Smolensk.

Napoleon disdained to attribute this disappointment to the ability of the enemy's general; he referred it to the incapacity of his own. He already discovered that his presence was necessary every where, which rendered it every where impossible. The circle of his operations was so much enlarged, that, being compelled to remain in the centre, his presence was wanting on the whole of the circumference. His generals, exhausted like himself, too independent of each other, too much separated, and at the same time too dependent upon him, ventured to do less of themselves, and frequently waited for his orders. His influence was weakened over so great an extent. It required too great a soul for so great a body; his, vast as it was, was not sufficient for the purpose.

But at length, on the 16th of July, the whole army was in motion. While all were hurrying and exerting themselves in this manner, he was still at Wilna, which he caused to be fortified. He there ordered a levy of eleven Lithuanian regiments. He established the duke of Bassano as governor of Lithuania, and as the centre of administrative, political, and even military communication between him, Europe, and the generals commanding the *corps de armée* which were not to follow him to Moscow.

This ostensible inactivity of Napoleon at Wilna lasted twenty days. Some thought that, finding himself in the centre of his operations with a strong reserve, he awaited the event, in readiness to direct his motions either towards Davoust, Murat, or Macdonald; others thought that the organization of Lithuania, and the politics of Europe, to which he was more proximate at Wilna, retained him in that city; or that he did not anticipate any obstacles worthy of him till he reached the Düna; a circumstance in which he was not deceived, but by which he was too much flattered. The precipitate evacuation of Lithuania by the Russians seemed to dazzle his judgment; of this Europe will be the best judge; his bulletins repeated his words.

"Here then is that Russian empire, so formidable at a distance! It is a desert, for which its scattered population is wholly insufficient. They will be vanquished by its very extent, which ought to defend them. They are barbarians. They are scarcely possessed of arms. They have no recruits in readiness. Alexander will require more time to collect them than he will take to reach Moscow. It is true that, from the moment of the passage of the Niemen, the atmosphere has been incessantly deluging or drying up the unsheltered soil; but this calamity is less an obstacle to the rapidity of our advance, than an impediment to the flight of the Russians. They are conquered without a combat by their weakness alone; by the memory of our victories; by the remorse which dictates the restitution of that Lithuania, which they have acquired neither by peace nor war, but solely by treachery."

To these motives of the stay, perhaps too protracted, which Napoleon made at Wilna, those who were nearest to his person have added another. They remarked to each other, "that a genius so vast as his, and always increasing in activity and audacity, was not now seconded as it had been formerly by a vigorous constitution. They were alarmed at finding their chief no longer insensible to the heat of a burning atmosphere; and they remarked to each other with melancholy forebodings, the tendency to corpulence by which his frame was now distinguished; the sure sign of a premature debility of system."

Some of them attributed this to his frequent use of the bath. They were ignorant, that, far from being a habit of luxury, this had become to him an indispensable relief from a bodily ailment of a serious and alarming character[17], which his policy carefully concealed, in order not to excite cruel expectations in his adversaries.

Such is the inevitable and unhappy influence of the most trivial causes over the destiny of nations. It will be shortly seen, when the profoundest combinations, which ought to have secured the success of the boldest, and perhaps the most useful enterprise in a European point of view, come to be developed;—how, at the decisive moment, on the plains of the Moskwa, nature paralysed the genius, and the man was wanting to the hero. The numerous battalions of Russia could not have defended her; a stormy day, a sudden attack of fever, were her salvation.

It will be only just and proper to revert to this observation, when, in examining the picture which I shall be forced to trace of the battle of the Moskwa, I shall be found repeating all the complaints, and even the reproaches, which an unusual inactivity and languor extorted from the most devoted friends and constant admirers of this great man. Most of them, as well as those who have subsequently given an account of the battle, were unaware of the bodily sufferings of a chief, who, in the midst of his depression, exerted himself to conceal their cause. That which was eminently a misfortune, these narrators have designated as a fault.

Besides, at 800 leagues' distance from one's home, after so many fatigues and sacrifices, at the instant when they saw the victory escape

---

17: The *dysuria*, or retention of urine.

from their grasp, and a frightful prospect revealed itself, it was natural for them to be severe; and they had suffered too much, to be quite impartial.

As for myself, I shall not conceal what I witnessed, in the persuasion that truth is of all tributes that which is alone worthy of a great man; of that illustrious captain, who had so often contrived to extract prodigious advantages from every occurrence, not excepting his reverses; of that man who raised himself to so great an eminence, that posterity will scarcely be enabled to distinguish the clouds scattered over a glory so brilliant.

CHAPTER 19
Murat Charges

Meantime, he was apprised that his orders were fulfilled, his army united, and that a battle claimed his presence. He at length departed from Wilna on the 16th of July, at half-past eleven at night; he stopped at Swentziani, while the heat of the 17th was most oppressive; on the 18th he was at Klubokoe: taking up his residence at a monastery, whence he observed that the village which it commanded bore more resemblance to an assemblage of savage huts than to European habitations.

An address of the Russians to the French soldiers had just been dispersed throughout his army. He found in it some idle abuse, coupled with a nugatory and unskilful invitation to desert. His anger was excited at its perusal; in his first agitation, he dictated a reply, which he tore; then a second, which experienced the same fate; at length a third, with which he expressed himself satisfied. It was that which was, at the time, read in the journals, under the signature of a French grenadier. In this manner he dictated even the most trivial letters, which issued from his cabinet or from his staff; he perpetually reduced his ministers and Berthier to the condition of being mere secretaries; his mind still retained its activity, notwithstanding his sinking frame; their union, however, began to fail; and this was one cause of our misfortunes.

In the midst of this occupation, he learned that Barclay had, on the 18th, abandoned his camp at Drissa, and that he was marching towards Witepsk. This movement opened his eyes. Detained by the check which Sebastiani had received near Druïa, and more especially by the rains and bad state of the roads, he found (though perhaps too late) that the occupation of Witepsk was urgent and decisive; that that city alone was eminently aggressive, inasmuch as it separated the two hostile rivers and armies. From that position, he would be enabled to turn the broken army of his rival, cut him off from his southern provinces, and crush his weakness with superior force. He concluded that, if Barclay had anticipated him in reaching that capital, he would doubtless defend it: and there, perhaps, he was to expect that so-much-coveted victory which had escaped him on the Vilia. He, therefore, instantly directed all his corps on Beszenkowiczi; thither he summoned Murat and Ney, who were then near Polotsk, where he left Oudinot. For himself, he proceeded from Klubokoe (where he was surrounded by his guard, the Italian army, and three divisions detached from Davoust), to Kamen, always in a carriage, except during the night, either from necessity, or, perhaps, with a view to keep his soldiers in ignorance of the inability of their chief to share their fatigues.

Till that time, the greater part of the army had proceeded with astonishment, at finding no enemy; they had now become habituated to the circumstance. By day the novelty of the places, and impatience to get to their journey's end, occupied their attention; at night the necessity of choosing or making for themselves a place of shelter; of finding food, and dressing it. The soldiers were so much engaged by so many cares, that they considered themselves less employed in making war than a troublesome journey; but if the war and the enemy were to fall back always thus, how much farther should they have to go in search of them? At length, on the 25th, the report of cannon was heard, and the army, as well as the emperor, indulged their hopes of a victory and peace.

This was in the direction of Beszenkowiczi, Prince Eugene had there encountered Doctorof, who commanded Barclay's rear-guard. In following his leader from Polotsk to Witepsk, he cleared his way on the left bank of the Düna to Beszenkowiczi, the bridge of which he burnt as he retired. The viceroy, on capturing this town, came in sight of the Düna, and re-established the passage; the few Russian troops left in observation on the other side feebly opposed the operation. When Napoleon contemplated, for the first time, this river, his new conquest, he censured sharply, and not unjustly, the defective construction of the bridge which made him master of the two banks.

It was no puerile vanity which induced him then to cross that river, but anxiety to see with his own eyes how far the Russian army had proceeded on its march from Drissa to Witepsk, and whether he might not attack it on its passage, or anticipate its arrival at the latter city. But the direction taken by the enemy's rear-guard, and the information obtained from some prisoners, convinced him that Barclay had been beforehand with him; that he had left Wittgenstein in front of Oudinot, and that the Russian general-in-chief was in Witepsk. He was, indeed, already prepared to dispute the possession of the defiles which cover that capital with Napoleon.

Napoleon having observed on the right bank of the river nothing but the remains of a rear-guard, returned to Beszenkowiczi. His various divisions arrived there at the same time by the northern and western roads. His orders of march had been executed with so much precision, that all the corps which had left the Niemen, at different epochs, and by different routes, notwithstanding obstacles of every description, after a month of separation, and at a hundred leagues' distance from the point of their departure, found themselves all reunited at Beszenkowiczi, where they arrived on the same day, and nearly at the same hour.

Great disorder was naturally the result; numerous columns of cavalry, infantry, and artillery presented themselves on all sides; contests took place for precedence; and each corps, exasperated with fatigue and hunger, was impatient to get to its destination. Meanwhile, the streets were blocked up with a crowd of orderlies, staff-officers, valets, saddle-horses, and baggage. They ran through the city in tumultuous groups; some looking for provisions, others for forage, and a few for lodgings; there was a constant crossing and jostling; and as the influx augmented every instant, chaos in a short time reigned throughout.

In one quarter, aides-de-camp, the bearers of urgent orders, vainly sought to force a passage; the soldiers were deaf to their remonstrances, and even to their orders: hence arose quarrels and outcries; the noise of which, united with the beating of drums, the oaths of the wagoners, the rumbling of the baggage-carts and cannon, the commands of the officers, and, finally, with the tumult of the regular contests which took place in the houses, the entrances of which, while one party attempted to force, others, already established there, prepared to defend.

At length, towards midnight, all these masses, which were nearly confounded together, got disentangled; the accumulation of troops gradually moved off in the direction of Ostrowno, or were distributed in Beszenkowiczi; and the most profound silence succeeded the most frightful tumult.

This great concentration, the multiplied orders which came from all parts, the rapidity with which the various corps were pushed forward, even during the night—all announced the expectation of a battle on the following day. In fact, Napoleon not having been able to anticipate the Russians in the possession of Witepsk, was determined to force them from that position; but the latter, after having entered by the right bank of the Düna, had passed through that city, and were now come to meet him, in order to defend the long defiles which protect it.

On the 25th of July, Murat proceeded towards Ostrowno with his cavalry. At the distance of two leagues from that village, Domon, Du Coëtlosquet, Carignan, and the 8th hussars, were advancing in column upon a broad road, lined by a double row of large birch trees. These hussars were near reaching the summit of a hill, on which they could only get a glimpse of the weakest portion of a corps, composed of three regiments of cavalry of the Russian guard, and six pieces of cannon. There was not a single rifleman to cover their line.

The colonels of the 8th imagined themselves preceded by two regiments of their division, which had marched across the fields on the right and left of the road, and from the view of which they were precluded by the bordering trees. But these corps had halted; and the 8th, already considerably in advance of them, still kept marching on, persuaded that what it perceived through the trees, at 150 paces' distance, in its front, were these two regiments, of which, without being aware of it, it had got the start.

The immobility of the Russians completed the error into which the chiefs of the 8th had fallen. The order to charge seemed to them to be a mistake; they sent an officer to reconnoitre the troop which was before them, and still marched on without any distrust. Suddenly they beheld their officer sabred, knocked down, made prisoner, and the enemy's cannon bringing down their hussars. They now hesitated no longer, and without losing time to extend their line under the enemy's fire, they dashed through the trees, and rushed forward to extinguish it. At the first onset they seized the cannon, dispersed the regiment that was in the centre of the enemy's line, and destroyed it. During the disorder of this first success, they observed the Russian regiment on the right, which they had passed, remaining motionless with astonishment; upon this they returned, and attacking it in the rear dispersed it. In the midst of this second victory, they perceived the third regiment on the enemy's left, which was giving way in confusion, and seeking to retreat; towards this third enemy they briskly returned, with all the men they could muster, and attacked and dispersed it in the midst of its retreat.

Animated by this success, Murat drove the enemy into the wood of Ostrowno, where he seemed to conceal himself. That monarch endeavoured to penetrate the wood, but a strong resistance obstructed the attempt.

The position of Ostrowno was well chosen and commanding; those posted there could see without being seen; it intersected the main road; it had the Düna on the right, a ravine in front, and thick woods on its surface and on the left. It was, moreover, in communication with magazines; it covered them, as well as Witepsk, the capital of these regions, which Ostermann had hurried to defend.

On his side, Murat, always as prodigal of his life, which was now that of a victorious king, as he had formerly been when only an obscure soldier, persisted in attacks upon these woods, notwithstanding the heavy fire which proceeded from them. But he was soon made sensible that a furious onset was fruitless here. The ground carried by the hussars of the 8th was disputed with him, and his advance-column, composed of the divisions Bruyères and Saint Germain, and of the 8th corps of infantry, was compelled to maintain itself there against an army.

They defended themselves as victors always do, by attacking. Each hostile corps, as it presented itself to assail our flanks, was in turn assaulted. Their cavalry were driven back into the woods, and their infantry broken at the point of the sabre. Our troops, nevertheless, were getting fatigued with victory, when the division Delzons arrived; the king promptly pushed it forward on the right, toward the line of the enemy's retreat, who now became uneasy, and no longer disputed the victory.

These defiles are several leagues in length. The same evening the viceroy rejoined Murat, and the next day they found the Russians in a new position. Pahlen and Konownitzin had united with Ostermann. After having repulsed the Russian left, the two French princes were pointing out to the troops of their right wing the position which was to serve them as a *point d'appui*, from which they were to make the attack, when suddenly a great clamour arose on their left: their eyes were instantly turned that way; the cavalry and infantry of that wing had twice attacked the enemy, and been twice repulsed; the Russians, emboldened by this success, were issuing in multitudes, and with frightful cries, from their woods. The audacity and fervour of attack had passed over to them, while the French exhibited the uncertainty and timidity of defence.

A battalion of Croats, and the 84th regiment, vainly attempted to make a stand; their line gradually decreased; the ground in front of them was strewed with their dead; behind them, the plain was covered with their wounded, who had retired from the battle, with those who carried them, and with many others, who, under the plea of supporting the wounded, or being wounded themselves, successively abandoned their ranks. A rout accordingly began. Already the artillery corps, who are always picked men, perceiving themselves no longer supported, began retiring with their pieces; a few minutes longer, and the troops of all arms, in their flight towards the same defile, would have there met each other; thence would have resulted a confusion, in which the voices and the efforts of their officers would have been lost, where all the elements of resistance would have been confounded and rendered useless.

It is said that Murat, on seeing this, darted forward in front of a regiment of Polish lancers; and that the latter, excited by the presence of the king, animated by his words, and, moreover, transported with rage at the sight of the Russians, followed him precipitately. Murat had only wished to stimulate them and impel them against the enemy; he had no intention of throwing himself with them into the midst of a conflict, in which he would neither be able to see nor to command; but the Polish lances were ready couched and condensed behind him; they covered the whole width of the ground; and they pushed him before them with all the rapidity of their steeds; he could neither detach himself from them nor stop; he had no resource but to charge in front of the regiment, just where he had stationed himself in order to harangue it; a resource to which, like a true soldier, he submitted with the best possible grace.

At the same time, general Anthouard ran to his artillerymen, and general Girardin to the 106th regiment, which he halted, rallied, and led back against the Russian right wing, whose position he carried, as well as two pieces of cannon and the victory; on his side, general Piré encountered and turned the left of the enemy. Fortune having again changed sides, the Russians withdrew into their forests.

Meanwhile, they persevered on the left in defending a thick wood, the advanced position of which broke our line. The 92nd regiment, intimidated by the heavy fire which issued from it, and bewildered by a shower of balls, remained immoveable, neither daring to advance nor retreat, restrained by two opposite fears—the dread of danger and the dread of shame—and escaping neither; but general Belliard hastened to reanimate them by his words, and general Roussel by his example; and the wood was carried.

By this success, a strong column which had advanced on our right, in order to turn it, was itself turned; Murat perceived this, and instantly drawing his sword, exclaimed, "Let the bravest follow me!" But this territory is intersected with ravines which protected the retreat of the Russians, who all plunged into a forest of two leagues in depth, which was the last natural curtain which concealed Witepsk from our view.

After so warm a contest, the king of Naples and the viceroy were hesitating about committing themselves to so covered a country, when the emperor came up: both hastened to his presence, in order to show him what had been done, and what still remained to be done. Napoleon immediately ascended the highest rising ground, which was nearest to the enemy. From thence his genius, soaring over every obstacle, soon penetrated the mystery of the forests, and the depths of the mountains before him; he gave his orders without hesitation; and the same woods which had arrested the audacity of the two princes, were traversed from end to end. In short, that very evening, Witepsk might have discerned from the summit of her double eminence our light troops emerging into the plain by which she is surrounded.

Here, every thing contributed to stop the emperor; the night, the multitude of hostile fires which covered the plain, an unknown country, which it was necessary to reconnoitre, in order to direct his divisions across it, and especially the time requisite to enable the crowd of soldiers to disengage themselves from the long and narrow defile through which they had to pass. A halt was therefore ordered, for the purpose of taking breath, reconnoitring, rallying, refreshing, and getting their arms ready for the next day. Napoleon slept in his tent, on an eminence to the left of the main road, and behind the village of Kukowiaczi.

CHAPTER 20

Lancers!

On the 27th, the emperor appeared at the advanced posts before daylight; its first rays exhibited to him at last the Russian army encamped on an elevated plain, which commands all the avenues of Witepsk. The river Luczissa, which has worn itself a deep channel, marked the foot of this position. In advance of it 10,000 horse and some infantry made a show of defending its approaches; the infantry was in the centre, on the main road; its left in woody uplands; all the cavalry to the right in double lines, supported by the Düna.

The front of the Russians was no longer opposite to our column, but upon our left; it had changed its direction with that of the river, which a winding had removed from us. The French column, after having crossed, by means of a narrow bridge, the ravine which divided it from the new field of battle, was obliged to deploy by a change of front to the left, with the right wing foremost, in order to preserve the support of the river on that side, and so confront the enemy: on the banks of this ravine, near the bridge, and to the left of the main-road, there was an isolated hillock which had already attracted the notice of the emperor. From that point he could see both armies, being stationed on the flank of the field of battle, like the second in a duel.

Two hundred Parisian *voltigeurs* of the 9th regiment of the line were the first to debouch; they were immediately pushed forward to the left, in front of the whole Russian cavalry, like them supporting themselves by the Düna, and marking the left of the new line; the 16th horse chasseurs followed, and then some light pieces. The Russians coolly allowed us to defile before them, and mature our attack.

Their inactivity was favourable to us; but the king of Naples, whose brain was intoxicated by the general notice he attracted, yielding to his usual impetuosity, urged the chasseurs of the 16th on the whole body of the Russian cavalry. All eyes beheld with terror that feeble French line, broken on its march by the deep ravines which intersected the ground, advance to attack the enemy's masses. These unfortunate men, feeling themselves sacrificed, proceeded with hesitating steps to certain destruction. In consequence, at the first movement made by the lancers of the Russian guard, they took to flight; but the ravine, which it was necessary to pass, obstructed their flight; they were overtaken, and precipitated into these shoals, where many of them perished.

At sight of this, Murat, grieved beyond measure, precipitated himself, sabre in hand, in the midst of this melée, with the sixty officers and horsemen surrounding him. His audacity so astonished the Russian lancers, that they halted. While this prince was engaged, and the *piqueur* who followed him saved his life by striking down an enemy whose arm was raised over his head, the remains of the 16th rallied, and went to seek shelter close to the 53rd regiment, which protected them.

This successful charge of the lancers of the Russian guard had carried them as far as the foot of the hillock from which Napoleon was directing the different corps. Some chasseurs of the French guard had just dismounted from their horses, according to custom, in order to form a circle around him; a few discharges from their carabines drove off the assailant lancers. The latter, being thus repulsed, encountered on their return the two hundred Parisian *voltigeurs*, whom the flight of the 16th horse chasseurs had left alone between the two armies. These they attacked, and all eyes were instantly fixed on the engagement.

Both armies concluded these foot soldiers to be lost; but though single-handed, they did not despair of themselves. In the first instance, their captains, by dint of hard fighting, obtained possession of a ground intersected by cavities and thickets which bordered on the Düna; there the whole party instantly united, urged by their warlike habits, by the desire of mutual support, and by the danger which stared them in the face. In this emergency, as always happens in imminent dangers, each looked to his neighbour; the young to their elders, and all of them to their chiefs, in order to read in their countenances what they had to hope, to fear, or to perform; each aspect was replete with confidence, and all, relying on their comrades, relied at the same time more upon themselves.

The ground was skilfully turned to account. The Russian lancers, entangled in the bushes, and obstructed by the crevices, couched their long lances in vain; they were struck by our people's balls while they were endeavouring to penetrate their ranks, and fell, wounded, to the earth; their bodies, and those of their horses, added to the difficulties of the ground. At length they became discouraged, and took to flight.

The joyful shouts of our army, the crosses of honour, which the emperor instantly sent to the bravest of the group, his words, afterwards perused by all Europe,—all taught these valiant soldiers the extent of a glory, which they had not yet estimated; noble actions generally appearing quite ordinary to those who perform them. They imagined themselves on the point of being killed or taken; and found themselves almost at the same instant victorious and rewarded.

Meanwhile, the army of Italy and the cavalry of Murat, followed by three divisions of the first corps, which had been confided, since they left Wilna, to count Lobau, attacked the main-road and the woods which formed the support of the enemy's left. The engagement was, in the first instance, very animated; but it terminated abruptly. The Russian vanguard retreated precipitately behind the ravine of the Luczissa, to escape being thrown into it. The enemy's army was then entirely collected on the opposite bank, and presented a united body of 80,000 men.

Their determined countenance, in a strong position, and in front of a capital, deceived Napoleon; he conceived that they would regard it as a point of honour to maintain their ground. It was only eleven o'clock; he ordered the attack to cease, in order to have an opportunity of exploring the whole front of the line, and preparing for a decisive battle on the following day. In the first instance, he proceeded to post himself on a rising ground among the light troops, in the midst of whom he breakfasted. Thence he observed the enemy's army, a ball from which wounded an officer very near him. The subsequent hours he spent in reconnoitring the ground, and in waiting for the arrival of the other corps.

Napoleon announced a battle for the following day. His parting words to Murat were these:—"To-morrow at five o'clock, the sun of Austerlitz!" They explain the cause of that suspension of hostilities in the middle of the day, in the midst of a success which filled the army with enthusiasm. They were astonished at this inactivity at the moment of overtaking an army, the pursuit of which had completely exhausted them. Murat, who had been daily deluded by a similar expectation, remarked to the emperor that Barclay only made a demonstration of boldness at that hour, in order to be enabled more tranquilly to effect his retreat during the night. Finding himself unable to convince his chief, he rashly proceeded to pitch his tent on the banks of the Luczissa, almost in the midst of the enemy. It was a position which gratified his desire of hearing the first symptoms of their retreat, his hope of disturbing it, and his adventurous character.

Murat was deceived, and yet he appeared to have been most clear-sighted; Napoleon was in the right, and yet, the event placed him in the wrong; such are the freaks of fortune! The emperor of the French had correctly appreciated the designs of Barclay. The Russian general, believing Bagration to be still near Orcha, had resolved upon fighting, in order to give him time to rejoin him. It was the intelligence which he received that very evening, of the retreat of Bagration by Novoï-Bikof towards Smolensk, which suddenly changed his determination.

In fact, by daybreak on the 28th, Murat sent word to the emperor that he was about to pursue the Russians, who had already disappeared. Napoleon still persisted in his opinion, obstinately affirming that the whole enemy's army was in front of him, and that it was necessary to advance with circumspection; this occasioned a considerable delay. At length he mounted his horse; every step he took destroyed his illusion; and he soon found himself in the midst of the camp which Barclay had just deserted.

Every thing about it exhibited the science of war; its advantageous site; the symmetry of all its parts; the exact and exclusive nicety in the use to which each of them had been destined; the order and neatness which thence resulted; in fine, nothing left behind, not one weapon, nor a single valuable; no trace, nothing in short, in this sudden nocturnal march, which could demonstrate, beyond the bounds of the camp, the route which the Russians had taken; there appeared more order in their defeat, than in our victory! Though conquered, their flight left us lessons by which conquerors never profit; whether it be that good fortune is contemptuous, or that it waits for misfortune to correct it.

A Russian soldier, who was surprised asleep under a bush, was the solitary result of that day, which was expected to be so decisive. We entered Witepsk, which was found equally deserted with the camp of the Russians. Some filthy Jews, and some Jesuits, were all that remained; they were interrogated, but without effect. All the roads were abortively reconnoitred. Were the Russians gone to Smolensk? Had they re-ascended the Düna? At length, a band of irregular Cossacks attracted us in the latter direction, while Ney explored the former. We marched six leagues over a deep sand, through a thick dust, and a suffocating heat. Night arrested our march in the neighbourhood of Aghaponovchtchina.

While parched, fevered, and exhausted by fatigue and hunger, the army met with nothing there but muddy water. Napoleon, the King of Naples, the Viceroy, and the Prince of Neufchatel, held a council in the imperial tents, which were pitched in the court-yard of a castle, situated upon an eminence to the left of the main road.

"That victory which was so fervently desired, so rapidly pursued, and rendered more necessary by the lapse of every succeeding day, had, it seemed, just escaped from our grasp, as it had at Wilna. True, we had come up with the Russian rear-guard; but was it that of their army? Was it not more likely that Barclay had fled towards Smolensk by way of Rudnia? Whither, then, must we pursue the Russians, in order to compel them to fight? Did not the necessity of organizing reconquered Lithuania, of establishing magazines and hospitals, of fixing a new centre of repose, of defence, and departure for a line of operations which prolonged itself in so alarming a manner;—did not every thing, in short, decidedly prove the necessity of halting on the borders of old Russia?"

An affray had just happened, not far from that, respecting which Murat was silent. Our vanguard had been repulsed; some of the cavalry had been obliged to dismount, in order to effect their retreat; others had been unable to bring off their extenuated horses, otherwise than by dragging them by the bridle. The emperor having interrogated Belliard on the subject, that general frankly declared, that the regiments were already very much weakened, that they were harassed to death, and stood in absolute need of rest; and that if they continued to march for six days longer, there would be no cavalry remaining, and that it was high time to halt.

To these motives were added, the effects of a consuming sun reflected from burning sands. Exhausted as he was, the emperor now decided; the course of the Düna and of the Boristhenes marked out the French line. The army was thus quartered on the banks of these two rivers, and in the interval between them; Poniatowski and his Poles at Mohilef; Davoust and the first corps at Orcha, Dubrowna, and Luibowiczi; Murat, Ney, the army of Italy and the guard, from Orcha and Dubrowna to Witepsk and Suraij. The advanced posts at Lyadi, Vinkowo, and Velij, opposite to those of Barclay and Bagration; for these two hostile armies, the one flying from Napoleon, across the Düna, by Drissa and Witepsk, the other, escaping Davoust across the Berezina and the Boristhenes, by way of Bobruisk, Bickof, and Smolensk, succeeded in forming a junction in the interval bounded by these two rivers.

The great divisions of the army detached from the central body were then stationed as follows: To the right, Dombrowski, in front of Bobruisk and opposed to the corps of 12,000 men commanded by the Russian general Hoertel.

To the left, the Duke of Reggio, and St. Cyr, at Polotsk and at

Bieloé, on the Petersburgh road, which was defended by Wittgenstein and 30,000 men.

At the extreme left were Macdonald and 38,000 Prussians and Poles, before Riga. They extended their line towards the right upon the Aa, and in the direction of Dünabourg.

At the same time, Schwartzenberg and Regnier, at the head of the Saxon and Austrian corps, occupied, towards Slonim, the interval between the Niemen and the Bug, covering Warsaw and the rear of the grand army, which was menaced by Tormasof. The Duke of Belluno was on the Vistula with a reserve of 40,000 men; while Augereau assembled an eleventh army at Stettin.

As to Wilna, the Duke of Bassano remained there, surrounded by the envoys of several courts. That minister governed Lithuania, communicated with all the chiefs, sent them the instructions which he received from Napoleon, and forwarded the provisions, recruits, and stragglers, as fast as they arrived.

As soon as the emperor had made up his mind, he returned to Witepsk with his guard: there, on the 28th of July, in entering the imperial head-quarters, he laid down his sword, and abruptly depositing it on his maps, with which his tables were covered, he exclaimed; "Here I stop! here I must look round me; rally; refresh my army, and organize Poland. The campaign of 1812 is finished; that of 1813 will do the rest."

CHAPTER 21
The Düna

With the conquest of Lithuania, the object of the war was attained, and, yet, the war appeared scarcely to have commenced; for places only had been vanquished, and not men. The Russian army was unbroken; its two wings, which had been separated by the vivacity of the first onset, had now united. We were in the finest season of the year. It was in this situation that Napoleon believed himself irrevocably decided to halt on the banks of the Boristhenes and the Düna. At that time, he could much more easily deceive others as to his intentions, as he actually deceived himself.

His line of defence was already traced upon his maps; the siege-equipage was proceeding towards Riga; the left of the army would rest on that strong place; hence, proceeding to Dünabourg and Polotsk, it would maintain a menacing defensive. Witepsk, so easy to fortify, and its woody heights, would serve as an entrenched camp for the centre. Thence, towards the south, the Berezina and its marshes, covered by the Boristhenes, supply no other passage but a few defiles; a very few troops would be sufficient to guard them. Further on, Bobruisk marked out the right of this great line, and orders were given to obtain possession of that fortress. In addition, an insurrection of the populous provinces of the south was calculated on; they would assist Schwartzenberg in expelling Tormasof, and the army would be increased by their numerous Cossacks. One of the greatest proprietors of these provinces, a nobleman in whom every thing was distinguished, even to his external appearance, hastened to join the liberators of his country. He it was whom the emperor intended for the leader of this insurrection.

In this position nothing would be wanting. Courland would support Macdonald; Samogitia, Oudinot; the fertile plains of Klubokoe, the emperor; the southern provinces would effect the rest. In addition, the grand magazine of the army was at Dantzic; its intermediate ones at Wilna and Minsk. In this manner the army would be connected with the country which it had just set free; and all things appertaining to that country—its rivers, marshes, productions, and inhabitants, would be united with us: all things would be agreed for the purposes of defence.

Such was Napoleon's plan. He was at that time seen exploring Witepsk and its environs, as if to reconnoitre places where he was likely to make a long residence. Establishments of all kinds were formed there. Thirty-six ovens, capable of baking at once 29,000 pounds of bread, were constructed. Neither was utility alone attended to; embellishment was also considered. Some stone houses spoiled the appearance of the square of the palace; the emperor ordered his guard to pull them down, and to clear away the rubbish. Indeed, he was already anticipating the pleasures of winter; Parisian actors must come to Witepsk; and as that city was abandoned, fair spectators must be attracted from Warsaw and Wilna.

His star at that time enlightened his path: happy had it been for him, if he had not afterwards mistaken the movements of his impatience for the inspirations of genius. But, whatever may be said, it was by himself alone that he suffered himself to be hurried on; for in him every thing proceeded from himself; and it was a vain attempt to seduce his prudence. In vain did one of his marshals then promise him an insurrection of the Russians, in consequence of the proclamations which the officers of his advanced guard had been instructed to disseminate. Some Poles had intoxicated that general with inconsiderate promises, dictated by the delusive hope common to all exiles, with which they flatter the ambition of the leaders who rely upon them.

But Murat was the individual whose incitements were most frequent and animated. Tired of repose, and insatiable of glory, that monarch, who considered the enemy to be within his grasp, was unable to repress his emotions. He quitted the advanced guard, went to Witepsk, and in a private interview with the emperor, gave way to his impetuosity. "He accused the Russian army of cowardice; according to him it had failed in the rendezvous before Witepsk, as if it had been an affair of a duel. It was a panic-struck army, which his light cavalry alone was sufficient to put to flight." This ebullition extorted a smile from Napoleon; but in order to moderate his fervour, he said to him, "Murat! the first campaign in Russia is finished; let us here plant our eagles. Two great rivers mark out our position; let us raise block-houses on that line; let our fires cross each other on all sides; let us form in square battalion; cannons at the angles and the exterior; let the interior contain our quarters and our magazines: 1813 will see us at Moscow—1814 at Petersburgh. The Russian war is a war of three years!"

It was thus that his genius conceived every thing in masses, and his eye expatiated over an army of 400,000 men as if it were a regiment.

That very day he loudly addressed an administrator in the following words: "As for you, sir, you must take care to provide subsistence for us in these quarters; for," added he, in a loud voice, and addressing himself to some of his officers, "we shall not repeat the folly of Charles the Twelfth." But his actions in a short time belied his words; and there was a general astonishment at his indifference to giving the necessary orders for so great an establishment. To the left no instructions were sent to Macdonald, nor was he supplied with the means of obtaining possession of Riga. To the right, it was Bobruisk which it was necessary to capture; this fortress stands in the midst of an extensive and deep marsh; and it was to a body of cavalry that the task of besieging it was committed.

Napoleon, in former times, scarcely ever gave orders without the possibility of being obeyed; but the prodigies of the war of Prussia had since occurred, and from that time the idea of impossibility was not admitted. His orders were always, that every thing must be attempted, because up to that time every thing had succeeded. This at first gave birth to great exertions, all of which, however, were not equally fortunate. Persons got discouraged; but their chief persevered; he had become accustomed to command every thing; those whom he commanded got accustomed not to execute every thing.

Meantime Dombrowski was left before that fortress with his Polish division, which Napoleon stated at 8000 men, although he knew very well that it did not at that time amount to more than 1200; but such was his custom; either because he calculated on his words being repeated, and that they would deceive the enemy; or that he wished, by this exaggerated estimate, to make his generals feel all that he expected from them.

Witepsk remained for survey. From the windows of its houses the eye looked down perpendicularly into the Düna, or to the very bottom of the precipices by which its walls are surrounded. In these countries the snow remains long upon the ground; it filters through its least solid parts, which it penetrates to a great depth, and which it dilutes and breaks down. Hence those deep and unexpected ravines, which no declination of the soil gives reason to foresee, which are imperceptible at some paces from their edge, and which on those vast plains surprised and suddenly arrested the charges of cavalry.

The French would not have required more than a month to render that city sufficiently strong as even to stand a regular siege: the natural strength of the place was such as to require little assistance from art, but that little was denied it. At the same time a few millions, which were indispensable to effect the levy of the Lithuanian troops, were refused to them. Prince Sangutsko was to have gone and commanded the insurrection in the South, but he was retained in the imperial headquarters.

But the moderation of the first discourses of Napoleon had not deceived the members of his household. They recollected that, at the first view of the deserted camp of Barclay, and of Witepsk abandoned, when he heard them congratulating each other on this conquest, he turned sharply round to them and exclaimed, "Do you think then that I have come so far to conquer these huts?" They also knew perfectly, that when he had a great object in view, he never devised any other than a vague plan, preferring to take counsel of opportunity; a system more conformable to the promptitude of his genius.

In other respects, the whole army was loaded with the favours of its commander. If he happened to meet with convoys of wounded, he stopped them, informed himself of their condition, of their sufferings, of the actions in which they had been wounded, and never quitted them without consoling them by his words, or making them partakers of his bounty.

He bestowed particular attention on his guard; he himself daily reviewed some part of them, lavishing commendation, and sometimes blame; but the latter seldom fell on any but the administrators; which pleased the soldiers, and diverted their complaints.

Every day he went and visited the ovens, tasted the bread, and satisfied himself of the regularity of all the distributions. He frequently sent wine from his table to the sentinel who was nearest to him. One day he assembled the elite of his guards for the purpose of giving them a new leader; he made them a speech, and with his own hand and sword introduced him to them; afterwards he embraced him in their presence. So many attentions were ascribed by some, to his gratitude for the past; by others, to his exigency for the future.

The latter saw clearly that Napoleon had at first flattered himself with the hope of receiving fresh overtures of peace from Alexander, and that the misery and debility of his army had occupied his attention. It was requisite to allow the long train of stragglers and sick sufficient time, the one for joining their corps, and the latter for reaching the hospitals. Finally, to establish these hospitals, to collect provisions, recruit the horses, and wait for the hospital-wagons, the artillery, and the pontoons, which were still laboriously dragging after us across the Lithuanian sands. His correspondence with Europe must also have been a source of occupation to him. To conclude, a destructive atmosphere stopped his progress! Such, in fact, is that climate; the atmosphere is always in the extreme—always excessive; it either parches or inundates, burns up or freezes, the soil and its inhabitants, for whose protection it appears expressly framed; a perfidious climate, the heat of which debilitated our bodies, in order to render them more accessible to the frosts by which they were shortly to be pierced.

The emperor was not the least sensible of its effects; but when he found himself somewhat refreshed by repose, when no envoy from Alexander made his appearance, and his first dispositions were completed, he was seized with impatience. He was observed to grow restless; whether it was that inactivity annoyed him, as it does all men of active habits, and that he preferred danger to the weariness of expectation, or that he was agitated by that desire of acquisition, which, with the greater part of mankind, has stronger efficacy than the pleasure of preserving, or the fear of losing.

It was then especially that the image of captive Moscow besieged him; it was the boundary of his fears, the object of his hopes: possessed of that, he would possess every thing. From that time it was foreseen that an ardent and restless genius, like his, and accustomed to short cuts, would not wait eight months, when he felt his object within his reach, and when twenty days were sufficient to attain it.

We must not, however, be too hasty in judging this extraordinary man by the weaknesses common to all men. We shall presently hear from himself;—we shall see how much his political position tended to complicate his military position. At a later period, we shall be less tempted to blame the resolution he was now about to take, when it is seen that the fate of Russia depended upon only one more day's health, which failed Napoleon, even on the very field of the Moskwa.

Meantime, he at first appeared hardly bold enough to confess to himself a project of such great temerity. But by degrees, he assumed courage to look it in the face. He then began to deliberate, and the state of great irresolution which tormented his mind affected his whole frame. He was observed to wander about his apartments, as if pursued by some dangerous temptation. Nothing could rivet his attention; he every moment began, quitted, and resumed his labour; he walked about without any object; inquired the hour, and looked at his watch; completely absorbed, he stopped, hummed a tune with an absent air, and again began walking about.

In the midst of his perplexity, he occasionally addressed the persons whom he met with such half sentences as "Well! what shall we do? Shall we stay where we are, or advance? How is it possible to stop short in the midst of so glorious a career?" He did not wait for their reply; but still kept wandering about, as if he was looking for something or somebody to terminate his indecision.

At length, quite overwhelmed with the weight of such an important consideration, and oppressed with so great an uncertainty, he would throw himself on one of the beds which he had caused to be laid on the floor of his apartments. His frame, exhausted by the heat, and the struggles of his mind, could only bear a covering of the slightest texture; it was in that state that he passed a portion of his days at Witepsk.

But when his body was at rest, his spirit was only the more active. "How many motives urged him towards Moscow! How support at Witepsk the *ennui* of seven winter months?—he, who till then had always been the assailant, was about to be reduced to a defensive position; a part unworthy of him, of which he had no experience, and adverse to his genius.

"Moreover, at Witepsk, nothing had been decided, and yet, at what a distance was he already from France! Europe, then, would at length behold him stopped, whom nothing had been able to stop. Would not the duration of the enterprise augment its danger? Ought he to allow Russia time to arm herself entirely? How long could he protract this uncertain condition without impairing the charm of his infallibility, (which the resistance of Spain had already enfeebled) and without engendering dangerous hopes in Europe? What would be thought, if it were known that a third of his army, dispersed or sick, were no longer in the ranks? It was indispensable, therefore, to dazzle the world speedily by the éclat of a great victory, and hide so many sacrifices under a heap of laurels."

Then, if he remained at Witepsk, he considered that he should have the *ennui*, the whole expense, all the inconveniences and anxieties of a defensive position to bear; while at Moscow there would be peace, abundance, a reimbursement of the expenses of the war, and immortal glory. He persuaded himself that audacity for him was henceforth the greatest prudence; that it is the same with all hazardous undertakings, as with faults, in which there is always risk at the beginning, but frequently gain at the conclusion; that the more inexcusable they are, the more they require to be successful. That it was indispensable, therefore, to consummate this undertaking, to push it to the utmost, astonish the universe, beat down Alexander by his audacity, and carry off a prize which should be a compensation for so many losses.

Thus it was, that the same danger which perhaps ought to have recalled him to the Niemen, or kept him stationary on the Düna, urged him towards Moscow! Such is the nature of false positions; every thing in them is perilous; temerity is prudence; there is no choice left but of errors; there is no hope but in the errors of the enemy, and in chance.

Having at last determined, he hastily arose, as if not to allow time to his own reflections to renew so painful a state of uncertainty; and already quite full of the plan which was to secure his conquest, he hastened to his maps; they presented to his view the cities of Smolensk and Moscow; "the great Moscow, the holy city;" names which he repeated with complacency, and which served to add new fuel to his ambitious flame. Fired with this prospect, his spirit, replete with the energy of his mighty conception, appears possessed by the genius of war. His voice deepens; his eye flashes fire; and his countenance darkens; his attendants retreat from his presence, struck with mingled awe and respect; but at length his plan is fixed; his determination taken; his order of march traced out. Instantly, the internal struggle by which he had been agitated subsided; and no sooner was he delivered of his terrible conception, than his countenance resumed its usual mild and tranquil character.

Chapter 22
The Generals

His resolution once taken, he was anxious that it should satisfy his friends; he conceived that by persuading them, they would be actuated by greater zeal, than by commanding their obedience. It was, moreover, by their sentiments that he was enabled to judge of those of the rest of his army; in short, like all other men, the silent discontent of his household disturbed him. Surrounded by disapproving countenances, and opinions contrary to his own, he felt himself uncomfortable. And, besides, to obtain their assent to his plan, was in some degree to make them share the responsibility which possibly weighed upon his mind.

But all the officers of his household opposed his plan, each in the way that marked his peculiar character; Berthier, by a melancholy countenance, by lamentations, and even tears; Lobau and Caulaincourt, by a frankness, which in the first was stamped by a cold and haughty roughness, excusable in so brave a warrior; and which in the second was persevering even to obstinacy, and impetuous even to violence. The emperor repelled their observations with some ill-humour; he exclaimed, addressing himself more especially to his aid-de-camp, as well as to Berthier, "that he had enriched his generals too much; that all they now aspired to was to follow the pleasures of the chase, and to display their brilliant equipages in Paris: and that, doubtless, they had become disgusted with war." When their honour was thus attacked, there was no longer any reply to be made; they merely bowed and remained silent. During one of his impatient fits, he told one of the generals of his guard, "you were born in a bivouac, and in a bivouac you will die."

As to Duroc, he first signified his disapprobation by a chilling silence, and afterwards by terse replies, reference to accurate reports, and brief remarks. To him the emperor replied, "that he saw clearly enough that the Russians wanted to draw him on; but that, nevertheless, he must proceed as far as Smolensk; that there he would establish his head-quarters; and that in the spring of 1813, if Russia did not previously make peace, she would be ruined; that Smolensk was the key of the two roads to Petersburgh and Moscow; that he must get possession of it; and that he would then be able to march on both those capitals at the same time, in order to destroy every thing in the one, and preserve every thing in the other."

Here the grand marshal observed to him, that he was not more likely to make peace at Smolensk, or even at Moscow, than he was at Witepsk; and that in removing to such a distance from France, the Prussians constituted an intermediate body, on whom little reliance could be placed. But the emperor replied, that on that supposition, as the Russian war no longer offered him any advantageous result, he ought to renounce it; and if so, he must turn his arms against Prussia, and compel her to pay the expenses of the war.

It was now Daru's turn. This minister is straightforward even to stiffness, and possesses immoveable firmness. The great question of the march upon Moscow produced a discussion which lasted during eight successive hours, and at which only Berthier was present. The emperor having desired his minister's opinion of the war, "It is not a national war," replied Daru; "the introduction of some English merchandize into Russia, and even the restoration of the kingdom of Poland, are not sufficient reasons for engaging in so distant a war; neither your troops nor ourselves understand its necessity or its objects, and to say the least, all things recommend the policy of stopping where we now are."

The emperor rejoined, "Did they take him for a madman? Did they imagine he made war from inclination? Had they not heard him say that the wars of Spain and Russia were two ulcers which ate into the vitals of France, and that she could not bear them both at once?

"He was anxious for peace; but in order to negotiate, two persons were necessary, and he was only one. Had a single letter from Alexander yet reached him?

"What, then, should he wait for at Witepsk? Two rivers, it was true, traced out the line of position; but, during the winter, there were no longer any rivers in this country. It was, therefore, a visionary line which they traced out; it was rather a line of demarcation than of separation. It was requisite, therefore, to constitute an artificial line; to construct towns and fortresses capable of defying the elements, and every species of scourge; to create every thing, land and atmosphere; for every thing was deficient, even provisions, unless, indeed, he chose to drain Lithuania, and render her hostile, or ruin ourselves; that if they were at Moscow, they might take what they pleased; here it was necessary to purchase every thing. Consequently," continued he, "you cannot enable me to live at Witepsk, nor shall I be able to defend you here: both of us, therefore, are here out of our proper element.

"That if he returned to Wilna, he might there indeed, be more easily supplied, but that he should not be in a better condition to defend himself; that in that case it would be necessary for him to fall back to the Vistula, and lose Lithuania. Whereas at Smolensk, he would be sure to gain either a decisive battle, or at least, a fortress and a position on the Dnieper.

"That he perceived clearly that their thoughts were dwelling on Charles the Twelfth; but that if the expedition to Moscow wanted a fortunate precedent, it was because it was deficient in a man capable of making it succeed; that in war, fortune went for one-half in every thing; that if people always waited for a complete assemblage of favourable circumstances, nothing would ever be undertaken; that we must begin, in order to finish; that there was no enterprise in which every thing concurred, and that, in all human projects, chance had its share; that, in short, it was not the rule which created the success, but the success the rule; and that, if he succeeded by new means, that success would create new principles.

"Blood has not yet been spilled," he added, "and Russia is too great to yield without fighting. Alexander can only negotiate after a great battle. If it is necessary, I will even proceed to the holy city in search of that battle, and I will gain it. Peace waits for me at the gates of Moscow. But with his honour thus saved, if Alexander still persists, I will negotiate with the Boyards, or even with the population of that capital; it is numerous, united, and consequently enlightened. It will understand its own interests, and comprehend the value of liberty." He concluded by saying, that "Moscow hated Petersburgh; that he would take advantage of their rivalry; that the results of such a jealousy were incalculable."

It was in this manner that the emperor, when animated by conversation and the banquet, revealed the nature of his hopes. Daru replied, "That war was a game which he played well, in which he was always the winner, and that it was natural to infer, that he took a pleasure in playing it. But that, in this case, it was not so much men as nature which it was necessary to conquer; that already the army was diminished one-third by desertion, sickness, or famine.

"If provisions failed at Witepsk, what would be the case farther on? The officers whom he had sent to procure them, either never reappeared, or returned with empty hands. That the small quantity of flour, or the few cattle which they had succeeded in collecting, were immediately consumed by the imperial guard; that the other divisions of the army were heard to murmur, that it exacted and absorbed every thing, that it constituted, as it were, a privileged class. The hospital and provision-wagons, as well as the droves of cattle, were not able to come up. The hospitals were insufficient for the sick; provisions, room, and medicines, were all wanting in them.

"All things consequently admonished them to halt, and with so much the more effect, as they could not calculate on the favourable disposition of the inhabitants beyond Witepsk. In conformity with his secret orders, they had been sounded, but without effect. How could men be roused to insurrection, for the sake of a liberty whose very name they did not understand? What influence could be obtained over a people almost savages, without property, and without wants? What could be taken from them? With what could they be tempted? Their only property was their life, which they carried with them into regions of almost infinite space."

Berthier added, "That if we were to proceed forward, the Russians would have in their favour our too-much elongated flanks, famine, and especially their formidable winter; while in staying where he was, the emperor would enlist the latter on his side, and render himself master of the war; that he would fix it within his reach, instead of following its deceitful, wandering, and undecided flight."

Such were the replies of Berthier and Daru. The emperor mildly listened to their observations, but oftener interrupted them by subtle arguments; begging the question, according to his wishes, or shifting it, when it became too pressing. But however disagreeable might be the truths which he was obliged to hear, he listened to them patiently, and replied with equal patience. Throughout this discussion, his conversation and whole deportment were remarkable for affability, simplicity, and good-humour, which, indeed, he almost always preserved in his own family; a circumstance which sufficiently explains why, notwithstanding so many misfortunes, he was so much beloved by those who lived on terms of intimacy with him.

Still dissatisfied, the emperor summoned successively several of the generals of his army; but his questions were such as indicated their answers; and many of these chiefs, born in the capacity of soldiers, and accustomed to obey his voice, were as submissive in these conversations as upon the field of battle.

Others waited the issue, in order to give their opinion; concealing their dread of a reverse, in the presence of a man who had always been fortunate, as well as their opinion, lest success might on some future day reproach them for it.

The greater part signified their approbation, being perfectly convinced that were they even to incur his displeasure by recommending him to stop, he would not be the less certain to advance. As it was necessary to incur fresh dangers, they preferred meeting them with an appearance of good-will. They found it more convenient to be wrong with him, than right against him.

But there was one individual, who, not content with approving his design, encouraged it. Prompted by a culpable ambition, he increased Napoleon's confidence, by exaggerating the force of his division. For after incurring so many fatigues, unaccompanied by danger, it was a great merit in those chiefs who preserved the greatest number of men around their eagles. The emperor was thus gratified on his weak side, and the time for rewards was approaching. In order to make himself more agreeable, the individual in question boldly took upon himself to vouch for the ardour of his soldiers, whose emaciated countenances but ill accorded with the flattery of their leader. The emperor gave credit to this ardour, because it pleased him, and because he only saw the soldiers at reviews; occasions when his presence, the military pomp, the mutual excitation produced by great assemblages, imparted fervour to the mind; when, in short, all things, even to the secret orders of the chiefs, dictated an appearance of enthusiasm.

But in fact it was only with his guard that he thus occupied his attention. In the army, the soldiers complained of his non-appearance. "They no longer saw him," they said, "except in days of battle, when they had to die for him, but never to supply them with the means of existence. They were all there to serve him, but he seemed no longer there to serve them."

In this manner did they suffer and complain, but without sufficiently considering that what they complained of was one of the inseparable evils of the campaign. The dispersion of the various *corps d'armée* being indispensable for the sake of procuring subsistence in these deserts, that necessity kept Napoleon at a distance from his soldiers. His guard could hardly find subsistence and shelter in his immediate neighbourhood; the rest were out of his sight. It is true that many imprudent acts had recently been committed; several convoys of provisions belonging to other corps were on their passage daringly retained at the imperial head-quarters, for the use of the guard, by whose order is not known. This violence, added to the jealousy which such bodies of men always inspire, created discontent in the army.

The emperor was ignorant of these complaints; but another cause of anxiety had occurred to torment him. He knew that at Witepsk alone, there were 3000 of his soldiers attacked by the dysentery, which was extending its ravages over his whole army. The rye which they were eating in soup was its principal cause. Their stomachs, accustomed to bread, rejected this cold and indigestible food, and the emperor was urging his physicians to find a remedy for its effects. One day he appeared less anxious. "Davoust," said he, "has found out what the medical men could not discover; he has just sent to inform me of it; all that is required is to roast the rye before preparing it;" and his eyes sparkled with hope as he questioned his physician, who declined giving any opinion until the experiment was tried. The emperor instantly called two grenadiers of his guard; he seated them at table, close to him, and made them begin the trial of this nourishment so prepared. It did not succeed with them, although he added to it some of his own wine, which he himself poured out for them.

Respect, however, for the conqueror of Europe, and the necessity of circumstances, supported them in the midst of their numerous privations. They saw that they were too deeply embarked; that a victory was necessary for their speedy deliverance; and that he alone could give it them. Misfortune, moreover, had purified the army; all that remained of it could not fail to be its elite both in mind and body. In order to have got so far as they had done, what trials had they not withstood! Suspense, and disgust with miserable cantonments, were sufficient to agitate such men. To remain, appeared to them insupportable; to retreat, impossible; it was, therefore, imperative to advance.

The great names of Smolensk and Moscow inspired no alarm. In ordinary times, and with ordinary men, that unknown region, that unvisited people, and the distance which magnifies all things, would have been sufficient to discourage. But these were the very circumstances which, in this case, were most attractive. The soldiers' chief pleasure was in hazardous situations, which were rendered more interesting by the greater proportion of danger they involved, and on which new dangers conferred a more striking air of singularity; emotions full of charm for active spirits, which had exhausted their taste for old things, and which, therefore, required new.

Ambition was, at that time, completely unshackled; every thing inspired the passion for glory; they had been launched into a boundless career. How was it possible to measure the ascendancy, which a powerful emperor must have acquired, or the strong impulse which he had given them?—an emperor, capable of telling his soldiers after the victory of Austerlitz, "I will allow you to name your children after me; and if among them there should prove one worthy of us, I will leave him every thing I possess, and name him my successor."

CHAPTER 23

Defeat at Inkowo

The junction of the two wings of the Russian army, in the direction of Smolensk, had compelled Napoleon also to approximate his various divisions. No signal of attack had yet been given, but the war involved him on all sides; it seemed to tempt his genius by success, and to stimulate it by reverses. On his left, Wittgenstein, equally in dread of Oudinot and Macdonald, remained between the two roads from Polotsk and Dünabourg, which meet at Sebez. The Duke of Reggio's orders had been to keep on the defensive. But neither at Polotsk nor at Witepsk was there any thing found in the country, which disclosed the position of the Russians. Tired of feeling nothing of them on any side, the marshal determined to go in quest of them himself. On the 1st of August, therefore, he left general Merle and his division on the Drissa, to protect his baggage, his great park of artillery, and his retreat; he pushed Verdier towards Sebez, and made him take a position on the high-road, in order to mask the movement which he was meditating. He himself, turning to the left with Legrand's infantry, Castex's cavalry, and Aubrey's light artillery, advanced as far as Yakoubowo, on the road to Osweïa.

As chance would have it, Wittgenstein, at the same moment, was marching from Osweïa to Yakoubowo; the hostile armies unexpectedly met each other in front of that village. It was late in the day; the shock was violent, but of short duration: night put an end to the combat, and postponed its decision.

The marshal found himself engaged, with a single division, in a deep and narrow pass, surrounded with woods and hills, all the declivities of which were opposed to us. He was hesitating, however, whether he should quit that contracted position, on which all the enemy's fire was about to be concentrated, when a young Russian staff-officer, scarcely emerged from boyhood, came dashing heedlessly into our posts, and allowed himself to be taken, with the despatches of which he was the bearer. We learned from them, that Wittgenstein was marching with all his forces to attack and destroy our bridges over the Düna. Oudinot felt it necessary to retreat, in order to rally and concentrate his forces in a less unfavourable position; in consequence, as frequently happens in retrograde marches, some stragglers and baggage fell into the hands of the Russians.

Wittgenstein, elated by this easy success, pushed it beyond all bounds. In the first transport of what he regarded as a victory, he ordered Koulnief, and 12,000 men, to pass the Drissa, in order to pursue d'Albert and Legrand. The latter had made a halt; Albert hastened to inform the marshal. They covered their detachment by a rising ground, watched all the movements of the Russian general, and observing him rashly venturing himself into a defile between them and the river, they rushed suddenly upon him, overthrew and killed him; taking from him also eight pieces of cannon, and 2000 men.

Koulnief, it was said, died like a hero; a cannon ball broke both his legs, and threw him prostrate on his own cannon; where, observing the French approaching, he tore off his decorations, and, in a transport of anger at his own temerity, condemned himself to die on the very spot where his error was committed, commanding his soldiers to leave him to his fate. The whole Russian army regretted him; it imputed this misfortune to one of those individuals whom the caprice of Paul had made into generals, at the period when that emperor was quite new to power, and conceived the idea of entering his peaceable inheritance in the character of a triumphant conqueror.

Rashness passed over with the victory from the Russian to the French camp; this unexpected success elated Casa-Bianca and his Corsican battalions; they forgot the error to which they were indebted for it, they neglected the recommendation of their general, and without reflecting that they were imitating the imprudence by which they had just profited, they precipitated themselves upon the flying footsteps of the Russians. They proceeded, headlong, in this manner for two leagues, and were only reminded of their temerity by finding themselves alone in presence of the Russian army. Verdier, forced to engage in order to support them, was already compromising the rest of his division, when the Duke of Reggio hurried up, relieved his troops from this peril, led them back behind the Drissa, and on the following day resumed his first position under the walls of Polotsk. There he found Saint-Cyr and the Bavarians, who increased the force of his corps to 35,000 men. As to Wittgenstein, he tranquilly took up his first position at Osweïa. The result of these four days was very unsatisfactory to the emperor.

Nearly about the same time intelligence was brought to Witepsk that the advanced guard of the viceroy had gained some advantages near Suraij; but that, in the centre, near the Dnieper, at Inkowo, Sebastiani had been surprised by superior numbers, and defeated.

Napoleon was then writing to the Duke of Bassano to announce daily fresh victories to the Turks. True or false was of no consequence, provided the communications produced the effect of suspending their treaty with Russia. He was still engaged in this task, when deputies from Red Russia arrived at Witepsk, and informed Duroc, that they had heard the report of the Russian cannon announcing the peace of Bucharest. That treaty, signed by Kutusoff, had just been ratified.

At this intelligence, which Duroc transmitted to Napoleon, the latter was deeply mortified. He was now no longer astonished at Alexander's silence. At first, it was the tardiness of Maret's negotiations to which he imputed this result; then, to the blind stupidity of the Turks, to whom their treaties of peace were always more fatal than their wars; lastly, the perfidious policy of his allies, all of whom, taking advantage of the distance, and in the obscurity of the seraglio, had, doubtless, dared to unite against their common dictator.

This event rendered a prompt victory still more necessary to him. All hope of peace was now at an end. He had just read the proclamations of Alexander. Being addressed to a rude people, they were necessarily unrefined: the following are some passages of them: "The enemy, with unexampled perfidy, has announced the destruction of our country. Our brave soldiers burn to throw themselves on his battalions, and to destroy them; but it is not our intention to allow them to be sacrificed on the altars of this Moloch. A general insurrection is necessary against the universal tyrant. He comes, with treachery in his heart, and loyalty on his lips, to chain us with his legions of slaves. Let us drive away this race of locusts. Let us carry the cross in our hearts, and the sword in our hands. Let us pluck his fangs from this lion's mouth, and overthrow the tyrant, whose object is to overthrow the earth."

The emperor was incensed. These reproaches, these successes, and these reverses, all contributed to stimulate his mind. The forward movement of Barclay, in three columns, towards Rudnia, which the check at Inkowo had disclosed, and the vigorous defensive operations of Wittgenstein, promised the approach of a battle. He had to choose between that, and a long and sanguinary defensive war, to which he was unaccustomed, which was difficult to maintain at such a distance from his reinforcements, and encouraging to his enemies.

Napoleon accordingly decided; but his decision, without being rash, was grand and bold, like the enterprise itself. Having determined to detach himself from Oudinot, he first caused him to be reinforced by Saint-Cyr's corps, and ordered him to connect himself with the Duke of Tarentum; having resolved also to march against the enemy, he did it by changing in front of him, and within his reach, but without his knowledge, the line of his operations at Witepsk for that of Minsk. His manoeuvre was so well combined; he had accustomed his lieutenants to so much punctuality, secrecy, and precision, that in four days, while the surprised hostile army could find no traces of the French army before it, the latter would by this plan find itself in a mass of 185,000 men on the left flank and rear of that enemy, which but just before had presumed to think of surprising him.

Meantime, the extent and the multiplicity of the operations, which on all sides claimed Napoleon's presence, still detained him at Witepsk. It was only by his letters, that he could make his presence universally felt. His head alone laboured for the whole, and he indulged himself in the thought that his urgent and repeated orders would suffice to make nature herself obedient to him.

The army only subsisted by its exertions, and from day to day; it had not provisions for twenty-four hours: Napoleon ordered that it should provide itself for fifteen days. He was incessantly dictating letters. On the 10th of August he addressed eight to the prince of Eckmühl, and almost as many to each of his other lieutenants. In the first, he concentrates every thing round himself, in conformity with his leading principle, "that war is nothing else than the art of assembling on a given point, a larger number of men than your enemy." It was in this spirit that he wrote to Davoust: "Send for Latour-Maubourg. If the enemy remain at Smolensk, as I have reason to suppose, it will be a decisive affair, and we cannot have too much numerical strength. Orcha will become the pivot of the army. Every thing leads me to believe that there will be a great battle at Smolensk; hospitals will, therefore, be requisite; they will be necessary at Orcha, Dombrowna, Mohilef, Kochanowo, Bobr, Borizof, and Minsk."

It was then particularly that he manifested extreme anxiety about the provisioning of Orcha. It was on the 10th of August, at the very moment when he was dictating this letter, that he gave his order of march. In four days, all his army would be assembled on the left bank of the Boristhenes, and in the direction of Liady. He departed from Witepsk on the 13th, after having remained there a fortnight.

Chapter 24

Consolation

It was the check at Inkowo which decided Napoleon; ten thousand Russian horse, in an affair with the advanced guard, had overthrown Sebastiani and his cavalry. The intrepidity and reputation of the defeated general, his report, the boldness of the attack, the hope, nay the urgent necessity, of a decisive engagement, all led the emperor to believe, that their numbers alone had carried the day, that the Russian army was between the Düna and the Dnieper, and that it was marching against the centre of his cantonments: this was actually the fact.

The grand army being dispersed, it was necessary to collect it together. Napoleon had resolved to defile with his guard, the army of Italy, and three of Davoust's divisions, before the front of attack of the Russians; to abandon his Witepsk line of operation, and take that of Orcha, and, lastly, to throw himself with 185,000 men on the left of the Dnieper and of the enemy's army. Covered by the river, his plan was to get beyond it, for the purpose of reaching Smolensk before it; if successful, he should have separated the Russian army not only from Moscow, but from the whole centre and south of the empire; it would be confined to the north; and he would have accomplished at Smolensk against Bagration and Barclay united, what he had in vain attempted at Witepsk against the army of Barclay alone.

Thus the line of operation of so large an army was about to be suddenly changed; 200,000 men, spread over a tract of more than fifty leagues, were to be all at once brought together, without the knowledge of the enemy, within reach of him, and on his left flank. This was, undoubtedly, one of those grand determinations which, executed with the unity and rapidity of their conception, change instantaneously the face of war, decide the fate of empires, and display the genius of conquerors.

As we marched from Orcha to Liady, the French army formed a long column on the left bank of the Dnieper. In this mass, the first corps, that of Davoust, was distinguished by the order and harmony which prevailed in its divisions. The fine appearance of the troops, the care with which they were supplied, and the attention that was paid to make them careful of their provisions, which the improvident soldier is apt to waste; lastly, the strength of these divisions, the happy result of this severe discipline, all caused them to be acknowledged as the model of the whole army.

Gudin's division was the only one wanting; owing to an ill-written order, it had been wandering for twenty-four hours in marshy woods; it arrived, however, but diminished by three hundred combatants; for such errors are not to be repaired but by forced marches, under which the weakest are sure to sink.

The emperor traversed in a day the hilly and woody tract which separates the Düna from the Boristhenes; it was in front of Rassasna that he crossed the latter river. Its distance from our home, the very antiquity of its name, every thing connected with it, excited our curiosity. For the first time, the waters of this Muscovite river were about to bear a French army, and to reflect our victorious arms. The Romans had known it only by their defeats: it was down this same stream that the savages of the North, the children of Odin and Rurik, descended to plunder Constantinople. Long before we could perceive it, our eyes sought it with ambitious impatience; we came to a narrow river, straitened between woody and uncultivated banks; it was the Boristhenes which presented itself to our view in this humble form. At this sight all our proud thoughts were lowered, and they were soon totally banished by the necessity of providing for our most urgent wants.

The emperor slept in his tent in advance of Rassasna; next day the army marched together, ready to draw up in order of battle, with the emperor on horseback in the midst of it. The advanced guard drove before it two *pulks* of Cossacks, who resisted only till they had gained time to destroy some bridges and some trusses of forage. The villages deserted by the enemy were plundered as soon as we entered them: we passed them in all possible haste and in disorder.

The streams were crossed by fords which were soon spoiled; the regiments which came afterwards passed over in other places, wherever they could. No one gave himself much concern about such details, which were neglected by the general staff: no person was left to point out the danger, where there was any, or the road, if there were several. Each *corps d'armée* seemed to be there for itself alone, each division, each individual to be unconnected with the rest; as if the fate of one had not depended on that of the other.

The army every where left stragglers behind it, and men who had lost their way, whom the officers passed without noticing; there would have been too many to find fault with; and besides, each was too much occupied with himself to attend to others. Many of these men were marauders, who feigned illness or a wound, to separate from the rest, which there was not time to prevent, and which will always be the case in large armies, that are urged forward with such precipitation, as individual order cannot exist in the midst of general disorder.

As far as Liady the villages appeared to us to be more Jewish than Polish; the Lithuanians sometimes fled at our approach; the Jews always remained; nothing could have induced them to forsake their wretched habitations; they might be known by their thick pronunciation, their voluble and hasty way of speaking, the vivacity of their motions, and their complexion, animated by the base passion of lucre. We noticed in particular their eager and piercing looks, their faces and features lengthened out into acute points, which a malicious and perfidious smile cannot widen; their tall, slim, and supple form; the earnestness of their demeanour, and lastly, their beards, usually red, and their long black robes, tightened round their loins by a leather girdle; for every thing but their filthiness distinguishes them from the Lithuanian peasants; every thing about them bespeaks a degraded people.

They seem to have conquered Poland, where they swarm, and the whole substance of which they extract. Formerly their religion, at present the sense of a reprobation too long universal, have made them the enemies of mankind; of old they attacked with arms, at present by cunning. This race is abhorred by the Russians, perhaps on account of its enmity to image-worship, while the Muscovites carry their adoration of images to idolatry. Finally, whether from superstition or rivalry of interests, they have forbidden them their country: the Jews were obliged to put up with their contempt, which their impotence repaid with hatred; but they detested our pillage still more. Enemies of all, spies to both armies, they sold one to the other from resentment or fear, according to occasion, and because there is nothing that they would not sell.

At Liady the Jews ended, and Russia proper commenced; our eyes were therefore relieved from their disgusting presence, but other wants made us regret them; we missed their active and officious services, which money could command, and their German jargon, the only language which we understood in these deserts, and which they all speak, because they require it in their traffic.

Chapter 25
Krasnoë

On the 15th of August, at three o'clock, we came in sight of Krasnoë, a town constructed of wood, which a Russian regiment made a show of defending; but it detained Marshal Ney no longer than the time necessary to come up with and overthrow it. The town being taken, there were seen beyond it 6000 Russian infantry in two columns, while several squadrons covered the retreat. This was the corps of Newerowskoi.

The ground was unequal, but bare, and suitable for cavalry. Murat took possession of it; but the bridges of Krasnoë were broken down, and the French cavalry was obliged to move off to the left, and to defile to a great distance in bad fords, in order to come up with the enemy. When our troops were in presence of the latter, the difficulty of the passage which they had just left behind them, and the bold countenance of the Russians, made them hesitate; they lost time in waiting for one another and deploying, but still the first effort dispersed the enemy's cavalry.

Newerowskoi finding himself uncovered, drew together his columns, and formed them into a full square so thick, that Murat's cavalry penetrated several times into it, without being able to break through or to disperse it.

It is even true that our first charges stopped short at the distance of 20 paces from the front of the Russians: whenever the latter found themselves too hard pressed, they faced about, steadily waited for us, and drove us back with their small arms; after which, profiting by our disorder, they immediately continued their retreat.

The Cossacks were seen striking with the shafts of their pikes such of their foot-soldiers as lengthened the line of march, or stepped out of their ranks; for our squadrons harassed them incessantly, watched all their movements, threw themselves into the smallest intervals, and instantly carried off all that separated from the main body; they even penetrated into it twice, but a little way, the horses remaining, as it were, stuck fast in that thick and obstinate mass.

Newerowskoi had one very critical moment: his column was marching on the left of the high-road through rye not yet cut, when all at once it was stopped by a long fence, formed of a stout palisade; his soldiers, pressed by our movements, had not time to make a gap in it, and Murat sent the Wurtembergers against them to make them lay down their arms; but while the head of the Russian column was surmounting the obstacle, their rearmost ranks faced about and stood firm. They fired ill, it is true, most of them into the air, like persons who are frightened; but so near, that the smoke, the flash of the reports of so many shot, frightened the Wurtemberg horses, and threw them into confusion.

The Russians embraced that moment to place between them and us that barrier which was expected to prove fatal to them. Their column profited by it to rally and gain ground. At length some French cannon came up, and they alone were capable of making a breach in this living fortress.

Newerowskoi hastened to reach a defile, where Grouchy was ordered to anticipate him; but Murat, deceived by a false report, had diverted the greatest part of that general's cavalry in the direction of Elnia; Grouchy had only 600 horse remaining. He made the 8th chasseurs dash forward to the defile, but it found itself too weak to stand against so strong a column. The vigorous and repeated charges made by that regiment, by the 6th hussars, and the 6th lancers, on the left flank of that dense mass, which was protected by the double row of birch-trees that lined the road on each side, were wholly insufficient, and Grouchy's applications for assistance were not attended to; either because the general who followed him was kept back by the difficulties of the ground, or that he was not sufficiently sensible of the importance of the combat. It was nevertheless great, since there was between Smolensk and Murat but this one Russian corps, and had that been defeated, Smolensk might have been surprised without defenders, taken without a battle, and the enemy's army cut off from his capital. But this Russian division at length gained a woody ground where its flanks were covered.

Newerowskoi retreated like a lion; still he left on the field of battle 1200 killed, 1000 prisoners, and eight pieces of cannon. The French cavalry had the honour of that day. The attack was as furious as the defence was obstinate; it had the more merit, having only the sword to employ against both sword and fire: the enlightened courage of the French soldier being besides of a more exalted nature than that of the Russian troops, mere docile slaves, who expose a less happy life, and bodies in which cold has extinguished sensibility.

As chance would have it, the day of this success was the emperor's birth-day. The army had no idea of celebrating it. In the disposition of the men and of the place, there was nothing that harmonized with such a celebration; empty acclamations would have been lost amid those vast deserts. In our situation, there was no other festival than the day of a complete victory.

Murat and Ney, however, in reporting their success to the emperor, paid homage to that anniversary. They caused a salute of 100 guns to be fired. The emperor remarked, with displeasure, that in Russia it was necessary to be more sparing of French powder; the answer was, that it was Russian powder which had been taken the preceding day. The idea of having his birth-day celebrated at the expense of the enemy drew a smile from Napoleon. It was admitted that this very rare species of flattery became such men.

Prince Eugene also considered it his duty to carry him his good wishes. The emperor said to him, "Every thing is preparing for a battle; I shall gain it, and we shall see Moscow." The prince kept silence, but as he retired, he returned for answer to the questions of Marshal Mortier, "Moscow will be our ruin!" Thus did disapprobation begin to be expressed. Duroc, the most reserved of all, the friend and confidant of the emperor, loudly declared, that he could not foresee the period of our return. Still it was only among themselves that the great officers indulged in such remarks, for they were aware that the decision being once taken, all would have to concur in its execution; that the more dangerous their situation became, the more need there was of courage; and that a word, calculated to abate zeal, would be treasonable; hence we saw those who by silence, nay even by words, opposed the emperor in his tent, appear out of it full of confidence and hope. This attitude was dictated by honour; the multitude has imputed it to flattery.

Newerowskoi, almost crushed, hastened to shut himself up in Smolensk. He left behind him some Cossacks to burn the forage; the houses were spared.

CHAPTER 26

Smolensk

While the grand army was thus ascending the Dnieper, along its left bank, Barclay and Bagration, placed between that river and the lake of Kasplia, towards Inkowo, believed themselves to be still in presence of the French army. They hesitated; twice hurried on by the counsel of quarter-master-general Toll, they resolved to force the line of our cantonments, and twice dismayed at so bold a determination, they stopped short in the midst of the movement they had commenced for that purpose. At length, too timid to take any other counsel than their own, they appeared to have left their decision to circumstances, and to await our attack, in order to regulate their defence by it.

It might also be perceived, from the unsteadiness of their movements, that there was not a good understanding between these two chiefs. In fact, their situation, their disposition, their very origin, every thing about them was at variance. On the one hand the cool valour, the scientific, methodical, and tenacious genius of Barclay, whose mind, German like his birth, was for calculating every thing, even the chances of the hazard, bent on owing all to his tactics, and nothing to fortune; on the other the martial, bold, and vehement instinct of Bagration, an old Russian of the school of Suwarrow, dissatisfied at being under a general who was his junior in the service—terrible in battle, but acquainted with no other book than nature, no other instructor than memory, no other counsels than his own inspirations.

This old Russian, on the frontiers of Russia proper, trembled with shame at the idea of retreating without fighting. In the army all shared his ardour; it was supported on the one hand by the patriotic pride of the nobles, by the success at Inkowo, by the inactivity of Napoleon at Witepsk, and by the severe remarks of those who were not responsible; on the other hand, by a nation of peasants, merchants, and soldiers, who saw us on the point of treading their sacred soil, with all the horror that such profanation could excite. All, in short, demanded a battle.

Barclay alone was against fighting. His plan, erroneously attributed to England, had been formed in his mind so far back as the year 1807; but he had to combat his own army as well as ours; and though commander-in-chief and minister, he was neither Russian enough, nor victorious enough, to win the confidence of the Russians. He possessed that of Alexander alone.

Bagration and his officers hesitated to obey him. The point was to defend their native land, to devote themselves for the salvation of all: it was the affair of each, and all imagined that they had a right to examine. Thus their ill fortune distrusted the prudence of their general; whilst, with the exception of a few chiefs, our good fortune trusted implicitly to the boldness, hitherto always prosperous of ours; for in success to command is easy; no one inquires whether it is prudence or fortune that guides. Such is the situation of military chiefs; when successful, they are blindly obeyed by all; when unfortunate, they are criticized by all.

Hurried away notwithstanding, by the general impulse, Barclay had just yielded to it for a moment, collected his forces near Rudnia, and attempted to surprise the French army, dispersed as it was. But the feeble blow which his advanced guard had just struck at Inkowo had alarmed him. He trembled, paused, and imagining every moment that he saw Napoleon approaching in front of him, on his right and every where excepting on his left, which was covered as he thought by the Dnieper, he lost several days in marches and counter-marches. He was thus hesitating, when all at once Newerowskoi's cries of distress resounded in his camp. To attack was now entirely out of the question: his troops ran to arms, and hurried towards Smolensk for the purpose of defending it.

Murat and Ney were already attacking that city: the former with his cavalry, at the place where the Boristhenes enters its walls; the latter, with his infantry, where it issues from them, and on woody ground intersected by deep ravines. The marshal's left was supported by the river, and his right by Murat, whom Poniatowski, coming direct from Mohilef, arrived to reinforce.

In this place two steep hills contract the channel of the Boristhenes; on these hills Smolensk is built. That city has the appearance of two towns, separated by the river and connected by two bridges. That on the right bank, the most modern, is wholly occupied by traders; it is open, but overlooks the other, of which it is nevertheless but a dependency.

The old town, occupying the plateau and slopes of the left bank, is surrounded by a wall twenty-five feet high, eighteen thick, three thousand fathoms in length, and defended by twenty-nine massive towers, a miserable earthen citadel of five bastions, which commands the Orcha road, and a wide ditch, which serves as a covered way. Some outworks and the suburbs intercept the view of the approaches to the Mohilef and Dnieper gates; they are defended by a ravine, which, after encompassing a great part of the town, becomes deeper and steeper as it approaches the Dnieper, on the side next to the citadel.

The deluded inhabitants were quitting the temples, where they had been praising God for the victories of their troops, when they saw them hastening up, bloody, vanquished, and flying before the victorious French army. Their disaster was unexpected, and their consternation so much the greater.

Meanwhile, the sight of Smolensk inflamed the impatient ardour of Marshal Ney: we know not whether he unseasonably called to mind the wonders of the Prussian war, when citadels fell before the sabres of our cavalry, or whether he at first designed only to reconnoitre this first Russian fortress: at any rate he approached too near; a ball struck him on the neck; incensed, he despatched a battalion against the citadel, through a shower of balls, which swept away two-thirds of his men; the remainder proceeded; nothing could stop them but the Russian walls; a few only returned. Little notice was taken of the heroic attempt which they had made, because it was a fault of their general's, and useless into the bargain.

Cooled by this check, Marshal Ney retired to a sandy and wooded height bordering the river. He was surveying the city and its environs, when he imagined that he could discern troops in motion on the other side of the river: he ran to fetch the emperor, and conducted him through coppices and dingles to avoid the fire of the place.

Napoleon, on reaching the height, beheld a cloud of dust enveloping long black columns, glistening with a multitude of arms: these masses approached so rapidly that they seemed to run. It was Barclay, Bagration, nearly 120,000 men: in short, the whole Russian army.

Transported with joy at this sight, Napoleon clapped his hands, exclaiming, "At last I have them!" There could be no doubt of it; this surprised army was hastening up to throw itself into Smolensk, to pass through it, to deploy under its walls, and at length to offer us that battle which was so ardently desired. The moment that was to decide the fate of Russia had at last arrived.

The emperor immediately went through the whole line, and allotted to each his place. Davoust, and next to him Count Lobau, were to deploy on the right of Ney: the guard in the centre, as a reserve, and farther off the army of Italy. The place of Junot and the Westphalians was indicated; but a false movement had carried them out of the way. Murat and Poniatowski formed the right of the army; those two chiefs already threatened the city: he made them draw back to the margin of a coppice, and leave vacant before them a spacious plain, extending from this wood as far as the Dnieper. It was a field of battle which he offered to the enemy. The French army, thus posted, had defiles and precipices at its back; but Napoleon concerned himself little about retreat; he thought only of victory.

Bagration and Barclay were meanwhile returning at full speed towards Smolensk; the first to save it by a battle, the other to cover the flight of its inhabitants and the evacuation of its magazines: he was determined to leave us nothing but its ashes. The two Russian generals arrived panting on the heights on the right bank; nor did they again take breath till they saw that they were still masters of the bridges which connect the two towns.

Napoleon then caused the enemy to be harassed by a host of riflemen, for the purpose of drawing him to the left bank of the river, and ensuring a battle for the following day. It is asserted that Bagration would have fallen in with his views, but that Barclay did not expose him to the temptation. He despatched him to Elnia, and took upon himself the defence of Smolensk.

Barclay had imagined that the greatest part of our army was marching upon Elnia, to get between Moscow and the Russian army. He deceived himself by the disposition, so common in war, of imputing to one's enemy designs contrary to those which he demonstrates. For the defensive, being uneasy in its nature, frequently magnifies the offensive, and fear, heating the imagination, causes it to attribute to the enemy a thousand projects of which he never dreamt. It is possible too that Barclay, having to cope with a colossal foe, felt authorized to expect from him gigantic movements.

The Russians themselves have since reproached Napoleon with not having adopted that manoeuvre; but have they considered, that to proceed thus to place himself beyond a river, a fortified town and a hostile army, to cut off the Russians from the road to their capital, would have been cutting off himself from all communication with his reinforcements, his other armies, and Europe? Those are not capable of appreciating the difficulties of such a movement who are astonished that it was not made, without preparation, in two days, across a river and a country both unknown, with such masses, and amidst another combination the execution of which was not yet completed.

Be that as it may, in the evening of the 16th, Bagration commenced his march for Elnia. Napoleon had just had his tent pitched in the middle of his first line, almost within reach of the guns of Smolensk, and on the brink of the ravine which encircles the city. He called Murat and Davoust: the former had just observed among the Russians movements indicative of a retreat. Every day since the passage of the Niemen, he had been accustomed to see them thus escape him; he did not therefore believe that there would be any battle the following day. Davoust was of a contrary opinion. As for the emperor, he had no hesitation in believing what he wished.

Chapter 27
Smolensk Occupied

On the 17th, by daybreak, the hope of seeing the Russian army drawn up before him awoke Napoleon; but the field which he had prepared for it remained empty: he persisted, nevertheless, in his illusion, in which Davoust participated; it was to his side that he proceeded. Dalton, one of the generals of that marshal, had seen some hostile battalions quit the city and range themselves in order of battle. The emperor seized this hope, which Ney, jointly with Murat, combated in vain.

But while he was still full of hopes and expectations, Belliard, tired of this uncertainty, ordered a few horse to follow him; he drove a band of Cossacks into the Dnieper, above the town, and saw on the opposite bank the road from Smolensk to Moscow covered with artillery, and troops on the march. There was no longer any doubt that the Russians were in full retreat. The emperor was apprised that he must renounce all hopes of a battle, but that his cannon might, from the opposite bank, annoy the retrograde march of the enemy.

Belliard even proposed to send part of the army across the river, to cut off the retreat of the Russian rear-guard, which was entrusted with the defence of Smolensk; but the party of cavalry sent to discover a ford went two leagues without finding one, and drowned several horses. There was nevertheless a wide and commodious crossing about a league above the city. Napoleon himself, in his agitation, turned his horse that way. He proceeded several *wersts* in that direction, tired himself, and returned.

From that moment he seemed to consider Smolensk as a mere place of passage, of which it was absolutely necessary to gain possession by main force, and without loss of time. But Murat, prudent when not heated by the presence of the enemy, and who, with his cavalry, had nothing to do in an assault, disapproved of this resolution.

To him so violent an effort appeared useless, when the Russians were retiring of their own accord; and in regard to the plan of overtaking them, he observed that, "since they would not fight, we had followed them far enough, and it was high time to stop."

The emperor replied: but the rest of their conversation was not overheard. As, however, the king afterwards declared that "he had thrown himself at the knees of his brother, and conjured him to stop, but that Napoleon saw nothing but Moscow; that honour, glory, rest, every thing for him was there; that this Moscow would be our ruin!"—it was obvious what had been the cause of their disagreement.

So much is certain, that when Murat quitted his brother-in-law, his face wore the expression of deep chagrin; his motions were abrupt; a gloomy and concentrated vehemence agitated him; and the name of Moscow several times escaped his lips.

Not far off, on the left bank of the Dnieper, a formidable battery had been placed, at the spot whence Belliard had perceived the retreat of the enemy. The Russians had opposed to us two still more formidable. Every moment our guns were shattered, and our ammunition-wagons blown up. It was into the midst of this volcano that the king urged his horse: there he stopped, alighted, and remained motionless. Belliard warned him that he was sacrificing his life to no purpose, and without glory. The king answered only by pushing on still farther. Those around him no longer doubted, that despairing of the issue of the war, and foreseeing future disasters, he was seeking death in order to escape them. Belliard, however, insisted, and observed to him, that his temerity would be the destruction of those about him. "Well then," replied Murat, "do you retire, and leave me here by myself." All refused to leave him; when the king angrily turning about, tore himself from this scene of carnage, like a man who is suffering violence.

Meanwhile a general assault had been ordered. Ney had to attack the citadel, and Davoust and Lobau the suburbs, which cover the walls of the city. Poniatowski, already on the banks of the Dnieper, with sixty pieces of cannon, was again to descend that river to the suburb which borders it, to destroy the enemy's bridges, and to intercept the retreat of the garrison. Napoleon gave orders, that, at the same time, the artillery of the guard should batter the great wall with its twelve-pounders, which were ineffective against so thick a mass. It disobeyed, and directed its fire into the covered way, which it cleared.

Every manoeuvre succeeded at once, excepting Ney's attack, the only one which ought to have been decisive, but which was neglected. The enemy was driven back precipitately within his walls; all who had not time to regain them perished; but, in mounting to the assault, our attacking columns left a long and wide track of blood, of wounded and dead.

It was remarked, that one battalion, which presented itself in flank to the Russian batteries, lost a whole rank of one of its platoons by a single bullet; twenty-two men were felled by the same blow.

Meanwhile the army, from an amphitheatre of heights, contemplated with silent anxiety the conduct of its brave comrades; but when it saw them darting through a shower of balls and grape shot, and persisting with an ardour, a firmness, and a regularity, quite admirable; then it was that the soldiers, warmed with enthusiasm, began clapping their hands. The noise of this glorious applause was such as even to reach the attacking columns. It rewarded the devotion of those warriors; and although in Dalton's single brigade, and in the artillery of Reindre, five chiefs of battalion, 1500 men, and the general himself fell, the survivors still say, that the enthusiastic homage which they excited, was a sufficient compensation to them for all their sufferings.

On reaching the walls of the place, they screened themselves from its fire, by means of the outworks and buildings, of which they had gained possession. The fire of musketry continued; and from the report, redoubled by the echo of the walls, it seemed to become more and more brisk. The emperor grew tired of this; he would have withdrawn his troops. Thus, the same blunder which Ney had made a battalion commit the preceding day, was repeated by the whole army; the one had cost 300 or 400 men, the other 5000 or 6000; but Davoust persuaded the emperor to persevere in his attack.

Night came on. Napoleon retired to his tent, which had been placed more prudently than the day before; and the Count Lobau, who had made himself master of the ditch, but could no longer maintain his ground there, ordered shells to be thrown into the city to dislodge the enemy. Thick black columns of smoke were presently seen rising from several points; these were soon lighted at intervals by flickering flashes, then by sparks, and at last, long spires of flame burst from all parts. It was like a great number of distinct fires. It was not long before they united and formed but one vast blaze, which whirling about as it rose, covered Smolensk, and entirely consumed it, with a dismal roaring.

Count Lobau was dismayed by so great a disaster, which he believed to be his own work. The emperor, seated in front of his tent, contemplated in silence this awful spectacle. It was as yet impossible to ascertain either the cause or the result, and the night was passed under arms.

About three in the morning, one of Davoust's subalterns ventured to the foot of the wall, which he scaled without noise. Emboldened by the silence which reigned around him, he penetrated into the city; all at once several voices and the Sclavonian accent were heard, and the Frenchman, surprised and surrounded, thought that he had nothing to do but to sell his life dearly, or surrender. The first rays of the dawn, however, showed him, in those whom he mistook for enemies, some of Poniatowski's Poles. They had been the first to enter the city, which Barclay had just evacuated.

After Smolensk had been reconnoitred and its approaches cleared, the army entered the walls: it traversed the reeking and blood-stained ruins with its accustomed order, pomp, and martial music, triumphing over the deserted wreck, and having no other witness of its glory but itself. A show without spectators, an almost fruitless victory, a sanguinary glory, of which the smoke that surrounded us, and seemed to be our only conquest, was but too faithful an emblem.

CHAPTER 28

Reconnoissance

When the emperor knew that Smolensk was entirely occupied, and its fires almost extinguished, and when day and the different reports had sufficiently instructed him; when, in short, he saw that there, as at the Niemen, at Wilna, at Witepsk, the phantom of victory, which allured him forward, and which he always imagined himself to be on the point of seizing, had once more eluded his grasp, he proceeded slowly towards his barren conquest. He inspected the field of battle, according to his custom, in order to appreciate the value of the attack, the merit of the resistance, and the loss on both sides.

He found it strewed with a great number of Russian dead, and very few of ours. Most of them, especially the French, had been stripped; they might be known by the whiteness of their skin, and by their forms less bony and muscular than those of the Russians. Melancholy review of the dead and dying! dismal account to make up and to render! The pain felt by the emperor might be inferred from the contraction of his features and his irritation; but in him policy was a second nature, which soon imposed silence on the first.

For the rest, this calculation of the dead the day after an engagement was as delusive as it was disagreeable; for most of ours had been previously removed, but those of the enemy left in sight; an expedient adopted with a view to prevent unpleasant impressions being made on our own troops, as well as from that natural impulse, which causes us to collect and assist our own dying, and to pay the last duties to our own dead, before we think of those belonging to the enemy.

The emperor, nevertheless, asserted in his bulletin, that his loss on the preceding day was much smaller than that of the Muscovites; that the conquest of Smolensk made him master of the Russian salt works, and that his minister of finance might reckon upon twenty-four additional millions. It is neither probable nor true, that he suffered himself to be the dupe of such illusions: yet it was believed, that he was then turning against himself that faculty of imposing upon others, of which he knew how to make so important a use.

Continuing his reconnoissance, he came to one of the gates of the citadel, near the Boristhenes, facing the suburb on the right bank, which was still occupied by the Russians. There, surrounded by Marshals Ney, Davoust, Mortier, the Grand-marshal Duroc, Count Lobau, and another general, he sat down on some mats before a hut, not so much to observe the enemy, as to relieve his heart from the load which oppressed it, and to seek, in the flattery or in the ardour of his generals, encouragement against facts and against his own reflections.

He talked long, vehemently, and without interruption. "What a disgrace for Barclay, to have given up, without fighting, the key of old Russia! and yet what a field of honour he had offered to him! how advantageous it was for him! a fortified town to support and take part in his efforts! the same town and a river to receive and cover the wreck of his army, if defeated!

"And what would he have had to fight? an army, numerous indeed, but straitened for want of room, and having nothing but precipices for its retreat. It had given itself up, in a manner, to his blows. Barclay had wanted nothing but resolution. It was therefore, all over with Russia. She had no army but to witness the fall of her cities, and not to defend them. For, in fact, on what more favourable ground could Barclay make a stand? what position would he determine to dispute? he, who had forsaken that Smolensk, called by him Smolensk the holy, Smolensk the strong, the key of Moscow, the Bulwark of Russia, which, as it had been given out, was to prove the grave of the French! We should presently see the effect of this loss on the Russians; we should see their Lithuanian soldiers, nay even those of Smolensk, deserting their ranks, indignant at the surrender of their capital without a struggle."

Napoleon added, that "authentic reports had made him acquainted with the weakness of the Russian divisions; that most of them were already much reduced; that they suffered themselves to be destroyed in detail, and that Alexander would soon cease to have an army. The rabble of peasants armed with pikes, whom we had just seen in the train of their battalions, sufficiently demonstrated to what shifts their generals were reduced."

While the emperor was thus talking, the balls of the Russian riflemen were whizzing about his ears; but he was worked up by his subject. He launched out against the enemy's general and army, as if he could have destroyed it by his reasoning, because he could not by victory. No one answered him; it was evident that he was not asking advice, but that he had been talking all this time to himself; that he was contending against his own reflections, and that, by this torrent of conjectures, he was seeking to impose upon himself, and endeavouring to make others participators in the same illusions.

Indeed, he did not give any one time to interrupt him. As to the weakness and disorganization of the Russian army, nobody believed it; but what could be urged in reply? He appealed to positive documents, those which had been sent to him by Lauriston; they had been altered, under the idea of correcting them: for the estimate of the Russian forces by Lauriston, the French minister in Russia, was correct; but, according to accounts less deserving of credit, though more flattering, this estimate had been diminished one-third.

After talking to himself for an hour, the emperor, looking at the heights on the right bank, which were nearly abandoned by the enemy, concluded with exclaiming, that "the Russians were women, and that they acknowledged themselves vanquished!" He strove to persuade himself that these people had, from their contact with Europe, lost their rude and savage valour. But their preceding wars had instructed them, and they had arrived at that point, at which nations still possess all their primitive virtues, in addition to those they have acquired.

At length, he again mounted his horse. It was then the Grand-marshal observed to one of us, that "if Barclay had committed so very great a blunder in refusing battle, the emperor would not have been so extremely anxious to convince us of it." A few paces farther, an officer, sent not long before to Prince Schwartzenberg, presented himself: he reported that Tormasof and his army had appeared in the north, between Minsk and Warsaw, and that they had marched upon our line of operation. A Saxon brigade taken at Kobrynn, the grand-duchy overrun, and Warsaw alarmed, had been the first results of this aggression; but Regnier had summoned Schwartzenberg to his aid. Tormasof had then retreated to Gorodeczna, where he halted on the 12th of August, between two defiles, in a plain surrounded by woods and marshes, but accessible in the rear of his left flank.

Regnier, skilful before an action, and an excellent judge of ground, knew how to prepare battles; but when the field became animated, when it was covered with men and horses, he lost his self-possession, and rapid movements seemed to dazzle him. At first, therefore, that general perceived at a glance the weak side of the Russians; he bore down upon it, but instead of breaking into it by masses and with impetuosity, he merely made successive attacks.

Tormasof, forewarned by these, had time to oppose, at first, regiments to regiments, then brigades to brigades, and lastly divisions to divisions. By favour of this prolonged contest, he gained the night, and withdrew his army from the field of battle, where a rapid and simultaneous effort might have destroyed it. Still, he lost some pieces of cannon, a great quantity of baggage, and four thousand men, and retired behind the Styr, where he was joined by Tchitchakof, who was hastening with the army of the Danube to his succour.

This battle, though far from decisive, preserved the grand-duchy: it confined the Russians, in this quarter, to the defensive, and gave the emperor time to win a battle.

During this recital, the tenacious genius of Napoleon was less struck with these advantages in themselves, than with the support they gave to the illusion which he had just been holding forth to us: accordingly, still adhering to his original idea, and without questioning the aid-de-camp, he turned round to his auditory, and, as if continuing his former conversation, he exclaimed: "There you see, the poltroons! they allow themselves to be beaten even by Austrians!" Then, casting around him a look of apprehension, "I hope," added he, "that none but Frenchmen hear me." He then asked if he might rely on the good faith of Prince Schwartzenberg, for which the aid-de-camp pledged himself; nor was he mistaken, though the event seemed to belie his confidence.

Every word which the emperor had uttered merely proved his disappointment, and that a great hesitation had again taken possession of his mind; for in him success was less communicative, and decision less verbose. At length he entered Smolensk. In the passage through its massive walls, Count Lobau exclaimed, "What a fine head for cantonments!" This was the same thing as advising him to stop there; but the emperor returned no other answer to this counsel than a stern look.

This look, however, soon changed its expression, when it had nothing to rest upon but ruins, among which our wounded were crawling, and heaps of smoking ashes, where lay human skeletons, dried and blackened by the fire. This great destruction confounded him. What a harvest of victory! That city where his troops were at length to find shelter, provisions, a rich booty, the promised reward for so many hardships, was but a ruin on which he should be obliged to bivouac! No doubt his influence over his men was great, but could it extend beyond nature? What would they think?

Here, it is right to observe, that the sufferings of the army did not want for an interpreter. He knew that his soldiers asked one another "for what purpose they had been marched eight hundred leagues, to find nothing but muddy water, famine, and bivouacs on heaps of ashes: for such were all their conquests; they possessed nothing but what they had brought with them. If it was necessary to drag every thing along with them, to transport France into Russia, wherefore had they been required to quit France?"

Several of the generals themselves began to tire: some stopped on account of illness, others murmured: "What better were they for his having enriched them, if they could not enjoy their wealth? for his having given them wives, if he made them widowers by a continual absence? for his having bestowed on them palaces, if he forced them to lie abroad incessantly on the bare ground, amidst frost and snow?—for every year the hardships of war increased; fresh conquests compelling them to go farther in quest of fresh enemies. Europe would soon be insufficient: he would want Asia too."

Several, especially of our allies, ventured to think, that we should lose less by a defeat than by a victory: a reverse would perhaps disgust the emperor with the war; at least it would place him more upon a level with us.

The generals who were nearest to Napoleon were astonished at his confidence. "Had he not already in some measure quitted Europe? and if Europe were to rise against him, he would have no subjects but his soldiers, no empire but his camp: even then, one-third of them, being foreigners, would become his enemies." Such was the language of Murat and Berthier. Napoleon, irritated at finding in his two chief lieutenants, and at the very moment of action, the same uneasiness with which he was himself struggling, vented his ill-humour against them: he overwhelmed them with it, as frequently happens in the household of princes, who are least sparing of those of whose attachment they are most sure; an inconvenience attending favour, which counterbalances its advantages.

After his spleen had vented itself in a torrent of words, he summoned them back; but this time, dissatisfied with such treatment, they kept aloof. The emperor then made amends for his hastiness by caresses, calling Berthier "his wife," and his fits of passion, "domestic bickerings."

Murat and Ney left him with minds full of sinister presentiments relative to this war, which at the first sight of the Russians they were themselves for carrying on with fury. For in them, whose character was entirely made up of action, inspiration, and first movements, there was no consistency: every thing was unexpected; the occasion hurried them away; impetuous, they varied in language, plans, and dispositions, at every step, just as the ground is incessantly varying in appearance.

Chapter 29

The Army Sickens

About the same time, Rapp and Lauriston presented themselves: the latter came from Petersburgh. Napoleon did not ask a single question of this officer on his arrival from the capital of his enemy. Aware, no doubt, of the frankness of his former aid-de-camp, and of his opinion respecting this war, he was apprehensive of receiving from him unsatisfactory intelligence.

But Rapp, who had followed our track, could not keep silence. "The army had advanced but a hundred leagues from the Niemen, and already it was completely altered. The officers who travelled post from the interior of France to join it, arrived dismayed. They could not conceive how it happened that a victorious army, without fighting, should leave behind it more wrecks than a defeated one.

"They had met with all who were marching to join the masses, and all who had separated from them; lastly, all who were not excited either by the presence of the chiefs, or by example, or by the war. The appearance of each troop, according to its distance from home, excited hope, anxiety, or pity.

"In Germany, as far as the Oder, where a thousand objects were incessantly reminding them of France, these recruits imagined themselves not wholly cut off from it; they were ardent and jovial; but beyond the Oder, in Poland, where the soil, productions, inhabitants, costumes, manners, in short every thing, to the very habitations, wore a foreign aspect; where nothing, in short, resembled a country which they regretted; they began to be dismayed at the distance they had traversed, and their faces already bore the stamp of fatigue and lassitude.

"By what an extraordinary distance must they then be separated from France, since they had already reached unknown regions, where every thing presented to them an aspect of such gloomy novelty! how many steps they had taken, and how many more they had yet to take!

The very idea of return was disheartening; and yet they were obliged to march on, to keep constantly marching! and they complained that ever since they left France, their fatigues had been gradually increasing, and the means of supporting them continually diminishing."

The truth is, that wine first failed them, then beer, even spirits; and, lastly, they were reduced to water, which in its turn was frequently wanting. The same was the case with dry provisions, and also with every necessary of life; and in this gradual destitution, depression of mind kept pace with the successive debilitation of the body. Agitated by a vague inquietude, they marched on amid the dull uniformity of the vast and silent forests of dark pines. They crept along these large trees, bare and stripped to their very tops, and were affrighted at their weakness amid this immensity. They then conceived gloomy and absurd notions respecting the geography of these unknown regions; and, overcome by a secret horror, they hesitated to penetrate farther into such vast deserts.

From these sufferings, physical and moral, from these privations, from these continual bivouacs, as dangerous near the pole as under the equator, and from the infection of the air by the putrefied carcases of men and horses that strewed the roads, sprang two dreadful epidemics—the dysentery and the typhus fever. The Germans first felt their ravages; they are less nervous and less sober than the French; and they were less interested in a cause which they regarded as foreign to them. Out of 22,000 Bavarians who had crossed the Oder, 11,000 only reached the Düna; and yet they had never been in action. This military march cost the French one-fourth, and the allies half of their army.

Every morning the regiments started in order from their bivouacs; but scarcely had they proceeded a few steps, before their widening ranks became lengthened out into small and broken files; the weakest, being unable to follow, dropped behind: these unfortunate wretches beheld their comrades and their eagles getting farther and farther from them: they still strove to overtake, but at length lost sight of them, and then sank disheartened. The roads and the margins of the woods were studded with them: some were seen plucking the ears of rye to devour the grain; and they would then attempt, frequently in vain, to reach the hospital, or the nearest village. Great numbers thus perished.

But it was not the sick only that separated from the army: many soldiers, disgusted and dispirited on the one hand, and impelled by a love of independence and plunder on the other, voluntarily deserted their colours; and these were not the least resolute: their numbers soon increased, as evil begets evil by example. They formed bands, and fixed their quarters in the mansions and villages adjacent to the military road. There they lived in abundance. Among them there were fewer French than Germans; but it was remarked, that the leader of each of these little independent bodies, composed of men of several nations, was invariably a Frenchman.

Rapp had witnessed all these disorders: on his arrival, his blunt honesty kept back none of these details from his chief; but the emperor merely replied, "I am going to strike a great blow, and all the stragglers will then rally."

With Sebastiani he was more explicit. The latter reminded him of his own words, when he had declared to him, at Wilna, that "he would not cross the Düna, for to proceed farther this year, would be hurrying to infallible destruction."

Sebastiani, like the others, laid great stress on the state of the army. "It is dreadful, I know," replied the emperor: "from Wilna, half of it consisted of stragglers; now they form two-thirds; there is, therefore, no time to be lost: we must extort peace; it is at Moscow. Besides, this army cannot now stop: with its composition, and in its disorganization, motion alone keeps it together. One may advance at the head of it, but not stop or go back. It is an army of attack, not of defence; an army of operation, not of position."

It was thus that he spoke to those immediately about him; but to the generals commanding his divisions, he held a different language. Before the former, he manifested the motives which urged him forward, from the latter he carefully concealed them, and seemed to agree with them as to the necessity of stopping. This may serve to explain the contradictions which were remarked in his own language.

Thus, the very same day, in the streets of Smolensk, surrounded by Davoust and his generals, whose corps had suffered most in the assault of the preceding day, he said, that in the capture of Smolensk he was indebted to them for an important success, and that he considered that city as an excellent head of cantonments.

"Now," continued he, "my line is well covered; we will stop here: behind this rampart, I can rally my troops, let them rest, receive reinforcements, and our supplies from Dantzic. Thus the whole of Poland is conquered and defended; this is a sufficient result; it is gathering, in two months, the fruit that might be expected only from two years of war: it is therefore sufficient. Betwixt this and the spring, we must organize Lithuania, and recompose an invincible army; then, if peace should not come to seek us in our winter quarters, we will go and conquer it at Moscow."

He then told the marshal in confidence, that his motive for ordering him to proceed beyond Smolensk, was only to drive off the Russians to the distance of a few marches; but he strictly forbade him to involve himself in any serious affair. At the same time, it is true, he committed the vanguard to Murat and to Ney, the two rashest of his officers; and, unknown to Davoust, he placed that prudent and methodical marshal under the command of the impetuous king of Naples. Thus his mind seemed to be wavering between two great resolutions, and the contradictions in his words were communicated to his actions. In this internal conflict, however, it was remarked, what an ascendance his enterprising genius had over his prudence, and how the former so disposed matters as to give birth to circumstances which must necessarily hurry him away.

Chapter 30

The Battle of Valoutina

Meanwhile the Russians still defended the suburb on the right bank of the Dnieper. On our side, the 18th, and the night of the 19th, were employed in rebuilding the bridges. On the 19th of August, before day, Ney crossed the river by the light of the suburb, which was on fire. At first, he saw there no enemies but the flames, and he began to climb the long and rugged declivity on which it stands. His troops proceeded slowly and with caution, making a thousand circuits to avoid the fire. The Russians had managed it with skill: it met our men at every point, and obstructed the principal avenues.

Ney, and the foremost of his soldiers, advanced in silence into this labyrinth of flames, with anxious eye and attentive ear, not knowing but that the Russians might be waiting on the summit of the steep, to pour suddenly upon them, to overthrow and drive them back into the flames and the river. But they breathed more freely, relieved from the weight of a great apprehension, when they perceived on the crest of the ravine, at the branching-off of the roads to Petersburgh and Moscow, nothing but a band of Cossacks, who immediately fled by those two roads. Having neither prisoners nor inhabitants, nor spies, the ground was, as at Witepsk, the only thing they could interrogate. But the enemy had left as many traces in one direction as in the other, so that the marshal paused in uncertainty between the two until mid-day.

During this interval, a passage had been effected across the Borishenes at several points; the roads to the two hostile capitals were reconnoitred to the distance of a league, and the Russian infantry was discovered in that leading to Moscow. Ney would soon have overtaken it; but as that road skirted the Dnieper, he had to cross the streams which fall into it. Each of them having scooped out its own bed, marked the bottom of a valley, the opposite side of which was a position where the enemy posted himself, and which it was necessary to carry: the first, that of the Stubna, did not detain him long; but the hill of Valoutina, at the foot of which runs the Kolowdnia, became the scene of an obstinate conflict.

The cause of this resistance has been attributed to an ancient tradition of national glory, which represented this field of battle as ground consecrated by victory. But this superstition, worthy even still of the Russian soldier, is far from the more enlightened patriotism of their generals. It was necessity that here compelled them to fight: we have seen that the Moscow road, on leaving Smolensk, skirted the Dnieper, and that the French artillery, on the other bank, traversed it with its fire. Barclay durst not take this road at night, for fear of risking his artillery, baggage, and the wagons with the wounded, the rolling of which would have betrayed his retreat.

The Petersburgh road quitted the river more abruptly: two marshy cross-roads branched off from it on the right, one at the distance of two leagues from Smolensk, the other at four; they ran through woods, and rejoined the high-road to Moscow, after a long circuit; the one at Bredichino, two leagues beyond Valoutina, the other farther off at Slobpnewa.

Into these defiles Barclay was bold enough to commit himself with so many horses and vehicles; so that this long and heavy column had thus to traverse two large arcs of a circle, of which the high-road from Smolensk to Moscow, which Ney soon attacked, was the chord. Every moment, as always happens in such cases, the overturning of a carriage, the sticking fast of a wheel, or of a single horse, in the mud, or the breaking of a trace, stopped the whole. The sound of the French cannon, meanwhile, drew nearer, and seemed to have already got before the Russian column, and to be on the point of reaching and closing the outlet which it was striving to gain.

At length, after an arduous march, the head of the enemy's convoy came in sight of the high-road at the moment when the French had only to force the height of Valoutina and the passage of Kolowdnia, in order to reach that outlet. Ney had furiously carried that of the Stubna; but Korf, driven back upon Valoutina, had summoned to his aid the column which preceded him. It is asserted that the latter, without order, and badly officered, hesitated to comply; but that Woronzof, aware of the importance of that position, prevailed upon its commander to turn back.

The Russians defended themselves to defend every thing, cannon, wounded, baggage: the French attacked in order to take every thing. Napoleon had halted a league and a half behind Ney. Conceiving that it was but an affair between his advanced guard and the rear of the enemy, he sent Gudin to the assistance of the marshal, rallied the other divisions, and returned to Smolensk. But this fight became a serious battle; 30,000 men were successively engaged in it on both sides: soldiers, officers, generals, encountered each other; the action was long, the struggle terrible; even night did not suspend it. At length, in possession of the plateau, exhausted by the loss of strength and blood, Ney finding himself surrounded only by dead, dying, and obscurity, became fatigued; he ordered his troops to cease firing, to keep silence, and present bayonets. The Russians hearing nothing more, were silent also, and availed themselves of the darkness to effect their retreat.

There was almost as much glory in their defeat as in our victory: the two chiefs carried their point, the one in conquering, the other in not being conquered till he had saved the Russian artillery, baggage, and wounded. One of the enemy's generals, the only one left unhurt on this field of carnage, endeavoured to escape from among our soldiers, by repeating the French word of command; he was recognized by the flashes of their fire-arms, and secured. Other Russian generals had perished, but the grand army sustained a still greater loss.

At the passage of the bridge over the Kolowdnia, which had been badly repaired, General Gudin, whose well-regulated valour loved to confront none but useful dangers, and who besides was not a bold rider, had alighted from his horse to cross the stream, when, at that moment, a cannon-ball skimming the surface of the ground, broke both his legs. When the tidings of this misfortune reached the emperor, they put a stop to every thing—to discussion and action. Every one was thunderstruck; the victory of Valoutina seemed no longer to be a success.

Gudin was conveyed to Smolensk, and there received the unavailing attentions of the emperor; but he soon expired. His remains were interred in the citadel of the city, which they honour: a worthy tomb for a soldier, who was a good citizen, a good husband, a good father, an intrepid general, just and mild, a man both of principle and talent; a rare assemblage of qualities in an age when virtuous men are too frequently devoid of abilities, and men of abilities without virtue. It was a fortunate chance that he was worthily replaced; Gérard, the oldest general of brigade of the division, took the command of it, and the enemy, who knew nothing of our loss, gained nothing by the dreadful blow he had dealt us.

The Russians, astonished at having been attacked only in front, conceived that all the military combinations of Murat were confined to following them on the high-road. They therefore styled him in derision, *"the general of the high roads,"* characterizing him thus from the event, which tends more commonly to deceive than to enlighten.

In fact, while Ney was attacking, Murat scoured his flanks with his cavalry, without being able to bring it into action; woods on the left, and morasses on the right, obstructed his movements. But while they were fighting in front, both were anticipating the effect of a flanking march of the Westphalians, commanded by Junot.

From the Stubna, the high-road, in order to avoid the marshes formed by the various tributary streams of the Dnieper, turned off to the left, ascended the heights, and went farther from the basin of the river, to which it afterwards returned in a more favourable situation. It had been remarked that a by-road, bolder and shorter, as they all are, ran straight across these low marshy grounds, between the Dnieper and the high-road, which it rejoined behind the plateau of Valoutina.

It was this cross-road which Junot pursued after crossing the river at Prudiszy. It soon led him into the rear of the left of the Russians, upon the flank of the columns which were returning to the assistance of their rear-guard. His attack was all that was wanted to render the victory decisive. Those who were engaged in front with Marshal Ney would have been daunted at hearing an attack in their rear; while the uncertainty and disorder into which, in the midst of an action, it would have thrown the multitude of men, horses, and carriages, crowded together in one road, would have been irreparable; but Junot, though personally brave, was irresolute as a general. His responsibility alarmed him.

Meanwhile Murat, judging that he must have come up, was astonished at not hearing his attack. The firmness of the Russians opposed to Ney led him to suspect the truth. He left his cavalry, and crossing the woods and marshes almost alone, he hastened to Junot, and upbraided him with his inaction. Junot alleged in excuse, that "He had no orders to attack; his Wurtemberg cavalry was shy, its efforts feigned, and it would never be brought to charge the enemy's battalions."

These words Murat answered by actions. He rushed on at the head of that cavalry, which, with a different leader, were quite different troops; he urged them on, launched them against the Russians, overthrew their tirailleurs, returned to Junot and said to him, "Now finish the business: your glory and your marshal's staff are still before you!" He then left him to rejoin his own troops, and Junot, confounded, remained motionless. Too long about Napoleon, whose active genius directed every thing, both the plan and the details, he had learned only to obey: he wanted experience in command; besides, fatigue and wounds had made him an old man before his time.

That such a general should have been selected for so important a movement, was not at all surprising; it was well known that the emperor was attached to him both from habit, (for he was his oldest aid-de-camp) and from a secret foible, for as the presence of that officer was mixed up with all the recollections of his victories and his glory, he disliked to part from him. It is also reasonable to suppose that it flattered his vanity, to see men who were his pupils commanding his armies; and it was moreover natural that he should have a firmer alliance on their attachment, than on that of any others.

When, however, on the following day he inspected the places themselves, and, at the sight of the bridge where Gudin fell, made the remark, that it was not there he ought to have debouched; when afterwards gazing, with an angry look, on the position which Junot had occupied, he exclaimed: "It was there, no doubt, that the Westphalians should have attacked! all the battle was there! what was Junot about?" his irritation became so violent, that nothing could at first allay it. He called Rapp, and told him to take the command from the Duke of Abrantes:—he would dismiss him from the army! he had lost his marshal's staff without retrieve! this blunder would probably block the road to Moscow against them; that to him, Rapp, he should entrust the Westphalians; that he would speak to them in their own language, and he would know how to make them fight. But Rapp refused the place of his old companion in arms; he appeased the emperor, whose anger always subsided quickly, as soon as it had vented itself in words.

But it was not merely on his left that the enemy had a narrow escape from being conquered; on his right he had run a still greater risk. Morand, one of Davoust's generals, had been despatched from that side through the forests; he marched along woody heights, and was, from the commencement of the action, on the flank of the Russians. A few paces more, and he would have debouched in the rear of their right. His sudden appearance would have infallibly decided the victory, and rendered it complete; but Napoleon, unacquainted with the localities, ordered him to be recalled to the spot where Davoust and himself had stopped.

In the army, we could not help asking ourselves, why the emperor, in making three officers, independent of one another, combine for the same object, had not made a point of being on the spot, to give their movements the unity indispensable, and without him impossible.

He, on the contrary, had returned to Smolensk, either from fatigue, or chiefly from not expecting so serious an affair; or finally, because, from the necessity of attending to every thing at once, he could not be in time, or completely any where. In fact, the business of his empire and of Europe, having been suspended by the preceding days of activity, had accumulated. It was necessary to clear out his portfolios, and to give circulation to both civil and political affairs, which began to clog; it was, besides, urgent and glorious to date from Smolensk.

When, therefore, Borelli, second in command of Murat's staff, came to inform him of the battle of Valoutina, he hesitated about receiving him; and so deeply was he engaged in the business before him, that a minister had to interfere to procure that officer admittance. The report of this officer agitated Napoleon. "What say you?" he exclaimed: "what! you are not enough! the enemy shows 60,000 men! Then it is a battle!" and he began storming at the disobedience and inactivity of Junot. When Borelli informed him of Gudin's mortal wound, Napoleon's grief was violent; he gave vent to it in repeated questions and expressions of regret; then with that strength of mind which was peculiar to him, he subdued his uneasiness, postponed his anger, suspended his chagrin, and giving himself up wholly to his occupation, he deferred until the morrow the charge of battles, for night had come on; but afterwards the hopes of a battle roused him, and he appeared next morning with the day on the fields of Valoutina.

CHAPTER 31

The Russian People

Ney's troops, and those of Gudin's division, deprived of their general, had drawn up there on the corpses of their companions and of the Russians, amidst the stumps of broken trees, on ground trampled by the feet of the combatants, furrowed with balls, strewed with the fragments of weapons, tattered garments, military utensils, carriages overthrown, and scattered limbs; for such are the trophies of war, such the beauties of a field of victory!

Gudin's battalions appeared to be melted down to platoons; the more they were reduced, the prouder they seemed to be: close to them, one still breathed the smell of burnt cartridges and gunpowder, with which the ground and their apparel were impregnated, and their faces yet quite begrimed. The emperor could not pass along their front without having to avoid, to step over, or to tread upon carcases, and bayonets twisted by the violence of the shock. But over all these horrors he threw a veil of glory. His gratitude transformed this field of death into a field of triumph, where, for some hours, satisfied honour and ambition held exclusive sway.

He was sensible that it was high time to encourage his soldiers by commendations and rewards. Never, therefore, were his looks more kind; and as to his language, "this battle was the most glorious achievement in our military history; the soldiers who heard him were men with whom one might conquer the world; the slain, warriors who had died an immortal death." He spoke thus, well aware that it is more especially amid such destruction that men think of immortality.

He was profuse in his rewards; on the 12th, 21st, 127th of the line, and the 17th light, he conferred eighty-seven decorations and promotions; these were Gudin's regiments. The 127th had, before this, marched without an eagle; for at that time it was necessary for a regiment to earn its colours in a field of battle, to prove, that in the sequel it would know how to preserve them there.

The emperor delivered the eagle to it with his own hands; he also satisfied Ney's corps. His favours were as great in themselves as they were in their form. The value of the gift was enhanced by the manner in which he bestowed it. He was successively surrounded by each regiment as by a family. There he appealed in a loud voice to the officers, subalterns, and privates, inquiring who were the bravest of all those brave men, or the most successful, and recompensing them on the spot. The officers named, the soldiers confirmed, the emperor approved: thus, as he himself observed, the elections were made instantaneously, in a circle, in his presence, and confirmed with acclamations by the troops.

These paternal manners, which made the private soldier the military comrade of the ruler of Europe; these forms, which revived the still-regretted usages of the republic, delighted the troops. He was a monarch, but the monarch of the Revolution; and they could not but love a fortunate sovereign who led them on to fortune; in him there was every thing to excite, and nothing to reproach them.

Never did field of victory exhibit a spectacle more capable of exalting; the presentation of that eagle so richly merited, the pomp of these promotions, the shouts of joy, the glory of those warriors, recompensed on the very spot where it had just been acquired; their valour proclaimed by a voice, every accent of which rung throughout attentive Europe; by that great captain whose bulletins would carry their names over the whole world, and more especially among their countrymen, and into the bosoms of their families, which they would at once cheer and make proud: how many favours at once! they were absolutely intoxicated with them: he himself seemed at first to allow himself to share their transports.

But when he was out of sight of his troops, the attitude of Ney and Murat, and the words of Poniatowski, who was as frank and judicious in council as he was intrepid in the field, tranquillized him; and when the close heat of the day began to overpower him, and he learned from the reports that his men had proceeded eight leagues without overtaking the enemy, the spell was entirely dissolved. On his return to Smolensk, the jolting of his carriage over the relics of the fight, the stoppages caused on the road by the long file of the wounded who were crawling or being carried back, and in Smolensk itself by the tumbrels of amputated limbs about to be thrown away at a distance; in a word, all that is horrible and odious out of fields of battle, completely disarmed him. Smolensk was but one vast hospital, and the loud groans which issued from it drowned the shout of glory which had just been raised on the fields of Valoutina.

The reports of the surgeons were frightful: in that country a spirit distilled from grain is used instead of wine and brandy made from grapes. Narcotic plants are mixed with it. Our young soldiers, exhausted with hunger and fatigue, conceived that this liquor would cheer them; but its perfidious heat caused them to throw out at once all the fire that was yet left in them, after which they sank exhausted, and became the victims of disease.

Others, less sober, or more debilitated, were seized with dizziness, stupefaction, and torpor; they squatted into the ditches and on the roads. Their half-open, watery, and lack-lustre eyes seemed to watch, with insensibility, death gradually seizing their whole frame; they expired sullenly and without a groan.

At Wilna, it had not been possible to establish hospitals for more than six thousand sick: convents, churches, synagogues, and barns, served to receive the suffering multitude. In these dismal places, which were sometimes unhealthy, but still too few, and too crowded, the sick were frequently without food, without beds, without covering, and without even straw and medicines. The surgeons were inadequate to the duty, so that every thing, even to the very hospitals, contributed to create disease, and nothing to cure.

At Witepsk, 400 wounded Russians were left on the field of battle: 300 more were abandoned in the town by their army; and as the inhabitants had been taken away, these unfortunate wretches remained three days before they were discovered, without assistance, huddled together pell-mell, dead and dying, amidst the most horrible filth and infection: they were at length collected together and mixed with our own wounded, who, like those of the Russians, amounted to 700. Our surgeons tore up their very shirts, and those of these poor creatures, to dress them; for there already began to be a scarcity of linen.

When at length the wounds of these unfortunate men were healed, and they required nothing but wholesome food to complete their cure, they perished for want of sustenance: few either of the French or Russians escaped. Those who were prevented from going in quest of food by the loss of a limb, or by debility, were the first to sink. These disasters occurred wherever the emperor was not in person; his presence bringing, and his departure carrying, every thing along with it; and his orders, in fact, not being scrupulously obeyed but within the circle of his own observation.

At Smolensk, there was no want of hospitals; fifteen spacious brick buildings were rescued from the flames: there were even found some wine, brandy, and a few medical stores; and our reserve wagons for the wounded at length rejoined us: but every thing ran short. The surgeons were at work night and day, but the very second night, all the materials for dressing the wounded were exhausted: there was no more linen, and they were forced to use paper, found in the archives, in its stead. Parchment served for splinters, and coarse cloth for compresses; and they had no other substitute for lint than tow and birch down (*coton du bouleau*).

Our surgeons were overwhelmed with dismay: for three days an hospital of a hundred wounded had been forgotten; an accident led to its discovery: Rapp penetrated into that abode of despair. I will spare my reader the horror of a description. Wherefore communicate those terrible impressions which harrow up the soul? Rapp did not spare them to Napoleon, who instantly caused his own wine, and a sum of money, to be distributed among such of those unfortunate men as a tenacious life still animated, or whom a disgusting food had supported.

But to the vehement emotion which these reports excited in the bosom of the emperor, was superadded an alarming consideration. The conflagration of Smolensk was no longer, he saw, the effect of a fatal and unforeseen accident of war, nor even the result of an act of despair: it was the result of cool determination. The Russians had studied the time and means, and taken as great pains to destroy, as are usually taken to preserve.

The same day the courageous answers of one of their popes (the only one found in Smolensk,) enlightened him still more in regard to the blind fury which had been excited in the whole Russian nation. His interpreter, alarmed by this animosity, conducted the pope to the emperor. The venerable priest first reproached him, with firmness, for his alleged sacrilegious acts: he knew not that it was the Russian general himself who had caused the storehouses and churches to be set on fire, and who had accused us of these outrages, in order that the mercantile class and the peasantry might not separate their cause from that of the nobility.

The emperor listened attentively. "But," said he to him at last, "has your church been burned?"—"No, sire," replied the pope; "God will be more powerful than you; he will protect it, for I have opened it to all the unfortunate people whom the destruction of the city has deprived of a home!"—"You are right," rejoined Napoleon, with emotion, "yes, God will watch over the innocent victims of war; he will reward you for your courage. Go, worthy priest, return to your post. Had all your popes followed your example, they had not basely betrayed the mission of peace which they received from heaven; if they had not abandoned the temples which their presence alone renders sacred, my soldiers would have spared your holy edifices; for we are all Christians, and your God is our God."

With these words, Napoleon sent back the priest to his temple with an escort and some succours. A heart-rending shriek arose at the sight of the soldiers penetrating into this asylum. A crowd of terrified women and children thronged about the altar; but the pope, raising his voice, cried; "be of good cheer: I have seen Napoleon; I have spoken to him. Oh! how have we been deceived, my children! the emperor of France is not the man that he has been represented to you. Learn that he and his soldiers worship the same God as we do. The war which he wages is not religious, it is a political quarrel with our emperor. His soldiers fight only our soldiers. They do not slaughter, as we have been assured, old men, women, and children. Cheer up, then, and let us thank God for being relieved from the painful duty of hating them as heathen, impious wretches, and incendiaries!" The pope then commenced a hymn of thanks, in which they all joined with tearful eyes.

But these very words demonstrated how much the nation had been deceived. The rest of the inhabitants had fled. Henceforward, then, it was not their army alone, it was the population, it was all Russia, that fled before us. The emperor felt that, with this population, one of his most powerful engines of conquest was escaping from his hands.

CHAPTER 32

Petersburgh Rejected

Ever since our arrival at Witepsk, Napoleon had in fact employed two of his officers to sound the sentiments of these people. The object was, to instil into them notions of liberty, and to compromise them in our cause by an insurrection more or less general. But there had been nothing to work upon excepting a few straggling savage boors, whom the Russians had perhaps left as spies amongst us. This attempt had only served to betray his plan, and to put the Russians on their guard against it.

This expedient, moreover, was repugnant to Napoleon, whose nature inclined him much more to the cause of kings than to that of nations. He employed it but carelessly. Subsequently, at Moscow, he received several addresses from different heads of families. They complained that they were treated by the nobility like herds of cattle, which they might sell or barter away at pleasure. They solicited Napoleon to proclaim the abolition of slavery, and in the event of his doing so, they offered to head partial insurrections, which they promised speedily to render general.

These offers were rejected. We should have seen, among a barbarous people, a barbarous liberty, an ungovernable, a horrible licentiousness: a few partial revolts had formerly furnished the standard of them. The Russian nobles, like the planters of St. Domingo, would have been ruined. The fear of this prevailed in the mind of Napoleon, and was confessed by him; it induced him to give up, for a time, all attempts to excite a movement which he could not have regulated.

Besides, these masters had conceived a distrust of their slaves. Amidst so many dangers, they distinguished this as the most urgent. They first wrought upon the minds of their unfortunate serfs, debased by all sorts of servitude. Their priests, whom they are accustomed to believe, imposed upon them by delusive language; they persuaded these peasants that we were legions of devils, commanded by Antichrist, infernal spirits, whose very look would excite horror, and whose touch would contaminate. Such of our prisoners as fell into their hands, remarked that these poor creatures would not again make use of the vessels which they had used, and that they reserved them for the most filthy animals.

As we advanced, however, our presence would have refuted all these clumsy fables. But behold! these nobles fell back with their serfs into the interior of the country, as at the approach of a dire contagion. Property, habitations, all that could detain them, and be serviceable to us, were sacrificed. They interposed famine, fire, and the desert, between them and us; for it was as much against their serfs as against Napoleon that this mighty resolution was executed. It was no longer, therefore, a war of kings that was to be prosecuted, but a war of class, a war of party, a war of religion, a national war, a combination of all sorts of war.

The emperor then first perceived the enormous magnitude of his enterprise; the farther he advanced, the more it became magnified. So long as he only encountered kings, to him, who was greater than all of them, their defeats were but sport; but the kings being conquered, he had now to do with people; and it was another Spain, but remote, barren, infinite, that he had found at the opposite extremity of Europe. He was daunted, hesitated, and paused.

At Witepsk, whatever resolution he might have taken, he wanted Smolensk, and till he should be at Smolensk, he seemed to have deferred coming to any determination. For this reason he was again seized with the same perplexity: it was now more embarrassing, as the flames, the prevalent epidemic, and the victims which surrounded him, had aggravated every thing; a fever of hesitation attacked him; his eyes turned towards Kief, Petersburgh, and Moscow.

At Kief he should envelop Tchitchakof and his army; he should rid the right flank and the rear of the grand army, of annoyance; he should cover the Polish provinces most productive of men, provisions, and horses; while fortified cantonments at Mohilef, Smolensk, Witepsk, Polotsk, Dünabourg, and Riga, would defend the rest. Behind this line, and during the winter, he might raise and organize all ancient Poland, and hurl it in the spring upon Russia, oppose nation to nation, and render the war equal.

At Smolensk, however, he was at the point where the Petersburgh and Moscow roads meet, 29 marches from the first of these capitals, and 15 from the other. In Petersburgh, the centre of the government, the knot to which all the threads of the administration were united, the brain of Russia, were her military and naval arsenals; in short, it was the only point of communication between Russia and England, of which he should possess himself. The victory of Polotsk, of which he had just received intelligence, seemed to urge him in that direction. By marching in concert with Saint-Cyr upon Petersburgh, he should envelop Wittgenstein, and cause Riga to fall before Macdonald.

On the other hand, in Moscow, it was the nobility, as well as the nation, that he should attack in its property, in its ancient honour; the road to that capital was shorter; it presented fewer obstacles and more resources; the Russian main army, which he could not neglect, and which he must destroy, was there, together with the chances of a battle, and the hope of giving a shock to the nation, by striking at its heart in this national war.

Of these three plans the latter appeared to him the only one practicable, in spite of the advancing season. The history of Charles XII. was, nevertheless, before his eyes; not that of Voltaire, which he had just thrown aside with impatience, judging it to be romantic and inaccurate, but the journal of Adlerfield, which he read, but which did not stop him. On comparing that expedition with his own, he found a thousand differences between them, on which he laid great stress; for who can be a judge in his own cause? and of what use is the example of the past, in a world where there never were two men, two things, or two situations exactly alike?

At any rate, about this period the name of Charles XII. was frequently heard to drop from his lips.

CHAPTER 33

Polotsk

But the news which arrived from all quarters excited his ardour quite as much as it had been at Witepsk. His lieutenants seemed to have done more than himself: the actions of Mohilef, Molodeczna, and Valoutina, were regular battles, in which Davoust, Schwartzenberg, and Ney, were conquerors; on his right, his line of operation seemed to be covered; the enemy's army was flying before him; on his left, the Duke of Reggio, after drawing Wittgenstein upon Polotsk, was attacked at Slowna, on the 17th of August. The attack of Wittgenstein was furious and obstinate; it failed; but he retained his offensive position, and Marshal Oudinot had been wounded. Saint-Cyr succeeded him in the command of that army, composed of about 30,000 French, Swiss, and Bavarians. The very next day this general, who disliked any command unless when he exercised it alone and in chief, availed himself of it, to give his measure to his own troops and to the enemy; but coolly, according to his character, and combining every thing.

From daybreak till five in the evening, he contrived to amuse the enemy by the proposal of an agreement to withdraw the wounded, and more especially by demonstrations of retreat. At the same time he silently rallied all his combatants, drew them up into three columns of attack, and concealed them behind the village of Spas and rising grounds.

At five o'clock, all being ready, and Wittgenstein's vigilance asleep, Saint-Cyr gave the signal: his artillery immediately began firing, and his columns rushed forward. The Russians, being taken by surprise, resisted in vain; their right was first broken, and their centre soon fled in disorder: they abandoned 1000 prisoners, 20 pieces of cannon, a field of battle covered with slain, and the offensive, which Saint-Cyr, being too weak, could only affect to resume, for the purpose of better defending himself.

In this short but severe and sanguinary conflict, the right wing of the Russians, which was supported by the Düna, made an obstinate resistance. It was necessary to charge it with the bayonet, amidst a thick fire of grape-shot; every thing succeeded, but when it was supposed that there was no more to do but to pursue, all was nearly lost; some Russian dragoons, according to some, and horse-guards, according to others, risked a charge on a battery of Saint-Cyr's; a French brigade placed to support it advanced, then suddenly turned its back and fled through the midst of our cannon, which it prevented from being fired. The Russians reached them pell-mell with our men; they sabred the gunners, upset the pieces, and pursued our horse so closely, that the latter, more and more terrified, ran in disorder upon their commander-in-chief and his staff, whom they overthrew. General Saint-Cyr was obliged to fly on foot. He threw himself into the bottom of a ravine, which sheltered him from the squall. The Russian dragoons were already close to Polotsk, when a prompt and skilful manoeuvre of Berkheim and the 4th French cuirassiers put an end to this warm affair. The Russians betook themselves to the woods.

The following day Saint-Cyr sent a body of men in pursuit of them, but merely to observe their retreat, to mark the victory, and to reap some more of its fruits. During the two succeeding months, up to the 18th of October, Wittgenstein kept at a respectful distance. The French general, on his part, confined his attention to observing the enemy, keeping up his communications with Macdonald, with Witepsk, and Smolensk, fortifying himself in his position of Polotsk, and, above all, finding there means of subsistence.

In this action of the 18th, four generals, four colonels, and many officers, were wounded. Among them the army remarked the Bavarian Generals Deroy and Liben. They expired on the 22nd of August. These generals were of the same age; they had belonged to the same regiment, had made the same campaigns, proceeded at nearly an equal pace in their perilous career, which was gloriously terminated by the same death, and in the same battle. It was thought right not to separate in the tomb these warriors, whom neither life nor death had been able to part; one grave received the remains of both.

On the news of this victory, the emperor sent to General Saint-Cyr the staff of Marshal of the empire. He placed a great number of crosses at his disposal, and subsequently approved most of the promotions which were applied for.

Notwithstanding this success, the determination to proceed beyond Smolensk was too perilous for Napoleon to decide on it alone: it was requisite that he should contrive to be drawn into it. Beyond Valoutina, Ney's corps, which was fatigued, had been replaced by that of Davoust. Murat as king, as brother-in-law to the emperor, and agreeably to his order, was to command it. Ney had submitted to this, less from condescension than from conformity of disposition. They agreed in their ardour.

But Davoust, whose methodical and tenacious genius was a complete contrast to the fiery impetuosity of Murat, and who was rendered proud by the remembrance of, and the titles derived from two great victories, was piqued at being placed in this dependence. These haughty chiefs, who were about the same age, had been companions in war, and had mutually witnessed each other's elevation; they were both spoiled by the habit of having obeyed only a great man, and were by no means fit to command one another; Murat, in particular, who was too often unable to command himself.

Davoust nevertheless obeyed, but with an ill grace, and imperfectly, as wounded pride generally does. He affected immediately to break off all direct correspondence with the emperor. The latter, surprised at this, ordered him to renew it, alleging his distrust of the reports of Murat. Davoust made a handle of this avowal, and again asserted his independence. Henceforward the vanguard had two leaders. Thus the emperor, fatigued, distressed, overloaded with business of every kind, and forced to show indulgence to his lieutenants, divided his power as well as his armies, in spite of his precepts and his former examples. Circumstances, which he had so often controlled, became stronger than him, and controlled him in their turn.

Meanwhile Barclay, having fallen back without resistance nearly as far as Dorogobouje, Murat had no need of Davoust, and no occasion presented itself for misunderstanding; but about eleven in the forenoon of the 23rd of August, a thick wood, a few *wersts* from that town, which the king wished to reconnoitre, was warmly disputed with him: he was obliged to carry it twice.

Murat, surprised at such a resistance at that early hour, pushed on, and piercing through this curtain, beheld the whole Russian army drawn up in order of battle. The narrow ravine of the Luja separated him from it: it was noon; the extent of the Russian lines, especially towards our right, the preparations, the hour, the place, which was that where Barclay had just rejoined Bagration; the choice of the ground, well suited for a general engagement; all gave him reason to anticipate a battle; and he sent a dispatch to the emperor to apprise him of it.

At the same time he ordered Montbrun to pass the ravine on his right with his cavalry, in order to reconnoitre and get upon the left of the enemy. Davoust, and his five divisions of infantry, extended themselves on that side; he protected Montbrun: the king recalled them to his left, on the high-road, designing, it is said, to support Montbrun's flank movement by some demonstrations in front.

Davoust replied, that "This would be sacrificing our right wing, through which the enemy would get behind us on the high-road, our only means of retreat; that thus he would force us to a battle, which he, Davoust, had orders to avoid, and which he would avoid, his force being insufficient, the position bad, and he being moreover under the command of a leader in whom he had but little confidence." He then wrote immediately to Napoleon, urging him to come up without loss of time, if he would not have Murat engage without him.

On this intelligence, which he received in the night of the 24th of August, Napoleon joyfully threw aside his indecision, which to this enterprising and decisive genius was absolute torture: he hurried forward with his guard, and proceeded twelve leagues without halting; but on the evening of the preceding day, the enemy's army had again disappeared.

On our side, his retreat was attributed to the movement of Montbrun; on the part of the Russians to Barclay, and to a bad position chosen by the chief of his staff, who had taken up ground in his own disfavour, instead of making it serve to his advantage. Bagration was the first who perceived it; his rage knew no bounds, and he proclaimed it treason.

Discord reigned in the Russian camp as well as in our advanced guard. Confidence in their commander, that strength of armies, was wanting; his every step seemed a blunder; each resolution that was taken the very worst. The loss of Smolensk had soured all; the junction of the two *corps d'armée* increased the evil; the stronger the Russian force felt itself, the weaker did its general seem to it. The outcry became general; another leader was loudly called for. A few prudent men, however, interposed: Kutusoff was announced, and the humbled pride of the Russians awaited him in order to fight.

The emperor, on his part, already at Dorogobouje, no longer hesitated; he knew that he carried every where with him the fate of Europe; that wherever he might be, that would always be the place where the destiny of nations would be decided; that he might therefore advance, fearless of the threatening consequences of the defection of the Swedes and Turks. Thus he neglected the hostile armies of Essen at Riga, of Wittgenstein before Polotsk, of Ertell before Bobruisk, and of Tchitchakof in Volhynia. They consisted of 120,000 men, whose number could not but keep gradually augmenting; he passed them, and suffered himself to be surrounded by them with indifference, assured that all these vain obstacles of war and policy would be swept away by the very first thunderbolt which he should launch.

And yet, his column of attack, which was 185,000 strong at his departure from Witepsk, was already reduced to 157,000; it was diminished by 28,000 men, half of whom occupied Witepsk, Orcha, Mohilef, and Smolensk. The rest had been killed or wounded, or were straggling, and plundering in his rear our allies and the French themselves.

But 157,000 men were sufficient to destroy the Russian army by a complete victory, and to take Moscow. As to his base of operation, notwithstanding the 120,000 Russians by whom it was threatened, it appeared to be secure. Lithuania, the Düna, the Dnieper, and lastly Smolensk, were or would soon be covered towards Riga and Dünabourg by Macdonald and 32,000 men; towards Polotsk, by Saint-Cyr, with 30,000; at Witepsk, Smolensk, and Mohilef, by Victor and 40,000; before Bobruisk, by Dombrowski and 12,000; and on the Bug by Schwartzenberg and Regnier, at the head of 45,000 men. Napoleon reckoned besides on the divisions of Loison and Durutte, 22,000 strong, which were already approaching Königsberg and Warsaw; and on reinforcements to the amount of 80,000, all of which would enter Russia before the middle of November.

He should thus have 280,000 men, including the Lithuanian and Polish levies, to support him, while, with 155,000 more, he made an incursion of 93 leagues; for such was the distance between Smolensk and Moscow.

But these 280,000 men were commanded by six different leaders, all independent of each other, and the most elevated of them, he who occupied the centre, and who seemed to be appointed to act as an intermediate link, to give some unity to the operations of the other five, was a minister of peace, and not of war. Besides, the same causes which had already diminished, by one-third, the French forces which first entered Russia, could not fail to disperse or to destroy a still greater proportion of all these reinforcements. Most of them were coming by detachments, formed provisionally into marching battalions under officers new to them, whom they were to leave the first day, without the incentive of discipline, *esprit de corps*, or glory, and traversing an exhausted country, which the season and the climate would be rendering daily more bare and more rude.

Meanwhile Napoleon beheld Dorogobouje in ashes, like Smolensk, especially the quarter of the merchants, those who had most to lose, whom their riches might have detained or brought back amongst us, and who, from their situation, formed a kind of intermediate class, a commencement of the third estate, which liberty was likely to seduce.

He was perfectly aware that he was quitting Smolensk, as he had come thither, with the hope of a battle, which the indecision and discord of the Russian generals had as yet deferred; but his resolution was taken; he would hear of nothing but what was calculated to support him in it. He persisted in pursuing the track of the enemy; his hardihood increased with their prudence; their circumspection he called pusillanimity, their retreat flight; he despised, that he might hope.

CHAPTER 34

Provisions

The emperor had proceeded with such expedition to Dorogobouje, that he was obliged to halt there, in order to wait for his army, and to leave Murat to pursue the enemy. He set out again on the 26th of August; the army marched in three columns abreast; the Emperor, Murat, Davoust, and Ney in the centre, on the high-road to Moscow; Poniatowski on the right; and the army of Italy on the left.

The principal column, that of the centre, found nothing on a road where its advanced guard itself had to subsist entirely on the leavings of the Russians; it could not digress from its direction, for want of time, in so rapid a march. Besides, the columns on the right and left consumed every thing on either side of it. In order to live better, it ought to have set out later every day, halted earlier, and then extended itself more on its flanks during the night; which could be done without imprudence when the enemy was so near at hand.

At Smolensk orders had been issued, as at Witepsk, to take, at starting, provisions for several days. The emperor was aware of the difficulty of collecting them, but he reckoned upon the diligence of the officers and the troops; they had warning,—that was sufficient; they would contrive to provide themselves with necessaries. They had acquired the habit of doing so; and it was really a curious sight to observe the voluntary and continual efforts of so many men to follow a single individual to such great distances. The existence of the army was a prodigy that was daily renewed, by the active, industrious, and intelligent spirit of the French and Polish troops, by their habit of surmounting all difficulties, and by their fondness for the hazards and irregularities of this dreadful game of an adventurous life.

In the train of each regiment there were a multitude of those diminutive horses with which Poland swarms, a great number of carts of the country, which required to be incessantly replaced with fresh ones, and a drove of cattle. The baggage-wagons were driven by soldiers, for they turned their hands to every trade. They were missed in the ranks, it is true; but here the want of provisions, the necessity for transporting every thing with them, excused this prodigious train: it required a second army, as it were, to carry or draw what was indispensable for the first.

In this prompt organization, adopted while marching, the army had accommodated itself to all the local customs and difficulties; the genius of the soldiers had admirably made the most of the scanty resources of the country. As to the officers, as the general orders always took for granted regular distributions which were never made, each of them, according to the degree of his zeal, intelligence, and firmness, appropriated to himself more or less of this spoil, and had converted individual pillage into regular contributions.

For it was only by excursions on the flanks and into an unknown country that any provisions could be procured. Every evening, when the army halted, and the bivouacs were established, detachments, rarely commanded by divisions, sometimes by brigades, and most commonly by regiments, went in quest of necessaries, and penetrated into the country; a few *wersts* from the road they found all the villages inhabited, and were not very hostilely received; but as they could not make themselves understood, and besides wanted every thing, and that instantaneously, the peasants were soon seized with a panic and fled into the woods, whence they issued again as no very formidable partisans.

The detachments meanwhile plentifully regaled themselves, and rejoined their corps next day or some days afterwards, laden with all that they had collected; and it frequently happened that they were plundered in their turn by their comrades belonging to the other corps whom they chanced to fall in with. Hence animosities, which would have infallibly led to most sanguinary intestine conflicts, had not all been subsequently overtaken by the same misfortune, and involved in the horrors of a common disaster.

Till the return of their detachments, the soldiers who remained with their eagles lived on what they could find on the military route; in general it consisted of new rye, which they bruised and boiled. Owing to the cattle which followed, there was less want of meat than of bread; but the length, and especially the rapidity of the marches, occasioned the loss of many of these animals: they were suffocated by the heat and dust; when, therefore, they came to water, they ran into it with such fury, that many of them were drowned, while others drank so immoderately, as to swell themselves out till they were unable to walk.

It was remarked, as before we reached Smolensk, that the divisions of the first corps continued to be the most numerous; their detachments, better disciplined, brought back more, and did less injury to the inhabitants. Those who remained with their colours lived on the contents of their knapsacks, the regular appearance of which relieved the eye, fatigued with a disorder that was nearly universal.

Each of these knapsacks, reduced to what was strictly necessary in point of apparel, contained two shirts, two pair of shoes with nails, and a pair of extra soles, a pair of pantaloons and half-gaiters of cloth; a few articles requisite to cleanliness, a bandage, and a quantity of lint, and sixty cartridges.

In the two sides were placed four biscuits of sixteen ounces each; under these, and at the bottom, was a long, narrow, linen bag, filled with ten pounds of flour. The whole knapsack and its contents, together with the straps and the hood, rolled up and fastened at top, weighed thirty-three pounds twelve ounces.

Each soldier carried also a linen bag, slung in form of a shoulder-belt, containing two loaves of three pounds each. Thus with his sabre, his loaded knapsack, three flints, his turn-screw, his belt and musket, he had to carry fifty-eight pounds weight, and was provided with bread for four days, biscuit for four, flour for seven, and sixty rounds of ammunition.

Behind it were carriages laden with provisions for six more days; but it was impossible to reckon with confidence on these vehicles, picked up on the spot, which would have been so convenient in any other country with a smaller army, and in a more regular war.

When the flour-bag was emptied, it was filled with any corn that could be found, and which was ground at the first mill, if any chanced to be met with; if not, by the hand-mills which followed the regiments, or which were found in the villages, for the Russians are scarcely acquainted with any others. It took sixteen men twelve hours to grind in one of them the corn necessary for one hundred and thirty men for one day.

As every house in this country has an oven, little want was felt on that score; bakers abounded; for the regiments of the first corps contained men of all trades, so that articles of food and clothing were all made or repaired by them during the march. They were colonies uniting the character of civilized and nomadic. The emperor had first conceived the idea, which the genius of the prince of Eckmühl had appropriated; he had every thing he wanted, time, place, and men to carry it into execution; but these three elements of success were less at the disposal of the other chiefs. Besides, their characters being more impetuous and less methodical, would scarcely have derived the same advantages from it; with a less organizing genius, they would therefore have had more obstacles to surmount; the emperor had not paid sufficient attention to these differences, which were productive of baneful effects.

Chapter 35
Murat & Davoust

It was from Slawkowo, a few leagues beyond Dorogobouje, that Napoleon sent orders, on the 27th of August, to marshal Victor, who was then on the Niemen, to advance to Smolensk. This marshal's left was to occupy Witepsk, his right Mohilef, and his centre Smolensk. There he would succour Saint-Cyr, in case of need, serve for a point of support to the army of Moscow, and keep up his communications with Lithuania.

It was also from the same imperial head-quarters that he published the details of his review at Valoutina, with the intention of proclaiming to the present and future ages the names even of the private soldiers who had there distinguished themselves. But he added, that at Smolensk "the conduct of the Poles had astonished the Russians, who had been accustomed to despise them." These words drew from the Poles an outcry of indignation, and the emperor smiled at an anger which he had foreseen, and the effects of which were designed to fall exclusively on the Russians.

On this march he took delight in dating from the heart of Old Russia a number of decrees, which would be circulated in the meanest hamlets of France; from the desire of appearing to be present every where at once, and filling the earth more and more with his power: the offspring of that inconceivable and expanding greatness of soul, whose ambition was at first a mere plaything, but finally coveted the empire of the world.

It is true that at the same time there was so little order about him at Slawkowo, that his guard burned, during the night, to warm themselves, the bridge which they were ordered to guard, and the only one by which he could, the next day, leave his imperial quarters. This disorder, however, like many others, proceeded not from insubordination, but from thoughtlessness; it was corrected as soon as it was perceived.

The very same day Murat drove the enemy beyond the Osma, a narrow river, but enclosed with high banks, and of great depth, like most of the rivers of this country, the effect of the snow, and which, at the period of its general melting, prevents inundations. The Russian rear-guard, covered by this obstacle, faced about and established itself on the heights of the opposite bank. Murat ordered the ravine to be examined, and a ford was discovered. It was through this narrow and insecure defile that he dared to march against the Russians, to venture between the river and their position; thus cutting off from himself all retreat, and turning a skirmish into a desperate action. In fact, the enemy descended in force from their height, and drove him back to the very brink of the ravine, into which they had well-nigh precipitated him. But Murat persisted in his error; he braved it out, and converted it into a success. The 4th lancers carried the position, and the Russians went to pass the night not far off; content with having made us purchase at a dear rate a quarter of a league of ground, which they would have given up to us for nothing during the night.

At the moment of the most imminent danger, a battery of the prince of Eckmühl twice refused to fire. Its commanding officer pleaded his instructions, which forbade him, upon pain of being broke, to fight without orders from Davoust. These orders arrived, in time, according to some, but too late according to others. I relate this incident, because, on the following day, it was the occasion of a violent quarrel between Murat and Davoust, in presence of the emperor, at Semlewo.

The king reproached the prince with his tardy circumspection, and more especially with an enmity which dated from the expedition to Egypt. In the vehemence of his passion he told him, that if there was any quarrel between them they ought to settle it by themselves, but that the army ought not to be made the sufferers for it.

Davoust, irritated in his turn, accused the king of temerity; according to him "his thoughtless ardour was incessantly compromising his troops, and wasting to no purpose, their lives, their strength, and their stores. It was right that the emperor should at last know what was daily occurring in his advanced guard. Every morning the enemy had disappeared before it; but this experience led to no alteration whatever in the march: the troops, therefore, set out late, all keeping the high-road, and forming a single column, and in this manner they advanced in the void till about noon.

"The enemy's rear-guard, ready to fight, was then discovered behind some marshy ravine, the bridges over which had been broken down, and which was commanded from the opposite bank. The light troops were instantly brought into action, then the first regiments of cavalry that were at hand, and then the artillery; but in general out of reach, or against straggling Cossacks, who were not worth the trouble. At length, after vain and sanguinary attempts made in front, the king took it into his head to reconnoitre the force and position of the enemy more accurately, and to manoeuvre; and he sent for the infantry.

"Then after having long waited in this endless column, the ravine was crossed on the left or on the right of the Russians, who retired under a fire of their small arms to a new position; where the same resistance, and the same mode of march and attack, exposed us to the same losses and the same delays.

"In this manner the king went on from position to position, till he came to one which was stronger or better defended. It was usually about five in the evening, sometimes later, rarely earlier; but in this case the tenacity of the Russians, and the hour, plainly indicated that their whole army was there, and was determined to pass the night on the spot.

"For it could not be denied that this retreat of the Russians was conducted with admirable order. The ground alone dictated it to them and not Murat. Their positions were so well chosen, taken so seasonably, and each defended so exactly in proportion to its strength, and the time which their general wished to gain, that in truth their movements seemed to form part of a plan which had been long determined on, carefully traced, and executed with scrupulous exactness.

"They never abandoned a post till the moment before they were likely to be driven from it.

"In the evening they established themselves early in a good position, leaving under arms no more troops than were absolutely necessary to defend it, while the remainder rested and refreshed themselves."

Davoust added that, "so far from profiting by this example, the king paid no regard either to the hour, the strength of the situation, or the resistance; that he dashed on among his tirailleurs, dancing about in front of the enemy's line, feeling it in every part; putting himself in a passion, giving his orders with loud shouts, and making himself hoarse with repeating them; exhausting every thing, cartouche-boxes, ammunition-wagons, men and horses, combatants and non-combatants, and keeping all the troops under arms till night had set in.

"Then, indeed, it was found necessary to desist, and to take up their quarters where they were; but they no longer knew where to find necessaries. It was really pitiful to hear the soldiers wandering in the dark, groping about, as it were, for forage, water, wood, straw, and provisions, and then, unable to find their bivouacs again, calling out to one another lest they should lose themselves, during the whole night. Scarcely had they time, not to sleep, but to prepare their food. Overwhelmed with fatigue, they cursed the hardships they had to endure, till daylight and the enemy came to rouse them again.

"It was not the advanced guard alone that suffered in this manner, but the whole of the cavalry. Every evening Murat had left behind him 20,000 men on horseback and under arms, on the high-road. This long column had remained all day without eating or drinking, amidst a cloud of dust, under a burning sky; ignorant of what was passing before it, advancing a few paces from one quarter of an hour to another, then halting to deploy among fields of rye, but without daring to take off the bridles and to allow their famished horses to feed, because the king kept them incessantly on the alert. It was to advance five or six leagues that they thus passed sixteen tedious hours—particularly arduous for the cuirassier horses, which had more to carry than the others, though weaker, as the largest horses in general are, and which required more food; hence their great carcasses were worn down to skeletons, their flanks collapsed, they crawled rather than walked, and every moment one was seen staggering, and another falling under his rider, who left him to his fate."

Davoust concluded with saying, that "in this manner the whole of the cavalry would perish; Murat, however, might dispose of that as he pleased, but as for the infantry of the first corps, so long as he had the command of it, he would not suffer it to be thrown away in that manner."

The king was not backward in replying. While the emperor was listening to them, he was at the same time playing with a Russian ball, which he kicked about with his foot. It seemed as if there was something in the misunderstanding between these chiefs which did not displease him. He attributed their animosity entirely to their ardour, well aware that of all passions glory is the most jealous.

The impatient ardour of Murat gratified his own. As the troops had nothing to live upon but what they found, every thing was consumed at the moment; for this reason it was necessary to make short work with the enemy, and to proceed rapidly. Besides, the general crisis in Europe was too strong, his situation too critical to remain there, and himself too impatient; he wished to bring matters to a close at any rate, in order to extricate himself.

The impetuosity of the king, therefore, seemed to suit his anxiety better than the methodical prudence of the Prince of Eckmühl. Accordingly, when he dismissed them, he said mildly to Davoust, that "one person could not possess every species of merit; that he knew better how to fight a battle than to push a rear-guard; and that if Murat had pursued Bagration in Lithuania, he would probably not have allowed him to escape." It is even asserted that he reproached the marshal with a restless disposition, an anxiety to appropriate to himself all the commands; less, indeed, from ambition than zeal, and that all might go on better; but yet this zeal had its inconveniences. He then sent them away with an injunction to agree better in future.

The two chiefs returned to their commands, and to their animosity. As the war was confined to the head of the column, that also was the scene of their disputes.

Chapter 36
Gjatz

On the 28th of August, the army crossed the vast plains of the government of Wiazma: it marched in all haste, the whole together, through fields, and several regiments abreast, each forming a short, close column. The high-road was left for the artillery, its wagons, and those carrying the sick and wounded. The emperor, on horseback, was seen every where: Murat's letters, and the approach to Wiazma, deceived him once more with the hope of a battle: he was heard calculating on the march the thousands of cannon-balls which he would require to crush the hostile army.

Napoleon had assigned its place to the baggage: he published an order for burning all vehicles which should be seen among the troops, not excepting carts loaded with provisions, for they might embarrass the movements of the columns, and compromise their safety in case of attack. Having met in his way with the carriage of General Narbonne, his aid-de-camp, he himself caused it to be set on fire, before the face of that general, and that instantaneously, without suffering it to be emptied; an order which was only severe, although it appeared harsh, because he himself began by enforcing its execution, which, however, was not followed up.

The baggage of all the corps was therefore assembled in the rear of the army: there was, from Dorogobouje, a long train of bat-horses and *kibitks*, harnessed with ropes; these vehicles were laden with booty, provisions, military effects, men appointed to take care of them; lastly, sick soldiers, and the arms of both, which were rusting in them. In this column were seen many of the tall dismounted cuirassiers, bestriding horses no bigger than our asses, because they could not follow on foot for want of practice and of boots. On this confused and disorderly multitude, as well as on most of the marauders on our flanks, the Cossacks might have made successful *coups de main*. They would thereby have harassed the army, and retarded its march, but Barclay seemed fearful of discouraging us: he put out his strength only against our advanced guard, and that but just sufficiently to slacken without stopping our progress.

This determination of Barclay's, the declining strength of the army, the quarrels between its chiefs, the approach of the decisive moment, gave uneasiness to Napoleon. At Dresden, at Witepsk, and even at Smolensk, he had hoped in vain for a communication from Alexander. At Ribky, on the 28th of August, he appeared to solicit one: a letter from Berthier to Barclay, in no other respect worthy of notice, concluded with these words: "The emperor directs me to request you to present his compliments to the emperor Alexander; tell him that neither the vicissitudes of war, nor any other circumstance, can diminish the friendship which he feels for him."

The same day, the 28th of August, the advanced-guard drove back the Russians as far as Wiazma; the army, thirsty from the march, the heat and the dust, was in want of water; the troops disputed the possession of a few muddy pools, and fought near the springs, which were soon rendered turbid and exhausted; the emperor himself was forced to put up with this muddy beverage.

During the night, the enemy destroyed the bridges over the Wiazma, plundered that town, and set it on fire. Murat and Davoust precipitately advanced to extinguish the flames. The enemy defended his conflagration, but the Wiazma was fordable near the ruins of the bridges: one part of the advanced-guard then attacked the incendiaries, and the other the fire, which they speedily subdued.

On this occasion some chosen men were sent to the advanced-guard, with orders to watch the enemy closely at Wiazma, and ascertain whether they, or our soldiers, were the real incendiaries. Their report entirely dissipated the doubts which the emperor might still have entertained as to the fatal resolution of the Russians. They found in this town some resources, which pillage would soon have wasted. In passing through the city, the emperor observed this disorder: he was exceedingly incensed, rode into the midst of the groups of soldiers, caused a suttler to be seized, and ordered him to be instantly tried and shot. But the meaning of the phrase from his lips was well known; it was known, also that the more vehement his paroxysms of anger, the sooner they were followed by indulgence. A moment afterwards, they, therefore, merely placed in his way the unfortunate man on his knees, with a woman and several children beside him, whom they passed off for his family. The emperor, who had already cooled, inquired what they wanted, and caused the man to be set at liberty.

He was still on horseback, when he saw Belliard, for fifteen years the companion in war of Murat, and then the chief of his staff, coming towards him. Surprised at seeing him, the emperor fancied some misfortune had happened. Belliard first relieved his apprehensions, and then added, that "Beyond the Wiazma, behind a ravine, on an advantageous position, the enemy had shown himself in force and ready for battle; that the cavalry on both sides immediately engaged, and as the infantry became necessary, the king in person put himself at the head of one of Davoust's divisions, and drew it out to lead it against the enemy; but that the marshal hastened up, calling to his men to halt, loudly censuring that manoeuvre, harshly reproaching the king for it, and forbidding his generals to obey him: that Murat then appealed to his dignity, to his military rank, to the exigency of the occasion, but in vain; that, finally, he had sent to declare to the emperor his disgust for a command so contested, and to tell him that he must choose between him and Davoust."

This intelligence threw Napoleon into a passion: he exclaimed, that "Davoust was unmindful of all subordination; that he forgot the respect due to his brother-in-law, to him whom he had appointed his lieutenant;" and he sent Berthier with orders that Compans' division, the same which had been the subject of the altercation, should be thenceforward under the command of the king. Davoust did not defend the manner, but merely the motive of his act, either from prejudice against the habitual temerity of the king, from spleen, or that he was a better judge of the ground, and the manoeuvre adapted to it, which is very possible.

Meanwhile the combat had finished, and Murat, whose attention was no longer diverted by the enemy, was wholly occupied with the thoughts of his quarrel. Shut up with Belliard, and hiding himself in a manner in his tent, as his memory recalled the expressions of the marshal, his blood became more and more inflamed with shame and rage. "He had been set at defiance, and publicly insulted, and Davoust still lived! What did he care for the anger of the emperor, and for his decision? it was for him to revenge his own wrong! What signified his rank? it was his sword alone that had made him a king, and it was to that alone he should appeal!" He was already snatching up his arms to go and attack Davoust, when Belliard stopped him, by urging existing circumstances, the example he ought to set to the army, the enemy to be pursued, and that it would be wrong to distress his friends and delight the foe by so desperate a proceeding.

The general says, that he then saw the king curse his crown, and strive to swallow the affront; but that tears of spite rolled down his cheeks and fell upon his clothes. Whilst he was thus tormenting himself, Davoust, obstinately persisting in his opinion, said that the emperor was misinformed, and remained quietly in his head-quarters.

Napoleon returned to Wiazma, where he was obliged to stop to ascertain the advantages that he might derive from his new conquest. The accounts which he received from the interior of Russia, represented the hostile government as appropriating to itself our successes, and inculcating the belief that the loss of so many provinces was the effect of a general plan of retreat, adopted beforehand. Papers seized at Wiazma stated that *Te Deum* had been sung at Petersburgh for pretended victories at Witepsk or Smolensk. "What!" he exclaimed in astonishment, "*Te Deum!* Dare they then lie to God as well as to men?"

For the rest, most of the intercepted Russian letters expressed the same astonishment. "While our villages are blazing," said they, "we hear nothing here but the ringing of bells, hymns of thanksgiving, and triumphant reports. It seems as if they would make us thank God for the victories of the French. Thus there is lying in the air, lying on earth, lying in words and in writing, lying to Heaven and earth, lying in every thing. Our great men treat Russia like a child, but there is no small degree of credulity in believing us to be so credulous."

Very just reflections, if means so gross had been employed to deceive those who were capable of writing such letters. At any rate, though these political falsehoods are generally resorted to, it was plain that when carried to such excess, they were a satire either on the governors or the governed, and, perhaps, on both.

During this time the advanced-guard pushed the Russians as far as Gjatz, exchanging a few balls with them,—an exchange which was almost always to the disadvantage of the French, the Russians taking care to employ only their long pieces, which would carry much farther than ours. Another remark which we made was, that from Smolensk the Russians had neglected to burn the villages and the mansions. As they are of a character which aims at effect, this obscure evil probably appeared to them to be a useless one. They were satisfied with the more signal conflagrations of their cities.

This defect, if that negligence proceeded from it, turned, as is frequently the case with all other defects, to the advantage of their enemies. In these villages, the French army found forage, corn, ovens for baking, and shelter. Others observed on this point, that all these devastations were allotted to Cossacks, to barbarians; and that these hordes, either from hatred or contempt of civilization, seemed to take a savage and particular pleasure in the destruction of the towns.

Chapter 37
Kutusoff

On the 1st of September, about noon, there was only a copse of fir-trees between Murat and Gjatz. The appearance of Cossacks obliged him to deploy his first regiments, but in his impatience he soon sent for some horse, and having himself driven the Russians from the wood which they occupied, he crossed it and found himself at the gates of Gjatz. This sight animated the French, and they instantly made themselves masters of the town as far as the river which parts it into two, and the bridges of which had been already set on fire.

There, as at Smolensk and Wiazma, whether by chance, or from the relic of a Tartar custom, the bazaar was on the Asiatic side, on the bank opposite to us. The Russian rear-guard, secured by the river, had time, therefore, to burn that whole quarter. Nothing but the promptitude of Murat saved the rest.

The troops crossed the Gjatz as they could, on planks, in a few boats, and by fording. The Russians disappeared behind the flames, whither our foremost riflemen followed them,—when they saw an inhabitant come forth, approach them, and cry out that he was a Frenchman. His joy and his accent confirmed his assertion. They conducted him to Davoust, who interrogated him.

According to the account of this man, there had been a great change in the Russian army. A violent clamour had been raised from its ranks against Barclay. It had been re-echoed by the nobility, by the merchants, by all Moscow. "That general, that minister, was a traitor; he caused all their divisions to be destroyed piece-meal; he was dishonouring the army by an interminable flight; yet, at the same time, they were labouring under the disgrace of an invasion, and their towns were in flames. If it was necessary to determine upon this ruin, they might as well sacrifice themselves at once; then, there would be at least some honour, whereas, to suffer themselves to be sacrificed by a stranger, was losing every thing, the honour of the sacrifice not excepted.

"But why employ this stranger? Was not the contemporary, the comrade, the rival of Suwarrow yet living? A Russian was wanted to save Russia!" And they all called for, all were anxious for Kutusoff and a battle. The Frenchman added, that Alexander had yielded; that the insubordination of Bagration, and the universal outcry, had obtained from him that general and a battle; and that, moreover, after drawing the invading army so far, the Russian emperor had himself judged a general engagement unavoidable.

Finally, he related, that the arrival of Kutusoff on the 29th of August at Tzarewozaimizcze, between Wiazma and Gjatz, and the announcement of a speedy battle, had intoxicated the enemy with twofold joy; that all had immediately marched towards Borodino,—not to continue their flight, but to fix themselves on this frontier of the government of Moscow, to root themselves to the soil, and defend it; in short, to conquer there or die.

An incident, otherwise not worthy of notice, seemed to confirm this intelligence; this was the arrival of a Russian officer with a flag of truce. He had so little to say, that it was evident from the first that he came only to observe. His manner was particularly displeasing to Davoust, who read in it something more than assurance. A French general having inconsiderately asked this stranger what we should find between Wiazma and Moscow, the Russian proudly replied, "Pultowa." This answer bespoke a battle; it pleased the French, who are fond of a smart repartee, and delight to meet with enemies worthy of themselves.

This officer was conducted back without precaution, as he had been brought. He saw that there was no obstacle to prevent access to our very head-quarters; he traversed our advanced posts without meeting with a single vidette; every where the same negligence was perceptible, and the temerity so natural to Frenchmen and to conquerors. Every one was asleep; there was no watchword, no patrols; our soldiers seemed to despise these details, as too trivial. Wherefore so many precautions? They attacked—they were victorious: it was for the Russians to defend themselves! This officer has since said, that he was tempted to take advantage that very night of our imprudence, but that he did not find any Russian corps within his reach.

The enemy, in his haste to burn the bridges over the Gjatz, left behind some of his Cossacks; they were taken and conducted to the emperor, who was approaching on horseback. Napoleon wished to question them himself. He sent for his interpreter, and caused two of these Scythians, whose strange dress and wild look were remarkable, to be placed by his side. In this manner he entered Gjatz, and passed through that town. The answers of these barbarians corresponded with the account of the Frenchman; and during the night of the 1st of September, all the reports from the advanced posts confirmed their accuracy.

Thus Barclay had, singly against all, supported till the very last moment that plan of retreat, which in 1807 he had vaunted to one of our generals as the only expedient for saving Russia. Among us, he was commended for having persisted in this prudent defensive system, in spite of the clamours of a proud nation irritated by misfortune, and before so aggressive an enemy.

He had, no doubt, failed in suffering himself to be surprised at Wilna, and for not considering the marshy course of the Berezina as the proper frontier of Lithuania; but it was remarked that, subsequently, at Witepsk and Smolensk, he had forestalled Napoleon; that on the Loutcheza, on the Dnieper, and at Valoutina, his resistance had been proportionate to time and place; that this petty warfare, and the losses occasioned by it, had been but too much in his favour; every retrograde step of his drawing us to a greater distance from our reinforcements, and carrying him nearer to his: in short, all that he had done, he had done judiciously, whether he had hazarded, defended, or abandoned.

And yet he had drawn upon himself general animadversion! But this was, in our opinion, his highest panegyric. We thought the better of him for despising public opinion, when it had gone astray; for having contented himself with watching our motions in order to profit by them, and for having proved that, most frequently, nations are saved in spite of themselves.

Barclay showed himself still greater during the rest of the campaign. This commander in chief, and minister at war, who had been deprived of the command, that it might be given to Kutusoff, voluntarily served under him, and was seen to obey with as much zeal as he had commanded.

CHAPTER 38

Impending Battle

The Russian army at length halted. Miloradowitch, with sixteen thousand recruits, and a host of peasants, bearing the cross and shouting, *"'Tis the will of God!"* hastened to join its ranks. We were informed that the enemy were turning up the whole plain of Borodino, and covering it with entrenchments, apparently with the determination of rooting themselves there, and not falling back any further.

Napoleon announced a battle to his army; he allowed it two days to rest, to prepare its arms, and to collect subsistence. He merely warned the detachments sent out in quest of provisions, that "if they did not return the following day, they would deprive themselves of the honour of fighting."

The emperor then endeavoured to obtain some information concerning his new adversary. Kutusoff was described to him as an old man, the groundwork of whose reputation had been formerly laid by a singular wound. He had since skilfully profited by circumstances. The very defeat of Austerlitz, which he had foreseen, added to his renown, which was further increased by his late campaigns against the Turks. His valour was incontestable, but he was charged with regulating its vehemence according to his private interest; for he calculated every thing. His genius was slow, vindictive, and, above all, crafty—the true Tartar character!—knowing the art of preparing an implacable war with a fawning, supple, and patient policy.

In other respects, he was more an adroit courtier than an able general: but formidable by his renown, by his address in augmenting it, and in making others concur in this object. He had contrived to flatter the whole nation, and every individual of it, from the general to the private soldier.

It was added, that there was in his person, in his language, nay, even in his very dress, his superstitious practices and his age, a remnant of

Suwarrow,—the stamp of an ancient Muscovite, an air of nationality, which rendered him dear to the Russians: at Moscow the joy at his appointment had been carried to intoxication; people embraced one another in the streets, and considered themselves as saved.

When Napoleon had learned these particulars, and given his orders, he awaited the event with that tranquillity of mind peculiar to extraordinary men. He quietly employed himself in exploring the environs of his head-quarters. He remarked the progress of agriculture; but at the sight of the Gjatz, which pours its waters into the Volga, he who had conquered so many rivers, felt anew the first emotions of his glory: he was heard to boast of being the master of those waves destined to visit Asia,—as if they were proceeding to announce his approach, and to open for him the way to that quarter of the globe.

On the 4th of September, the army, still divided into three columns, set out from Gjatz and its environs. Murat had gone on a few leagues before. Ever since the arrival of Kutusoff, troops of Cossacks had been incessantly hovering about the heads of our columns. Murat was exasperated at seeing his cavalry forced to deploy against so feeble an obstacle. We are assured that on that day, from one of those first impulses worthy of the ages of chivalry, he dashed suddenly and alone towards their line, stopped short a few paces from them, and there, sword in hand, made a sign for them to retire, with an air and gesture so commanding, that these barbarians obeyed, and fell back in amazement.

This circumstance, which was related to us immediately, was received without incredulity. The martial air of that monarch, the brilliancy of his chivalrous dress, his reputation, and the novelty of such an action, caused this momentary ascendancy to appear true, in spite of its improbability; for such was Murat, a theatrical monarch by the splendour of his dress, and truly a king by his extraordinary valour and his inexhaustible activity; bold as the attack, and always armed with that air of superiority, that threatening audacity, which is the most dangerous of offensive weapons.

He had not marched long, however, before he was forced to halt. At Griednewa, between Gjatz and Borodino, the high-road suddenly descends into a deep ravine, whence it again rises as suddenly to a spacious height, which Kutusoff had ordered Konownitzin to defend. That general at first made a vigorous resistance against the foremost troops of Murat; but as the army closely followed the latter, every moment gave increased energy to the attack, and diminished that of the defence; presently the advanced-guard of the viceroy engaged on the right of the Russians, where a charge by the Italian chasseurs was withstood for a moment by the Cossacks, which excited astonishment; they became intermixed.

Platof himself admitted that in this affair an officer was wounded near him, at which he was by no means surprised; but that he nevertheless caused the sorcerer who accompanied him to be flogged before all his Cossacks, loudly charging him with laziness for neglecting to turn aside the balls by his conjurations, as he had been expressly directed to do.

Konownitzin was vanquished and retired; on the 5th his bloody track was followed to the vast convent of Kolotskoi,—fortified as habitations were of old in those too highly vaunted Gothic ages, when civil wars were so frequent; when every place, not excepting even these sacred abodes of peace, was transformed into a military post.

Konownitzin, threatened on the right and left, made no other stand either at Kolotskoi or at Golowino; but when the advanced-guard debouched from that village, it beheld the whole plain and the woods infested with Cossacks, the rye crops spoiled, the villages sacked; in short, a general destruction. By these signs it recognized the field of battle, which Kutusoff was preparing for the grand army. Behind these clouds of Scythians were perceived three villages; they presented a line of a league. The intervals between them, intersected by ravines and wood, were covered with the enemy's riflemen. In the first moment of ardour, some French horse ventured into the midst of these Russians, and were cut off.

Napoleon then appeared on a height, from which he surveyed the whole country, with that eye of a conqueror which sees every thing at once and without confusion; which penetrates through obstacles, sets aside accessories, discovers the capital point, and fixes it with the look of an eagle, like prey on which he is about to dart with all his might and all his impetuosity.

He knew that, a league before him, at Borodino, the Kologha, a river running in a ravine, along the margin of which he proceeded a few *wersts*, turned abruptly to the left, and discharged itself into the Moskwa. He guessed that a chain of considerable heights alone could have opposed its course, and so suddenly changed its direction. These were, no doubt, occupied by the enemy's army, and on this side it could not be easily attacked. But the Kologha, both banks of which he followed, while it covered the right of the position, left their left exposed.

The maps of the country were insufficient; at any rate, as the ground necessarily sloped towards the principal stream, which was the most considerable merely from being the lowest, it followed, that the ravines which ran into it must rise, become shallower, and be at length lost, as they receded from the Kologha. Besides, the old road to Smolensk, which ran on its right, sufficiently marked their commencement; why should it have been formerly carried to a distance from the principal stream of water, and consequently from the most habitable places, if not to avoid the ravines and the hills which bordered them?

The demonstrations of the enemy agreed with these inductions of his experience,—no precautions, no resistance in front of their right and their centre; but before their left a great number of troops, a marked solicitude to profit by the slightest accidents of the ground, in order to dispute it, and finally, a formidable redoubt; this was, of course, their weak side, since they covered it with such care. Nay, more; it was on the flank of the high-road, and on that of the grand army, that this redoubt was situated; it was therefore of the utmost importance to carry it, if he would advance: Napoleon gave orders to that effect.

How much the historian is at a loss for words to express the *coup d'oeil* of a man of genius!

The villages and the woods were immediately occupied; on the left and in the centre were the army of Italy, Compans' division, and Murat; on the right, Poniatowski. The attack was general; for the army of Italy and the Polish army appeared at once on the two wings of the grand imperial column. These three masses drove back the Russian rear-guards upon Borodino, and the whole war was concentrated on a single point.

This curtain being withdrawn, the first Russian redoubt was discovered; too much detached in advance of their position, which it defended without being defended by it. The nature of the ground had compelled the choice of this insulated situation.

Compans skilfully availed himself of the undulations of the ground; its elevations served as platforms to his guns for battering the redoubt, and screened his infantry while drawing up into columns of attack. The 61st marched foremost; the redoubt was taken by a single effort, and with the bayonet; but Bagration sent reinforcements, by which it was retaken. Three times did the 61st recover it from the Russians, and three times was it driven out again; but at length it maintained itself in it, covered with blood and half destroyed.

Next day, when the emperor reviewed that regiment, he inquired where was its third battalion? "In the redoubt," was the reply of the colonel. But the affair did not stop there; a neighbouring wood still swarmed with Russian light troops, who sallied every moment from this retreat to renew their attacks, which were supported by three divisions: at length the attack of Schewardino by Morand, and of the woods of Elnia by Poniatowski, completely disheartened the troops of Bagration, and Murat's cavalry cleared the plain. It was chiefly the firmness of a Spanish regiment that foiled the enemy; they at last gave way, and that redoubt, which had been their advanced post, became ours.

At the same time the emperor assigned its place to each corps; the rest of the army formed in line, and a general discharge of musketry, accompanied at intervals with that of a few cannon, ensued. It continued till each party had fixed its limit, and darkness had rendered their fire uncertain.

One of Davoust's regiments then sought to take its rank in the first line. Owing to the darkness, it passed beyond it, and got into the midst of the Russian cuirassiers, who attacked it, threw it into disorder, took from it three pieces of cannon, and killed or took three hundred men. The rest immediately fell into platoons, forming a shapeless mass, but making so formidable a resistance, that the enemy could not again break it; and this regiment, with diminished numbers, finally regained its place in the line of battle.

Chapter 39
Napoleon's Strategy

The emperor encamped behind the army of Italy, on the left of the high-road; the old guard formed in square around his tents. As soon as the fire of small arms had ceased, the fires were kindled. Those of the Russians burned brightly, in an immense semicircle; ours gave a pale, unequal, and irregular light,—the troops arriving late and in haste, on an unknown ground, where nothing was prepared for them, and where there was a want of wood, especially in the centre and on the left.

The emperor slept little. On General Caulaincourt's return from the conquered redoubt, as no prisoners had fallen into our hands, Napoleon surprised, kept asking him repeatedly, "Had not his cavalry then charged apropos? Were the Russians determined to conquer or die?"—The answer was, that "being fanaticised by their leaders, and accustomed to fight with the Turks, who gave no quarter, they would be killed sooner than surrender." The emperor then fell into a deep meditation; and judging that a battle of artillery would be the most certain, he multiplied his orders to bring up, with all speed, the parks which had not yet joined him.

That very same night, a cold mizzling rain began to fall, and the autumn set in with a violent wind. This was an additional enemy, which it was necessary to take into account; for this period of the year corresponded with the age on which Napoleon was entering, and every one knows the influence of the seasons of the year on the like seasons of life.

During that night how many different agitations! The soldiers and the officers had to prepare their arms, to repair their clothing, and to combat cold and hunger; for their life was a continual combat. The generals, and the emperor himself, were uneasy, lest their defeat of the preceding day should have disheartened the Russians, and they should escape us in the dark. Murat had anticipated this; we imagined several times that we saw their fires burn more faintly, and that we heard the noise of their departure; but day alone eclipsed the light of the enemy's bivouacs.

This time there was no need to go far in quest of them. The sun of the 6th found the two armies again, and displayed them to each other, on the same ground where it had left them the evening before. There was a general feeling of exultation.

The emperor took advantage of the first rays of dawn, to advance between the two lines, and to go from height to height along the whole front of the hostile army. He saw the Russians crowning all the eminences, in a vast semicircle, two leagues in extent, from the Moskwa to the old Moscow road. Their right bordered the Kologha, from its influx into the Moskwa to Borodino; their centre, from Gorcka to Semenowska, was the salient part of their line. Their right and left receded. The Kologha rendered their right inaccessible.

The emperor perceived this immediately, and as, from its distance, this wing was not more threatening than vulnerable, he took no account of it. For him then the Russian army commenced at Gorcka, a village situated on the high-road, and at the point of an elevated plain which overlooks Borodino and the Kologha. This sharp projection is surrounded by the Kologha, and by a deep and marshy ravine; its lofty crest, to which the high-road ascends on leaving Borodino, was strongly entrenched, and formed a separate work on the right of the Russian centre, of which it was the extremity.

On its left, and within reach of its fire, rose a detached hill, commanding the whole plain; it was crowned by a formidable redoubt, provided with twenty-one pieces of cannon. In front and on its right it was encompassed by the Kologha and by ravines; its left inclined to and supported itself upon a long and wide plateau, the foot of which descended to a muddy ravine, a branch of the Kologha. The crest of this plateau, which was lined by the Russians, declined and receded as it ran towards the left, in front of the grand army; it then kept rising as far as the yet smoking ruins of the village of Semenowska. This salient point terminated Barclay's command and the centre of the enemy: it was armed with a strong battery, covered by an entrenchment.

Here began the left wing of the Russians under Bagration. The less elevated crest which it occupied undulated as it gradually receded to Utitza, a village on the old Moscow road, where the field of battle ended. Two hills, armed with redoubts, and bearing diagonally upon the entrenchment of Semenowska, which flanked them, marked the front of Bagration.

From Semenowska to the wood of Utitza there was an interval of about twelve hundred paces. It was the nature of the ground which had decided Kutusoff thus to refuse this wing; for here the ravine, which was under the plateau in the centre, just commenced. It was scarcely an obstacle; the slopes of its banks were very gentle, and the summits suitable for artillery were at some distance from its margin. This side was evidently the most accessible, since the redoubt of the 61st, which that regiment had taken the preceding day, no longer defended the approach: this was even favoured by a wood of large pines, extending from the redoubt just mentioned to that which appeared to terminate the line of the Russians.

But their left wing did not end there. The emperor knew that behind this wood was the old Moscow road; that it turned round the left wing of the Russians, and passing behind their army, ran again into the new Moscow road in front of Mojaisk. He judged that it must be occupied; and, in fact, Tutchkof, with his *corps d'armée*, had placed himself across it at the entrance of a wood; he had covered himself by two heights, on which he had planted artillery.

But this was of little consequence, because, between this detached corps and the last Russian redoubt, there was a space of five or six hundred fathoms and a covered ground. If we did not begin with overwhelming Tutchkof, we might therefore occupy it, pass between him and the last of Bagration's redoubts, and take the left wing of the enemy in flank; but the emperor could not satisfy himself on this point, as the Russian advanced posts and the woods forbade his farther advance, and intercepted his view.

Having finished his reconnoissance, he formed his plan. "Eugene shall be the pivot!" he exclaimed: "it is the right that must commence. As soon as, under cover of the wood, it has taken the redoubt opposite to it, it must make a movement to the left, and march on the Russian flank, sweeping and driving back their whole army upon their right and into the Kologha."

The general plan thus conceived, he applied himself to the details. During the night, three batteries, of sixty guns each, must be opposed to the Russian redoubts; two facing their left, the third before their centre. At daybreak, Poniatowski and his army, reduced to five thousand men, must advance on the old Smolensk road, turning the wood on which the French right wing and the Russian left were supported. He would flank the one and annoy the other; the army would wait for the report of his first shots.

Instantly, the whole of the artillery should commence upon the left of the Russians, its fire would open their ranks and redoubts, and Davoust and Ney should rush upon them; they should be supported by Junot and his Westphalians, by Murat and his cavalry, and lastly, by the emperor himself, with 20,000 guards. It was against these two redoubts that the first efforts should be made; it was by them that he would penetrate into the hostile army, thenceforth mutilated, and whose centre and right would then be uncovered, and almost enveloped.

Meanwhile, as the Russians showed themselves in redoubled masses on their centre and their right, threatening the Moscow road, the only line of operation of the grand army; as in throwing his chief force and himself on their left, Napoleon was about to place the Kologha between him and that road, his only retreat, he resolved to strengthen the army of Italy which occupied it, and joined with it two of Davoust's divisions and Grouchy's cavalry. As to his left, he judged that one Italian division, the Bavarian cavalry, and that of Ornano, about 10,000 men, would suffice to cover it. Such were the plans of Napoleon.

Chapter 40
Orders

He was on the heights of Borodino, taking a last survey of the whole field of battle, and confirming himself in his plan, when Davoust hastened up. This marshal had just examined the left of the Russians with so much the more care, as it was the ground on which he was to act, and he mistrusted his own eyes.

He begged the emperor "to place at his disposal his five divisions, 35,000 strong, and to unite with them Poniatowski, whose force was too weak to turn the enemy by itself. Next day he would set this force in motion; he would cover its march with the last shades of night, and with the wood on which the Russian left wing was supported, and beyond which he would pass by following the old road from Smolensk to Moscow; then, all at once, by a precipitate manoeuvre, he would deploy 40,000 French and Poles on the flank and in the rear of that wing. There, while the emperor would occupy the front of the Muscovites by a general attack, he would march impetuously from redoubt to redoubt, from reserve to reserve, driving every thing from left to right on the high-road of Mojaisk, where they should put an end at once to the Russian army, the battle, and the war."

The emperor listened attentively to the marshal; but after meditating in silence for some minutes, he replied, "No! it is too great a movement; it would remove me too far from my object, and make me lose too much time."

The Prince of Eckmühl, however, from conviction, persisted in his point; he undertook to accomplish his manoeuvre before six in the morning; he protested that in another hour the greatest part of its effect would be produced. Napoleon, impatient of contradiction, sharply replied with this exclamation, "Ah! you are always for turning the enemy; it is too dangerous a manoeuvre!" The marshal, after this rebuff, said no more: he then returned to his post, murmuring against a prudence which he thought unseasonable, and to which he was not accustomed; and he knew not to what cause to attribute it, unless the looks of so many allies, who were not to be relied on, an army so reduced, a position so remote, and age, had rendered Napoleon less enterprising than he was.

The emperor, having decided, had returned to his camp, when Murat, whom the Russians had so often deceived, persuaded him that they were going to run away once more without fighting. In vain did Rapp, who was sent to observe their attitude, return and say, that he had seen them entrenching themselves more and more; that they were numerous, judiciously disposed, and appeared determined much rather to attack, if they were not anticipated, than to retreat: Murat persisted in his opinion, and the emperor, uneasy, returned to the heights of Borodino.

He there perceived long black columns of troops covering the high-road, and spreading over the plain; then large convoys of wagons, provisions, and ammunition, in short all the dispositions indicative of a stay and a battle. At that very moment, though he had taken with him but few attendants, that he might not attract the notice and the fire of the enemy, he was recognized by the Russian batteries, and a cannon-shot suddenly interrupted the silence of that day.

For, as it frequently happens, nothing was so calm as the day preceding that great battle. It was like a thing mutually agreed upon! Wherefore do each other useless injury? was not the next day to decide every thing? Besides, each had to prepare itself; the different corps, their arms, their force, their ammunition; they had to resume all their unity, which on a march is always more or less deranged. The generals had to observe their reciprocal dispositions of attack, defence, and retreat, in order to adapt them to each other and the ground, and to leave as little as possible to chance.

Thus these two colossal foes, on the point of commencing their terrible contest, watched each other attentively, measured one another with their eyes, and silently prepared for a tremendous conflict.

The emperor, who could no longer entertain doubts of a battle, returned to his tent to dictate the order of it. There he meditated on his awful situation. He had seen that the two armies were equal; about 120,000 men, and 600 pieces of cannon on either side. The Russians had the advantage of ground, of speaking but one language, of one uniform, of being a single nation, fighting for the same cause, but a great number of irregular troops and recruits.

The French had as many men, but more soldiers; for the state of his corps had just been submitted to him: he had before his eyes an account of the strength of his divisions, and as it was neither a review, nor a distribution, but a battle that was in prospect, this time the statements were not exaggerated. His army was reduced indeed, but sound, supple, nervous,—like those manly bodies, which, having just lost the plumpness of youth, display forms more masculine and strongly marked.

Still, during the last few days that he had marched in the midst of it, he had found it silent, from that silence which is imposed by great expectation or great astonishment; like nature, the moment before a violent tempest, or crowds at the instant of an extraordinary danger.

He felt that it wanted rest of some kind or other, but that there was no rest for it but in death or victory; for he had brought it into such a necessity of conquering, that it must triumph at any rate. The temerity of the situation into which he had urged it was evident, but he knew that of all faults that was the one which the French most willingly forgave; that in short they doubted neither of themselves nor of him, nor of the general result, whatever might be their individual hardships.

He reckoned, moreover, on their habit and thirst of glory, and even on their curiosity; no doubt they wished to see Moscow, to be able to say that they had been there, to receive there the promised reward, perhaps to plunder, and, above all, there to find repose. He did not observe in them enthusiasm, but something more firm: an entire confidence in his star, in his genius, the consciousness of their superiority, and the proud assurance of conquerors, in the presence of the vanquished.

Full of these sentiments, he dictated a proclamation, simple, grave, and frank, as befitted such circumstances, and men who were not just commencing their career, and whom, after so many sufferings, it would have been idle to pretend to exalt.

Accordingly he addressed himself solely to the reason of all, or what is the same thing, to the real interest of each; he finished with glory, the only passion to which he could appeal in these deserts, the last of the noble motives by which it was possible to act upon soldiers always victorious, enlightened by an advanced civilization and long experience; in short, of all the generous illusions, the only one that could have carried them so far. This harangue will some day be deemed admirable: it was worthy of the commander and of the army; it did honour to both.

"Soldiers!" said he, "here is the battle which you have so ardently desired. Victory will now depend upon yourselves; it is necessary for us; it will give us abundance, good winter-quarters, and a speedy return home! Behave as you did at Austerlitz, at Friedland, at Witepsk, and at Smolensk, and afford to remotest posterity occasion to cite your conduct on that day: let it be said of you, 'He was in that great battle under the walls of Moscow.'"

Chapter 41
We Have Them at Last!

About the middle of the day, Napoleon remarked an extraordinary movement in the enemy's camp; in fact, the whole Russian army was drawn up and under arms, and Kutusoff, surrounded with every species of religious and military pomp, took his station in the middle of it. He had made his popes and his archimandrites dress themselves in those splendid and majestic insignia, which they have inherited from the Greeks. They marched before him, carrying the venerated symbols of their religion, and particularly that divine image, formerly the protectress of Smolensk, which, by their account, had been miraculously saved from the profanation of the sacrilegious French.

When the Russian saw that his soldiers were sufficiently excited by this extraordinary spectacle, he raised his voice, and began by putting them in mind of heaven, the only country which remains to the slave. In the name of the religion of equality, he endeavoured to animate these serfs to defend the property of their masters; but it was principally by exhibiting to them that holy image which had taken refuge in their ranks, that he appealed to their courage, and raised their indignation.

Napoleon, in his mouth, "was a universal despot! the tyrannical disturber of the world! a poor worm! an arch-rebel, who had overturned their altars, and polluted them with blood; who had exposed the true ark of the Lord, represented by the holy image, to the profanation of men, and the inclemency of the seasons." He then told them of their cities reduced to ashes; reminded them that they were about to fight for their wives and children; added a few words respecting the emperor, and concluded by appealing to their piety and their patriotism. These were the virtues of instinct with this rude and simple people, who had not yet advanced beyond sensations, but who, for that very reason, were so much more formidable as soldiers; less diverted from obedience by reasoning; confined by slavery to a narrow circle, in which they are reduced to a small number of sensations, which are the only sources of their wants, wishes, and ideas.

As to other characteristics, proud for want of comparison, and credulous as they are proud, from ignorance—worshippers of images, idolaters as much as Christians can be; for they had converted that religion of the soul, which is wholly intellectual and moral, into one entirely physical and material, to bring it to the level of their brute and short capacity.

This solemn spectacle, however, their general's address, the exhortations of their officers, and the benedictions of their priests, served to give a thorough tincture of fanaticism to their courage. All, even to the meanest soldier, fancied themselves devoted by God himself to the defence of Heaven and their consecrated soil.

With the French there was no solemnity, either religious or military, no review, no means of excitation: even the address of the emperor was not distributed till very late, and read the next morning so near the time of action, that several corps were actually engaged before they could hear it. The Russians, however, whom so many powerful motives should have inflamed, added to their invocations the sword of St. Michael, thus seeking to borrow aid from all the powers of heaven; while the French sought for it only within themselves, persuaded that real strength exists only in the heart, and that *there* is to be found the "celestial host."

Chance so ordered it, that on that very day the emperor received from Paris the portrait of the King of Rome, that infant whose birth had been hailed by the empire with the same transports of joy and hope as it had been by the emperor. Every day since that happy event, the emperor, in the interior of his palace, had given loose when near his child, to the expression of the most tender feelings; when, therefore, in the midst of these distant fields, and all these menacing preparations, he saw once more that sweet countenance, how his warlike soul melted! With his own hand he exhibited this picture outside his tent; he then called his officers, and even some of the soldiers of his old guard, desirous of sharing his pleasure with these veteran grenadiers, of showing his private family to his military family, and making it shine as a symbol of hope in the midst of imminent peril.

In the evening, an aid-de-camp of Marmont, who had been despatched from the field of battle near Salamanca, arrived at that of the Moskwa. This was the same Fabvier, who has since made such a figure in our civil dissensions. The emperor received graciously the aid-de-camp of the vanquished general. On the eve of a battle, the fate of which was so uncertain, he felt disposed to be indulgent to a defeat; he listened to all that was said to him respecting the scattered state of his forces in Spain, and the number of commanders-in-chief, and admitted the justice of it all; but he explained his reasons, which it enters not into our province to mention here.

With the return of night also returned the apprehension, that under cover of its shades, the Russian army might escape from the field of battle. Napoleon's anxiety was so great as to prevent him from sleeping. He kept calling incessantly to know the hour, inquiring if any noise was heard, and sending persons to ascertain if the enemy was still before him. His doubts on this subject were so strong, that he had given orders that his proclamation should not be read to his troops until the next morning, and then only in case of the certainty of a battle.

Tranquillized for a few moments, anxiety of an opposite description again seized him. He became frightened at the destitute state of the soldiers. Weak and famished as they were, how could they support a long and terrible shock? In this danger he looked upon his guard as his sole resource; it seemed to be his security for both armies. He sent for Bessières, that one of his marshals in whom he had the greatest confidence for commanding it; he wished to know if this chosen reserve wanted nothing;—he called him back several times, and repeated his pressing questions. He desired that these old soldiers should have three days' biscuit and rice distributed among them from their wagons of reserve; finally, dreading that his orders had not been obeyed, he got up once more, and questioned the grenadiers on guard at the entrance of his tent, if they had received these provisions. Satisfied by their answer, he went in, and soon fell into a doze.

Shortly after, he called once more. His aid-de-camp found him now supporting his head with both hands; he seemed, by what was heard, to be meditating on the vanities of glory. "What is war? A trade of barbarians, the whole art of which consists in being the strongest on a given point!" He then complained of the fickleness of fortune, which he said, he began to experience. Seeming to revert to more encouraging ideas, he recollected what had been told him of the tardiness and carelessness of Kutusoff, and expressed his surprise that Beningsen had not been preferred to him. He thought of the critical situation into which he had brought himself, and added, "that a great day was at hand, that there would be a terrible battle." He asked Rapp if he thought we should gain the victory? "No doubt;" was the reply, "but it will be sanguinary." "I know it," resumed Napoleon, "but I have 80,000 men; I shall lose 20,000, I shall enter Moscow with 60,000; the stragglers will there rejoin us, and afterwards the battalions on the march, and we shall be stronger than we were before the battle." In this estimate he seemed to include neither his guard nor the cavalry.

Again assailed by his first anxiety, he sent once more to examine the attitude of the Russians; he was informed that their fires burned with equal brightness, and that by the number of these, and the moving shadows surrounding them, it was supposed that it was not merely a rear-guard, but a whole army that kept feeding them. The certainty of their presence at last quieted the emperor, and he tried to take some rest.

But the marches which he had just made with the array, the fatigues of the preceding days and nights, so many cares, and his intense and anxious expectation, had worn him out; the chillness of the atmosphere had struck to him; an irritating fever, a dry cough, and excessive thirst consumed him. During the remainder of the night, he made vain attempts to quench the burning thirst which consumed him. This fresh disorder was complicated with an old complaint; he had been struggling since the day before with a painful attack of that cruel disorder[18], which had been long threatening him.

At last, just at five o'clock, one of Ney's officers came to inform him that the marshal was still in sight of the Russians, and wished to begin the attack. This news seemed to restore the strength of which the fever had deprived him. He arose, called his officers, and sallied out, exclaiming, "We have them at last! Forward! Let us go and open the gates of Moscow!"

18: A retention of urine.

Chapter 42
The Battle of Borodino

It was half-past five in the morning, when Napoleon arrived near the redoubt which had been conquered on the 5th of September. There he waited for the first dawn of day, and for the first fire of Poniatowski's infantry. The sun rose. The emperor, showing it to his officers, exclaimed, "Behold the sun of Austerlitz!" But it was opposite to us. It rose on the Russian side, made us conspicuous to their fire, and dazzled us. We then first perceived, that owing to the darkness, our batteries had been placed out of reach of the enemy, and it was necessary to push them more forward. The enemy allowed this to be done: he seemed to hesitate in being the first to break the awful silence.

The emperor's attention was then directed towards his right, when, all at once, near seven o'clock, the battle began upon his left. Shortly after, he was informed, that one of the regiments of Prince Eugene, the 106th, had got possession of the village of Borodino, and its bridge, which it should have destroyed; but that being carried away by the ardour of success, it had crossed that passage, in spite of the cries of its general, in order to attack the heights of Gorcka, where it was overwhelmed by the front and flank fires of the Russians. It was added, that the general who commanded that brigade had been already killed, and that the 106th regiment would have been entirely destroyed had it not been for the 92nd, which voluntarily ran up to its assistance, and collected and brought back its survivors.

It was Napoleon himself who had just ordered his left wing to make a violent attack. Probably, he had only reckoned on a partial execution of his orders, and wished to keep the enemy's attention directed to that side. But he multiplied his orders, used the most violent excitations, and engaged a battle in front, the plan of which he had conceived in an oblique order.

During this action, the emperor judging that Poniatowski was closing with the enemy on the old Moscow road, gave him the signal to attack. Suddenly, from that peaceful plain, and the silent hills, volumes of fire and smoke were seen spouting out, followed by a multitude of explosions, and the whistling of bullets, tearing the air in every direction. In the midst of this noise, Davoust, with the divisions Compans and Dessaix, and thirty pieces of cannon in front, advanced rapidly to the first Russian redoubt.

The enemy's musketry began, and was answered only by the French cannon. The French infantry marched without firing: it was hurrying on to get within reach of and extinguish that of the enemy, when Compans, the general of that column, and his bravest soldiers, were wounded and fell: the rest, disconcerted, halted under the shower of balls, in order to return it, when Rapp, rushing to replace Compans, again led his soldiers on, with fixed bayonets, and at a running pace against the enemy's redoubt.

He was himself just on the point of reaching it, when he was, in his turn, hit; it was his twenty-second wound. A third general, who succeeded him, also fell. Davoust himself was wounded. Rapp was carried to the emperor, who said to him, "What, Rapp, always hit! What are they doing above, then?" The aid-de-camp answered, that it would require the guard to finish. "No!" replied Napoleon, "I shall take good care of that; I have no wish to see it destroyed; I shall gain the battle without it."

Ney, then, with his three divisions, reduced to 10,000 men, hastened into the plain to the assistance of Davoust. The enemy divided his fire. Ney rushed forward. The 57th regiment of Compans' division, finding itself supported, took fresh courage; by a last effort it succeeded in reaching the enemy's entrenchments, scaled them, mingled with the Russians, put them to the bayonet, overthrew and killed the most obstinate of them. The rest fled, and the 57th maintained itself in its conquest. At the same time Ney made so furious an attack on the two other redoubts, that he wrested them from the enemy.

It was now mid-day; the left Russian line being thus forced, and the plain cleared, the emperor ordered Murat to proceed with his cavalry, and complete the victory. An instant was sufficient for that prince to show himself on the heights and in the midst of the enemy, who again made his appearance there; for the second Russian line and the reinforcements, led on by Bagawout and sent by Tutchkof, had come to the assistance of the first line. They all rushed forward, resting upon Semenowska, in order to retake their redoubts. The French, who were still in the disorder of victory, were astonished and fell back.

The Westphalians, whom Napoleon had just sent to the assistance of Poniatowski, were then crossing the wood which separated that prince from the rest of the army; through the dust and smoke they got a glimpse of our troops, who were retreating. By the direction of their march, they guessed them to be enemies, and fired upon them. They persisted in their mistake, and thereby increased the disorder.

The enemy's cavalry vigorously followed up their advantage; they surrounded Murat, who forgot himself in his endeavours to rally his troops; they were already stretching out their arms to lay hold of him, when he threw himself into the redoubt, and escaped from them. But there he found only some unsteady soldiers whose courage had forsaken them, and running round the parapet in a state of the greatest panic. They only wanted an outlet to run away.

The presence of the king and his cries first restored confidence to a few. He himself seized a musket; with one hand he fought, with the other he elevated and waved his plume, calling to his men, and restoring them to their first valour by that authority which example gives. At the same time Ney had again formed his divisions. Their fire stopped the enemy's cuirassiers, and threw their ranks into disorder. They let go their hold, Murat was at last disengaged, and the heights were reconquered.

Scarcely had the king escaped this peril, when he ran into another; with the cavalry of Bruyère and Nansouty, he rushed upon the enemy, and by obstinate and repeated charges overthrew the Russian lines, pushed and drove them back on their centre, and, within an hour, completed the total defeat of their left wing.

But the heights of the ruined village of Semenowska, where the left of the enemy's centre commenced, were still untouched; the reinforcements which Kutusoff incessantly drew from his right, supported it. Their commanding fire was poured down upon Ney and Murat's troops, and stopped their victory; it was indispensable to acquire that position. Maubourg with his cavalry first cleared the front; Friand, one of Davoust's generals, followed him with his infantry. Dufour and the 15th light were the first to climb the steep; they dislodged the Russians from the village, the ruins of which were badly entrenched. Friand, although wounded, followed up and secured this advantage.

Chapter 43
Exhaustion

This vigorous action opened up to us the road to victory; it was necessary to rush into it; but Murat and Ney were exhausted: they halted, and while they were rallying their troops, they sent to Napoleon to ask for reinforcements. Napoleon was then seized with a hesitation which he never before displayed; he deliberated long with himself, and at last, after repeated orders and counter-orders to his young guard, he expressed his belief that the appearance of Friand and Maubourg's troops on the heights would be sufficient, the decisive moment not appearing to him to be yet arrived.

But Kutusoff took advantage of the respite which he had no reason to expect; he summoned the whole of his reserve, even to the Russian guards, to the support of his uncovered left wing. Bagration, with all these reinforcements, re-formed his line, his right resting on the great battery which Prince Eugene was attacking, his left on the wood which bounded the field of battle towards Psarewo. His fire cut our ranks to pieces; his attack was violent, impetuous, and simultaneous; infantry, artillery, and cavalry, all made a grand effort. Ney and Murat stood firm against this tempest; the question with them was no longer about following up the victory, but about retaining it.

The soldiers of Friand, drawn up in front of Semenowska, repelled the first charges, but when they were assailed with a shower of balls and grape shot, they began to give way; one of their leaders got tired, and gave orders to retreat. At that critical moment, Murat ran up to him, and seizing him by the collar, exclaimed, "What are you about?" The colonel, pointing to the ground, covered with half his troops, answered, "You see well enough that it is impossible to stand here."—"Very well, I will remain!" exclaimed the king. These words stopped the officer: he looked Murat steadily in the face, and turning round, coolly said, "You are right! Soldiers, face to the enemy! Let us go and be killed!"

Meanwhile, Murat had just sent back Borelli to the emperor to ask for assistance; that officer pointed to the clouds of dust which the charges of the cavalry were raising upon the heights, which had hitherto remained tranquil since they had been taken. Some cannon-balls also for the first time fell close to where Napoleon was stationed; the enemy seemed to be approaching; Borelli insisted, and the emperor promised his young guard. But, scarcely had it advanced a few paces, when he himself called out to it to halt. The Count de Lobau, however, made it advance by degrees, under pretence of dressing the line. Napoleon perceiving it, repeated his order.

Fortunately, the artillery of the reserve advanced at that moment, to take a position on the conquered heights; Lauriston had obtained the emperor's consent to that manoeuvre, but it was rather a permission than an order. Shortly after, however, he thought it so important, that he urged its execution with the only movement of impatience he exhibited during the whole of that day.

It is not known whether his doubts as to the results of Prince Poniatowski and Prince Eugene's engagement on his right and left kept him in uncertainty; what is certain is, that he seemed to be apprehensive lest the extreme left of the Russians should escape from the Poles, and return to take possession of the field of battle in the rear of Ney and Murat. This at least was one of the causes of his retaining his guard in observation upon that point. To such as pressed him, his answer was, "that he wished to have a better view; that his battle was not yet begun; that it would be a long one; that they must learn to wait; that time entered into every thing; that it was the element of which all things are composed; that nothing was yet sufficiently clear." He then inquired the hour, and added, "that the hour of his battle was not yet come; that it would begin in two hours."

But it never began: the whole of that day he was sitting down, or walking about leisurely, in front, and a little to the left of the redoubt which had been conquered on the 5th, on the borders of a ravine, at a great distance from the battle, of which he could scarcely see any thing after it got beyond the heights; not at all uneasy when he saw it return nearer to him, nor impatient with his own troops, or the enemy. He merely made some gestures of melancholy resignation, on every occasion, when they came to inform him of the loss of his best generals. He rose several times to take a few turns, but immediately sat down again.

Every one around him looked at him with astonishment. Hitherto, during these great shocks, he had displayed an active coolness;

but here it was a dead calm, a nerveless and sluggish inactivity. Some fancied they traced in it that dejection which is generally the follower of violent sensations: others, that he had already become indifferent to every thing, even to the emotion of battles. Several remarked, that the calm constancy and *sang-froid* which great men display on these great occasions, turn, in the course of time, to phlegm and heaviness, when age has worn out their springs. Those who were most devoted to him, accounted for his immobility by the necessity of not changing his place too much, when he was commanding over such an extent, in order that the bearers of intelligence might know where to find him. Finally, there were others who, on much better grounds, attributed it to the shock which his health had sustained, to a secret malady, and to the commencement of a violent indisposition.

The generals of artillery, who were surprised at their stagnation, quickly availed themselves of the permission to fight which was just given them. They very soon crowned the heights. Eighty pieces of cannon were discharged at once. The Russian cavalry was first broken by that brazen line, and obliged to take refuge behind its infantry.

The latter advanced in dense masses, in which our balls at first made wide and deep holes; they still, however, continued to advance, when the French batteries crushed them by a second discharge of grape-shot. Whole platoons fell at once; their soldiers were seen trying to keep together under this terrible fire. Every instant, separated by death, they closed together over her, treading her under foot.

At last they halted, not daring to advance farther, and yet unwilling to retreat; either because they were struck, and, as it were, petrified with horror, in the midst of this great destruction, or that Bagration was wounded at that moment; or, perhaps, because their generals, after the failure of their first disposition, knew not how to change it, from not possessing, like Napoleon, the great art of putting such great bodies into motion at once, in unison, and without confusion. In short, these listless masses allowed themselves to be mowed down for two hours, making no other movement than their fall. It was a most horrible massacre; and our brave and intelligent artillerymen could not help admiring the motionless, blind, and resigned courage of their enemies.

The victors were the first to be tired out. They became impatient at the tardiness of this battle of artillery. Their ammunition being entirely exhausted, they came to a decision, in consequence of which Ney moved forward, extending his right, which he made to advance rapidly, and again turn the left of the new front opposed to him. Davoust and Murat seconded him, and the remnants of Ney's corps became the conquerors over the remains of Bagration's.

The battle then ceased in the plain, and became concentrated on the rest of the enemy's heights, and near the great redoubt, which Barclay with the centre and the right, continued to defend obstinately against Eugene.

In this manner, about mid-day, the whole of the French right wing, Ney, Davoust, and Murat, after annihilating Bagration and the half of the Russian line, presented itself on the half-opened flank of the remainder of the hostile army, of which they could see the whole interior, the reserves, the abandoned rears, and even the commencement of the retreat.

But as they felt themselves too weak to throw themselves into that gap, behind a line still formidable, they called aloud for the guard: "The young guard! only let it follow them at a distance! Let it show itself, and take their place upon the heights! They themselves will then be sufficient to finish!"

General Belliard was sent by them to the emperor. He declared, "that from their position, the eye could penetrate, without impediment, a far as the road to Mojaisk, in the rear of the Russian army; that they could see there a confused crowd of flying and wounded soldiers, and carriages retreating; that it was true there was still a ravine and a thin copse between them, but that the Russian generals were so confounded, that they had no thought of turning these to any advantage; that in short, only a single effort was required to arrive in the middle of that disorder, to seal the enemy's discomfiture, and terminate the war!"

The emperor, however, still hesitated, and ordered that general to go and look again, and to return and bring him word. Belliard, surprised, went and returned with all speed; he reported, "that the enemy began to think better of it; that the copse was already lined with his marksmen: that the opportunity was about to escape; that there was not a moment to be lost, otherwise it would require a second battle to terminate the first!"

But Bessières, who had just returned from the heights, to which Napoleon had sent him to examine the attitude of the Russians, asserted, that, "far from being in disorder, they had retreated to a second position, where they seemed to be preparing for a fresh attack." The emperor then said to Belliard, "That nothing was yet sufficiently unravelled: that to make him give his reserves, he wanted to see more clearly upon his chess-board." This was his expression; which he repeated several times, at the same time pointing on one side to the old Moscow road, of which Poniatowski had not yet made himself master; on the other, to an attack of the enemy's cavalry in the rear of our left wing; and, finally, to the great redoubt, against which the efforts of prince Eugene had been ineffectual.

Belliard, in consternation, returned to the king of Naples, and informed him of the impossibility of obtaining the reserve from the emperor; he said, "he had found him still seated in the same place, with a suffering and dejected air, his features sunk, and a dull look; giving his orders languishingly, in the midst of these dreadful warlike noises, to which he seemed completely a stranger!" At this account, Ney, furious and hurried away by his ardent and unmeasured character, exclaimed, "Are we then come so far, to be satisfied with a field of battle? What business has the emperor in the rear of the army? There, he is only within reach of reverses, and not of victory. Since he will no longer make war himself, since he is no longer the general, as he wishes to be the emperor every where, let him return to the Tuilleries, and leave us to be generals for him!"

Murat was more calm; he recollected having seen the emperor the day before, as he was riding along, observing that part of the enemy's line, halt several times, dismount, and with his head resting upon the cannon, remain there some time in the attitude of suffering. He knew what a restless night he had passed, and that a violent and incessant cough cut short his breathing. The king guessed that fatigue, and the first attacks of the equinox, had shaken his weakened frame, and that in short, at that critical moment, the action of his genius was in a manner chained down by his body; which had sunk under the triple load of fatigue, of fever, and of a malady which, probably, more than any other, prostrates the moral and physical strength of its victims.

Still, farther incitements were not wanting; for shortly after Belliard, Daru, urged by Dumas, and particularly by Berthier, said in a low voice to the emperor, "that from all sides it was the cry that the moment for sending the guard was now come." To which Napoleon replied, "And if there should be another battle to-morrow, where is my army?" The minister urged no farther, surprised to see, for the first time, the emperor putting off till the morrow, and adjourning his victory.

Chapter 44
Caulaincourt

Barclay, however, with the right, kept up a most obstinate struggle with Prince Eugene. The latter, immediately after the capture of Borodino, passed the Kologha in the face of the enemy's great redoubt. There, particularly, the Russians had calculated upon their steep heights, encompassed by deep and muddy ravines, upon our exhaustion, upon their entrenchments, defended by heavy artillery, and upon 80 pieces of cannon, planted on the borders of these banks, bristling with fire and flames! But all these elements, art, and nature, every thing failed them at once: assailed by a first burst of that *French fury*, which has been so celebrated, they saw Morand's soldiers appear suddenly in the midst of them, and fled in disorder.

Eighteen hundred men of the 30th regiment, with general Bonnamy at their head, had just made that great effort.

It was there that Fabvier, the aid-de-camp of Marmont, who had arrived but the day before from the heart of Spain, made himself conspicuous; he went as a volunteer, and on foot, at the head of the most advanced sharp-shooters, as if he had come there to represent the army of Spain, in the midst of the grand army; and, inspired with that rivalry of glory which makes heroes, wished to exhibit it at the head, and the first in every danger.

He fell wounded in that too famous redoubt; for the triumph was short-lived; the attack wanted concert, either from precipitation in the first assailant, or too great slowness in those who followed. They had to pass a ravine, whose depth protected them from the enemy's fire. It is affirmed that many of our troops halted there. Morand, therefore, was left alone in the face of several Russian lines. It was yet only ten o'clock. Friand, who was on his right, had not yet commenced the attack of Semenowska; and, on his left, the divisions Gérard, Broussier, and the Italian guard, were not yet in line.

This attack, besides, should not have been made so precipitately: the intention had been only to keep Barclay in check, and occupied on that side, the battle having been arranged to begin by the right wing, and pivot on the left. This was the emperor's plan, and we know not why he himself altered it at the moment of its execution; for it was he who, on the first discharge of the artillery, sent different officers in succession to Prince Eugene, to urge his attack.

The Russians, recovering from their first surprise, rushed forward in all directions. Kutusoff and Yermoloff advanced at their head with a resolution worthy of so great an occasion. The 30th regiment, single against a whole army, ventured to attack it with the bayonet; it was enveloped, crushed, and driven out of the redoubt, where it left a third of its men, and its intrepid general pierced through with twenty wounds. Encouraged by their success, the Russians were no longer satisfied with defending themselves, but attacked in their turn. Then were seen united, on that single point, all the skill, strength, and fury, which war can bring forth. The French stood firm for four hours on the declivity of that volcano, under the shower of iron and lead which it vomited forth. But to do this required all the skill and determination of Prince Eugene; and the idea so insupportable to long-victorious soldiers, of confessing themselves vanquished.

Each division changed its general several times. The viceroy went from one to the other, mingling entreaties and reproaches, and, above all, reminding them of their former victories. He sent to apprise the emperor of his critical situation; but Napoleon replied, "That he could not assist him; that he must conquer; that he had only to make a greater effort; that the heat of the battle was there." The prince was rallying all his forces to make a general assault, when suddenly his attention was diverted by furious cries proceeding from his left.

Ouwarof, with two regiments of cavalry, and some thousand Cossacks, had attacked his reserve, and thrown it into disorder. He ran thither instantly, and, seconded by Generals Delzons and Ornano, soon drove away that troop, which was more noisy than formidable; after which he returned to put himself at the head of a decisive attack.

It was about that time that Murat, forced to remain inactive on the plain where he commanded, had sent, for the fourth time, to his brother-in-law, to complain of the losses which his cavalry were sustaining from the Russian troops, protected by the redoubts which were opposed to Prince Eugene. "He only requested the cavalry of the guard, with whose assistance he could turn the entrenched heights, and destroy them along with the army which defended them."

The emperor seemed to give his consent, and sent in search of Bessières, who commanded these horse-guards. Unfortunately they could not find the marshal, who, by his orders, had gone to look at the battle somewhat nearer. The emperor waited nearly an hour without the least impatience, or repeating his order; and when the marshal returned, he received him with a pleasant look, heard his report quietly, and allowed him to advance as far as he might judge it desirable.

But it was too late; he could no longer think of making the whole Russian army prisoners, or perhaps of taking entire possession of Russia; the field of battle was all he was likely to gain. He had allowed Kutusoff leisure to reconnoitre his positions; that general had fortified all the points of difficult approach which remained to him, and his cavalry covered the plain.

The Russians had thus, for the third time, renewed their left wing, in the face of Ney and Murat. The latter summoned the cavalry of Montbrun, who had been killed. General Caulaincourt succeeded him; he found the aides-de-camp of the unfortunate Montbrun in tears for the loss of their commander. "Follow me," said he to them, "weep not for him, but come and avenge his death!"

The king pointed out to him the enemy's fresh wing; he must break through it, and push on as far as the breast of their great battery; when there, during the time that the light cavalry is following up his advantage, he, Caulaincourt, must turn suddenly, on the left with his cuirassiers, in order to take in the rear that terrible redoubt whose front fire is still mowing the ranks of the viceroy.

Caulaincourt's reply was, "You shall see me there presently, alive or dead." He immediately set off, overthrew all before him, and turning suddenly round on the left with his cuirassiers, was the first to enter the bloody redoubt, when he was struck dead by a musket-ball. His conquest was his tomb.

They ran immediately to acquaint the emperor with this victory, and the loss which it had occasioned. The grand-equerry, brother of the unfortunate general, listened, and was at first petrified; but he soon summoned courage against this misfortune, and, but for the tears which silently coursed down his cheeks, you might have thought that he felt nothing. The emperor, uttering an exclamation of sorrow, said to him, "You have heard the news, do you wish to retire?" But as at that moment we were advancing against the enemy, the grand-equerry made no reply; he did not retire; he only half uncovered himself to thank the emperor, and to refuse.

While this determined charge of cavalry was executing, the viceroy, with his infantry, was on the point of reaching the mouth of this volcano, when suddenly he saw its fires extinguished, its smoke disappear, and its summit glittering with the moveable and resplendent armour of our cuirassiers. These heights, hitherto Russian, had at last become French; he hastened forward to share and terminate the victory, and to strengthen himself in that position.

But the Russians had not yet abandoned it; they returned with greater obstinacy and fury to the attack; successively as they were beat back by our troops, they were again rallied by their generals, and finally the greater part perished at the foot of these works, which they had themselves raised.

Fortunately, their last attacking column presented itself towards Semenowska and the great redoubt, without its artillery, the progress of which had, no doubt, been retarded by the ravines. Belliard had barely time to collect thirty cannon against this infantry. They came almost close to the mouths of our pieces, which overwhelmed them so apropos, that they wheeled round and retreated without being even able to deploy. Murat and Belliard then said, that if they could have had at that moment ten thousand infantry of the reserve, their victory would have been decisive; but that, being reduced to their cavalry, they considered themselves fortunate to keep possession of the field of battle.

On his side, Grouchy, by sanguinary and repeated charges on the left of the great redoubt, secured the victory, and scoured the plain. But it was impossible to pursue the fugitive Russians; fresh ravines, with armed redoubts behind them, protected their retreat. There they defended themselves with fury until the approach of night, covering in this manner the great road to Moscow, their holy city, their magazine, their depot, their place of refuge.

From this second range of heights, their artillery overwhelmed the first which they had abandoned to us. The viceroy was obliged to conceal his panting, exhausted, and thinned lines in the hollows of the ground, and behind the half-destroyed entrenchments. The soldiers were obliged to get upon their knees, and crouch themselves up behind these shapeless parapets. In that painful posture they remained for several hours, kept in check by the enemy, who stood in check of them.

It was about half-past three o'clock when this last victory was achieved; there had been several such during the day; each corps successively beat that which was opposed to it, without being able to take advantage of its success to decide the battle; as, not being supported in proper time by the reserve, each halted exhausted. But at last all the first obstacles were overcome; the firing gradually slackened, and got to a greater distance from the emperor. Officers were coming in to him from all parts. Poniatowski and Sebastiani, after an obstinate contest, were also victorious. The enemy halted, and entrenched himself in a new position. It was getting late, our ammunition was exhausted, and the battle ended.

Belliard then returned for the third time to the emperor, whose sufferings appeared to have increased. He mounted his horse with difficulty, and rode slowly along the heights of Semenowska. He found a field of battle imperfectly gained, as the enemy's bullets, and even their musket-balls, still disputed the possession of it with us.

In the midst of these warlike noises, and the still burning ardour of Ney and Murat, he continued always in the same state, his gait desponding, and his voice languid. The sight of the Russians, however, and the noise of their continued firing, seemed again to inspire him; he went to take a nearer view of their last position, and even wished to drive them from it. But Murat, pointing to the scanty remains of our own troops, declared that it would require the guard to finish; on which, Bessières continuing to insist, as he always did, on the importance of this *corps d'elite*, objected "the distance the emperor was from his reinforcements; that Europe was between him and France; that it was indispensable to preserve, at least, that handful of soldiers, which was all that remained to answer for his safety." And as it was then nearly five o'clock, Berthier added, "that it was too late; that the enemy was strengthening himself in his last position; and that it would require a sacrifice of several more thousands, without any adequate results." Napoleon then thought of nothing but to recommend the victors to be prudent. Afterwards he returned, still at the same slow pace, to his tent, that had been erected behind that battery which was carried two days before, and in front of which he had remained ever since the morning, an almost motionless spectator of all the vicissitudes of that terrible day.

As he was thus returning, he called Mortier to him, and ordered him "to make the young guard now advance, but on no account to pass the new ravine which separated us from the enemy." He added, "that he gave him in charge to guard the field of battle; that that was all required of him; that he was at liberty to do whatever he thought necessary for that purpose, and nothing more." He recalled him shortly after to ask "if he had properly understood him; recommended him to make no attack; but merely to guard the field of battle." An hour afterwards he sent to him to reiterate the order, "neither to advance nor retreat, whatever might happen."

CHAPTER 45

The Imperfect Victory

After he had retired to his tent, great mental anguish was added to his previous physical dejection. He had seen the field of battle; places had spoken much more loudly than men; the victory which he had so eagerly pursued, and so dearly bought, was incomplete. Was this he who had always pushed his successes to the farthest possible limits, whom Fortune had just found cold and inactive, at a time when she was offering him her last favours?

The losses were certainly immense, and out of all proportion to the advantages gained. Every one around him had to lament the loss of a friend, a relation, or a brother; for the fate of battles had fallen on the most distinguished. Forty-three generals had been killed or wounded. What a mourning for Paris! what a triumph for his enemies! what a dangerous subject for the reflections of Germany! In his army, even in his very tent, his victory was silent, gloomy, isolated, even without flatterers!

The persons whom he had summoned, Dumas and Daru, listened to him, and said nothing; but their attitude, their downcast eyes, and their silence, spoke more eloquently than words.

It was now ten o'clock. Murat, whom twelve hours' fighting had not exhausted, again came to ask him for the cavalry of his guard. "The enemy's army," said he, "is passing the Moskwa in haste and disorder; I wish to surprise and extinguish it." The emperor repelled this sally of immoderate ardour; afterwards he dictated the bulletin of the day.

He seemed pleased at announcing to Europe, that neither he nor his guard had been at all exposed. By some this care was regarded as a refinement of self-love; but those who were better informed thought very differently. They had never seen him display any vain or gratuitous passion, and their idea was, that at that distance, and at the head of an army of foreigners, who had no other bond of union but victory, he had judged it indispensable to preserve a select and devoted body.

His enemies, in fact, would have no longer any thing to hope from fields of battle; neither his death, as he had no need to expose his person in order to insure success, nor a victory, as his genius was sufficient at a distance, even without bringing forward his reserve. As long, therefore, as this guard remained untouched, his real power and that which he derived from opinion would remain entire. It seemed to be a sort of security to him, against his allies, as well as against his enemies: on that account he took so much pains to inform Europe of the preservation of that formidable reserve; and yet it scarcely amounted to 20,000 men, of whom more than a third were new recruits.

These were powerful motives, but they did not at all satisfy men who knew that excellent reasons may be found for committing the greatest faults. They all agreed, "that they had seen the battle which had been won in the morning on the right, halt where it was favourable to us, and continue successively in front, a contest of mere strength, as in the infancy of the art! it was a battle without any plan, a mere victory of soldiers, rather than of a general! Why so much precipitation to overtake the enemy, with an army panting, exhausted, and weakened? and when we had come up with him, why neglect to complete his discomfiture, and remain bleeding and mutilated, in the midst of an enraged nation, in immense deserts, and at 800 leagues' distance from our resources?"

Murat then exclaimed, "That in this great day he had not recognized the genius of Napoleon!" The viceroy confessed "that he had no conception what could be the reason of the indecision which his adopted father had shown." Ney, when he was called on for his opinion, was singularly obstinate in advising him to retreat.

Those alone who had never quitted his person, observed, that the conqueror of so many nations had been overcome by a burning fever, and above all by a fatal return of that painful malady which every violent movement, and all long and strong emotions excited in him. They then quoted the words which he himself had written in Italy fifteen years before: "Health is indispensable in war, and nothing can replace it;" and the exclamation, unfortunately prophetic, which he had uttered on the plains of Austerlitz: "Ordener is worn out. One is not always fit for war; I shall be good for six years longer, after which I must lie by."

During the night, the Russians made us sensible of their vicinity, by their unseasonable clamours. Next morning there was an alert, close to the emperor's tent. The old guard was actually obliged to run to arms; a circumstance which, after a victory, seemed insulting. The army remained motionless until noon, or rather it might be said that there was no longer an army, but a single vanguard. The rest of the troops were dispersed over the field of battle to carry off the wounded, of whom there were 20,000. They were taken to the great abbey of Kolotskoi, two leagues in the rear.

Larrey, the surgeon-in-chief, had just taken assistants from all the regiments; the ambulances had rejoined, but all was insufficient. He has since complained, in a printed narrative, that no troop had been left him to procure the most necessary articles in the surrounding villages.

The emperor then rode over the field of battle; never did one present so horrible an appearance. Every thing concurred to make it so; a gloomy sky, a cold rain, a violent wind, houses burnt to ashes, a plain turned topsy-turvy, covered with ruins and rubbish, in the distance the sad and sombre verdure of the trees of the North; soldiers roaming about in all directions, and hunting for provisions, even in the haversacks of their dead companions; horrible wounds, for the Russian musket-balls are larger than ours; silent bivouacs, no singing or story-telling—a gloomy taciturnity.

Round the eagles were seen the remaining officers and subalterns, and a few soldiers, scarcely enough to protect the colours. Their clothes had been torn in the fury of the combat, were blackened with powder, and spotted with blood; and yet, in the midst of their rags, their misery, and disasters, they had a proud look, and at the sight of the emperor, uttered some shouts of triumph, but they were rare and excited; for in this army, capable at once of analysis and enthusiasm, every one was sensible of the position of all.

French soldiers are not easily deceived; they were astonished to find so many of the enemy killed, so great a number wounded, and so few prisoners, there being not 800 of the latter. By the number of these, the extent of a victory had been formerly calculated. The dead bodies were rather a proof of the courage of the vanquished, than the evidence of a victory. If the rest retreated in such good order, proud, and so little discouraged, what signified the gain of a field of battle? In such extensive countries, would there ever be any want of ground for the Russians to fight on?

As for us, we had already too much, and a great deal more than we were able to retain. Could that be called conquering it? The long and straight furrow which we had traced with so much difficulty from Kowno, across sands and ashes, would it not close behind us, like that of a vessel on an immense ocean! A few peasants, badly armed, might easily efface all traces of it.

In fact they were about to carry off, in the rear of the army, our wounded and our marauders. Five hundred stragglers soon fell into their hands. It is true that some French soldiers, arrested in this manner, affected to join these Cossacks; they assisted them in making fresh captures, until finding themselves sufficiently numerous, with their new prisoners, they collected together suddenly and rid themselves of their unsuspecting enemies.

The emperor could not value his victory otherwise than by the dead. The ground was strewed to such a degree with Frenchmen, extended prostrate on the redoubts, that they appeared to belong more to them than to those who remained standing. There seemed to be more victors killed there, than there were still living.

Amidst the crowd of corpses which we were obliged to march over in following Napoleon, the foot of a horse encountered a wounded man, and extorted from him a last sign of life or of suffering. The emperor, hitherto equally silent with his victory, and whose heart felt oppressed by the sight of so many victims, gave an exclamation; he felt relieved by uttering cries of indignation, and lavishing the attentions of humanity on this unfortunate creature. To pacify him, somebody remarked that it was only a Russian, but he retorted warmly, "that after victory there are no enemies, but only men!" He then dispersed the officers of his suite, in order to succour the wounded, who were heard groaning in every direction.

Great numbers were found at the bottom of the ravines, into which the greater part of our men had been precipitated, and where many had dragged themselves, in order to be better protected from the enemy, and the violence of the storm. Some groaningly pronounced the name of their country or their mother; these were the youngest: the elder ones waited the approach of death, some with a tranquil, and others with a sardonic air, without deigning to implore for mercy or to complain; others besought us to kill them outright: these unfortunate men were quickly passed by, having neither the useless pity to assist them, nor the cruel pity to put an end to their sufferings.

One of these, the most mutilated (one arm and his trunk being all that remained to him) appeared so animated, so full of hope, and even of gaiety, that an attempt was made to save him. In bearing him along, it was remarked that he complained of suffering in the limbs, which he no longer possessed; this is a common case with mutilated persons, and seems to afford additional evidence that the soul remains entire, and that feeling belongs to it alone, and not to the body, which can no more feel than it can think.

The Russians were seen dragging themselves along to places where dead bodies were heaped together, and offered them a horrible retreat. It has been affirmed by several persons, that one of these poor fellows lived for several days in the carcase of a horse, which had been gutted by a shell, and the inside of which he gnawed. Some were seen straightening their broken leg by tying a branch of a tree tightly against it, then supporting themselves with another branch, and walking in this manner to the next village. Not one of them uttered a groan.

Perhaps, when far from their own homes, they looked less for compassion. But certainly they appeared to support pain with greater fortitude than the French; not that they suffered more courageously, but that they suffered less; for they have less feeling in body and mind, which arises from their being less civilized, and from their organs being hardened by the climate.

During this melancholy review, the emperor in vain sought to console himself with a cheering illusion, by having a second enumeration made of the few prisoners who remained, and collecting together some dismounted cannon: from seven to eight hundred prisoners, and twenty broken cannon, were all the trophies of this imperfect victory.

Chapter 46
The Russians Retreat

At the same time, Murat kept pushing the Russian rear-guard as far as Mojaisk: the road which it uncovered on its retreat was perfectly clear, and without a single fragment of men, carriages, or dress. All their dead had been buried, for they have a religious respect for the dead.

At the sight of Mojaisk, Murat fancied himself already in possession of it, and sent to inform the emperor that he might sleep there. But the Russian rear-guard had taken a position outside the walls of the town, and the remains of their army were placed on a height behind it. In this way they covered the Moscow and the Kalouga roads.

Perhaps Kutusoff hesitated which of these two roads to take, or was desirous of leaving us in uncertainty as to the one he had taken, which was the case. Besides, the Russians felt it a point of honour to bivouac at only four leagues from the scene of our victory. That also allowed them time to disencumber the road behind them and clear away their fragments.

Their attitude was equally firm and imposing as before the battle, which we could not help admiring; but something of this was also attributable to the length of time we had taken to quit the field of Borodino, and to a deep ravine which was between them and our cavalry. Murat did not perceive this obstacle, but General Dery, one of his officers, guessed it. He went and reconnoitred the ground, close to the gates of the town, under the Russian bayonets.

But the king of Naples, quite as fiery as at the beginning of the campaign, or of his military life, made nothing of the obstacle; he summoned his cavalry, called to them furiously to advance, to charge and break through these battalions, gates, and walls! In vain his aid-de-camp urged the impossibility of effecting his orders; he pointed out to him the army on the opposite heights, which commanded Mojaisk, and the ravine where the remains of our cavalry were about to be swallowed up. Murat, in greater fury than ever, insisted "that they must march, and if there was any obstacle, they would see it." He then made use of insulting phrases to urge them on, and his orders were about to be carried,—with some delay, nevertheless, for there was generally an understanding to retard their execution, in order to give him time to reflect, and to allow time for a counter-order, which had been anticipated to arrive before any misfortune happened, which was not always the case, but was so this time. Murat was satisfied with wasting his cannon and powder on some drunken and straggling Cossacks by whom he was almost surrounded, and who attacked him with frightful howls.

This skirmish, however, was sufficiently serious to add to the losses of the preceding day, as general Belliard was wounded in it. This officer, who was a great loss to Murat, was employed in reconnoitring the left of the enemy's position. As it was approachable, the attack should have been made on that side, but Murat never thought of any thing but striking what was immediately before him.

The emperor only arrived on the field of battle at nightfall, escorted by a very feeble detachment. He advanced towards Mojaisk, at a still slower pace than the day before, and so completely absent, that he neither seemed to hear the noise of the engagement, nor that of the bullets which were whistling around him.

Some one stopped him, and pointed out to him the enemy's rear-guard between him and the town; and on the heights behind, the fires of an army of 50,000 men. This sight was a proof of the incompleteness of his victory, and how little the enemy were discouraged; but he seemed quite insensible of it; he listened to the reports with a dejected and listless air, and returned to sleep at a village some little distance off, which was within reach of the enemy's fire.

The Russian autumn had triumphed over him: had it not been for that, perhaps the whole of Russia would have yielded to our arms on the plains of the Moskwa: its premature inclemency was a most seasonable assistance to their empire. It was on the 6th of September, the very day before the great battle! that a hurricane announced its fatal commencement. It struck Napoleon. Ever since the night of that day, it has been seen that a wearying fever had dried up his blood, and oppressed his spirits, and that he was quite overcome by it during the battle; the suffering he endured from this, added to another still more severe, for the five following days arrested his march, and bound up his genius. This it was which preserved Kutusoff from total ruin at Borodino, and allowed him time to rally the remainder of his army, and withdraw it from our pursuit.

On the 9th of September we found Mojaisk uncovered, and still standing: but beyond it the enemy's rear-guard on the heights which command it, and which their army had occupied the day before. Some of our troops entered the town for the purpose of passing through it in pursuit of the enemy, and others to plunder and find lodgings for themselves. They found neither inhabitants nor provisions, but merely dead bodies, which they were obliged to throw out of the windows, in order to get themselves under cover, and a number of dying soldiers, who were all collected into one spot. These last were so numerous, and had been so scattered about, that the Russians had not dared to set fire to the habitations; but their humanity, which was not always so scrupulous, had given way to the desire of firing on the first French they saw enter, which they did with shells: the consequence was, that this wooden town was soon set fire to, and a part of the unfortunate wounded whom they had abandoned were consumed in the flames.

While we were making attempts to save them, fifty voltigeurs of the 33rd climbed the heights, of which the enemy's cavalry and artillery still occupied the summit. The French army, which had halted under the walls of Mojaisk, was surprised at seeing this handful of men, scattered about on this uncovered declivity, teasing with their fire thousands of the enemy's cavalry. All at once what had been foreseen happened; several of the enemy's squadrons put themselves in motion, and in an instant surrounded these bold fellows, who immediately formed, and kept facing and firing at them in all directions; but they were so few in the midst of a large plain, and the number of cavalry about them was so great, that they soon disappeared from our eyes. A general exclamation of sorrow burst from the whole of our lines. Every one of the soldiers with his neck stretched, and his eye fixed, followed the enemy's movements, and endeavoured to distinguish the fate of his companions in arms. Some were lamenting the distance they were at, and wishing to march; others mechanically loaded their muskets or crossed their bayonets with a threatening air, as if they had been near enough to assist them. Their looks were sometimes as animated as if they were fighting, and at other times as much distressed as if they had been beat. Others advised and encouraged them, forgetting that they were out of reach of hearing.

Several volleys of smoke, ascending from amidst the black mass of horses, prolonged the uncertainty. Some cried out, that it was our men firing, and still defending themselves, and that they were not yet beat. In fact, a Russian commanding officer had just been killed by the officer commanding these *tirailleurs*. This was the way in which he replied to the summons to surrender. Our anxiety lasted some minutes longer, when all at once the army set up a cry of joy and admiration at seeing the Russian cavalry, intimidated at this bold resistance, separate in order to escape their well-directed fire, disperse, and at last allow us to see once more this handful of brave fellows master of this extensive field of battle, of which it only occupied a few feet.

When the Russians saw that we were manoeuvring seriously to attack them, they disappeared without leaving us any traces to follow them. This was the same they had done at Witepsk and Smolensk, and what was still more remarkable, the second day after their great disaster. At first there was some uncertainty whether to follow the road to Moscow or that to Kalouga, after which Murat and Mortier proceeded, at all hazards, towards Moscow.

They marched for two days, with no other food than horse-flesh and bruised wheat, without finding a single person or thing by which to discover the Russian army. That army, although its infantry only formed one confused mass, did not leave behind it a single fragment; such was the national spirit and habit of obedience in it, collectively and singly, and so thoroughly unprovided were we with every kind of information, as well as resources, in this deserted and thoroughly hostile country.

The army of Italy was advancing at some leagues' distance on the left of the great road, and surprised some of the armed peasantry, who were not accustomed to fighting; but their master, with a dagger in his hand, rushed upon our soldiers like a madman: he exclaimed that he had no longer a religion, empire, or country to defend, and that life was odious to him; they were willing, however, to leave him that, but as he attempted to kill the soldiers who surrounded him, pity yielded to anger, and his wish was gratified.

Near Krymskoié, on the 11th of September, the hostile army again made its appearance, firmly established in a strong position. It had returned to its plan of looking more to the ground, in its retreat, than to the enemy. The duke of Treviso at first satisfied Murat of the impossibility of attacking it; but the smell of powder soon intoxicated that monarch. He committed himself, and obliged Dufour, Mortier, and their infantry, to advance to his support. This consisted of the remains of Friand's division, and the young guard. There were lost, without the least utility, 2000 men of that reserve which had been so unseasonably spared on the day of battle; and Mortier was so enraged, that he wrote to the emperor, that he would no longer obey Murat's orders. For it was by letter that the generals of the vanguard communicated with Napoleon. He had remained for three days at Mojaisk, confined to his apartment, still consumed by a burning fever, overwhelmed with business, and worn out with anxiety. A violent cold had deprived him of the use of his voice. Compelled to dictate to seven persons at once, and unable to make himself heard, he wrote on different papers the heads of his despatches. When any difficulty arose, he explained himself by signs.

There was a moment when Bessières enumerated to him all the generals who were wounded on the day of the battle. This fatal list affected him so poignantly, that by a violent effort he recovered his voice, and interrupted the marshal by the sudden exclamation, "Eight days at Moscow, and there will be an end of it!"

Meantime, although he had hitherto placed all his futurity in that capital, a victory so sanguinary and so little decisive lowered his hopes. His instructions to Berthier of the 11th of September for marshal Victor exhibited his distress: "The enemy, attacked at the heart, no longer trifles with us at the extremities. Write to the duke of Belluno to direct all, infantry, cavalry, artillery, and isolated soldiers to Smolensk, in order to be forwarded from thence to Moscow."

In the midst of these bodily and mental sufferings, which he carefully concealed from his army, Davoust obtained access to him; his object was to offer himself again, notwithstanding his wound, to take the command of the vanguard, promising that he would contrive to march night and day, reach the enemy, and compel him to fight, without squandering, as Murat did, the strength and lives of the soldiers. Napoleon only answered him by extolling in high terms the audacious and inexhaustible ardour of his brother-in-law.

He had just before heard, that the enemy's army had again been found; that it had not retired upon his right flank, towards Kalouga, as he had feared it would; that it was still retreating, and that his vanguard was already within two days' march of Moscow. That great name, and the great hopes which he attached to it, revived his strength, and on the 12th of September, he was sufficiently recovered to set out in a carriage, in order to join his vanguard.

CHAPTER 47

Moscow

We have seen how the Emperor Alexander, surprised at Wilna amidst his preparations for defence, retreated with his disunited army, and was unable to rally it till it was at the distance of a hundred leagues from that city, between Witepsk and Smolensk. That Prince, hurried along in the precipitate retreat of Barclay, sought refuge at Drissa, in a camp injudiciously chosen and entrenched at great expense; a mere point in the space, on so extensive a frontier, and which served only to indicate to the enemy the object of his manoeuvres.

Alexander, however, encouraged by the sight of this camp, and of the Düna, took breath behind that river. It was there that he first consented to receive an English agent, so important did he deem it to appear till that moment faithful to his engagements with France. Whether he acted with real good faith, or merely made a show of doing so, we know not: so much is certain, that at Paris, after his success, he affirmed, on his honour, to Count Daru, that, "notwithstanding the accusations of Napoleon, this was his first infraction of the treaty of Tilsit."

At the same time he caused Barclay to issue addresses, designed to corrupt the French and their allies, similar to those which had so irritated Napoleon at Klubokoe;—attempts which the French regarded as contemptible, and the Germans as unseasonable.

In other respects, the Emperor had given his enemies but a mean opinion of his military talents: this opinion was founded on his having neglected the Berezina, the only natural line of defence of Lithuania; on his eccentric retreat towards the north, when the rest of his army was fleeing southward; and lastly, on his ukase relative to recruiting, dated Drissa, which assigned to the recruits, for their places of rendezvous, several towns that were almost immediately occupied by the French. His departure from the army, as soon as it began to fight, was also a subject of remark.

As to his political measures in his new and in his old provinces, and his proclamations from Polotsk to his army, to Moscow, to his great nation, it was admitted that they were singularly adapted to persons and places. It appears, in fact, that in the political means which he employed there was a very striking gradation of energy.

In the recently acquired portion of Lithuania, houses, inhabitants, crops, in short every thing had been spared, either from hurry or designedly. The most powerful of the nobles had alone been carried off: their defection might have set too dangerous an example, and had they still further committed themselves, their return in the sequel would have been more difficult; besides, they were hostages.

In the provinces of Lithuania which had been of old incorporated with the empire, where a mild administration, favours judiciously bestowed, and a longer habit of subjection, had extinguished the recollection of independence, the inhabitants were hurried away with all they could carry with them. Still it was not deemed expedient to require of subjects professing a different religion, and a nascent patriotism, the destruction of property: a levy of five men only out of every five hundred males was ordered.

But in Russia Proper, where religion, superstition, ignorance, patriotism, all went hand in hand with the government, not only had the inhabitants been obliged to retreat with the army, but every thing that could not be removed had been destroyed. Those who were not destined to recruit the regulars, joined the militia or the Cossacks.

The interior of the empire being then threatened, it was for Moscow to set an example. That capital, justly denominated by its poets, *"Moscow with the golden cupolas,"* was a vast and motley assemblage of two hundred and ninety-five churches, and fifteen hundred mansions, with their gardens and dependencies. These palaces of brick, and their parks, intermixed with neat houses of wood, and even thatched cottages, were spread over several square leagues of irregular ground: they were grouped round a lofty triangular fortress; the vast double enclosure of which, half a league in circuit, contained, the one, several palaces, some churches, and rocky and uncultivated spots; the other, a prodigious bazaar, the town of the merchants and shopkeepers, where was displayed the collected wealth of the four quarters of the globe.

These edifices, these palaces, nay, the very shops themselves, were all covered with polished and painted iron: the churches, each surmounted by a terrace and several steeples, terminating in golden balls, then the crescent, and lastly the cross, reminded the spectator of the history of this nation: it was Asia and its religion, at first victorious, subsequently vanquished, and finally the crescent of Mahomet surmounted by the cross of Christ.

A single ray of sun-shine caused this splendid city to glisten with a thousand varied colours. At sight of it the traveller paused, delighted and astonished. It reminded him of the prodigies with which the oriental poets had amused his childhood. On entering it, a nearer view served but to heighten his astonishment: he recognized the nobles by the manners, the habits, and the different languages of modern Europe; and by the rich and light elegance of their dress. He beheld, with surprise, the luxury and the Asiatic form of those of the merchants; the Grecian costumes of the common people, and their long beards. He was struck by the same variety in the edifices: and yet all this was tinged with a local and sometimes harsh colour, such as befits the country of which Moscow was the ancient capital.

When, lastly, he observed the grandeur and magnificence of so many palaces, the wealth which they displayed, the luxury of the equipages, the multitude of slaves and servants, the splendour of those gorgeous spectacles, the noise of those sumptuous festivities, entertainments, and rejoicings, which incessantly resounded within its walls, he fancied himself transported into a city of kings, into an assemblage of sovereigns, who had brought with them their manners, customs, and attendants from all parts of the world.

They were, nevertheless, only subjects; but opulent and powerful subjects; grandees, vain of their ancient nobility, strong in their collected numbers, and in the general ties of consanguinity contracted during the seven centuries which this capital had existed. They were landed proprietors, proud of their existence amidst their vast possessions; for almost the whole territory of the government of Moscow belongs to them, and they there reign over a million of serfs. Finally, they were nobles, resting, with a patriotic and religious pride, upon "the cradle and the tomb of their nobility"—for such is the appellation which they give to Moscow.

It seems right, in fact, that here the nobles of the most illustrious families should be born and educated; that hence they should launch into the career of honours and glory; and lastly, that hither, when satisfied, discontented, or undeceived, they should bring their disgust, or their resentment to pour it forth; their reputation, in order to enjoy it, to exercise its influence on the young nobility; and to recruit, at a distance from power, of which they have nothing farther to expect, their pride, which has been too long bowed down near the throne.

Here their ambition, either satiated or disappointed, has assumed, amidst their own dependents, and as it were beyond the reach of the court, a greater freedom of speech: it is a sort of privilege which time has sanctioned, of which they are tenacious, and which their sovereign respects. They become worse courtiers, but better citizens. Hence the dislike of their princes to visit this vast repository of glory and of commerce, this city of nobles whom they have disgraced or disgusted, whose age or reputation places them beyond their power, and to whom they are obliged to show indulgence.

To this city necessity brought Alexander: he repaired thither from Polotsk, preceded by his proclamations, and looked for by the nobility and the mercantile class. His first appearance was amidst the assembled nobility. There every thing was great—the circumstance, the assembly, the speaker, and the resolutions which he inspired. His voice betrayed emotion. No sooner had he ceased, than one general simultaneous, unanimous cry burst from all hearts:—"Ask what you please, sire! we offer you every thing! take our all!"

One of the nobles then proposed the levy of a militia; and in order to its formation, the gift of one peasant in twenty-five: but a hundred voices interrupted him, crying, that "the country required a greater sacrifice; that it was necessary to grant one serf in ten, ready armed, equipped, and supplied with provisions for three months." This was offering, for the single government of Moscow, eighty thousand men, and a great quantity of stores.

This sacrifice was immediately voted without deliberation—some say with enthusiasm, and that it was executed in like manner, so long as the danger was at hand. Others have attributed the concurrence of this assembly to so urgent a proposition, to submission alone—a sentiment indeed, which, in the presence of absolute power, absorbs every other.

They add, that, on the breaking up of the meeting, the principal nobles were heard to murmur among themselves against the extravagance of such a measure. "Was the danger then so pressing? Was there not the Russian army, which, as they were told, still numbered four hundred thousand men, to defend them? Why then deprive them of so many peasants! The service of these men would be, it was said, only temporary; but who could ever wish for their return? It was, on the contrary, an event to be dreaded. Would these serfs, habituated to the irregularities of war, bring back their former submission? Undoubtedly not: they would return full of new sentiments and new ideas, with which they would infect the villages; they would there propagate a refractory spirit, which would give infinite trouble to the master by spoiling the slave."

Be this as it may, the resolution of that meeting was generous, and worthy of so great a nation. The details are of little consequence. We well know that it is the same everywhere; that every thing in the world loses by being seen too near; and lastly, that nations ought to be judged by the general mass and by results.

Alexander then addressed the merchants, but more briefly: he ordered that proclamation to be read to them, in which Napoleon was represented as "a perfidious wretch; a Moloch, who, with treachery in his heart and loyalty on his lips, was striving to sweep Russia from the face of the earth."

It is said that, at these words, the masculine and highly coloured faces of the auditors, to which long beards imparted a look at once antique, majestic and wild, were inflamed with rage. Their eyes flashed fire; they were seized with a convulsive fury: their stiffened arms, their clenched fists, the gnashing of their teeth, and subdued execrations, expressed its vehemence. The effect was correspondent. Their chief, whom they elect themselves, proved himself worthy of his station: he put down his name the first for fifty thousand roubles. It was two-thirds of his fortune, and he paid it the next day.

These merchants are divided into three classes: it was proposed to fix the contribution for each; but one of the assembly, who was included in the lowest class, declared that his patriotism would not brook any limit, and he immediately subscribed a sum far surpassing the proposed standard: the others followed his example more or less closely. Advantage was taken of their first emotions. Every thing was at hand that was requisite to bind them irrevocably while they were yet together, excited by one another, and by the words of their sovereign.

This patriotic donation amounted, it is said, to two millions of roubles. The other governments repeated, like so many echoes, the national cry of Moscow. The Emperor accepted all; but all could not be given immediately: and when, in order to complete his work, he claimed the rest of the promised succours, he was obliged to have recourse to constraint; the danger which had alarmed some and inflamed others, having by that time ceased to exist.

CHAPTER 48

The City Abandoned

Meanwhile Smolensk was soon reduced; Napoleon at Wiazma, and consternation in Moscow. The great battle was not yet lost, and already people began to abandon that capital.

The governor-general, Count Rostopchin, told the women, in his proclamations, that "he should not detain *them*, as the less fear the less danger there would be; but that their brothers and husbands must stay, or they would cover themselves with infamy." He then added encouraging particulars concerning the hostile force, which consisted, according to his statement, of "one hundred and fifty thousand men, who were reduced to the necessity of feeding on horse-flesh. The Emperor Alexander was about to return to his faithful capital; eighty-three thousand Russians, both recruits and militia, with eighty pieces of cannon, were marching towards Borodino, to join Kutusoff."

He thus concluded: "If these forces are not sufficient, I will say to you, 'Come, my friends, and inhabitants of Moscow, let us march also! we will assemble one hundred thousand men: we will take the image of the Blessed Virgin, and one hundred and fifty pieces of cannon, and put an end to the business at once!'"

It has been remarked as a purely local singularity, that most of these proclamations were in the scriptural style and in poetic prose.

At the same time a prodigious balloon was constructed, by command of Alexander, not far from Moscow, under the direction of a German artificer. The destination of this winged machine was to hover over the French army, to single out its chief, and destroy him by a shower of balls and fire. Several attempts were made to raise it, but without success, the springs by which the wings were to be worked having always broken.

Rostopchin, nevertheless, affecting to persevere, is said to have caused a great quantity of rockets and other combustibles to be prepared. Moscow itself was designed to be the great infernal machine, the sudden nocturnal explosion of which was to consume the Emperor and his army. Should the enemy escape this danger, he would at least no longer have an asylum or resources; and the horror of so tremendous a calamity, which would be charged to his account, as had been done in regard to the disasters of Smolensk, Dorogobouje, Wiazma, and Gjatz, would not fail to rouse the whole of Russia.

Such was the terrible plan of this noble descendant of one of the greatest Asiatic conquerors. It was conceived without effort, matured with care, and executed without hesitation. This Russian nobleman has since visited Paris. He is a steady man, a good husband, an excellent father: he has a superior and cultivated mind, and in society his manners are mild and pleasing: but, like some of his countrymen, he combines an antique energy with the civilization of modern times.

His name henceforth belongs to history: still he had only the largest share in the honour of this great sacrifice. It had been previously commenced at Smolensk, and it was he who completed it. This resolution, like every thing great and entire, was admirable; the motive sufficient and justified by success; the devotedness unparalleled, and so extraordinary, that the historian is obliged to pause in order to fathom, to comprehend, and to contemplate it.[19]

One single individual, amidst a vast empire nearly overthrown, surveys its danger with steady eye: he measures, he appreciates it, and ventures, perhaps uncommissioned, to devote all the public and private interests a sacrifice to it. Though but a subject, he decides the lot of the state, without the countenance of his sovereign; a noble, he decrees the destruction of the palaces of all the nobles, without their consent; the protector, from the post which he occupies, of a numerous population, of a multitude of opulent merchants and traders, of one of the largest capitals in Europe, he sacrifices their fortunes, their establishments, nay, the whole city: he himself consigns to the flames

---

19: A Count Rostopchin, we know, has written that he had no hand in that great event: but we cannot help following the opinion of the Russians and French, who were witnesses of and actors in this grand drama. All, without exception, persist in attributing to that nobleman the entire honour of that generous resolution. Several even seem to think, that if Count Rostopchin, who is yet animated by the same noble spirit, which will render his name imperishable, still refuses the immortality of so great an action, it is that he may leave all the glory of it to the patriotism of the nation, of which he is become one of the most remarkable characters.

the finest and the richest of his palaces, and proud and satisfied, he quietly remains among the resentful sufferers who have been injured or utterly ruined by the measure.

What motive then could be so just and so powerful as to inspire him with such astonishing confidence? In deciding upon the destruction of Moscow, his principal aim was not to famish the enemy, since he had contrived to clear that great city of provisions; nor to deprive the French army of shelter, since it was impossible to suppose that out of eight thousand houses and churches, dispersed over so vast a space, there should not be left buildings enough to serve as barracks for one hundred and fifty thousand men.

He was no doubt aware also that by such a step he would counteract that very important point of what was supposed to be the plan of campaign formed by Alexander, whose object was thought to be to entice forward and to detain Napoleon, till winter should come upon him, seize him, and deliver him up defenceless to the whole incensed nation. For it was natural to presume that these flames would enlighten that conqueror; they would take from his invasion its end and aim. They would of course compel him to renounce it while it was yet time, and decide him to return to Lithuania, for the purpose of taking up winter quarters in that country—a determination which was likely to prepare for Russia a second campaign more dangerous than the first.

But in this important crisis Rostopchin perceived two great dangers; the one, which threatened the national honour, was that of a disgraceful peace dictated at Moscow, and forced upon his sovereign; the other was a political rather than a military danger, in which he feared the seductions of the enemy more than his arms, and a revolution more than a conquest.

Averse, therefore, to any treaty, this governor foresaw that in the populous capital, which the Russians themselves style the oracle, the example of the whole empire, Napoleon would have recourse to the weapon of revolution, the only one that would be left him to accomplish his purpose. For this reason he resolved to raise a barrier of fire between that great captain and all weaknesses, from whatever quarter they might proceed, whether from the throne or from his countrymen, either nobles or senators; and more especially between a population of serfs and the soldiers of a free nation; in short, between the latter and that mass of artisans and tradesmen, who form in Moscow the commencement of an intermediate class—a class for which the French Revolution was specially adapted.

All the preparations were made in silence, without the knowledge either of the people, the proprietors of all classes, or perhaps of their Emperor. The nation was ignorant that it was sacrificing itself. This is so strictly true, that, when the moment for execution arrived, we heard the inhabitants who had fled to the churches, execrating this destruction. Those who beheld it from a distance, the most opulent of the nobles, mistaken like their peasants, charged us with it; and in short, those by whom it was ordered threw the odium of it upon us, having engaged in the work of destruction in order to render us objects of detestation, and caring but little about the maledictions of so many unfortunate creatures, provided they could throw the weight of them upon us.

The silence of Alexander leaves room to doubt whether he approved this grand determination or not. What part he took in this catastrophe is still a mystery to the Russians: either they are ignorant on the subject, or they make a secret of the matter:—the effect of despotism, which enjoins ignorance or silence.

Some think that no individual in the whole empire excepting the sovereign, would have dared to take on himself so heavy a responsibility. His subsequent conduct has disavowed without disapproving. Others are of opinion that this was one of the causes of his absence from the army, and that, not wishing to appear either to order or to defend, he would not stay to be a witness of the catastrophe.

As to the general abandonment of the houses, all the way from Smolensk, it was compulsory, the Russian army defending them till they were carried sword in hand, and describing us every where as destructive monsters. The country suffered but little from this emigration. The peasants residing near the high road escaped through by-ways to other villages belonging to their lords, where they found accommodation.

The forsaking of their huts made of trunks of trees laid one upon another, which a hatchet suffices for building, and of which a bench, a table, and an image, constitute the whole furniture, was scarcely any sacrifice for serfs, who had nothing of their own, whose persons did not even belong to themselves, and whose masters were obliged to provide for them, since they were their property, and the source of all their income.

These peasants, moreover, in removing their carts, their implements, and their cattle, carried every thing with them, most of them being able to supply themselves with habitation, clothing, and all other necessaries: for these people are still in but the first stage of civilization, and far from that division of labour which denotes the extension and high improvement of commerce and society.

But in the towns, and especially in the great capital, how could they be expected to quit so many establishments, to resign so many conveniences and enjoyments, so much wealth, moveable and immoveable? and yet it cost little or no more to obtain the total abandonment of Moscow than that of the meanest village. There, as at Vienna, Berlin, and Madrid, the principal nobles hesitated not to retire on our approach: for with them to remain would seem to be the same as to betray. But here, tradesmen, artisans, day-labourers, all thought it their duty to flee like the most powerful of the grandees. There was no occasion to command: these people have not yet ideas sufficient to judge for themselves, to distinguish and to discover differences; the example of the nobles was sufficient. The few foreigners who remained at Moscow might have enlightened them; some of these were exiled, and terror drove away the rest.

It was, besides, an easy task to excite apprehensions of profanation, pillage, and devastation in the minds of people so cut off from other nations, and in the inhabitants of a city which had been so often plundered and burnt by the Tartars. With these examples before their eyes, they could not await an impious and ferocious enemy but for the purpose of fighting him: the rest must necessarily shun his approach with horror, if they would save themselves in this life and in the next: obedience, honour, religion, fear, every thing in short enjoined them to flee, with all that they could carry off.

A fortnight before our arrival, the departure of the archives, the public chests and treasure, and that of the nobles and the principal merchants, together with their most valuable effects, indicated to the rest of the inhabitants what course to pursue. The governor, already impatient to see the city evacuated, appointed superintendents to expedite the emigration.

On the 3rd of September, a Frenchwoman, at the risk of being torn in pieces by the furious Muscovites, ventured to leave her hiding-place. She wandered a long time through extensive quarters, the solitude of which astonished her, when a distant and doleful sound thrilled her with terror. It was like the funeral dirge of this vast city; fixed in motionless suspense, she beheld an immense multitude of persons of both sexes in deep affliction, carrying their effects and their sacred images, and leading their children along with them. Their priests, laden with the sacred symbols of religion, headed the procession. They were invoking heaven in hymns of lamentation, in which all of them joined with tears.

On reaching the gates of the city, this crowd of unfortunate creatures passed through them with painful hesitation: turned their eyes once more towards Moscow, they seemed to be bidding a last farewell to their holy city: but by degrees their sobs and the doleful tones of their hymns died away in the vast plains by which it is surrounded.

Chapter 49
Fili

Thus was this population dispersed in detail or in masses. The roads to Cazan, Wladimir, and Yaroslaf were covered to the distance of forty leagues by fugitives on foot, and several unbroken files of vehicles of every kind. At the same time the measures of Rostopchin to prevent dejection and to preserve order, detained many of these unfortunate people till the very last moment.

To this must be added the appointment of Kutusoff, which had revived their hopes, the false intelligence of a victory at Borodino, and for the less affluent, the hesitation natural at the moment of abandoning the only home which they possessed; lastly, the inadequacy of the means of transport, notwithstanding the quantity of vehicles, which is peculiarly great in Russia; either because heavy requisitions for the exigencies of the army had reduced their number; or because they were too small, as it is customary to make them very light, on account of the sandy soil and the roads, which may be said to be rather marked out than constructed.

It was just then that Kutusoff, though defeated at Borodino, sent letters to all quarters announcing that he was victorious. He deceived Moscow, Petersburg, and even the commanders of the other Russian armies. Alexander communicated this false intelligence to his allies. In the first transports of his joy he hastened to the altars, loaded the army and the family of his general with honours and money, gave directions for rejoicings, returned thanks to heaven, and appointed Kutusoff field-marshal for this defeat.

Most of the Russians affirm that their emperor was grossly imposed upon by this report. They are still unacquainted with the motives of such a deception, which at first procured Kutusoff unbounded favours, that were not withdrawn from him, and afterwards, it is said, dreadful menaces, that were not put in execution.

If we may credit several of his countrymen, who were perhaps his enemies, it would appear that he had two motives. In the first place, he wished not to shake, by disastrous intelligence, the little firmness which, in Russia, Alexander was generally, but erroneously thought to possess. In the second, as he was anxious that his despatch should arrive on the very name-day of his Sovereign, it is added that his object was to obtain the rewards for which this kind of anniversaries furnishes occasion.

But at Moscow the erroneous impression was of short continuance. The rumour of the destruction of half his army was almost immediately propagated in that city, from the singular commotion of extraordinary events, which has been known to spread almost instantaneously to prodigious distances. Still, however, the language of the chiefs, the only persons who durst speak, continued haughty and threatening: many of the inhabitants, trusting to it, remained; but they were every day more and more tormented by a painful anxiety. Nearly at one and the same moment, they were transported with rage, elevated with hope, and overwhelmed with fear.

At one of those moments when, either prostrate before the altars, or in their own houses before the images of their saints, they had no hope but in heaven, shouts of joy suddenly resounded: the people instantly thronged the streets and public places to learn the cause. Intoxicated with joy, their eyes were fixed on the cross of the principal church. A vulture had entangled himself in the chains which supported it and was held suspended by them. This was a certain presage to minds whose natural superstition was heightened by extraordinary anxiety; it was thus that their God would seize and deliver Napoleon into their power.

Rostopchin took advantage of all these movements, which he excited or checked according as they were favourable to him or otherwise. He caused the most diminutive to be selected from the prisoners taken from the enemy, and exhibited to the people, that the latter might derive courage from the sight of their weakness: and yet he emptied Moscow of every kind of supplies, in order to feed the vanquished, and to famish the conquerors. This measure was easily carried into effect, as Moscow was provisioned in spring and autumn by water only, and in winter by sledges.

He was still preserving with a remnant of hope the order that was necessary, especially in such a flight, when the effects of the disaster at Borodino appeared. The long train of wounded, their groans, their garments and linen dyed with gore; their most powerful nobles struck and overthrown like the others—all this was a novel and alarming sight to a city which had for such a length of time been exempt from the horrors of war. The police redoubled its activity; but the terror which it excited could not long make head against a still greater terror.

Rostopchin once more addressed the people. He declared that "he would defend Moscow to the last extremity; that the tribunals were already closed, but that was of no consequence; that there was no occasion for tribunals to try the guilty." He added, that "in two days he would give the signal." He recommended to the people to "arm themselves with hatchets, and especially with three-pronged forks, as the French were not heavier than a sheaf of corn." As for the wounded, he said he should cause "masses to be said and the water to be blessed in order to their speedy recovery. Next day," he added, "he should repair to Kutusoff, to take final measures for exterminating the enemy. And then," said he, "we will send these guests to the devil; we will despatch the perfidious wretches, and fall to work to reduce them to powder."

Kutusoff had in fact never despaired of the salvation of the country. After employing the militia during the battle of Borodino to carry ammunition and to assist the wounded, he had just formed with them the third rank of his army. At Mojaisk, the good face which he had kept up had enabled him to gain sufficient time to make an orderly retreat, to pick his wounded, to abandon such as were incurable, and to embarrass the enemy's army with them. Subsequently at Zelkowo, a check had stopped the impetuous advance of Murat. At length, on the 13th of September, Moscow beheld the fires of the Russian bivouacs.

There the national pride, an advantageous position, and the works with which it was strengthened, all induced a belief that the general had determined to save the capital or to perish with it. He hesitated, however, and whether from policy or prudence, he at length abandoned the governor of Moscow to his full responsibility.

The Russian army in this position of Fili, in front of Moscow, numbered ninety-one thousand men, six thousand of whom were Cossacks, sixty-five thousand veteran troops, (the relics of one hundred and twenty-one thousand engaged at the Moskwa,) and twenty thousand recruits, armed half with muskets and half with pikes.

The French army, one hundred and thirty thousand strong the day before the great battle, had lost about forty thousand men at Borodino, and still consisted of ninety thousand. Some regiments on the march and the divisions of Laborde and Pino had just rejoined it: so that on its arrival before Moscow it still amounted to nearly one hundred thousand men. Its march was retarded by six hundred and seven pieces of cannon, two thousand five hundred artillery carriages, and five thousand baggage wagons; it had no more ammunition than would suffice for one engagement. Kutusoff perhaps calculated the disproportion between his effective force and ours. On this point, however, nothing but conjecture can be advanced, or he assigned purely military motives for his retreat.

So much is certain, that the old general deceived the governor to the very last moment. He even swore to him "by his grey hair that he would perish with him before Moscow," when all at once the governor was informed, that in a council of war held at night in the camp, it had been determined to abandon the capital without a battle.

Rostopchin was incensed, but not daunted by this intelligence. There was now no time to be lost, no farther pains were taken to conceal from Moscow the fate that was destined for it; indeed it was not worth while to dissemble for the sake of the few inhabitants who were left; and besides it was necessary to induce them to seek their safety in flight.

At night, therefore, emissaries went round, knocking at every door and announcing the conflagration. Fusees were introduced at every favourable aperture, and especially into the shops covered with iron of the tradesmen's quarter. The fire engines were carried off: the desolation attained its highest pitch, and each individual, according to his disposition, was either overwhelmed with distress or urged to a decision. Most of those who were left formed groups in the public places; they crowded together, questioned each other, and reciprocally asked advice: many wandered about at random, some depressed with terror, others in a frightful state of exasperation. At length the army, the last hope of the people, deserted them: the troops began to traverse the city, and in their retreat they hurried along with them the still considerable remnant of its population.

They departed by the gate of Kolomna, surrounded by a multitude of women, children, and aged persons in deep affliction. The fields were covered with them. They fled in all directions, by every path across the country, without provisions, and laden with such of their effects as in their agitation they had first laid their hands on. Some, for want of horses, had harnessed themselves to carts, and thus dragged along their infant children, a sick wife, or an infirm father, in short, whatever they held most dear. The woods afforded them shelter, and they subsisted on the charity of their countrymen.

On that day, a terrific scene terminated this melancholy drama. This, the last day of Moscow, having arrived, Rostopchin collected together all whom he had been able to retain and arm. The prisons were thrown open. A squalid and disgusting crew tumultuously issued from them. These wretches rushed into the streets with a ferocious joy. Two men, a Russian and a Frenchman, the one accused of treason, the other of political indiscretion, were selected from among this horde, and dragged before Rostopchin, who reproached the Russian with his crime. The latter was the son of a tradesman: he had been apprehended while exciting the people to insurrection. A circumstance which occasioned alarm was the discovery that he belonged to a sect of German *illuminati*, called Martinists, a society of superstitious independents. His audacity had never failed him in prison. It was imagined for a moment that the spirit of equality had penetrated into Russia. At any rate he did not impeach any accomplices.

At this crisis his father arrived. It was expected that he would intercede for his son: on the contrary, he insisted on his death. The governor granted him a few moments, that he might once more speak to and bless him. "What, I! I bless a traitor:" exclaimed the enraged Russian, and turning to his son, he, with a horrid voice and gesture, pronounced a curse upon him.

This was the signal for his execution. The poor wretch was struck down by an ill-directed blow of a sabre. He fell, but wounded only, and perhaps the arrival of the French might have saved him, had not the people perceived that he was yet alive. They forced the barriers, fell upon him, and tore him to pieces.

The Frenchman during this scene was petrified with terror. "As for thee," said Rostopchin, turning towards him, "being a Frenchman, thou canst not but wish for the arrival of the French army: be free, then, but go and tell thy countrymen, that Russia had but a single traitor, and that he is punished." Then addressing himself to the wretches who surrounded him, he called them sons of Russia, and exhorted them to make atonement for their crimes by serving their country. He was the last to quit that unfortunate city, and he then rejoined the Russian army.

From that moment the mighty Moscow belonged neither to the Russians nor to the French, but to that guilty horde, whose fury was directed by a few officers and soldiers of the police. They were organized, and each had his post allotted to him, in order that pillage, fire, and devastation might commence every where at once.

Chapter 50
Moscow Entered

That very day (September the 14th), Napoleon, being at length persuaded that Kutusoff had not thrown himself on his right flank, rejoined his advanced guard. He mounted his horse a few leagues from Moscow. He marched slowly and cautiously, sending scouts before him to examine the woods and the ravines, and to ascend all the eminences to look out for the enemy's army. A battle was expected: the ground favoured the opinion: works were begun, but had all been abandoned, and we experienced not the slightest resistance.

At length the last eminence only remained to be passed: it is contiguous to Moscow, which it commands. It is called *the Hill of Salvation*, because, on its summit, the inhabitants, at sight of their holy city, cross and prostrate themselves. Our scouts had soon gained the top of this hill. It was two o'clock: the sun caused this great city to glisten with a thousand colours. Struck with astonishment at the sight, they paused, exclaiming, "Moscow! Moscow!" Every one quickened his pace; the troops hurried on in disorder; and the whole army, clapping their hands, repeated with transport, "Moscow! Moscow!" just as sailors shout "Land! land!" at the conclusion of a long and toilsome voyage.

At the sight of this gilded city, of this brilliant knot uniting Asia and Europe, of this magnificent emporium of the luxury, the manners, and the arts of the two fairest divisions of the globe, we stood still in proud contemplation. What a glorious day had now arrived! It would furnish the grandest, the most brilliant recollection of our whole lives. We felt that at this moment all our actions would engage the attention of the astonished universe; and that every one of our movements, however trivial, would be recorded by history.

On this immense and imposing theatre we marched, accompanied, as it were, by the acclamations of all nations: proud of exalting our grateful age above all other ages, we already beheld it great from our greatness, and completely irradiated by our glory.

At our return, already so ardently wished for, with what almost respectful consideration, with what enthusiasm should we be received by our wives, our countrymen, and even by our parents! We should form, during the rest of our lives, a particular class of beings, at whom they would not look but with astonishment, to whom they would not listen but with mingled curiosity and admiration! Crowds would throng about us wherever we passed; they would catch up our most unmeaning words. This miraculous conquest would surround us with a halo of glory: henceforward people would fancy that they breathed about us an air of prodigy and wonder.

When these proud thoughts gave place to more moderate sentiments, we said to ourselves, that this was the promised term of our labours; that at length we should pause, since we could no longer be surpassed by ourselves, after a noble expedition, the worthy parallel to that of Egypt, and the successful rival of all the great and glorious wars of antiquity.

At that moment, dangers, sufferings were all forgotten. Was it possible to purchase too dearly the proud felicity of being able to say, during the rest of life, "I belonged to the army of Moscow!"

Well, comrades, even now, amidst our abasement, and though it dates from that fatal city, is not this reflection of a noble exultation sufficiently powerful to console us, and to make us proudly hold up our heads, bowed down by misfortune?

Napoleon himself hastened up. He paused in transport: an exclamation of joy escaped his lips. Ever since the great battle, the discontented marshals had shunned him: but at the sight of captive Moscow, at the intelligence of the arrival of a flag of truce, struck with so important a result, and intoxicated with all the enthusiasm of glory, they forgot their grievances. They pressed around the emperor, paying homage to his good fortune, and already tempted to attribute to his genius the little pains he had taken on the 7th to complete his victory.

But in Napoleon first emotions were of short duration. He had too much to think of, to indulge his sensations for any length of time. His first exclamation was: "There, at last, is that famous city!" and the second: "It was high time!"

His eyes, fixed on that capital, already expressed nothing but impatience: in it he beheld in imagination the whole Russian empire. Its walls enclosed all his hopes,—peace, the expenses of the war, immortal glory: his eager looks therefore intently watched all its outlets. When will its gates at length open? When shall he see that deputation come forth, which will place its wealth, its population, its senate, and the principal of the Russian nobility at our disposal? Henceforth that enterprise in which he had so rashly engaged, brought to a successful termination by dint of boldness, will pass for the result of a high combination; his imprudence for greatness: henceforth his victory at the Moskwa, incomplete as it was, will be deemed his greatest achievement. Thus all that might have turned to his ruin will contribute to his glory: that day would begin to decide whether he was the greatest man in the world, or the most rash; in short, whether he had raised himself an altar, or dug himself a grave.

Anxiety, however, soon began to take possession of his mind. On his left and right he already beheld Prince Eugene and Poniatowski approaching the hostile city; Murat, with his scouts, had already reached the entrance of the suburbs, and yet no deputation appeared: an officer, sent by Miloradowitch, merely came to declare that his general would set fire to the city, if his rear was not allowed time to evacuate it.

Napoleon granted every demand. The first troops of the two armies were, for a time, intermingled. Murat was recognized by the Cossacks, who, familiar as the nomadic tribes, and expressive as the people of the south, thronged around him: then, by their gestures and exclamations, they extolled his valour and intoxicated him with their admiration. The king took the watches of his officers, and distributed them among these barbarous warriors. One of them called him his *hettman*.

Murat was for a moment tempted to believe that in these officers he should find a new Mazeppa, or that he himself should become one: he imagined that he had gained them over. This momentary armistice, under the actual circumstances, sustained the hopes of Napoleon, such need had he to delude himself. He was thus amused for two hours.

Meanwhile the day was declining, and Moscow continued dull, silent, and as it were inanimate. The anxiety of the emperor increased; the impatience of the soldiers became more difficult to be repressed. Some officers ventured within the walls of the city. "Moscow is deserted!"

At this intelligence, which he angrily refused to credit, Napoleon descended the Hill of Salvation, and approached the Moskwa and the Dorogomilow gate. He paused once more, but in vain, at the entry of that barrier. Murat urged him. "Well!" replied he, "enter then, since they wish it!" He recommended the strictest discipline; he still indulged hopes. "Perhaps these inhabitants do not even know how to surrender: for here every thing is new; they to us, and we to them."

Reports now began to succeed each other: they all agreed. Some Frenchmen, inhabitants of Moscow, ventured to quit the hiding-place which for some days had concealed them from the fury of the populace, and confirmed the fatal tidings. The emperor called Daru. "Moscow deserted!" exclaimed he: "what an improbable story! We must know the truth of it. Go and bring me the boyars." He imagined that those men, stiff with pride, or paralysed with terror, were fixed motionless in their houses: and he, who had hitherto been always met by the submission of the vanquished, provoked their confidence, and anticipated their prayers.

How, indeed, was it possible for him to persuade himself, that so many magnificent palaces, so many splendid temples, so many rich mercantile establishments, were forsaken by their owners, like the paltry hamlets through which he had recently passed. Daru's mission however was fruitless. Not a Muscovite was to be seen; not the least smoke rose from a single chimney; not the slightest noise issued from this immense and populous city; its three hundred thousand inhabitants seemed to be struck dumb and motionless by enchantment: it was the silence of the desert!

But such was the incredulity of Napoleon, that he was not yet convinced, and waited for farther information. At length, an officer, determined to gratify him, or persuaded that whatever the Emperor willed must necessarily be accomplished, entered the city, seized five or six vagabonds, drove them before his horse to the Emperor, and imagined that he had brought him a deputation. From the first words they uttered, Napoleon discovered that the persons before him were only indigent labourers.

It was not till then that he ceased to doubt the entire evacuation of Moscow, and lost all the hopes that he had built upon it. He shrugged his shoulders, and with that contemptuous look with which he met every thing that crossed his wishes, he exclaimed, "Ah! the Russians know not yet the effect which the taking of their capital will produce upon them!"

CHAPTER 51

The Kremlin

It was now an hour since Murat, and the long and close column of his cavalry, had entered Moscow; they penetrated into that gigantic body, as yet untouched, but inanimate. Struck with profound astonishment at the sight of this complete solitude, they replied to the taciturnity of this modern Thebes, by a silence equally solemn. These warriors listened, with a secret shuddering, to the steps of their horses resounding alone, amid these deserted palaces. They were astonished to hear nothing but themselves amid such numerous habitations. No-one thought of stopping or of plundering, either from prudence, or because great civilized nations respect themselves in enemies' capitals, in the presence of those great centres of civilization.

Meanwhile they were silently observing that mighty city, which would have been truly remarkable had they met with it in a flourishing and populous country, but which was still more astonishing in these deserts. It was like a rich and brilliant oasis. They had at first been struck by the sudden view of so many magnificent palaces; but they now perceived that they were intermingled with mean cottages; a circumstance which indicated the want of gradation between the classes, and that luxury was not generated there, as in other countries, by industry, but preceded it; whereas, in the natural order, it ought to be its more or less necessary consequence.

Here more especially prevailed inequality—that bane of all human society, which produces pride in some, debasement in others, corruption in all. And yet such a generous abandonment of every thing demonstrated that this excessive luxury, as yet however entirely borrowed, had not rendered these nobles effeminate.

They thus advanced, sometimes agitated by surprise, at others by pity, and more frequently by a noble enthusiasm. Several cited events of the great conquests which history has handed down to us;

but it was for the purpose of indulging their pride, not to draw lessons from them; for they thought themselves too lofty and beyond all comparison: they had left behind them all the conquerors of antiquity. They were exalted by that which is second to virtue only, by glory. Then succeeded melancholy; either from the exhaustion consequent on so many sensations, or the effect of the operation produced by such an immeasurable elevation, and of the seclusion in which we were wandering on that height, whence we beheld immensity, infinity, in which our weakness was lost: for the higher we ascend, the more the horizon expands, and the more conscious we become of our own insignificance.

Amid these reflections, which were favoured by a slow pace, the report of fire-arms was all at once heard: the column halted. Its last horses still covered the fields; its centre was in one of the longest streets of the city; its head had reached the Kremlin. The gates of that citadel appeared to be closed. Ferocious cries issued from within it: men and women, of savage and disgusting aspect, appeared fully armed on its walls. In a state of filthy inebriety, they uttered the most horrible imprecations. Murat sent them an amicable message, but to no purpose. It was found necessary to employ cannon to break open the gate.

We penetrated partly without opposition, partly by force, among these wretches. One of them rushed close to the king, and endeavoured to kill one of his officers. It was thought sufficient to disarm him, but he again fell upon his victim, rolled him on the ground, and attempted to suffocate him; and even after his arms were seized and held, he still strove to tear him with his teeth. These were the only Muscovites who had waited our coming, and who seemed to have been left behind as a savage and barbarous token of the national hatred.

It was easy to perceive, however, that there was no unison in this patriotic fury. Five hundred recruits, who had been forgotten in the Kremlin, beheld this scene without stirring. At the first summons they dispersed. Farther on, we overtook a convoy of provisions, the escort of which immediately threw down its arms. Several thousand stragglers and deserters from the enemy, voluntarily remained in the power of our advanced guard. The latter left to the corps which followed the task of picking them up; and these to others, and so on: hence they remained at liberty in the midst of us, till the conflagration and pillage of the city having reminded them of their duty, and rallied them all in one general feeling of antipathy, they went and rejoined Kutusoff.

Murat, who had been stopped but a few moments by the Kremlin, dispersed this crew which he despised. Ardent and indefatigable as in Italy and Egypt, after a march of nine hundred leagues, and sixty battles fought to reach Moscow, he traversed that proud city without deigning to halt in it, and pursuing the Russian rear-guard, he boldly, and without hesitation, took the road for Wladimir and Asia.

Several thousand Cossacks, with four pieces of cannon, were retreating in that direction. The armistice was at an end. Murat, tired of this peace of half a day, immediately ordered it to be broken by a discharge of carbines. But our cavalry considered the war as finished; Moscow appeared to them to be the term of it, and the advanced posts of the two empires were unwilling to renew hostilities. A fresh order arrived, and the same hesitation prevailed. At length Murat, irritated at this disobedience, gave his orders in person; and the firing, with which he seemed to threaten Asia, but which was not destined to cease till we reached the banks of the Seine, was renewed.

Chapter 52

Fire!

Napoleon did not enter Moscow till after dark. He stopped in one of the first houses of the Dorogomilow suburb. There he appointed Marshal Mortimer governor of that capital. "Above all," said he to him, "no pillage? For this you shall be answerable to me with your life. Defend Moscow against all, whether friend or foe."

That night was a gloomy one: sinister reports followed one upon the heels of another. Some Frenchmen, resident in the country, and even a Russian officer of police, came to denounce the conflagration. He gave all the particulars of the preparations for it. The Emperor, alarmed by these accounts, strove in vain to take some rest. He called every moment, and had the fatal tidings repeated to him. He nevertheless entrenched himself in his incredulity, till about two in the morning, when he was informed that the fire had actually broken out.

It was at the exchange, in the centre of the city, in its richest quarter. He instantly issued orders upon orders. As soon as it was light, he himself hastened to the spot, and threatened the young guard and Mortimer. The Marshal pointed out to him some houses covered with iron; they were closely shut up, still untouched and uninjured without, and yet a black smoke was already issuing from them. Napoleon pensively entered the Kremlin.

At the sight of this half Gothic and half modern palace of the Ruriks and the Romanofs, of their throne still standing, of the cross of the great Ivan, and of the finest part of the city, which is overlooked by the Kremlin, and which the flames, as yet confined to the bazaar, seemed disposed to spare, his former hopes revived. His ambition was flattered by this conquest. "At length then," he exclaimed, "I am in Moscow, in the ancient palace of the Czars, in the Kremlin!" He examined every part of it with pride, curiosity, and gratification.

He required a statement of the resources afforded by the city; and in this brief moment given to hope, he sent proposals of peace to the Emperor Alexander. A superior officer of the enemy's had just been found in the great hospital; he was charged with the delivery of this letter. It was by the baleful light of the flames of the bazaar that Napoleon finished it, and the Russian departed. He was to be the bearer of the news of this disaster to his sovereign, whose only answer was this conflagration.

Daylight favoured the efforts of the Duke of Treviso, to subdue the fire. The incendiaries kept themselves concealed. Doubts were entertained of their existence. At length, strict injunctions being issued, order restored, and alarm suspended, each took possession of a commodious house, or sumptuous palace, under the idea of there finding comforts that had been dearly purchased by long and excessive privations.

Two officers had taken up their quarters in one of the buildings of the Kremlin. The view hence embraced the north and west of the city. About midnight they were awakened by an extraordinary light. They looked and beheld palaces filled with flames, which at first merely illuminated, but presently consumed these elegant and noble structures. They observed that the north wind drove these flames directly towards the Kremlin, and became alarmed for the safety of that fortress in which the flower of their army and its commander reposed. They were apprehensive also for the surrounding houses, where our soldiers, attendants and horses, weary and exhausted, were doubtless buried in profound sleep. Sparks and burning fragments were already flying over the roofs of the Kremlin, when the wind, shifting from north to west, blew them in another direction.

One of these officers, relieved from apprehension respecting his corps, then composed himself again to sleep, exclaiming, "Let others look to it now; 'tis no affair of ours." For such was the unconcern produced by the multiplicity of events and misfortunes, and such the selfishness arising from excessive suffering and fatigue, that they left to each only just strength and feeling sufficient for his personal service and preservation.

It was not long before fresh and vivid lights again awoke them. They beheld other flames rising precisely in the new direction which the wind had taken towards the Kremlin, and they cursed French imprudence and want of discipline, to which they imputed this disaster. But three times did the wind thus change from north to west, and three times did these hostile fires, as if obstinately bent on the destruction of the imperial quarters, appear eager to follow this new direction.

At this sight a strong suspicion seized their minds. Can the Muscovites, aware of our rash and thoughtless negligence, have conceived the hope of burning with Moscow our soldiers, heavy with wine, fatigue and sleep; or rather, have they dared to imagine that they should involve Napoleon in this catastrophe; that the loss of such a man would be fully equivalent to that of their capital; that it was a result sufficiently important to justify the sacrifice of all Moscow to obtain it; that perhaps Heaven, in order to grant them so signal a victory, had decreed so great a sacrifice; and lastly, that so immense a colossus required a not less immense funeral pile?

Whether this was their plan we cannot tell, but nothing less than the Emperor's good fortune was required to prevent its being realized. In fact, not only did the Kremlin contain, unknown to us, a magazine of gunpowder; but that very night, the guards, asleep and carelessly posted, suffered a whole park of artillery to enter and draw up under the windows of Napoleon.

It was at this moment that the furious flames were driven from all quarters with the greatest violence towards the Kremlin; for the wind, attracted no doubt by this vast combustion, increased every moment in strength. The flower of the army and the Emperor would have been destroyed, if but one of the brands that flew over our heads had alighted on one of the powder-wagons. Thus upon each of the sparks that were for several hours floating in the air, depended the fate of the whole army.

At length the day, a gloomy day, appeared: it came to add to the horrors of the scene, and to deprive it of its brilliancy. Many of the officers sought refuge in the halls of the palace. The chiefs, and Mortimer himself, overcome by the fire with which, for thirty six hours, they had been contending, there dropped down from fatigue and despair.

They said nothing and we accused ourselves. Most of us imagined that want of discipline in our troops and intoxication had begun the disaster, and that the high wind had completed it. We viewed ourselves with a sort of disgust. The cry of horror which all Europe would not fail to set up terrified us. Filled with consternation by so tremendous a catastrophe, we accosted each other with downcast looks: it sullied our glory; it deprived us of the fruits of it; it threatened our present and our future existence; we were now but an army of criminals, whom Heaven and the civilized world would severely judge. From these overwhelming thoughts and paroxysms of rage against the incendiaries, we were roused only by an eagerness to obtain intelligence; and all the accounts began to accuse the Russians alone of this disaster.

In fact, officers arrived from all quarters, and they all agreed. The very first night, that of the 14th, a fire-balloon had settled on the palace of Prince Trubetskoi, and consumed it: this was a signal. Fire had been immediately set to the Exchange: Russian police soldiers had been seen stirring it up with tarred lances. Here howitzer shells, perfidiously placed, had discharged themselves in the stoves of several houses, and wounded the military who crowded round them. Retiring to other quarters which were still standing, they sought fresh retreats; but when they were on the point of entering houses closely shut up and uninhabited, they had heard faint explosions within; these were succeeded by a light smoke, which immediately became thick and black, then reddish, and lastly the colour of fire, and presently the whole edifice was involved in flames.

All had seen hideous-looking men, covered with rags, and women resembling furies, wandering among these flames, and completing a frightful image of the infernal regions. These wretches, intoxicated with wine and the success of their crimes, no longer took any pains to conceal themselves: they proceeded in triumph through the blazing streets; they were caught, armed with torches, assiduously striving to spread the conflagration: it was necessary to strike down their hands with sabres to oblige them to loose their hold. It was said that these banditti had been released from prison by the Russian generals for the purpose of burning Moscow; and that in fact so grand, so extreme a resolution could have been adopted only by patriotism and executed only by guilt.

Orders were immediately issued to shoot all the incendiaries on the spot. The army was on foot. The old guard which exclusively occupied one part of the Kremlin, was under arms: the baggage, and the horses ready loaded, filled the courts; we were struck dumb with astonishment, fatigue and disappointment, on witnessing the destruction of such excellent quarters. Though masters of Moscow, we were forced to go and bivouac without provisions outside its gates.

While our troops were yet struggling with the conflagration, and the army was disputing their prey with the flames, Napoleon, whose sleep none had dared to disturb during the night, was awoke by the two-fold light of day and of the fire. His first feeling was that of irritation, and he would have commanded the devouring element; but he soon paused and yielded to impossibility. Surprised that when he had struck at the heart of an empire, he should find there any other sentiment than submission and terror, he felt himself vanquished, and surpassed in determination.

This conquest, for which he had sacrificed every thing, was like a phantom which he had pursued, and which at the moment when he imagined he had grasped it, vanished in a mingled mass of smoke and flame. He was then seized with extreme agitation; he seemed to be consumed by the fires which surrounded him. He rose every moment, paced to and fro, and again sat down abruptly. He traversed his apartments with quick steps: his sudden and vehement gestures betrayed painful uneasiness: he quitted, resumed, and again quitted, an urgent occupation, to hasten to the windows and watch the progress of the conflagration. Short and incoherent exclamations burst from his labouring bosom. "What a tremendous spectacle!—It is their own work!—So many palaces!—What extraordinary resolution!—What men!—These are Scythians indeed!"

Between the fire and him there was an extensive vacant space, then the Moskwa and its two quays; and yet the panes of the windows against which he leaned felt already burning to the touch, and the constant exertions of sweepers, placed on the iron roofs of the palace, were not sufficient to keep them clear of the numerous flakes of fire which alighted upon them.

At this moment a rumour was spread that the Kremlin was undermined: this was confirmed, it was said, by Russians, and by written documents. Some of his attendants were beside themselves with fear; while the military awaited unmoved what the orders of the Emperor and fate should decree: And to this alarm the Emperor replied only with a smile of incredulity.

But he still walked convulsively; he stopped at every window, and beheld the terrible, the victorious element furiously consuming his brilliant conquest; seizing all the bridges, all the avenues to his fortress, inclosing, and as it were besieging him in it; spreading every moment among the neighbouring houses; and, reducing him within narrower and narrower limits, confining him at length to the site of the Kremlin alone.

We already breathed nothing but smoke and ashes. Night approached, and was about to add darkness to our dangers: the equinoxial gales, in alliance with the Russians, increased in violence. The King of Naples and Prince Eugene hastened to the spot: in company with the Prince of Neufchatel they made their way to the Emperor, and urged him by their entreaties, their gestures, and on their knees, and insisted on removing him from this scene of desolation. All was in vain.

Napoleon, in possession of the palace of the Czars, was bent on not yielding that conquest even to the conflagration, when all at once the shout of "the Kremlin is on fire!" passed from mouth to mouth, and roused us from the contemplative stupor with which we had been seized. The Emperor went out to ascertain the danger. Twice had the fire communicated to the building in which he was, and twice had it been extinguished; but the tower of the arsenal was still burning. A soldier of the police had been found in it. He was brought in, and Napoleon caused him to be interrogated in his presence. This man was the incendiary: he had executed his commission at the signal given by his chief. It was evident that every thing was devoted to destruction, the ancient and sacred Kremlin itself not excepted.

The gestures of the Emperor betokened disdain and vexation: the wretch was hurried into the first court, where the enraged grenadiers dispatched him with their bayonets.

Chapter 53
Napoleon Leaves Moscow

This incident had decided Napoleon. He hastily descended the northern staircase, famous for the massacre of the Strelitzes, and desired to be conducted out of the city, to the distance of a league on the road to Petersburgh, toward the imperial palace of Petrowsky.

But we were encircled by a sea of fire, which blocked up all the gates of the citadel, and frustrated the first attempts that were made to depart. After some search, we discovered a postern gate leading between the rocks to the Moskwa. It was by this narrow passage that Napoleon, his officers and guard escaped from the Kremlin. But what had they gained by this movement? They had approached nearer to the fire, and could neither retreat nor remain where they were; and how were they to advance? how force a passage through the waves of this ocean of flame? Those who had traversed the city, stunned by the tempest, and blinded by the ashes, could not find their way, since the streets themselves were no longer distinguishable amidst smoke and ruins.

There was no time to be lost. The roaring of the flames around us became every moment more violent. A single narrow winding street completely on fire, appeared to be rather the entrance than the outlet to this hell. The Emperor rushed on foot and without hesitation into this narrow passage. He advanced amid the crackling of the flames, the crash of floors, and the fall of burning timbers, and of the red-hot iron roofs which tumbled around him. These ruins impeded his progress. The flames which, with impetuous roar, consumed the edifices between which we were proceeding spreading beyond the walls, were blown about by the wind, and formed an arch over our heads. We walked on a ground of fire, beneath a fiery sky, and between two walls of fire. The intense heat burned our eyes, which we were nevertheless obliged to keep open and fixed on the danger. A consuming atmosphere, glowing ashes, detached flames, parched our throats, and rendered our respiration short and dry; and we were already almost suffocated by the smoke. Our hands were burned, either in endeavouring to protect our faces from the insupportable heat, or in brushing off the sparks which every moment covered and penetrated our garments.

In this inexpressible distress, and when a rapid advance seemed to be our only mean of safety, our guide stopped in uncertainty and agitation. Here would probably have terminated our adventurous career, had not some pillagers of the first corps recognised the Emperor amidst the whirling flames: they ran up and guided him towards the smoking ruins of a quarter which had been reduced to ashes in the morning.

It was then that we met the Prince of Eckmühl. This marshal, who had been wounded at the Moskwa, had desired to be carried back among the flames to rescue Napoleon, or to perish with him. He threw himself into his arms with transport; the emperor received him kindly, but with that composure which in danger he never lost for a moment.

To escape from this vast region of calamities, it was further necessary to pass a long convoy of powder, which was defiling amidst the fire. This was not the least of his dangers, but it was the last, and by nightfall he arrived at Petrowsky.

Next morning, the 17th of September, Napoleon cast his first looks towards Moscow, hoping to see that the conflagration had subsided. He beheld it again raging with the utmost violence: the whole city appeared like a vast spout of fire rising in whirling eddies to the sky, which it deeply coloured. Absorbed by this melancholy contemplation, he preserved a long and gloomy silence, which he broke only by the exclamation, "This forebodes great misfortunes to us!"

The effort which he had made to reach Moscow had expended all his means of warfare. Moscow had been the term of his projects, the aim of all his hopes, and Moscow was no more! What was now to be done? Here this decisive genius was forced to hesitate. He, who in 1805 had ordered the sudden and total abandonment of an expedition, prepared at an immense cost, and determined at Bologne-sur-Mer on the surprise and annihilation of the Austrian army, in short, all the operations of the campaign between Ulm and Munich exactly as they were executed; the same man, who, the following year, dictated at Paris with the same infallibility all the movements of his army as far as Berlin, the day fixed for his entrance into that capital, and the appointment of the governor whom he destined for it—he it was, who, astonished in his turn, was now undecided what course to pursue. Never had he communicated his most daring projects to the most confidential of his ministers but in the order for their execution; he was now constrained to consult, and put to the proof, the moral and physical energies of those about him.

In doing this, however, he still preserved the same forms. He declared, therefore, that he should march for Petersburg. This conquest was already marked out on his maps, hitherto so prophetic: orders were even issued to the different corps to hold themselves in readiness. But his decision was only a feint: it was but a better face that he strove to assume, or an expedient for diverting his grief for the loss of Moscow: so that Berthier, and more especially Bessières, soon convinced him that he had neither time, provisions, roads, nor a single requisite for so extensive an excursion.

At this moment he was apprised that Kutusoff, after having fled eastward, had suddenly turned to the south, and thrown himself between Moscow and Kalouga. This was an additional motive against the expedition to Petersburg; there was a threefold reason for marching upon this beaten army for the purpose of extinguishing it; to secure his right flank and his line of operation; to possess himself of Kalouga and Toula, the granary and arsenal of Russia; and lastly, to open a safe, short, new, and virgin retreat to Smolensk and Lithuania.

Some one proposed to return upon Wittgenstein and Witepsk. Napoleon was undecided between all these plans. That for the conquest of Petersburg alone flattered him: the others appeared but as ways of retreat, as acknowledgments of error; and whether from pride, or policy which will not admit itself to be in the wrong, he rejected them.

Besides, where was he to stop in a retreat? He had so fully calculated on concluding a peace at Moscow, that he had no winter quarters provided in Lithuania. Kalouga had no temptations for him. Wherefore lay waste fresh provinces? It would be wiser to threaten them, and leave the Russians something to lose, in order to induce them to conclude a peace by which it might be preserved. Would it be possible to march to another battle, to fresh conquests, without exposing a line of operation, covered with sick, stragglers, wounded and convoys of all sorts? Moscow was the general rallying point; how could it be changed? What other name would have any attraction?

Lastly, and above all, how relinquish a hope to which he had made so many sacrifices, when he knew that his letter to Alexander had just passed the Russian advanced posts; when eight days would be sufficient for receiving an answer so ardently desired; when he wanted that time to rally and re-organize his army, to collect the relics of Moscow, the conflagration of which had but too strongly sanctioned pillage, and to draw his soldiers from that vast infirmary!

Scarcely indeed a third of that army and of that capital now existed. But himself and the Kremlin were still standing: his renown was still entire, and he persuaded himself that those two great names, Napoleon and Moscow, combined, would be sufficient to accomplish every thing. He determined, therefore, to return to the Kremlin, which a battalion of his guard had unfortunately preserved.

Chapter 54
Moscow Destroyed

The camps which he traversed on his way thither presented an extraordinary sight. In the fields, amidst thick and cold mud, large fires were kept up with mahogany furniture, windows, and gilded doors. Around these fires, on a litter of damp straw, imperfectly sheltered by a few boards, were seen the soldiers, and their officers, splashed all over with mud, and blackened with smoke, seated in arm-chairs or reclined on silken couches. At their feet were spread or heaped Cashmere shawls, the rarest furs of Siberia, the gold stuffs of Persia, and silver plates, off which they had nothing to eat but a black dough baked in the ashes, and half broiled and bloody horse-flesh. Singular assemblage of abundance and want, of riches and filth, of luxury and wretchedness!

Between the camp and the city were met troops of soldiers dragging along their booty, or driving before them, like beasts of burden, Muscovites bending under the weight of the pillage of their capital; for the fire brought to view nearly twenty thousand inhabitants, previously unobserved in that immense city. Some of these Muscovites of both sexes were well dressed; they were tradespeople. They came with the wreck of their property to seek refuge at our fires. They lived pell-mell with our soldiers, protected by some, and tolerated, or rather scarcely remarked by others.

About ten thousand of the enemy's troops were in the same predicament. For several days they wandered about among us free, and some of them even still armed. Our soldiers met these vanquished enemies without animosity, or without thinking of making them prisoners; either because they considered the war as at an end, from thoughtlessness, or from pity, and because when not in battle the French delight in having no enemies. They suffered them to share their fires; nay, more, they allowed them to pillage in their company. When some degree of order was restored, or rather when the officers had organized this marauding as a regular system of forage, the great number of these Russian stragglers then attracted notice. Orders were given to secure them; but seven or eight thousand had already escaped. It was not long before we had to fight them.

On entering the city, the Emperor was struck by a sight still more extraordinary: a few houses scattered among the ruins were all that was left of the mighty Moscow. The smell issuing from this colossus, overthrown, burned, and calcined, was horrible. Heaps of ashes, and at intervals, fragments of walls or half demolished pillars, were now the only vestiges that marked the site of streets.

The suburbs were sprinkled with Russians of both sexes, covered with garments nearly burned. They flitted like spectres among the ruins; squatted in the gardens, some of them were scratching up the earth in quest of vegetables, while others were disputing with the crows for the relics of the dead animals which the army had left behind. Farther on, others again were seen plunging into the Moskwa to bring out some of the corn which had been thrown into it by command of Rostopchin, and which they devoured without preparation, sour and spoiled as it already was.

Meanwhile the sight of the booty, in such of the camps where every thing was yet wanting, inflamed the soldiers whom their duty or stricter officers had kept with their colours. They murmured. "Why were they to be kept back? Why were they to perish by famine and want, when every thing was within their reach! Was it right to leave the enemy's fires to destroy what might be saved? Why was such respect to be paid them?" They added, that "as the inhabitants of Moscow had not only abandoned, but even endeavoured utterly to destroy it, all that they could save would be legitimately acquired; that the remains of that city, like the relics of the arms of the conquered, belonged by right to the victors, as the Muscovites had turned their capital into a vast machine of war, for the purpose of annihilating us."

The best principled and the best disciplined were those who argued thus, and it was impossible to reply. Too rigid scruples at first prevented the issuing of orders for pillage; it was now permitted, unrestrained by regulations. Urged by the most imperious necessities, all hurried to share in the spoil, the soldiers of the elite, and even officers themselves. Their chiefs were obliged to shut their eyes: only such guards as were absolutely indispensable were left with the eagles and the fasces.

The Emperor saw his whole army dispersed over the city. His progress was obstructed by a long file of marauders going in quest of booty, or returning with it; by tumultuous assemblages of soldiers grouped around the entrances of cellars, or the doors of palaces, shops, and churches, which the fire had nearly reached, and into which they were endeavouring to penetrate.

His steps were impeded by the fragments of furniture of every kind which had been thrown out of the windows to save it from the flames, or by rich pillage which had been abandoned from caprice for some other booty; for such is the way with soldiers; they are incessantly beginning their fortune afresh, taking every thing without discrimination, loading themselves beyond measure, as if they could carry all they find; then, after they have gone a few steps, compelled by fatigue to throw away the greatest part of their burden.

The roads were obstructed; the open places, like the camps, were turned into markets, whither every one repaired to exchange superfluities for necessaries. There, the rarest articles, the value of which was not known to their possessors, were sold at a low price; others, of deceitful appearance, were purchased at a price far beyond their worth. Gold, as being more portable, was bought at an immense loss with silver, which the knapsacks were incapable of holding. Everywhere soldiers were seen seated on bales of merchandize, on heaps of sugar and coffee, amidst wines and the most exquisite liqueurs, which they were offering in exchange for a morsel of bread. Many, in an intoxication aggravated by inanition, had fallen near the flames, which reached them, and put an end to their lives.

Most of the houses and palaces which had escaped the fire served nevertheless for quarters for the officers, and all that they contained was respected. All of them beheld with pain this vast destruction, and the pillage which was its necessary consequence. Some of our men belonging to the elite were charged with taking too much pleasure in collecting what they were able to save from the flames; but their number was so few that they were mentioned by name. In these ardent men, war was a passion which presupposed the existence of others. It was not covetousness, for they did not hoard; they spent lavishly what they picked up, taking in order to give, believing that one hand washed the other, and that they had paid for every thing with the danger.

Besides, on such an occasion, there is scarcely any distinction to be made, unless in the motive: some took with regret, others with pleasure, and all from necessity. Amidst wealth which had ceased to belong to any individual, ready to be consumed, or to be buried in ashes, they were placed in a quite novel situation, where right and wrong were confounded, and for which no rule was laid down. The most delicate, either from principle, or because they were richer than others, bought of the soldiers the provision and apparel which they required: some sent agents to plunder for them; and the most necessitous were forced to help themselves with their own hands.

As to the soldiers, many of them being embarrassed with the fruits of their pillage, became less active, less thoughtless: in danger they began to calculate, and in order to save their booty, they did what they would have disdained to do to save themselves.

It was amidst this confusion that Napoleon again entered Moscow. He had allowed this pillage, hoping that his army, scattered over the ruins, would not ransack them in vain. But when he learned that the disorder increased; that the old guard itself was seduced; that the Russian peasants, who were at length allured thither with provisions, for which he caused them to be liberally paid for the purpose of drawing others, were robbed of the provisions which they brought us, by our famished soldiers; when he was informed that the different corps, destitute of every thing, were ready to fight for the relics of Moscow; that, finally, all the existing resources were wasted by this irregular pillage; he then issued strict orders, and forbade his guard to leave their quarters. The churches, in which our cavalry had sheltered themselves, were restored to the Greek worship. The business of plunder was ordered to be taken in turn by the corps like any other duty, and directions were at length given for securing the Russian stragglers.

But it was too late. These soldiers had fled: the affrighted peasants returned no more; great quantities of provisions were spoiled. The French army have sometimes fallen into this fault, but on the present occasion the fire pleads their excuse: no time was to be lost in anticipating the flames. It is, however, a remarkable fact, that at the first command perfect order was restored.

Some writers, and even French ones, have ransacked these ruins in quest of traces of outrages which might have been committed in them. There were very few. Most of our men behaved generously, considering the small number of inhabitants, and the great number of enemies, that they met with. But if in the first moments of pillage some excesses were committed, ought this to appear surprising in an army exasperated by such urgent wants, such severe sufferings, and composed of so many different nations?

Misfortune having since humbled these warriors, reproaches have, as is always the case, been raised against them. Who can be ignorant that such disorders have always been the bad side of great wars, the inglorious part of glory; that the renown of conquerors casts its shadow like every thing else in this world! Does there exist a creature ever so diminutive, on every side of which the sun, great as is that luminary, can shine at once? It is therefore a law of nature, that large bodies have large shadows.

For the rest, people have been too much astonished at the virtues as well as at the vices of that army. They were the virtues of the moment, the vices of the age; and for this very reason, the former were less praiseworthy, and the latter less reprehensible, inasmuch as they were, if I may so express myself, enjoined by example and circumstances. Thus every thing is relative, which does not exclude fixed principles and absolute good as the point of departure and aim. But here the question relates to the judgment formed of this army and its chief; and he who would form a correct judgment of them must put himself in their place. As, then, this position is very elevated, very extraordinary, very complicated, few minds are capable of attaining it, embracing the whole of it, and appreciating all its necessary results.

Chapter 55
'I Must Have Peace'

Meanwhile Kutusoff, on leaving Moscow, had drawn Murat towards Kolomna, to the point where the Moskwa intersects the road. Here, under favour of the night, he suddenly turned to the south, proceeding by way of Podol, to throw himself between Moscow and Kalouga. This nocturnal march of the Russians around Moscow, the ashes and flames of which were wafted to them by the violence of the wind, was melancholy and religious. They advanced by the baleful light of the conflagration, which was consuming the centre of their commerce, the sanctuary of their religion, the cradle of their empire! Filled with horror and indignation, they all kept a sullen silence, which was unbroken save by the dull and monotonous sound of their footsteps, the roaring of the flames, and the howling of the tempest. The dismal light was frequently interrupted by livid and sudden flashes. The brows of these warriors might then be seen contracted by a savage grief, and the fire of their sombre and threatening looks answered these flames, which they regarded as our work; it already betrayed that ferocious revenge which was rankling in their hearts, which spread throughout the whole empire, and to which so many Frenchmen fell victims.

At that solemn moment, Kutusoff in a firm and noble tone informed his sovereign of the loss of his capital. He declared, that, "in order to preserve the fertile provinces of the south, and his communication with Tormasof and Tchitchakof, he had been obliged to abandon Moscow, but emptied of the inhabitants, who were the life of it; that as the people are the soul of every empire, so wherever the Russian people were, there would be Moscow and the whole empire of Russia."

Here, however, he seemed to bend under the weight of his grief. He admitted that "this wound was deep and could never be effaced;"

but soon recovering himself, he added, that "the loss of Moscow made but one city less in the empire, that it was the sacrifice of a part for the salvation of the whole. He was throwing himself on the flank of the enemy's long line of operation, keeping him as it were blockaded by his detachments: there he should watch his movements, cover the resources of the empire, and again complete his army;" and already (on the 16th of September) he announced, that "Napoleon would be forced to abandon his fatal conquest."

It is said that on the receipt of this intelligence Alexander was thunderstruck. Napoleon built hopes on the weakness of his rival, and the Russians at the same time dreaded the effect of that weakness. The Czar belied both these hopes and these fears. In his addresses to his subjects he exhibited himself great as his misfortune; "No pusillanimous dejection!" he exclaimed: "Let us vow redoubled courage and perseverance! The enemy is in deserted Moscow as in a tomb, without means of domination or even of existence. He entered Russia with three hundred thousand men of all countries, without union or any national or religious bond;—he has lost half of them by the sword, famine, and desertion: he has but the wreck of this army in Moscow; he is in the heart of Russia, and not a single Russian is at his feet.

"Meanwhile, our forces are increasing and inclosing him. He is in the midst of a mighty population, encompassed by armies which are waiting for, and keeping him in check. To escape famine, he will soon be obliged to direct his flight through the close ranks of our brave soldiers. Shall we then recede, when all Europe is looking on and encouraging us? Let us on the contrary set it an example, and kiss the hand which has chosen us to be the first of the nations in the cause of virtue and independence." He concluded with an invocation to the Almighty.

The Russians entertain different opinions respecting their general and their Emperor. We, for our part, as enemies, can only judge of our enemies by their actions. Now such were their words, and their actions corresponded with them. Comrades! let us do them justice! their sacrifice was complete, without reserve, without tardy regrets. They have since claimed nothing, even in the enemy's capital which they preserved. Their renown has therefore remained great and unsullied. They have known real glory; and when a more advanced civilization shall have spread among all classes of that great nation, it will have its brilliant era, and will sway in its turn the sceptre of glory, which it seems to be decreed that the nations of the earth shall successively relinquish to each other.

This circuitous march made by Kutusoff, either from indecision or stratagem, turned out fortunate for him. Murat lost all trace of him for three days. The Russian employed this interval in studying the ground and entrenching himself. His advanced guard had nearly reached Woronowo, one of the finest domains belonging to Count Rostopchin, when that nobleman proceeded forward before it. The Russians supposed that he was going to take a last look at this mansion, when all at once the edifice was wrapt from their sight by clouds of smoke.

They hurried on to extinguish the fire, but Rostopchin himself rejected their aid. They beheld him amid the flames which he was encouraging, smiling at the demolition of this splendid mansion, and then with a firm hand penning these words, which the French, shuddering with surprise, read on the iron gate of a church which was left standing: "For eight years I have been embellishing this country seat, where I have lived happily in the bosom of my family. The inhabitants of this estate, to the number of 1,720, will leave it on your approach, while I have set fire to my house, that it might not be polluted by your presence. Frenchmen, I have relinquished to you my two houses at Moscow, with their furniture, worth half a million of roubles. Here you will find nothing but ashes."

It was near this place that Murat came up with Kutusoff. On the 29th of September there was a smart engagement of cavalry towards Czerikowo, and another, on the 4th of October, near Vinkowo. But there, Miloradowitch, too closely pressed, turned round furiously, with twelve thousand horse, upon Sebastiani. He brought him into such danger, that Murat, amidst the fire, dictated a proposal for a suspension of arms, announcing to Kutusoff the approach of a flag of truce. It was Lauriston that he expected. But as the arrival of Poniatowski at that moment gave us some superiority, the king made no use of the letter which he had written; he fought till nightfall, and repulsed Miloradowitch.

Meanwhile the conflagration at Moscow, which commenced in the night of the 14th of September, suspended through our exertions during the day of the 15th, revived in the following night, and raging in its utmost violence on the 16th, 17th, and 18th, abated on the 19th. It ceased on the 20th. That very day, Napoleon, whom the flames had driven from the Kremlin, returned to the palace of the czars. He invited thither the looks of all Europe. He there awaited his convoys, his reinforcements, and the stragglers of his army; certain that all his men would be rallied by his victory, by the allurements of such vast booty, by the astonishing sight of captive Moscow, and above all, by his own glory, which from the top of this immense pile of ruins, still shone attractive like a beacon upon a rock.

Twice, however, on the 22nd and 28th of September, letters from Murat had well nigh drawn Napoleon from this fatal abode. They announced a battle; but twice the orders for departure, written in consequence, were burned. It seemed as though the war was finished for our Emperor, and that he was only waiting for an answer from Petersburg. He nourished his hopes with the recollections of Tilsit and Erfurt. Was it possible that at Moscow he should have less ascendancy over Alexander? Then, like men who have long been favourites of fortune, what he ardently wished he confidently expected.

His genius possessed besides that extraordinary faculty, which consisted in throwing aside the most important occupation whenever he pleased, either for the sake of variety or of rest: for in him the power of volition surpassed that of imagination. In this respect he reigned over himself as much as he did over others.

Thus Paris diverted his attention from Petersburg. His affairs were as yet divided, and the couriers, which in the first days succeeded each other without intermission, served to engage him. But the rapidity with which he transacted business soon left him nothing to do. His expresses, which at first came from France in a fortnight, ceased to arrive. A few military posts, placed in four towns reduced to ashes, and in wooden houses rudely palisaded, were not sufficient to guard a road of ninety-three leagues: for we had not been able to establish more than a few echelons, and those at too great distances, on too long a line of operation, broken at every point where it was touched by the enemy; and for which a few peasants and a handful of Cossacks were quite sufficient.

Still no answer was received from Alexander. The uneasiness of Napoleon increased, and his means of distraction diminished. The activity of his genius, accustomed to the government of all Europe, had nothing wherewith to occupy itself but the management of one hundred thousand men; and then, the organization of his army was so perfect, that this was scarcely any occupation. Here every thing was fixed; he held all the wires in his hand: he was surrounded by ministers who could tell him immediately, at any hour of the day, the position of each man in the morning or at night, whether alone or not, whether with his colours, or in the hospital, or on leave of absence, or wherever else he might be, and that from Moscow to

Paris—to such a degree of perfection had the science of military administration been brought, so experienced and well chosen were the officers, and so much was required by their commander.

But eleven days had now elapsed; still Alexander was silent, and still did Napoleon hope to overcome his rival in obstinacy: thus losing the time which he ought to have gained, and which is always serviceable to defence against attack.

From this period all his actions indicated to the Russians still more strongly than at Witepsk, that their mighty foe was resolved to fix himself in the heart of their empire. Moscow, though in ashes, received an intendant and municipalities. Orders were issued to provision it for the winter. A theatre was formed amidst the ruins. The first-rate actors of Paris were said to have been sent for. An Italian singer strove to reproduce in the Kremlin the evening entertainments of the Tuileries. By such means Napoleon expected to dupe a government, which the habit of reigning over error and ignorance had rendered an adept in all these deceptions.

He was himself sensible of the inadequacy of these means, and yet September was past, October had begun. Alexander had not deigned to reply! it was an affront! he was exasperated. On the 3rd of October, after a night of restlessness and anger, he summoned his marshals. "Come in," said he, as soon as he perceived them, "hear the new plan which I have conceived; Prince Eugene, read it." They listened. "We must burn the remains of Moscow, march by Twer to Petersburg, where we shall be joined by Macdonald. Murat and Davoust will form the rear-guard."—The Emperor, all animation, fixed his sparkling eyes on his generals, whose frigid and silent countenances expressed nothing but astonishment.

Then exalting himself in order to rouse them—"What!" said he, "and are *you* not inflamed by this idea? Was there ever so great a military achievement? Henceforth this conquest is the only one that is worthy of us! With what glory we shall be covered, and what will the whole world say, when it learns that in three months we have conquered the two great capitals of the North!"

But Davoust, as well as Daru, objected to him, "the season, the want of supplies, a sterile desert and artificial road, that from Twer to Petersburg, running for a hundred leagues through morasses, and which three hundred peasants might in one day render impassable. Why keep proceeding northward? why go to meet winter, to provoke and to defy it?—it was already too near; and what was to become of the six thousand wounded still in Moscow? were they then to be left to the mercy of Kutusoff? That general would not fail to follow close at our heels. We should have at once to attack and to defend ourselves, and to march, as though we were fleeing to a conquest."

These officers have declared that they then proposed various plans; a useless trouble with a prince whose genius outstripped all other imaginations, and whom their objections would not have stopped, had he been really determined to march to Petersburg. But that idea was in him only a sally of anger, an inspiration of despair, on finding himself obliged in the face of Europe to give way, to relinquish a conquest, and to retreat.

It was more especially a threat to frighten his officers as well as the enemy, and to bring about and promote a negotiation which Caulaincourt was to open. That officer had pleased Alexander; he was the only one of the grandees of Napoleon's court who had acquired any influence over his rival; but for some months past, Napoleon had kept him at a distance, because he had not been able to persuade him to approve his expedition.

It was nevertheless to this very man that he was that day obliged to have recourse, and to disclose his anxiety. He sent for him; but when alone with him, he hesitated. Taking him by the arm, he walked to and fro a long time in great agitation, while his pride prevented him from breaking so painful a silence: at length it yielded, but in a threatening manner. He was to beg the enemy to solicit peace, as if he deigned to grant it.

After a few words, which were scarcely articulate, he said, that "he was about to march to Petersburg. He knew that the destruction of that city would no doubt give pain to his grand-equerry. Russia would then rise against the Emperor Alexander: there would be a conspiracy against that monarch; he would be assassinated, which would be a most unfortunate circumstance. He esteemed that prince, and should regret him, both for his own sake and that of France. His character, he added, was suitable to our interests; no prince could replace him with such advantage to us. He thought therefore of sending Caulaincourt to him, to prevent such a catastrophe."

The Duke of Vicenza, however, more obstinate, than susceptible of flattery, did not alter his tone. He maintained that "these overtures would be useless; that so long as the Russian territory was not entirely evacuated, Alexander would not listen to any proposals; that Russia was sensible of all her advantage at this season of the year; nay, more, that this step would be detrimental to himself, inasmuch as it would demonstrate the need which Napoleon had of peace, and betray all the embarrassment of our situation."

He added, "that the higher the rank of the negotiator whom he selected, the more clearly he would show his anxiety; that of course he himself would be more likely to fail than any other, especially as he should go with this certainty." The Emperor abruptly terminated the conversation by these words: "Well, then, I will send Lauriston."

The latter asserts, that he added fresh objections to the preceding, and that, being urged by the Emperor, he recommended to him to begin his retreat that very day by way of Kalouga. Napoleon, irritated at this, acrimoniously replied, that "he liked simple plans, less circuitous routes, high roads, the road by which he had come, yet he would not retread it but with peace." Then showing to him, as he had done to the Duke of Vicenza, the letter which he had written to Alexander, he ordered him to go and obtain of Kutusoff a safe-conduct to Petersburg. The last words of the Emperor to Lauriston were: "I want peace, I must have peace, I absolutely will have peace; only save my honour!"

Chapter 56
Cossacks

The general set out, and reached the advanced posts on the 5th of October. Hostilities were instantly suspended, the interview granted; but Wolkonsky, aide-de-camp to Alexander, and Beningsen were there without Kutusoff. Wilson asserts, that the Russian generals and officers, suspecting their commander, and accusing him of weakness, had raised a cry of treason, and that the latter had not dared to leave his camp.

Lauriston's instructions purported that he was to address himself to no one but Kutusoff. He therefore peremptorily rejected any intermediate communication, and seizing, as he said, this occasion for breaking off a negotiation which he disapproved, he retired, in spite of all the solicitations of Wolkonsky, and determined to return to Moscow. In that case, no doubt, Napoleon, exasperated, would have fallen upon Kutusoff, overthrown him and destroyed his army, as yet very incomplete, and have forced him into a peace. In case of less decisive success, he would at least have been able to retire without loss upon his reinforcements.

Beningsen unfortunately desired an interview with Murat. Lauriston paused. The chief of the Russian staff, an abler negotiator than soldier, strove to charm the new king by demonstrations of respect; to seduce him by praises; to deceive him with smooth words, breathing nothing but a weariness of war and the hope of peace: and Murat, tired of battles, anxious respecting their result, and as it is said, regretting his throne, now that he had no hope of a better, suffered himself to be charmed, seduced and deceived.

Beningsen was equally successful in persuading his own commander, and the leader of our vanguard; he sent in great haste for Lauriston, and had him conducted to the Russian camp, where Kutusoff was waiting for him at midnight. The interview began ill. Konownitzin and Wolkonsky wished to be present. This shocked the French general: he insisted that they should retire, and they complied.

As soon as Lauriston was alone with Kutusoff, he explained his motives and his object, and applied for a safe-conduct to Petersburg. The Russian general replied, that a compliance with this demand exceeded his powers; but he immediately proposed to send Wolkonsky with the letter from Napoleon to Alexander, and offered an armistice till the return of that officer. He accompanied these proposals with pacific protestations, which were repeated by all his generals.

"According to their account," they all deplored the continuance of the war. And for what reason? Their nations, like their Emperors, ought to esteem, to love, and to be allies of one another. It was their ardent wish that a speedy peace might arrive from Petersburg. Wolkonsky could not make "haste enough." They pressed round Lauriston, drawing him aside, taking him by the hand, and lavishing upon him those caressing manners which they have inherited from Asia.

It was soon demonstrated that the chief point in which they were all agreed was to deceive Murat and his Emperor; and in this they succeeded. These details transported Napoleon with joy. Credulous from hope, perhaps from despair, he was for some moments dazzled by these appearances; eager to escape from the inward feeling which oppressed him, he seemed desirous to deaden it by resigning himself to an expansive joy. He summoned all his generals; he triumphantly "announced to them a very speedy peace. They had but to wait another fortnight. None but himself was acquainted with the Russian character. On the receipt of his letter, Petersburg would be full of bonfires."

But the armistice proposed by Kutusoff was unsatisfactory to him, and he ordered Murat to break it instantly; but notwithstanding, it continued to be observed, the cause of which is unknown.

This armistice was a singular one. If either party wished to break it, three hours notice was to be sufficient. It was confined to the fronts of the two camps, but did not extend to their flanks. Such at least was the interpretation put upon it by the Russians. We could not bring up a convoy, or send out a foraging party, without fighting; so that the war continued everywhere, excepting where it could be favourable to us.

In the first of the succeeding days, Murat took it into his head to show himself at the enemy's advanced posts. There, he was gratified by the notice which his fine person, his reputation for bravery, and his rank procured him. The Russian officers took good care not to displease him; they were profuse of all the marks of respect calculated to strengthen his illusion. He could give his orders to their vedettes just as he did to the French. If he took a fancy to any part of the ground which they occupied, they cheerfully gave it up to him.

Some Cossack chiefs even went so far as to affect enthusiasm, and to tell him that they had ceased to acknowledge any other as Emperor but him who reigned at Moscow. Murat believed for a moment that they would no longer fight against him. He went even farther. Napoleon was heard to exclaim, while reading his letters, "Murat, King of the Cossacks! What folly!" The most extravagant ideas were conceived by men on whom fortune had lavished all sorts of favours.

As for the Emperor, who could scarcely be deceived, he had but a few moments of a factitious joy. He soon complained "that an annoying warfare of partisans hovered around him; that notwithstanding all these pacific demonstrations, he was sensible that bodies of Cossacks were prowling on his flanks and in his rear. Had not one hundred and fifty dragoons of his old guard been surprised and routed, by a number of these barbarians? And this two days after the armistice, on the road to Mojaisk, on his line of operation, that by which the army communicated with its magazines, its reinforcements, its depots, and himself with Europe!"

In fact two convoys had just fallen into the enemy's hands on that road: one through the negligence of its commander, who put an end to his life in despair; and the other through the cowardice of an officer, who was about to be punished when the retreat commenced. To the destruction of the army he owed his escape.

Our soldiers, and especially our cavalry, were obliged every morning to go to a great distance in quest of provisions for the evening and the next day; and as the environs of Moscow and Vinkowo became gradually more and more drained, they were daily necessitated to extend their excursions. Both men and horses returned worn out with fatigue, that is to say such of them as returned at all; for we had to fight for every bushel of rye, and for every truss of forage. It was a series of incessant surprises, skirmishes, and losses. The peasantry took a part in it. They punished with death such of their number as the prospect of gain had allured to our camp with provisions. Others set fire to their own villages, to drive our foragers out of them, and to give them up to the Cossacks whom they had previously summoned, and who kept us there in a state of siege.

It was the peasantry also who took Vereïa, a town in the neighbourhood of Moscow. One of their priests is said to have planned and executed this *coup-de-main*. He armed the inhabitants, obtained some troops from Kutusoff; then on the 10th of October, before daybreak, he caused the signal of a false attack to be given in one quarter, while in another he himself rushed upon our palisades, destroyed them, penetrated into the town, and put the whole garrison to the sword.

Thus the war was every where; in our front, on our flanks and in our rear: the army was weakening, and the enemy becoming daily more enterprising. This conquest was destined to fare like many others, which are won in the mass, and lost in detail.

Murat himself at length grew uneasy. In these daily skirmishes he saw half of the remnant of his cavalry melted away. At the advanced posts, or on meeting with our officers, those of the Russians, either from weariness, vanity, or military frankness carried to indiscretion, exaggerated the disasters which threatened us. They showed us those "wild-looking horses, scarcely at all broken in, whose long manes swept the dust of the plain. Did not this tell us that a numerous cavalry was joining them from all quarters, while ours was gradually perishing? Did not the continual discharges of fire-arms within their line apprise us that a multitude of recruits were there training under favour of the armistice?"

And in fact, notwithstanding the long journeys which they had to make, all these recruits joined the army. There was no occasion to defer calling them together as in other years, till deep snows, obstructing all the roads excepting the high road, rendered their desertion impossible. Not one failed to obey the national appeal; all Russia rose: mothers, it was said, wept for joy on learning that their sons had been selected for soldiers: they hastened to acquaint them with this glorious intelligence, and even accompanied them to see them marked with the sign of the Crusaders, to hear them cry, *'Tis the will of God!*

The Russian officers added, "that they were particularly astonished at our security on the approach of their mighty winter, which was their natural and most formidable ally, and which they expected every moment: they pitied us and urged us to fly. In a fortnight, your nails will drop off, and your arms will fall from your benumbed and half-dead fingers."

The language of some of the Cossack chiefs was also remarkable. They asked our officers, "if they had not, in their own country, corn enough, air enough, graves enough—in short, room enough to live and die? Why then did they come so far from home to throw away their lives and to fatten a foreign soil with their blood?" They added, that "this was a robbery of their native land, which, while living, it is our duty to cultivate, to defend and to embellish; and to which after our death we owe our bodies, which we received from it, which it has fed, and which in their turn ought to feed it."

The Emperor was not ignorant of these warnings, but he would not suffer his resolution to be shaken by them. The uneasiness which had again seized him betrayed itself in angry orders. It was then that he caused the churches of the Kremlin to be stripped of every thing that could serve for a trophy to the grand army. These objects, devoted to destruction by the Russians themselves, belonged, he said, to the conquerors by the twofold right conferred by victory, and still more by the conflagration.

It required long efforts to remove the gigantic cross from the steeple of Ivan the Great, to the possession of which the Russians attached the salvation of their empire. The Emperor determined that it should adorn the dome of the invalids, at Paris. During the work it was remarked that a great number of ravens kept flying round this cross, and that Napoleon, weary of their hoarse croaking, exclaimed, that "it seemed as if these flocks of ill-omened birds meant to defend it." We cannot pretend to tell all that he thought in this critical situation, but it is well known that he was accessible to every kind of presentiment.

His daily excursions, always illumined by a brilliant sun, in which he strove himself to perceive and to make others recognize his star, did not amuse him. To the sullen silence of inanimate Moscow was superadded that of the surrounding deserts, and the still more menacing silence of Alexander. It was not the faint sound of the footsteps of our soldiers wandering in this vast sepulchre, that could rouse our Emperor from his reverie, and snatch him from his painful recollections and still more painful anticipations.

His nights in particular became irksome to him. He passed part of them with Count Daru. It was then only that he admitted the danger of his situation. "From Wilna to Moscow what submission, what point of support, rest or retreat, marks his power? It is a vast, bare and desert field of battle, in which his diminished army is imperceptible, insulated, and as it were lost in the horrors of an immense void. In this country of foreign manners and religion, he has not conquered a single individual; he is in fact master only of the ground on which he stands. That which he has just quitted and left behind him is no more his than that which he has not yet reached. Insufficient for these vast deserts, he is lost as it were in their immense space."

He then reviewed the different resolutions of which he still had the choice. "People imagined," he said, "that he had nothing to do but march, without considering that it would take a month to refit his army and to evacuate his hospitals; that if he relinquished his wounded, the Cossacks would celebrate daily triumphs over his sick and his stragglers. He would appear to fly. All Europe would resound with the report! Europe, which envied him, which was seeking a rival under whom to rally, and which imagined that it had found such a rival in Alexander."

Then appreciating all the power which he derived from the notion of his infallibility, he shuddered at the idea of giving it the first blow. "What a frightful series of dangerous wars would date from his first retrograde step! Let not then his inactivity be censured! As if I did not know," added he, "that in a military point of view Moscow is of no value! But Moscow is not a military position, it is a political position. People look upon me as general there, when in fact I am Emperor!" He then exclaimed that "in politics a person ought never to recede, never to retrograde, never to admit himself to be wrong, as it lessened his consideration; that when mistaken, he ought to persevere, in order to give him the appearance of being in the right."

On this account he adhered to his own opinion with that tenacity which, on other occasions, was his best quality, but in this case his worst defect.

His distress meanwhile increased. He knew that he could not rely on the Prussian army: an intimation from too authentic a source, addressed to Berthier, extinguished his confidence in the support of the Austrians. He was sensible that Kutusoff was playing with him, but he had gone so far, that he could neither advance nor stay where he was, nor retreat, nor fight with honour and success. Thus alternately impelled and held back by all that can decide and dissuade, he remained upon those ashes, ceasing to hope, but continuing to desire.

The letter of which Lauriston was the bearer had been dispatched on the 6th of October; the answer to it could scarcely arrive before the 20th; and yet in spite of so many threatening demonstrations, the pride, the policy, and perhaps the health of Napoleon induced him to pursue the worst of all courses, that of waiting for this answer, and of trusting to time which was destroying him. Daru, like his other grandees, was astonished to find in him no longer that prompt decision, variable and rapid as the circumstances that called it forth; they asserted, that his genius could no longer accommodate itself to them; they placed it to the account of his natural obstinacy, which led to his elevation, and was likely to cause his downfall.

But in this extremely critical warlike position, which by its complication with a political position, became the most delicate which ever existed, it was not to be expected that a character like his, which had hitherto been so great from its unshaken constancy, would make a speedy renunciation of the object which he had proposed to himself ever since he left Witepsk.

Chapter 57
Stay or Go?

Napoleon however, was completely aware of his situation. To him every thing seemed lost if he receded in the face of astonished Europe, and every thing saved if he could yet overcome Alexander in determination. He appreciated but too well the means that were left him to shake the constancy of his rival; he knew that the number of effective troops, that his situation, the season, in short every thing would become daily more and more unfavourable to him; but he reckoned upon that force of illusion which gave him his renown. Till that day he had borrowed from it a real and never-failing strength; he endeavoured therefore to keep up by specious arguments the confidence of his people, and perhaps also the faint hope that was yet left to himself.

Moscow, empty of inhabitants, no longer furnished him with any thing to lay hold of. "It is no doubt a misfortune," said he, "but this misfortune is not without its advantage. Had it been otherwise, he would not have been able to keep order in so large a city, to overawe a population of three hundred thousand souls, and to sleep in the Kremlin without having his throat cut. They have left us nothing but ruins, but at least we are quiet among them. Millions have no doubt slipped through our hands, but how many millions is Russia losing! Her commerce is ruined for a century to come. The nation is thrown back fifty years; this, of itself, is an important result. When the first moment of enthusiasm is past, this reflection will fill them with consternation." The conclusion which he drew was, that so violent a shock would convulse the throne of Alexander, and force that prince to sue for peace.

If he reviewed his different *corps d'armée*, as their reduced battalions now presented but a narrow front, which he had traversed in a moment, this diminution vexed him; and whether he wished to dissemble for the sake of his enemies or his own people, he declared that the practice hitherto pursued, of ranging the men three deep, was wrong, and that two were sufficient; he therefore ordered that in future his infantry should be drawn up in two ranks only.

Nay, more, he insisted that the inflexibility of the *states of situation* should give way to this illusion. He disputed their results. The obstinacy of Count Lobau could not overcome his: he was desirous no doubt of making his aide-de-camp understand what he wished others to believe, and that nothing could shake his resolution.

Murat, nevertheless, transmitted to him tidings of the distress of his advanced guard. They terrified Berthier; but Napoleon sent for the officer who brought them, pressed him with his interrogatories, daunted him with his looks, brow-beat him with his incredulity. The assertions of Murat's envoy lost much of their assurance. Napoleon took advantage of his hesitation to keep up the hopes of Berthier, and to persuade him that matters were not yet so very urgent; and he sent back the officer to Murat's camp with the opinion which he would no doubt propagate, that the Emperor was immoveable, that he doubtless had his reasons for thus persisting, and that they must all redouble their exertions.

Meanwhile the attitude of his army seconded his wishes. Most of the officers persevered in their confidence. The common soldiers, who, seeing their whole lives in the present moment and expecting but little from the future, concerned themselves but little about it, retained their thoughtlessness, the most valuable of their qualities. The rewards, however, which the Emperor bestowed profusely upon them in the daily reviews, were received only with a sedate joy, mingled with some degree of dejection. The vacant places that were just filled up were yet dyed with blood. These favours were threatening.

On the other hand, ever since they had left Wilna many of them had thrown away their winter garments, that they might load themselves with provisions. Their shoes were worn by the length of the way, and the rest of their apparel by the actions in which they had been engaged; but, in spite of all, their attitude was still lofty. They carefully concealed their wretched plight from the notice of the Emperor, and appeared before him with their arms bright and in the best order. In this first court of the palace of the Czars, eight hundred leagues from their resources, and after so many battles and bivouacs, they were anxious to appear still clean, ready and smart; for herein consists the pride of the soldier: here they piqued themselves upon it the more on account of the difficulty, in order to astonish, and because man prides himself on every thing that requires extraordinary effort.

The Emperor complaisantly affected to know no better, catching at every thing to keep up his hopes, when all at once the first snows fell. With them fell all the illusions with which he had endeavoured to surround himself. From that moment he thought of nothing but retreat, without, however, pronouncing the word, and yet no positive order for it could be obtained from him. He merely said, that in twenty days the army must be in winter-quarters, and he urged the departure of his wounded. On this, as on other occasions, he would not consent to the voluntary relinquishment of any thing, however trifling; there was a deficiency of horses for his artillery, now too numerous for an army so reduced; it did not signify, and he flew into a passion at the proposal to leave part of it in Moscow. "No; the enemy would make a trophy of it."—and he insisted that every thing should go along with him.

In this desert country, he gave orders for the purchase of twenty thousand horses, and he expected forage for two months to be provided, on a tract where the most distant and dangerous excursions were not sufficient for the supply of the passing day. Some of his officers were astonished to hear orders which it was so impossible to execute; but we have already seen that he sometimes issued such orders to deceive his enemies, and most frequently to indicate to his own troops the extent of his necessities, and the exertions which they ought to make for the purpose of supplying them.

His distress manifested itself only in some paroxysms of ill humour. It was in the morning at his levee. There, amid the assembled chiefs, in whose anxious looks he imagined he could read disapprobation, he seemed desirous to awe them by the severity of his attitude, by his sharp tone and his abrupt language. From the paleness of his face, it was evident that Truth, whose best time for obtaining a hearing is in the darkness of night, had oppressed him grievously by her presence, and tired him with her unwelcome light. Sometimes, on these occasions, his bursting heart would overflow, and pour forth his sorrows around him by movements of impatience; but so far from lightening his grief, he aggravated them by those acts of injustice for which he reproached himself, and which he was afterwards anxious to repair.

It was to Count Daru alone that he unbosomed himself frankly, but without weakness. He said, "he should march upon Kutusoff, crush or drive him back, and then turn suddenly towards Smolensk." Daru, who had before approved this course, replied, that "it was now too late; that the Russian army was reinforced, his own weakened; his victory forgotten; that the moment his troops should turn their faces towards France, they would slip away from him by degrees; that each soldier, laden with booty, would try to get the start of the army, for the purpose of selling it in France."—"What then is to be done?" exclaimed the Emperor. "Remain here," replied Daru, "make one vast entrenched camp of Moscow and pass the winter in it. He would answer for it that there would be no want of bread and salt: the rest foraging on a large scale would supply. Such of the horses as they could not procure food for might be salted down. As to lodgings, if there were not houses enough, the cellars might make up the deficiency. Here we might stay till the return of spring, when our reinforcements and all Lithuania in arms should come to relieve, to join us, and to complete the conquest."

After listening to this proposal the Emperor was for some time silent and thoughtful; he then replied, "This is a lion's counsel! But what would Paris say? what would they do there? what have they been doing for the last three weeks that they have not heard from me? who knows what would be the effect of a suspension of communications for six months! No; France would not accustom itself to my absence, and Prussia and Austria would take advantage of it."

Still Napoleon did not decide either to stay or to depart. Overcome in this struggle of obstinacy, he deferred from day to day the avowal of his defeat. Amid the dreadful storm of men and elements which was gathering around him, his ministers and his aides-de-camp saw him pass whole days in discussing the merits of some new verses which he had received, or the regulations for the Comédie Française at Paris, which he took three evenings to finish. As they were acquainted with his deep anxiety, they admired the strength of his genius, and the facility with which he could take off or fix the whole force of his attention on whatever he pleased.

It was merely remarked that he prolonged his meals, which had hitherto been so simple and so short. He seemed desirous of stifling thought by repletion. He would then pass whole hours, half reclined, as if torpid, and awaiting, with a novel in his hand, the catastrophe of his terrible history. On beholding this obstinate and inflexible character struggling with impossibility, his officers would then observe to one another, that having arrived at the summit of his glory, he no doubt foresaw that from his first retrograde step would date its decline; that for this reason he continued immoveable, clinging to and lingering a few moments longer on this elevation.

Kutusoff, meanwhile, was gaining that time which we were losing. His letters to Alexander described "his army as being in the midst of abundance; his recruits arriving from all quarters and being trained; his wounded recovering in the bosom of their families; the peasants, some in arms, some on the look out from the tops of steeples, while others were stealing into our habitations and even into the Kremlin. Rostopchin received from them a daily report of what was passing at Moscow, as before its capture. If they undertook to be our guides, it was for the purpose of delivering us into his hands. His partisans were every day bringing in some hundreds of prisoners. Every thing concurred to destroy the enemy's army and to strengthen his own; to serve him and to betray us; in a word, the campaign, which was over for us, was but just about to begin for them."

Kutusoff neglected no advantage. He made his camp ring with the news of the victory of Salamanca. "The French," said he, "are expelled from Madrid. The hand of the Most High presses heavily upon Napoleon. Moscow will be his prison, his grave, and that of all his grand army. We shall soon take France in Russia!" It was in such language that the Russian general addressed his troops and his Emperor; and nevertheless he still kept up appearances with Murat. At once bold and crafty, he contrived slowly to prepare a sudden and impetuous warfare, and to cover his plans for our destruction with demonstrations of kindness and honeyed words.

At length, after several days of illusion, the charm was dispelled. A Cossack completely dissolved it. This barbarian fired at Murat, at the moment when that prince came as usual to show himself at the advanced posts. Murat was exasperated; he declared to Miloradowitch that an armistice which was incessantly violated was at an end; and that thenceforward each ought to put confidence in himself alone.

At the same time he apprised the Emperor, that a woody country on his left might favour attempts against his flank and rear; that his first line, backed against a ravine, might be precipitated into it; that in short the position which he occupied, in advance of a defile, was dangerous, and rendered a retrograde movement absolutely necessary. But Napoleon would not consent to this step, though he had at first pointed out Woronowo as a more secure position. In this war, still in his view rather political than military, he dreaded above all the appearance of receding. He preferred risking every thing.

At the same time, on the 13th of October, he sent back Lauriston to Murat, to examine the position of the vanguard. As to the Emperor, either from a tenacious adherence to his first hope, or that any disposition which might be construed into a preparation for retreat, equally shocked his pride and his policy, a singular negligence was remarked in his preparations for departure. He nevertheless thought of it, for that very day he traced his plan of retreat by Woloklamsk, Zubtzow, and Bieloé, on Witepsk. A moment afterwards he dictated another on Smolensk. Junot received orders to burn on the 21st, at Kolotskoi, all the muskets of the wounded, and to blow up the ammunition wagons. D'Hilliers was to occupy Elnia, and to form magazines at that place. It was not till the 17th, at Moscow, that Berthier thought of causing leather to be distributed for the first time among the troops.

This major-general was a wretched substitute for his principal on this critical occasion. In a strange country and climate, he recommended no new precaution, and he expected the minutest details to be dictated by his Emperor. They were forgotten. This negligence or want of foresight was attended with fatal consequences. In an army, each division of which was commanded by a marshal, a prince, or even a king, one relied perhaps too much on the other. Besides, Berthier gave no orders of himself; he thought it enough to repeat exactly the very letter of Napoleon's commands; for, as to their spirit, either from fatigue or habit, he was incessantly confounding the positive with the conjectural parts of those instructions.

Napoleon meanwhile rallied his *corps d'armée*. The reviews which he held in the Kremlin were more frequent; he formed all the dismounted cavalry into battalions, and lavishly distributed rewards. The division of Claparede, the trophies and all the wounded that could be removed, set out for Mojaisk; the rest were collected in the great foundling hospital; French surgeons were placed there; and the Russian wounded, intermixed with ours, were intended to serve them for a safeguard.

But it was too late. Amid these preparations, and at the moment when Napoleon was reviewing Ney's divisions in the first court of the Kremlin, a report was all at once circulated around him, that the report of cannon was heard towards Vinkowo. It was some time before any one durst apprise him of the circumstance; some from incredulity or uncertainty, and dreading the first movement of his impatience; others from love of ease, hesitating to provoke a terrible signal, or apprehensive of being sent to verify this assertion, and of exposing themselves to a fatiguing excursion.

Duroc, at length, took courage. The Emperor was at first agitated, but quickly recovering himself, he continued the review. An aide-de-camp, young Beranger, arrived shortly after with the intelligence that Murat's first line had been surprised and overthrown, his left turned by favour of the woods, his flank attacked, his retreat cut off; that twelve pieces of cannon, twenty ammunition wagons, and thirty wagons belonging to the train were taken, two generals killed, three or four thousand men lost and the baggage; and lastly, that the King was wounded. He had not been able to rescue the relics of his advanced guard from the enemy, but by repeatedly charging their numerous troops which already occupied the high road in his rear, his only retreat.

Our honour however was saved. The attack in front, directed by Kutusoff, was feeble; Poniatowski, at some leagues distance on the right, made a glorious resistance; Murat and his carbineers, by supernatural exertions, checked Bagawout, who was ready to penetrate our left flank, and restored the fortune of the day. Claparede and Latour-Maubourg cleared the defile of Spaskaplia, two leagues in the rear of our line, which was already occupied by Platof. Two Russian generals were killed, and others wounded: the loss of the enemy was considerable, but the advantage of the attack, our cannon, our position, the victory in short, were theirs.

As for Murat, he no longer had an advanced guard. The armistice had destroyed half the remnant of his cavalry. This engagement finished it; the survivors, emaciated with hunger, were so few as scarcely to furnish a charge. Thus had the war recommenced. It was now the 18th of October.

At these tidings Napoleon recovered the fire of his early years. A thousand orders general and particular, all differing, yet all in unison and all necessary, burst at once from his impetuous genius. Night had not yet arrived, and the whole army was already in motion for Woronowo; Broussier was sent in the direction of Fominskoë, and Poniatowski toward Medyn. The Emperor himself quitted Moscow before daylight on the 19th of October. "Let us march upon Kalouga," said he, "and woe be to those whom I meet with by the way!"

CHAPTER 58

The Retreat Begins

In the southern part of Moscow, near one of its gates, one of its most extensive suburbs is divided by two high roads; both run to Kalouga: the one, that on the right, is the more ancient; the other is new. It was on the first that Kutusoff had just beaten Murat. By the same road Napoleon left Moscow on the 19th of October, announcing to his officers his intention to return to the frontiers of Poland by Kalouga, Medyn, Yuknow, Elnia, and Smolensk. One of them, Rapp, observed that "it was late, and that winter might overtake them by the way." The Emperor replied, "that he had been obliged to allow time to the soldiers to recruit themselves, and to the wounded collected in Moscow, Mojaisk, and Kolotskoi, to move off towards Smolensk." Then pointing to a still serene sky, he asked, "if in that brilliant sun they did not recognize his star?" But this appeal to his fortune, and the sinister expression of his looks, belied the security which he affected.

Napoleon entered Moscow with ninety thousand fighting men, and twenty thousand sick and wounded, and quitted it with more than a hundred thousand combatants. He left there only twelve hundred sick. His stay, notwithstanding daily losses, had therefore served to rest his infantry, to complete his stores, to augment his force by ten thousand men, and to protect the recovery or the retreat of a great part of his wounded. But on this very first day he could perceive, that his cavalry and artillery might be said rather to crawl than to march.

A melancholy spectacle added to the gloomy presentiments of our chief. The army had ever since the preceding day been pouring out of Moscow without intermission. In this column of one hundred and forty thousand men and about fifty thousand horses of all kinds, a hundred thousand combatants marching at the head with their knapsacks, their arms, upwards of five hundred and fifty pieces of cannon, and two thousand artillery-wagons, still exhibited a formidable appearance, worthy of soldiers who had conquered the world. But the rest, in an alarming proportion, resembled a horde of Tartars after a successful invasion. It consisted of three or four files of infinite length, in which there was a mixture, a confusion of chaises, ammunition wagons, handsome carriages, and vehicles of every kind. Here trophies of Russian, Turkish, and Persian colours, and the gigantic cross of Ivan the Great—there, long-bearded Russian peasants carrying or driving along our booty, of which they constituted a part: others dragging even wheelbarrows filled with whatever they could remove. The fools were not likely to proceed in this manner till the conclusion of the first day: their senseless avidity made them think nothing of battles and a march of eight hundred leagues.

In these followers of the army were particularly remarked a multitude of men of all nations, without uniform and without arms, and servants swearing in every language, and urging by dint of shouts and blows the progress of elegant carriages, drawn by pigmy horses harnessed with ropes. They were filled with provisions, or with the booty saved from the flames. They carried also French women with their children. Formerly these females were happy inhabitants of Moscow; they now fled from the hatred of the Muscovites, which the invasion had drawn upon their heads; the army was their only asylum.

A few Russian girls, voluntary captives, also followed. It looked like a caravan, a wandering nation, or rather one of those armies of antiquity returning loaded with slaves and spoil after a great devastation. It was inconceivable how the head of this column could draw and support such a heavy mass of equipages in so long a route.

Notwithstanding the width of the road and the shouts of his escort, Napoleon had great difficulty to obtain a passage through this immense throng. No doubt the obstruction of a defile, a few forced marches and a handful of Cossacks, would have been sufficient to rid us of all this encumbrance: but fortune or the enemy had alone a right to lighten us in this manner. As for the Emperor, he was fully sensible that he could neither deprive his soldiers of this fruit of so many toils, nor reproach them for securing it. Besides, the provisions concealed the booty, and could he, who could not give his troops the subsistence which he ought to have done, forbid their carrying it along with them? Lastly, in failure of military conveyances, these vehicles would be the only means of preservation for the sick and wounded.

Napoleon, therefore, extricated himself in silence from the immense train which he drew after him, and advanced on the old road leading to Kalouga. He pushed on in this direction for some hours, declaring that he should go and beat Kutusoff on the very field of his victory. But all at once, about mid-day, opposite to the castle of Krasnopachra, where he halted, he suddenly turned to the right with his army, and in three marches across the country gained the new road to Kalouga.

The rain, which overtook him in the midst of this manoeuvre, spoiled the cross-roads, and obliged him to halt in them. This was a most unfortunate circumstance. It was not without difficulty that our cannon were drawn out of the sloughs.

At any rate the Emperor had masked his movement by Ney's corps and the relics of Murat's cavalry, which had remained behind the Motscha and at Woronowo. Kutusoff, deceived by this feint, was still waiting for the grand army on the old road, whilst on the 23rd of October, the whole of it, transferred to the new one, had but one march to make in order to pass quietly by him, and to get between him and Kalouga.

A letter from Berthier to Kutusoff, dated the first day of this flanking march, was at once a last attempt at peace, and perhaps a *ruse de guerre*. No satisfactory answer was returned to it.

Chapter 59
Malo-Yaroslawetz

On the 23rd the imperial quarters were at Borowsk. That night was an agreeable one for the Emperor: he was informed that at six in the evening Delzons and his division had, four leagues in advance of him, found Malo-Yaroslawetz and the woods which command it unoccupied: this was a strong position within reach of Kutusoff, and the only point where he could cut us off from the new road to Kalouga.

The Emperor wished first to secure this advantage by his presence; the order to march was even given, but withdrawn, we know not why. He passed the whole of that evening on horseback, not far from Borowsk, on the left of the road, the side on which he supposed Kutusoff to be. He reconnoitred the ground in the midst of a heavy rain, as if he anticipated that it might become a field of battle. Next day, the 24th, he learned that the Russians had disputed the possession of Malo-Yaroslawetz with Delzons. Owing either to confidence or uncertainty in his plans, this intelligence gave him very little concern.

He quitted Borowsk, therefore, late and leisurely, when the noise of a very smart engagement reached where he was; he then became uneasy, hastened to an eminence and listened. "Had the Russians anticipated him? Was his manoeuvre thwarted? Had he not used sufficient expedition in that march, the object of which was to pass the left flank of Kutusoff?"

In reality there was in this whole movement a little of that torpor which succeeds a long repose. Moscow is but one hundred and ten *wersts* from Malo-Yaroslawetz; four days would have been sufficient to go that distance; we took six. The army, laden with provisions and pillage, was heavy, and the roads were deep. A whole day had been sacrificed to the passage of the Nara and its morass, as also to the rallying of the different corps. It is true that in defiling so near the enemy it was necessary to march close, that we might not present to him too long a flank. Be this as it may, we may date all our calamities from that delay.

The Emperor was still listening; the noise increased. "Is it then a battle?" he exclaimed. Every discharge agitated him, for the chief point with him was no longer to conquer, but to preserve, and he urged on Davoust, who accompanied him; but he and that marshal did not reach the field of battle till dark, when the firing was subsiding and the whole was over.

The Emperor saw the end of the battle, but without being able to assist the viceroy. A band of Cossacks from Twer had nearly captured one of his officers, who was only a very short distance from him.

It was not till then that an officer, sent by Prince Eugene, came to him to explain the whole affair. "The troops had," he said, "in the first place, been obliged to cross the Louja at the foot of Malo-Yaroslawetz, at the bottom of an elbow which the river makes in its course; and then to climb a steep hill: it is on this rapid declivity, broken by pointed crags, that the town is built. Beyond is an elevated plain, surrounded with wood from which run three roads, one in front, coming from Kalouga, and two on the left, from Lectazowo, the entrenched camp of Kutusoff.

"On the preceding day Delzons found no enemy there; but he did not think it prudent to place his whole division in the upper town, beyond a river and a defile, and on the margin of a precipice, down which it might have been thrown by a nocturnal surprise. He remained, therefore, on the low bank of the Louja, sending only two battalions to occupy the town and to watch the elevated plain.

"The night was drawing to a close; it was four o'clock, and all were already asleep in Delzons's bivouacs, excepting a few sentinels, when Doctorof's Russians suddenly rushed in the dark out of the wood with tremendous shouts. Our sentinels were driven back on their posts, the posts on their battalions, the battalions on the division: and yet it was not a *coup-de-main*, for the Russians had brought up cannon. At the very commencement of the attack, the firing had conveyed the tidings of a serious affair to the viceroy, who was three leagues distant."

The report added, that "the Prince had immediately hastened up with some officers, and that his divisions and his guard had precipitately followed him. As he approached, a vast amphitheatre, where all was bustle, opened before him; the Louja marked the foot of it, and a multitude of Russian riflemen already disputed its banks."

Behind them from the summit of the declivities on which the

town was situated, their advanced guard poured their fire on Delzons: beyond that, on the elevated plain, the whole army of Kutusoff was hastening up in two long black columns, by the two roads from Lectazowo. They were seen stretching and entrenching themselves on this bare slope, upon a line of about half a league, where they commanded and embraced every thing by their number and position: they were already placing themselves across the old road to Kalouga, which was open the preceding day, which we might have occupied and travelled if we had pleased, but which Kutusoff would henceforward have it in his power to defend inch by inch.

The enemy's artillery had at the same time taken advantage of the heights which bordered the river on their side; their fire traversed the low ground in the bend of the river, in which were Delzons and his troops. The position was untenable, and hesitation would have been fatal. It was necessary to get out of it either by a prompt retreat, or by an impetuous attack; but it was before us that our retreat lay, and the viceroy gave orders for the attack.

After crossing the Louja by a narrow bridge, the high road from Kalouga runs along the bottom of a ravine which ascends to the town, and then enters Malo-Yaroslawetz. The Russians, in mass occupied this hollow way: Delzons and his Frenchmen rushed upon them head foremost; the Russians were broken and overthrown; they gave way and presently our bayonets glistened on the heights.

Delzons, conceiving himself sure of the victory, announced it as won. He had nothing but a pile of buildings to storm, his soldiers hesitated. He himself advanced and was encouraging them by his words, gestures and example, when a ball struck him on the forehead, and extended him on the ground. His brother threw himself upon him, covered him with his body, clasped him in his arms, and would have borne him off out of the fire and the fray, but a second ball hit him also, and both expired together.

This loss left a great void, which required to be filled up. Guilleminot succeeded Delzons, and the first thing he did was to throw a hundred grenadiers into a church and church-yard, in the walls of which they made loop-holes. This church stood on the left of the high road, which it commanded, and to this edifice we owed the victory. Five times on that day was this post passed by the Russian columns, which were pursuing ours, and five times did its fire, seasonably poured upon their flank and rear, harass them and slacken their progress: afterwards when we resumed the offensive, this position placed them between two fires and ensured the success of our attacks.

Scarcely had that general made this disposition when he was assailed by hosts of Russians; he was driven back towards the bridge, where the viceroy had stationed himself, in order to judge how to act and prepare his reserves. At first the reinforcements which he sent came up but slowly one after another; and as is almost always the case, each of them, being inadequate to any great effort, was successively destroyed without result.

At length the whole of the 14th division was engaged: the combat was then carried, for the third time, to the heights. But when the French had passed the houses, when they had removed from the central point from which they set out; when they had reached the plain, where they were exposed, and where the circle expanded; they could advance no farther: overwhelmed by the fire of a whole army they were daunted and shaken: fresh Russians incessantly came up; our thinned ranks gave way and were broken; the obstacles of the ground increased their confusion: they again descended precipitately and abandoned every thing.

Meanwhile the shells having set fire to the wooden town behind them, in their retreat they were stopped by the conflagration; one fire drove them back upon another; the Russian recruits, wrought up to a pitch of fanatic fury, closely pursued them; our soldiers became enraged; they fought man to man: some were seen seizing each other by one hand, striking with the other, until both victors and vanquished rolled down precipices into the flames, without losing their hold. There the wounded expired, either suffocated by the smoke, or consumed by the fire. Their blackened and calcined skeletons soon presented a hideous sight, when the eye could still discover in them the traces of a human form.

All, however, were not equally intent on doing their duty. There was one officer, a man who was known to talk very big, and who, at the bottom of a ravine, wasted the time for action in making speeches. In this place of security he kept about him a sufficient number of troops to authorize his remaining himself, leaving the rest to expose themselves in detail, without unison and at random.

The 15th division was still left. The viceroy summoned it: as it advanced, it threw a brigade into the suburb on the left, and another into the town on the right. It consisted of Italians, recruits, who had never before been in action. They ascended, shouting enthusiastically, ignorant of the danger or despising it, from that singular disposition, which renders life less dear in its flower than in its decline, either because while young we fear death less from the feeling of its distance, or because at that age, rich in years and prodigal of every thing, we squander life as the wealthy do their fortune.

The shock was terrible: every thing was reconquered for the fourth time, and lost in like manner. More eager to begin than their seniors, they were sooner disheartened, and returned flying to the old battalions, which supported and were obliged to lead them back to the danger.

The Russians, emboldened by their incessantly increasing numbers and success, then descended by their right to gain possession of the bridge and to cut off our retreat. Prince Eugene had nothing left but his last reserve: he and his guard now took part in the combat. At this sight, and at his call, the remains of the 13th, 14th, and 15th divisions mustered their courage; they made a powerful and a last effort, and for the fifth time the combat was transferred to the heights.

At the same time Colonel Peraldi and the Italian chasseurs overthrew with their bayonets the Russians, who were already approaching the left of the bridge, and inebriated by the smoke and the fire, through which they had passed, by the havoc which they made, and by their victory, they pushed forward without stopping on the elevated plain, and endeavoured to make themselves masters of the enemy's cannon: but one of those deep clefts, with which the soil of Russia is intersected, stopped them in the midst of a destructive fire; their ranks opened, the enemy's cavalry attacked them, and they were driven back to the very gardens of the suburbs. There they paused and rallied: all, both French and Italians, obstinately defended the upper avenues of the town, and the Russians being at length repulsed, drew back and concentrated themselves on the road to Kalouga, between the woods and Malo-Yaroslawetz.

In this manner eighteen thousand Italians and French crowded together at the bottom of a ravine, defeated fifty thousand Russians, posted over their heads, and seconded by all the obstacles that a town built on a steep declivity is capable of presenting.

The army, however, surveyed with sorrow this field of battle, where seven generals and four thousand Italians had been killed or wounded. The sight of the enemy's loss afforded no consolation; it was not twice the amount of ours, and their wounded would be saved. It was moreover recollected that in a similar situation Peter I., in sacrificing ten Russians for one Swede, thought that he was not sustaining merely an equal loss, but even gaining by so terrible a bargain. But what caused the greatest pain, was the idea that so sanguinary a conflict might have been spared.

In fact, the fires which were discovered on our left, in the night between the 23rd and 24th, had apprised us of the movement of the Russians towards Malo-Yaroslawetz; and yet the French army had marched thither languidly; a single division, thrown to the distance of three leagues from all succour, had been carelessly risked; the *corps d'armée* had remained out of reach of each other. Where were now the rapid movements of Marengo, Ulm, and Eckmühl? Why so slow and drawling a march on such a critical occasion? Was it our artillery and baggage that had caused this tardiness? Such was at least the most plausible presumption.

Chapter 60
The Emperor Draws His Sword

When the Emperor heard the report of this combat, he was a few paces to the right of the high road, at the bottom of a ravine, close to the rivulet and village of Ghorodinia, in the habitation of a weaver, an old, crazy, filthy, wooden hut. Here he was half a league from Malo-Yaroslawetz, at the commencement of the bend of the Louja. It was in this worm-eaten dwelling, and in a dirty dark room, parted off into two by a cloth, that the fate of the army and of Europe was about to be decided.

The first hours of the night passed in receiving reports. All agreed that the enemy was making preparations against the next day for a battle, which all were disposed to decline. About eleven o'clock Bessières entered. This marshal owed his elevation to honourable services, and above all to the affection of the Emperor, who had become attached to him as to a creation of his own. It is true, that a man could not be a favourite with Napoleon, as with any other monarch; that it was necessary at least to have followed and been of some service to him, for he sacrificed little to the agreeable; in short, it was requisite that he should have been more than a witness of so many victories; and the Emperor when fatigued, accustomed himself to see with eyes which he believed to be of his own formation.

He had sent this marshal to examine the attitude of the enemy. Bessières had obeyed: he had carefully explored the front of the Russian position. "It is," said he, "unassailable!"—"Oh heavens!" exclaimed the Emperor, clasping his hands, "are you sure you are right? Are you not mistaken? Will you answer for that?" Bessières repeated his assertion: he affirmed that "three hundred grenadiers would there be sufficient to keep in check a whole army." Napoleon then crossed his arms with a look of consternation, hung his head, and remained as if overwhelmed with the deepest dejection. "His army was victorious and himself conquered. His route was intercepted, his manoeuvre, thwarted: Kutusoff, an old man, a Scythian, had been beforehand with him! And he could not accuse his star. Did not the sun of France seem to have followed him to Russia? Was not the road to Malo-Yaroslawetz open but the preceding day? It was not his fortune then that had failed him, but he who had been wanting to his fortune?"

Absorbed in this abyss of painful reflections, he fell into so profound a stupor, that none of those about him could draw from him a single word. Scarcely could a nod of the head be obtained from him by dint of importunity. At length he strove to get some rest: but a feverish anxiety prevented him from closing his eyes. During all the rest of that cruel night he kept rising, lying down again, and calling incessantly, but yet not a single word betrayed his distress: it was only from the agitation of his body that the anguish of his mind was to be inferred.

About four in the morning, one of his orderly officers, the Prince d'Aremberg, came to inform him that under favour of the night, the woods and some inequalities of ground, Cossacks were slipping in between him and his advanced posts. The Emperor had just sent off Poniatowski on his right to Kremenskoe. So little did he expect the enemy from that side, that he had neglected to order out any scouts on his right flank. He therefore slighted the report of his orderly officer.

No sooner did the sun appear above the horizon on the 25th, than he mounted his horse, and advanced on the Kalouga road, which to him was now nothing more than the road to Malo-Yaroslawetz. To reach the bridge of that town, he had to cross the plain, about a league in length and breadth, embraced by the bend of the Louja: a few officers only attended him. The four squadrons of his usual escort, not having been previously apprised, hastened to rejoin, but had not yet overtaken him. The road was covered with sick-wagons, artillery, and vehicles of luxury: it was the interior of the army, and every one was marching on without mistrust.

In the distance, towards the right, a few small bodies of men were first seen running, and then large black lines advancing. Outcries were presently heard: some women and attendants on the army were met running back, too much affrighted and out of breath, either to listen to any thing, or to answer any question. At the same time the file of vehicles stopped in uncertainty; disorder arose in it: some endeavoured to proceed, others to turn back; they crossed, jostled and upset one another: and the whole was soon a scene of complete uproar and confusion.

The Emperor looked on and smiled, still advancing, and believing it to be a groundless panic. His aides-de-camp suspected that it was Cossacks whom they saw, but they marched in such regular platoons that they still had doubts on the subject; and if those wretches had not howled at the moment of attack, as they all do to stifle the sense of danger, it is probable that Napoleon would not have escaped them. A circumstance which increased the peril was, that their cries were at first mistaken for acclamations, and their hurrahs for shouts of *Vive l'Empereur!*

It was Platof and six thousand Cossacks, who in the rear of our victorious advanced-guard, had ventured to cross the river, the low plain and the high road, carrying all before them; and it was at the very moment when the Emperor, perfectly tranquil in the midst of his army, and the windings of a deep river, was advancing, refusing belief to so audacious a plan, that they put it in execution.

When they had once started, they approached with such speed, that Rapp had but just time to say to the Emperor, "It is the Cossacks!—turn back!" The Emperor, whose eyes deceived him, or who disliked running away, stood firm, and was on the point of being surrounded, when Rapp seized the bridle of his horse, and turned him round, crying. "Indeed you must!" And really it was high time to fly, although Napoleon's pride would not allow him to do so. He drew his sword, the Prince of Neufchatel and the grand equerry did the same; then placing themselves on the left side of the road, they waited the approach of the horde, from which they were not forty paces distant. Rapp had barely time to turn himself round to face these barbarians, when the foremost of them thrust his lance into the chest of his horse with such violence as to throw him down. The other aides-de-camp, and a few horse belonging to the guard, extricated the general. This action, the bravery of Lecoulteux, the efforts of a score of officers and chasseurs, and above all the thirst of these barbarians for plunder, saved the Emperor. And yet they needed only to have stretched out their hands and seized him; for, at the same moment, the horde, in crossing the high road, overthrew every thing before them, horses, men, and carriages, wounding and killing some, and dragging them into the woods for the purpose of plundering them; then, loosing the horses harnessed to the guns, they took them along with them across the country. But they had only a momentary victory; a triumph of surprise. The cavalry of the guard galloped up; at this sight they let go their prey and fled; and this torrent subsided, leaving indeed melancholy traces, but abandoning all that it was hurrying away in its course.

Some of these barbarians, however, carried their audacity even to insolence. They were seen retiring at a foot-pace across the interval between our squadrons, and coolly reloading their arms. They reckoned upon the heaviness of our cavalry of the elite, and the swiftness of their own horses, which they urge with a whip. Their flight was effected without disorder; they faced round several times, without waiting indeed till within reach of fire, so that they left scarcely any wounded and not one prisoner. At length they enticed us on to ravines covered with bushes, where we were stopped by their artillery, which was waiting for them. All this furnished subject for reflection. Our army was worn down; and the war had begun again with new and undiminished spirit.

The Emperor, struck with astonishment that the enemy had dared to attack him, halted until the plain was cleared; after which he returned to Malo-Yaroslawetz, where the viceroy pointed out to him the obstacles which had been conquered the preceding day.

The ground itself spoke sufficiently. Never was field of battle more terribly eloquent. Its marked features; its ruins covered with blood; the streets, the line of which could no longer be recognized but by the long train of the dead, whose heads were crushed by the wheels of the cannon, the wounded, who were still seen issuing from the rubbish and crawling along, with their garments, their hair, and their limbs half consumed by the fire, and uttering lamentable cries; finally, the doleful sound of the last melancholy honours which the grenadiers were paying to the remains of their colonels and generals who had been slain—all attested the extreme obstinacy of the conflict. In this scene the Emperor, it was said, beheld nothing but glory: he exclaimed, that "the honour of so proud a day belonged exclusively to Prince Eugene." This sight, nevertheless, aggravated the painful impression which had already seized him. He then advanced to the elevated plain.

CHAPTER 61

The Road to Kalouga

Can you ever forget, comrades, the fatal field which put a stop to the conquest of the world, where the victories of twenty years were blasted, where the great edifice of our fortune began to totter to its foundation? Do you not still figure to yourselves the blood-stained ruins of that town, those deep ravines, and the woods which surround that elevated plain and convert it, as it were, into a tented field? On one side were the French, quitting the north, which they shunned; on the other, at the entrance of the wood, were the Russians, guarding the south, and striving to drive us back upon their mighty winter. In the midst of this plain, between the two armies, was Napoleon, his steps and his eyes wandering from south to west, along the roads to Kalouga and Medyn, both which were closed against him. On that to Kalouga, were Kutusoff and one hundred and twenty thousand men, ready to dispute with him twenty leagues of defiles; towards Medyn he beheld a numerous cavalry: it was Platof and those same hordes which had just penetrated into the flank of the army, had traversed it through and through, and burst forth, laden with booty, to form again on his right flank, where reinforcements and artillery were waiting for them. It was on that side that the eyes of the Emperor were fixed longest; it was there that he received the reports of his officers and consulted his maps: then, oppressed with regret and gloomy forebodings, he slowly returned to his head-quarters.

Murat, Prince Eugene, Berthier, Davoust and Bessières followed him. This mean habitation of an obscure artisan contained within it an Emperor, two Kings, and three Generals. Here they were about to decide the fate of Europe, and of the army which had conquered it. Smolensk was the goal. Should they march thither by Kalouga, Medyn or Mojaisk? Napoleon was seated at a table, his head supported by his hands, which concealed his features, as well as the anguish which they no doubt expressed.

A silence fraught with such imminent destinies continued to be respected, until Murat, whose actions were always the result of impetuous feeling, became weary of this hesitation. Yielding to the dictates of his genius, which was wholly directed by his ardent temperament, he was eager to burst from that uncertainty, by one of those first movements which elevate to glory, or hurry to destruction.

Rising, he exclaimed, that "he might possibly be again accused of imprudence, but that in war circumstances decided and gave to every thing its name; that where there is no other course than to attack, prudence becomes temerity and temerity prudence; that to stop was impossible, to fly dangerous, consequently they ought to pursue. What signified the menacing attitude of the Russians and their impenetrable woods? For his part he cared not for them. Give him but the remnant of his cavalry, and that of the guard, and he would force his way into their forests and their battalions, overthrow all before him, and open anew to the army the road to Kalouga."

Here Napoleon, raising his head, extinguished all this fire, by saying, that "we had exhibited temerity enough already; that we had done too much for glory, and it was high time to give up thinking of any thing but how to save the rest of the army."

Bessières, either because his pride revolted from the idea of obeying the King of Naples, or from a desire to preserve uninjured the cavalry of the guard, which he had formed, for which he was answerable to Napoleon, and which he exclusively commanded; Bessières, finding himself supported, then ventured to add, that "neither the army nor even the guard had sufficient spirit left for such efforts. It was already said in both, that as the means of conveyance were inadequate, henceforth the victor, if overtaken, would fall a prey to the vanquished; that of course every wound would be mortal. Murat would therefore be but feebly seconded. And in what a position! its strength had just been but too well demonstrated. Against what enemies! had they not remarked the field of the preceding day's battle, and with what fury the Russian recruits, only just armed and clothed, had there fought and fell?" The Marshal concluded by voting in favour of retreat, which the Emperor approved by his silence.

The Prince of Eckmühl immediately observed, that, "as a retreat was decided upon, he proposed that it should be by Medyn and Smolensk." But Murat interrupted Davoust, and whether from enmity or from that discouragement which usually succeeds the rejection of a rash measure, he declared his astonishment, "that any one should dare to propose so imprudent a step to the Emperor. Had Davoust sworn the destruction of the army? Would he have so long and so heavy a column trail along, without guides and in uncertainty, on an unknown track, within reach of Kutusoff, presenting its flank to all the attacks of the enemy? Would he, Davoust, defend it? Why—when in our rear Borowsk and Vereïa would lead us without danger to Mojaisk—why reject that safe route? There, provisions must have been collected, there every thing was known to us, and we could not be misled by any traitor."

At these words Davoust, burning with a rage which he had great difficulty to repress, replied, that "he proposed a retreat through a fertile country, by an untouched, plentiful and well supplied route, villages still standing, and by the shortest road, that the enemy might not avail himself of it, to cut us off from the route from Mojaisk to Smolensk, recommended by Murat. And what a route! a desert of sand and ashes, where convoys of wounded would increase our embarrassment, where we should meet with nothing but ruins, traces of blood, skeletons and famine!

"Moreover, though he deemed it his duty to give his opinion when it was asked, he was ready to obey orders contrary to it with the same zeal as if they were consonant with his suggestions; but that the Emperor alone had a right to impose silence on him, and not Murat, who was not his Sovereign, and never should be!"

The quarrel growing warm, Bessières and Berthier interposed. As for the Emperor, still absorbed in the same attitude, he appeared insensible to what was passing. At length he broke up this council with the words, "Well, gentlemen, I will decide."

He decided on retreat, and by that road which would carry him most speedily to a distance from the enemy; but it required another desperate effort before he could bring himself to give an order of march so new to him. So painful was this effort, that in the inward struggle which it occasioned, he lost the use of his senses. Those who attended him have asserted, that the report of another warm affair with the Cossacks, towards Borowsk, a few leagues in the rear of the army, was the last shock which induced him finally to adopt this fatal resolution.

It is a remarkable fact, that he issued orders for this retreat northward, at the very moment that Kutusoff and his Russians, dismayed by the defeat of Malo-Yaroslawetz, were retiring southward.

CHAPTER 62

Wilson—the Englishman

The very same night a similar anxiety had agitated the Russian camp. During the combat of Malo-Yaroslawetz, Kutusoff had approached the field of battle, groping his way, as it were, pausing at every step, and examining the ground, as if he was afraid of its sinking beneath him; he did not send off the different corps which were dispatched to the assistance of Doctorof, till the orders for that purpose were absolutely extorted from him. He durst not place himself in person across Napoleon's way, till an hour when general battles are not to be apprehended.

Wilson, warm from the action, then hastened to him.—Wilson, that active bustling Englishman, whom we had seen in Egypt, in Spain, and every where else, the enemy of the French and of Napoleon. He was the representative of the allies in the Russian army; he was in the midst of Kutusoff's army an independent man, an observer, nay, even a judge—infallible motives of aversion; his presence was odious to the old Russian general; and as hatred never fails to beget hatred, both cordially detested each other.

Wilson reproached him with his excessive dilatoriness; he reminded him that five times in one day it had caused them to lose the victory, in the battle of Vinkowo, on the 18th of October. In fact, on that day Murat would have been destroyed, had Kutusoff fully occupied the front of the French by a brisk attack, while Beningsen was turning their left wing. But either from negligence, or that tardiness which is the fault of age, or as several Russians assert, because Kutusoff was more envious of Beningsen than inimical to Napoleon, the veteran had attacked too faintly, and too late, and had stopped too soon.

Wilson continued to insist on his agreeing to a decisive engagement on the following day, and on his refusal, he asked, "Was he then determined to open a free passage for Napoleon? to allow him to escape with his victory? What a cry of indignation would be raised in Petersburgh, in London, throughout all Europe! Did he not already hear the murmurs of his own troops?"

Kutusoff, irritated at this, replied, that "he would certainly rather make a bridge of gold for the enemy than compromise his army, and with it the fate of the whole empire. Was not Napoleon fleeing? why then stop him and force him to conquer? The season was sufficient to destroy him: of all the allies of Russia, they could rely with most confidence on winter; and he should wait for its assistance. As for the Russian army, it was under his command, and it would obey him in spite of the clamours of Wilson; Alexander, when informed of his proceedings, would approve them. What did he care for England? was it for her that he was fighting? He was a true-born Russian, his fondest wish was to see Russia delivered, and delivered she would be without risking the chance of another battle; and as for the rest of Europe, it was nothing to him whether it was under the dominion of France or England."

Thus was Wilson repulsed, and yet Kutusoff, shut up with the French army in the elevated plain of Malo-Yaroslawetz, was compelled to put himself into the most threatening attitude. He there drew up, on the 25th, all his divisions, and seven hundred pieces of artillery. No doubts were any longer entertained in the two armies that a decisive day had arrived: Wilson was of that opinion himself. He remarked that the Russian lines had at their back a muddy ravine, across which there was an unsafe bridge. This only way of retreat, in the sight of an enemy, appeared to him to be impracticable. Kutusoff was now in such a situation that he must either conquer or perish; and the Englishman was hugging himself at the prospect of a decisive engagement: whether its issue proved fatal to Napoleon or dangerous to Russia, it must be bloody, and England could not but be a gainer by it.

Still uneasy, however, he went at night through the ranks: he was delighted to hear Kutusoff swear that he was at length going to fight; he triumphed on seeing all the Russian generals preparing for a terrible conflict; Beningsen alone had still his doubts on the subject. The Englishman, nevertheless, considering that the position no longer admitted of falling back, at length lay down to wait for daylight, when about three in the morning a general order for retreat awoke him. All his efforts were ineffectual. Kutusoff had resolved to direct his flight southward, first to Gonczarewo, and then beyond Kalouga; and at the Oka every thing was by this time ready for his passage.

It was at that very instant that Napoleon ordered his troops to retire northward on Mojaisk. The two armies therefore turned their backs on each other, mutually deceiving each other by means of their rear-guards.

On the part of Kutusoff, Wilson asserts, that his retreat was like a rout. Cavalry, cannon, carriages, and battalions thronged from all sides to the entrance of the bridge, against which the Russian army was backed. There all these columns, hurrying from the right, the left, and the centre, met, clashed, and became blended into so enormous and so dense a mass, that it lost all power of motion. It took several hours to disentangle it and to clear the passage. A few balls discharged by Davoust, which he regarded as thrown away, fell among this confused crowd.

Napoleon needed but to have advanced upon this disorderly rabble. It was after the greatest effort, that of Malo-Yaroslawetz, had been made, and when he had nothing to do but to march, that he retreated. But such is war! in which it is impossible to attempt too much or to be too daring. One army knows not what the other is doing. The advanced posts are the exterior of these two great hostile bodies, by means of which they overawe one another. What an abyss there is between two armies that are in the presence of each other!

Besides, it was perhaps because the Emperor had been wanting in prudence at Moscow that he was now deficient in audacity: he was worn out; the two affairs with the Cossacks had disgusted him: he felt for his wounded; so many horrors disheartened him, and like men of extreme resolutions, having ceased to hope for a complete victory, he determined upon a precipitate retreat.

From that moment he had nothing in his view but Paris, just as on leaving Paris he saw nothing but Moscow. It was on the 26th of October that the fatal movement of our retreat commenced. Davoust with twenty-five thousand men remained as a rear-guard. While he advanced a few paces, and, without being aware of it, spread consternation among the Russians, the grand army in astonishment turned its back on them. It marched with downcast eyes, as if ashamed and humbled. In the midst of it, its commander, gloomy and silent, seemed to be anxiously measuring his line of communication with the fortresses on the Vistula.

For the space of more than two hundred and fifty leagues it offered but two points where he could halt and rest, the first, Smolensk, and the second, Minsk. He had made these two towns his two great depots, where immense magazines were established. But Wittgenstein, still before Polotsk, threatened the left flank of the former, and Tchitchakof, already at Bresklitowsky, the right flank of the latter. Wittgenstein's force was gaining strength by recruits and fresh corps which he was daily receiving, and by the gradual diminution of that of Saint Cyr.

Napoleon, however, reckoned upon the Duke of Belluno and his thirty-six thousand fresh troops. The *corps d'armée* had been at Smolensk ever since the beginning of September. He reckoned also upon detachments being sent from his depots, on the sick and wounded who had recovered, and on the stragglers, who would be rallied and formed at Wilna into marching battalions. All these would successively come into line, and fill up the chasms made in his ranks by the sword, famine, and disease. He should therefore have time to regain that position on the Düna and the Borysthenes, where he wished it to be believed that his presence, added to that of Victor, Saint Cyr, and Macdonald, would overawe Wittgenstein, check Kutusoff, and threaten Alexander even in his second capital.

He therefore proclaimed that he was going to take post on the Düna. But it was not upon that river and the Borysthenes that his thoughts rested: he was sensible that it was not with a harassed and reduced army that he could guard the interval between those two rivers and their courses, which the ice would speedily efface. He placed no reliance on a sea of snow six feet deep, with which winter would speedily cover those parts, but to which it would also give solidity: the whole then would be one wide road for the enemy to reach him, to penetrate into the intervals between his wooden cantonments, scattered over a frontier of two hundred leagues, and to burn them.

Had he at first stopped there, as he declared he should on his arrival at Witepsk; had he there taken proper measures for preserving and recruiting his army; had Tormasof, Tchitchakof and Hoertel been driven out of Volhynia; had he raised a hundred thousand Cossacks in those rich provinces; his winter-quarters would then have been habitable. But now, nothing was ready for him there; and not only was his force inadequate to the purpose, but Tchitchakof, a hundred leagues in his rear, would still threaten his communications with Germany and France and his retreat. It was therefore at a hundred leagues beyond Smolensk, in a more compact position, behind the morasses of the Berezina, it was to Minsk, that it was necessary to repair in search of winter-quarters, from which he was forty marches distant.

But should he arrive there in time? He had reason to think so. Dombrowski and his Poles, placed around Bobruisk, would be sufficient to keep Ertell in check. As for Schwartzenberg, that general had been victorious; he was at the head of forty-two thousand Austrians, Saxons, and Poles, whom Durutte, and his French division, from Warsaw, would augment to more than fifty thousand men. He had pursued Tormasof as far as the Styr.

It was true that the Russian army of Moldavia had just formed a junction with the remnant of the army of Volhynia; that Tchitchakof, an active and resolute general, had assumed the command of fifty-five thousand Russians; that the Austrian had paused and even thought it prudent, on the 23rd of September, to retire behind the Bug; but he was to have recrossed that river at Bresklitowsky, and Napoleon knew no more.

At any rate, without a defection, which it was too late to foresee, and which a precipitate return could alone prevent, he flattered himself that Schwartzenberg, Regnier, Durutte, Dombrowski, and twenty thousand men, divided between Minsk, Slonim, Grodno, and Wilna—in short, that seventy thousand men; would not allow sixty thousand Russians to gain possession of his magazines and to cut off his retreat.

CHAPTER 63

A Land in Flames

Napoleon, reduced to such hazardous conjectures, arrived quite pensive at Vereïa, when Mortier presented himself before him. But I perceive that, hurried along, just as we then were, by the rapid succession of violent scenes and memorable events, my attention has been diverted from a fact worthy of notice. On the 23rd of October, at half-past one in the morning, the air was shaken by a tremendous explosion which for a moment astonished both armies, though amid such mighty expectations scarcely any thing now excited astonishment.

Mortier had obeyed his orders; the Kremlin was no more: barrels of powder had been placed in all the halls of the palace of the Czars, and one hundred and eighty-three thousand pounds under the vaults which supported them. The marshal, with eight thousand men, had remained on this volcano, which a Russian howitzer-shell might have exploded. Here he covered the march of the army upon Kalouga and the retreat of our different convoys towards Mojaisk.

Among these eight thousand men there were scarcely two thousand on whom Mortier could rely: the others were dismounted cavalry, men of different countries and regiments, under new officers, without similar habits, without common recollections, in short, without any bond of union, who formed rather a rabble than an organized body; they could scarcely fail in a short time to disperse.

This marshal was looked upon as a devoted victim. The other chiefs, his old companions in glory, had left him with tears in their eyes, as well as the Emperor, who said to him, "that he relied on his good fortune; but still in war we must sometimes make part of a fire." Mortier had resigned himself without hesitation. His orders were to defend the Kremlin, and on retreating to blow it up, and to burn what yet remained of the city. It was from the castle of Krasnopachra, on the 21st of October, that Napoleon had sent him his last orders. After executing them, Mortier was to march upon Vereïa and to form the rear-guard of the army.

In this letter Napoleon particularly recommended to him "to put the men still remaining in the hospitals into the carriages belonging to the young guard, those of the dismounted cavalry, and any others that he might find. The Romans," added he, "awarded civic crowns to those who saved citizens: so many soldiers as he should save, so many crowns would the Duke of Treviso deserve. He must put them on his horses and those of any of his troops. It was thus that he, Napoleon, acted at St. Jean d'Acre. He ought so much the more to take this measure, since, as soon as the convoy should have rejoined the army, there would be plenty of horses and carriages, which the consumption would have rendered useless for its supply. The Emperor hoped that he should have to testify his satisfaction to the Duke of Treviso for having saved him five hundred men. He must begin with the officers and then with the subalterns, and give the preference to Frenchmen. He would therefore assemble all the generals and officers under his command, to make them sensible of the importance of this measure, and how well they would deserve of the Emperor if they saved him five hundred men."

Meanwhile, as the grand army was leaving Moscow, the Cossacks were penetrating into the suburbs, and Mortier had retired towards the Kremlin, as a remnant of life retires towards the heart, when death has begun to seize the extremities. These Cossacks were the scouts to ten thousand Russians under the command of Winzingerode.

This foreigner, inflamed with hatred of Napoleon, and animated by the desire of retaking Moscow and naturalizing himself in Russia by this signal exploit, pushed on to a considerable distance from his men; he traversed, running, the Georgian colony, hastened towards the Chinese town and the Kremlin, met with advanced posts, mistook them, fell into an ambuscade, and finding himself a prisoner in a city which he had come to take, he suddenly changed his part, waving his handkerchief in the air, and declaring that he had brought a flag of truce.

He was conducted to the Duke of Treviso. There he claimed, in a high tone, the protection of the law of nations, which, he said, was violated in his person. Mortier replied, that "a general-in-chief, coming in this manner, might be taken for a rash soldier, but never for a flag of truce, and that he must immediately deliver his sword." The Russian general, having no longer any hope of imposing upon him, complied and admitted his imprudence.

At length, after four days' resistance, the French bid an eternal adieu to that fatal city. They carried with them four hundred wounded, and, on retiring, deposited, in a safe and secret place, a fire-work skilfully prepared, which a slow fire was already consuming; its progress was minutely calculated; so that it was known at what hour the fire would reach the immense heap of powder buried among the foundations of these condemned palaces.

Mortier hastened his flight; but while he was rapidly retiring, some greedy Cossacks and squalid Muscovites, allured probably by the prospect of pillage, approached; they listened, and emboldened by the apparent quiet which pervaded the fortress, they ventured to penetrate into it; they ascended, and their hands, eager after plunder, were already stretched forth, when in a moment they were all destroyed, crushed, hurled into the air, with the buildings which they had come to pillage, and thirty thousand stand of arms that had been left behind there: and then their mangled limbs, mixed with fragments of walls and shattered weapons, blown to a great distance, descended in a horrible shower.

The earth shook under the feet of Mortier. At Feminskoe, ten leagues off, the Emperor heard the explosion, and he himself, in that tone of anger in which he sometimes addressed Europe, published the following day a bulletin, dated from Borowsk, to this effect, that "the Kremlin, the arsenal, the magazines were all destroyed; that the ancient citadel, which dated from the origin of the monarchy, and the first palace of the Czars, no longer existed; that Moscow was now but a heap of ruins, a filthy and unwholesome sink, without importance, either political or military. He had abandoned it to Russian beggars and plunderers to march against Kutusoff, to throw himself on the left wing of that general, to drive him back, and then to proceed quietly to the banks of the Düna, where he should take up his winter-quarters." Then, apprehensive lest he should appear to be retreating, he added, that "there he should be within eighty leagues of Wilna and Petersburg, a double advantage; that is to say, twenty marches nearer to his resources and his object." By this remark he hoped to give to his retreat the air of an offensive march.

It was on this occasion that he declared, that "he had refused to give orders for the destruction of the whole country which he was quitting; he felt a repugnance to aggravate the miseries of its inhabitants. To punish the Russian incendiary and a hundred wretches who make war like Tartars, he would not ruin nine thousand proprietors, and leave two hundred thousand serfs, innocent of all these barbarities, absolutely destitute of resources."

He had not then been soured by misfortune; but in three days every thing had changed. After coming in collision with Kutusoff, he retreated through this same town of Borowsk, and no sooner had he passed through it than it ceased to exist. It was thus that in future all was destined to be burned behind him. While conquering, he had preserved: when retiring, he resolved to destroy: either from necessity, to ruin the enemy and to retard his march, every thing being imperative in war; or by way of reprisal, the dreadful consequence of wars of invasion, which in the first place authorize every means of defence, while these afterwards operate as motives to those of attack.

It must be admitted, however, that the aggression in this terrible species of warfare was not on the side of Napoleon. On the 19th of October, Berthier had written to Kutusoff, proposing "to regulate hostilities in such a manner that they might not inflict on the Muscovite empire more evils than were inseparable from a state of war; the devastation of Russia being as detrimental to that empire as it was painful to Napoleon." But Kutusoff replied, that "it was not in his power to restrain the Russian patriotism," which amounted to an approval of the Tartar war made upon us by his militia, and authorized us in some measure to repay them in their own coin.

The like flames consumed Vereïa, where Mortier rejoined the Emperor, bringing to him Winzingerode. At sight of that German general, all the secret resentments of Napoleon took fire; his dejection gave place to anger, and he discharged all the spleen that oppressed him upon his enemy. "Who are you?" he exclaimed, crossing his arms with violence as if to grasp and to restrain himself, "a man without country! You have always been my personal enemy. When I was at war with the Austrians, I found you in their ranks. Austria is become my ally, and you have entered into the Russian service. You have been one of the warmest instigators of the present war. Nevertheless you are a native of the states of the Confederation of the Rhine; you are my subject. You are not an ordinary enemy, you are a rebel; I have a right to bring you to trial! *Gendarmes d'elite*, seize this man!" The *gendarmes* remained motionless, like men accustomed to see these violent scenes terminate without effect, and sure of obeying best by disobeying.

The Emperor resumed: "Do you see, sir, this devastated country, these villages in flames? To whom are these disasters to be charged? to fifty adventurers like yourself, paid by England, who has thrown them upon the continent; but the weight of this war will ultimately fall on those who have excited it. In six months I shall be at Petersburg, and I will call them to account for all this swaggering."

Then addressing the aide-de-camp of Winzingerode, who was a prisoner like himself, "As for you, Count Narischkin," said he, "I have nothing to upbraid you with; you are a Russian, you are doing your duty; but how could a man of one of the first families in Russia become the aide-de-camp of a foreign mercenary? Be the aide-de-camp of a Russian general; that employment will be far more honourable."

Till then General Winzingerode had not had an opportunity to answer this violent language, except by his attitude: it was calm as his reply. "The Emperor Alexander," he said, "was his benefactor and that of his family: all that he possessed he owed to him; gratitude had made him his subject; he was at the post which his benefactor had allotted to him, and consequently he was only doing his duty."

Napoleon added some threats, but in a less violent strain, and he confined himself to words, either because he had vented all his wrath in the first explosion, or because he merely designed to frighten the Germans who might be tempted to abandon him. Such at least was the interpretation which those about him put upon his violence. It was disapproved; no account was taken of it, and each was eager to accost the captive general, to tranquillize and to console him. These attentions were continued till the army reached Lithuania, where the Cossacks retook Winzingerode and his aide-de-camp. The Emperor had affected to treat this young Russian nobleman with kindness, at the same time that he stormed so loudly against his general—a proof that there was calculation even in his wrath.

CHAPTER 64

The Field of Borodino Again

On the 28th of October we again beheld Mojaisk. That town was still full of wounded; some were carried away and the rest collected together and left, as at Moscow, to the generosity of the Russians. Napoleon had proceeded but a few *wersts* from that place, when the winter began. Thus, after an obstinate combat, and ten days' marching and countermarching, the army, which had brought from Moscow only fifteen rations of flour per man, had advanced but three days' march in its retreat. It was in want of provisions and overtaken by the winter.

Some men had already sunk under these hardships. In the first days of the retreat, on the 26th of October, carriages, laden with provisions, which the horses could no longer draw, were burned. The order for setting fire to all behind the army then followed; in obedience to it, powder-wagons, the horses of which were already worn out, were blown up together with the houses. But at length, as the enemy had not again shown himself, we seemed to be but once more setting out on a toilsome journey; and Napoleon, on again seeing the well-known road, was recovering his confidence, when, towards evening, a Russian chasseur, who had been made prisoner, was sent to him by Davoust.

At first he questioned him carelessly; but as chance would have it, this Russian had some knowledge of roads, names, and distances. He answered, that "the whole Russian army was marching by Medyn upon Wiazma." The Emperor then became attentive. Did Kutusoff mean to forestall him there, as at Malo-Yaroslawetz, to cut off his retreat upon Smolensk, as he had done that upon Kalouga, and to coop him up in this desert without provisions, without shelter, and in the midst of a general insurrection? His first impulse, however, inclined him to reject this notion; for, whether owing to pride or experience, he was accustomed not to give his adversaries credit for that ability which he should have displayed in their place.

In this instance, however, he had another motive. His security was but affected: for it was evident that the Russian army was taking the Medyn road, the very one which Davoust had recommended for the French army: and Davoust, either from vanity or inadvertence, had not confided this alarming intelligence to his dispatch alone. Napoleon feared its effects on his troops, and therefore affected to disbelieve and to despise it; but at the same time he gave orders that his guard should march next day in all haste, and so long as it should be light, as far as Gjatz. Here he proposed to afford rest and provisions to this flower of his army, to ascertain, so much nearer, the direction of Kutusoff's march, and to be beforehand with him at that point.

But he had not consulted the season, which seemed to avenge the slight. Winter was so near at hand, that a blast of a few minutes was sufficient to bring it on, sharp, biting, intense. We were immediately sensible that it was indigenous to this country, and that we were strangers in it. Every thing was altered: roads, faces, courage: the army became sullen, the march toilsome, and consternation began.

Some leagues from Mojaisk, we had to cross the Kologa. It was but a large rivulet; two trees, the same number of props, and a few planks were sufficient to ensure the passage: but such was the confusion and inattention, that the Emperor was detained there. Several pieces of cannon, which it was attempted to get across by fording, were lost. It seemed as if each *corps d'armée* was marching separately as if there was no staff, no general order, no common tie, nothing that bound these corps together. In reality the elevation of each of their chiefs rendered them too independent of one another. The Emperor himself had become so exceedingly great, that he was at an immeasurable distance from the details of his army; and Berthier, holding an intermediate place between him and officers, who were all kings, princes, or marshals, was obliged to act with a great deal of caution. He was besides wholly incompetent to the situation.

The Emperor, stopped by the trifling obstacle of a broken bridge, confined himself to a gesture expressive of dissatisfaction and contempt; to which Berthier replied only by a look of resignation. On this particular point he had received no orders from the Emperor: he therefore conceived that he was not to blame; for Berthier was a faithful echo, a mirror, and nothing more. Always ready, clear and distinct, he reflected, he repeated the Emperor, but added nothing, and what Napoleon forgot was forgotten without retrieve.

After passing the Kologa, we marched on, absorbed in thought, when some of us, raising our eyes, uttered an exclamation of horror. Each instantly looked around him, and beheld a plain trampled, bare and devastated, all the trees cut down within a few feet from the surface, and farther off craggy hills, the highest of which appeared to be the most misshapen. It had all the appearance of an extinguished and destroyed volcano. The ground was covered all around with fragments of helmets and cuirasses, broken drums, gun-stocks, tatters of uniforms, and standards dyed with blood.

On this desolate spot lay thirty thousand half-devoured corpses. A number of skeletons, left on the summit of one of the hills, overlooked the whole. It seemed as if death had here fixed his empire; it was that terrible redoubt, the conquest and the grave of Caulaincourt. Presently the cry, "It is the field of the great battle!" formed a long and doleful murmur. The Emperor passed quickly. Nobody stopped. Cold, hunger, and the enemy urged us on: we merely turned our faces as we proceeded to take a last melancholy look at the vast grave of so many companions in arms, uselessly sacrificed, and whom we were obliged to leave behind.

It was here that we had inscribed with the sword and blood one of the most memorable pages of our history. A few relics yet recorded it, and they would soon be swept away. Some day the traveller will pass with indifference over this plain, undistinguished from any other; but when he shall learn that it was the theatre of the great battle, he will turn back, long survey it with inquisitive looks, impress its minutest features on his greedy memory, and doubtless exclaim, What men! what a commander! what a destiny! These were the soldiers, who thirteen years before in the south attempted a passage to the East, through Egypt, and were dashed against its gates. They afterwards conquered Europe, and hither they came by the north to present themselves again before that same Asia, to be again foiled. What then urged them into this roving and adventurous life? They were not barbarians, seeking a more genial climate, more commodious habitations, more enchanting spectacles, greater wealth: on the contrary, they possessed all these advantages, and all possible pleasures; and yet they forsook them, to live without shelter, and without food, to fall daily and in succession, either slain or mutilated. What necessity drove them to this?—Why, what but confidence in a leader hitherto infallible! the ambition to complete a great work gloriously begun! the intoxication of victory, and above all, that insatiable thirst of fame, that powerful instinct, which impels man to seek death, in order to obtain immortality.

Chapter 65

Burning Wagons

While the army was passing this fatal field in grave and silent meditation, one of the victims of that sanguinary day was perceived, it is said, still living, and piercing the air with his groans. It was found by those who ran up to him that he was a French soldier. Both his legs had been broken in the engagement; he had fallen among the dead, where he remained unnoticed. The body of a horse, gutted by a shell, was at first his asylum; afterwards, for fifty days, the muddy water of a ravine, into which he had rolled, and the putrefied flesh of the dead, had served for dressing for his wounds and food for the support of his languishing existence. Those who say that they discovered this man affirm that they saved him.

Farther on, we again beheld the great abbey or hospital of Kolotskoi, a sight still more hideous than that of the field of battle. At Borodino all was death, but not without its quiet; there at least the battle was over; at Kolotskoi it was still raging. Death here seemed to be pursuing his victims, who had escaped from the engagement, with the utmost malignity; he penetrated into them by all their senses at once. They were destitute of every thing for repelling his attacks, excepting orders, which it was impossible to execute in these deserts, and which, moreover, issuing from too high and too distant a quarter, passed through too many hands to be executed.

Still, in spite of famine, cold, and the most complete destitution, the devotedness of a few surgeons and a remnant of hope, still supported a great number of wounded in this pestiferous abode. But when they saw the army repass, and that they were about to be left behind, the least infirm crawled to the threshold of the door, lined the way, and extended towards us their supplicating hands.

The Emperor had just given orders that each carriage, of whatever kind it might be, should take up one of these unfortunate creatures, that the weakest should be left, as at Moscow, under the protection of such of the wounded and captive Russian officers as had been recovered by our attentions. He halted to see this order carried into execution, and it was at a fire kindled with his forsaken wagons that he and most of his attendants warmed themselves. Ever since morning a multitude of explosions proclaimed the numerous sacrifices of this kind which it already had been found necessary to make.

During this halt, an atrocious action was witnessed. Several of the wounded had just been placed in the suttlers' carts. These wretches, whose vehicles were overloaded with the plunder of Moscow, murmured at the new burden imposed upon them; but being compelled to admit it, they held their peace. No sooner, however, had the army recommenced its march, than they slackened their pace, dropped behind their columns, and taking advantage of a lonely situation, they threw all the unfortunate men committed to their care into the ditches. One only lived long enough to be picked up by the next carriages that passed: he was a general, and through him this atrocious procedure became known. A shudder of horror spread throughout the column; it reached the Emperor; for the sufferings of the army were not yet so severe and so universal as to stifle pity, and to concentrate all his affections within the bosom of each individual.

In the evening of this long day, as the imperial column approached Gjatz, it was surprised to find Russians quite recently killed on the way. It was remarked, that each of them had his head shattered in the same manner, and that his bloody brains were scattered near him. It was known that two thousand Russian prisoners were marching on before, and that their guard consisted of Spaniards, Portuguese, and Poles. On this discovery, each, according to his disposition, was indignant, approved, or remained indifferent. Around the Emperor these various feelings were mute. Caulaincourt broke out into the exclamation, that "it was an atrocious cruelty. Here was a pretty specimen of the civilization which we were introducing into Russia! What would be the effect of this barbarity on the enemy? Were we not leaving our wounded and a multitude of prisoners at his mercy? Did he want the means of wreaking the most horrible retaliation?"

Napoleon preserved a gloomy silence, but on the ensuing day these murders had ceased. These unfortunate people were then merely left to die of hunger in the enclosures where, at night, they were confined like cattle. This was no doubt a barbarity too; but what could we do? Exchange them? the enemy rejected the proposal. Release them? they would have gone and published the general distress, and, soon joined by others, they would have returned to pursue us. In this mortal warfare, to give them their lives would have been sacrificing our own. We were cruel from necessity. The mischief arose from our having involved ourselves in so dreadful an alternative.

Besides, in their march to the interior of Russia, our soldiers, who had been made prisoners, were not more humanely treated, and there, certainly, imperious necessity was not an excuse.

At length the troops arrived with the night at Gjatz; but this first day of winter had been cruelly occupied. The sight of the field of battle, and of the two forsaken hospitals, the multitude of wagons consigned to the flames, the Russians with their brains blown out, the excessive length of the march, the first severities of winter, all concurred to render it horrible: the retreat became a flight; and Napoleon, compelled to yield and run away, was a spectacle perfectly novel.

Several of our allies enjoyed it with that inward satisfaction which is felt by inferiors, when they see their chiefs at length thwarted, and obliged in their turn to give way. They indulged that miserable envy that is excited by extraordinary success, which rarely occurs without being abused, and which shocks that equality which is the first want of man. But this malicious joy was soon extinguished and lost in the universal distress.

The wounded pride of Napoleon justified the supposition of such reflections. This was perceived in one of the halts of that day: there, on the rough furrows of a frozen field, strewed with wrecks both Russian and French, he attempted, by the energy of his words, to relieve himself from the weight of the insupportable responsibility of so many disasters. "He had in fact dreaded this war, and he devoted its author to the execration of the whole world. It was —— whom he accused of this; it was that Russian minister, sold to the English, who had fomented it, and the traitor had drawn into it both Alexander and himself."

These words, uttered before two of his generals, were heard with that silence enjoined by old respect, added to that which is due to misfortune. But the Duke of Vicenza, perhaps too impatient, betrayed his indignation by a gesture of anger and incredulity, and, abruptly retiring, put an end to this painful conversation.

Chapter 66
Wiazma

From Gjatz the Emperor proceeded in two marches to Wiazma. He there halted to wait for Prince Eugene and Davoust, and to reconnoitre the road of Medyn and Yucknow, which runs at that place into the high road to Smolensk. It was this cross-road which might bring the Russian army from Malo-Yaroslawetz on his passage. But on the first of November, after waiting thirty-six hours, Napoleon had not seen any *avant-courier* of that army; he set out, wavering between the hope that Kutusoff had fallen asleep, and the fear that the Russian had left Wiazma on his right, and proceeded two marches farther towards Dorogobouje to cut off his retreat. At any rate, he left Ney at Wiazma, to collect the first and fourth corps, and to relieve, as the rear-guard, Davoust, whom he judged to be fatigued.

He complained of the tardiness of the latter; he wrote to reproach him with being still five marches behind him, when he ought to have been no more than three days later; he considered the genius of that marshal as too methodical to direct, in a suitable manner, so irregular a march.

The whole army, and the corps of Prince Eugene in particular, repeated these complaints. They said, that "owing to his spirit of order and obstinacy, Davoust had suffered the enemy to overtake him at the Abbey of Kalotskoi; that he had there done ragamuffin Cossacks the honour of retiring before them, step by step, and in square battalions, as if they had been Mamelukes; that Platof, with his cannon, had played at a distance on the deep masses which he had presented to him; that then only the marshal had opposed to them merely a few slender lines, which had speedily formed again, and some light pieces, the first fire of which had produced the desired effect; but that these manoeuvres and regular foraging excursions had occasioned a great loss of time, which is always valuable in retreat, and especially amidst famine, through which the most skilful manoeuvre was to pass with all possible expedition."

In reply to this, Davoust urged his natural horror of every kind of disorder, which had at first led him to attempt to introduce regularity into this flight; he had endeavoured to cover the wrecks of it, fearing the shame and the danger of leaving for the enemy these evidences of our disastrous state.

He added, that, "people were not aware of all that he had had to surmount; he had found the country completely devastated, houses demolished, and the trees burned to their very roots; for it was not to him who came last, that the work of general destruction had been left; the conflagration preceded him. It appeared as if the rear-guard had been totally forgotten! No doubt, too, people forgot the frozen road rough with the tracks of all who had gone before him; as well as the deep fords and broken bridges, which no one thought of repairing, as each corps, when not engaged, cared but for itself alone."

Did they not know besides, that the whole tremendous train of stragglers, belonging to the other corps, on horseback, on foot, and in vehicles, aggravated these embarrassments, just as in a diseased body all the complaints fly to and unite in the part most affected? Every day he marched between these wretches and the Cossacks, driving forward the one and pressed by the other.

Thus, after passing Gjatz, he had found the slough of Czarewo-Zaimcze without a bridge, and completely encumbered with carriages. He had dragged them out of the marsh in sight of the enemy, and so near to them that their fires lighted his labours, and the sound of their drums mingled with that of his voice. For the marshal and his generals could not yet resolve to relinquish to the enemy so many trophies; nor did they make up their minds to it, till after superfluous exertions, and in the last extremity, which happened several times a day.

The road was in fact crossed every moment by marshy hollows. A slope, slippery as glass with the frost, hurried the carriages into them and there they stuck; to draw them out it was necessary to climb the opposite ascent by an icy road, where the horses, whose shoes were worn quite smooth, could not obtaining a footing, and where every moment they and their drivers dropped exhausted one upon the other. The famished soldiers immediately fell upon these luckless animals and tore them to pieces; then at fires, kindled with the remains of their carriages, they broiled the yet bleeding flesh and devoured it.

Meanwhile the artillerymen, a chosen corps, and their officers, all brought up in the first school in the world, kept off these unfortunate wretches whenever they could, and took the horses from their own chaises and wagons, which they abandoned to save the guns. To these they harnessed their horses, nay even themselves: the Cossacks, observing this disaster from a distance, durst not approach; but with their light pieces mounted on sledges they threw their balls into all this disorder, and served to increase it.

The first corps had already lost ten thousand men: nevertheless, by dint of efforts and sacrifices, the viceroy and the Prince of Eckmühl were, on the 2nd of November, within two leagues of Wiazma. It is certain that the same day they might have passed that town, joined Ney, and avoided a disastrous engagement. It is affirmed, that such was the opinion of Prince Eugene, but that Davoust believed his troops to be too much fatigued, on which the viceroy, sacrificing himself to his duty, staid to share a danger which he foresaw. Davoust's generals say, on the contrary, that Prince Eugene, who was already encamped, could not find in his heart to make his soldiers leave their fires and their meal, which they had already begun, and the cooking of which always cost them a great deal of trouble.

Be that as it may, during the deceptive tranquillity of that night, the advanced-guard of the Russians arrived from Malo-Yaroslawetz, our retreat from which place had put an end to theirs: it skirted along the two French corps and that of Poniatowski, passed their bivouacs, and disposed its columns of attack against the left flank of the road, in the intermediate two leagues which Davoust and Eugene had left between themselves and Wiazma.

Miloradowitch, whom we denominated the Russian Murat, commanded this advanced-guard. He was, according to his countrymen, an indefatigable and successful warrior, impetuous as that soldier-king, of a stature equally remarkable, and, like him, a favourite of fortune. He was never known to be wounded, though numbers of officers and soldiers had fallen around him, and several horses had been killed under him. He despised the principles of war: he even made an art of not following the rules of that art, pretending to surprise the enemy by unexpected blows, for he was prompt in decision; he disdained to make any preparations, leaving places and circumstances to suggest what was proper to be done, and guiding himself only by sudden inspirations. In other respects, a general in the field of battle alone, he was destitute of foresight in the management of any affairs, either public or private, a notorious spendthrift, and, what is rare, not less upright than prodigal.

It was this general, with Platof and twenty thousand men, whom we had now to fight.

Chapter 67
Hard Pressed

On the 3rd of November, Prince Eugene was proceeding towards Wiazma, preceded by his equipages and his artillery, when the first light of day showed him at once his retreat threatened by an army on his left; behind him his rear-guard cut off; and on his left the plain covered with stragglers and scattered vehicles, fleeing before the lances of the enemy. At the same time, towards Wiazma, he heard Marshal Ney, who should have assisted him, fighting for his own preservation.

That Prince was not one of those generals, the offspring of favour, to whom every thing is unexpected and cause of astonishment, for want of experience. He immediately looked the evil in the face, and set about remedying it. He halted, turned about, deployed his divisions on the right of the high road, and checked in the plain the Russian columns, who were striving to cut him off from that road. Their foremost troops, overpowering the right of the Italians, had already seized one point, of which they kept possession, when Ney despatched from Wiazma one of his regiments, which attacked them in the rear and dislodged them.

At the same time Compans, a general of Davoust's, joined the Italian rear-guard with his division. They cleared a way for themselves, and while they, united with the Viceroy, were engaged, Davoust with his column passed rapidly behind them, along the left side of the high road, then crossing it as soon as he had got beyond them, he claimed his place in the order of battle, took the right wing, and found himself between Wiazma and the Russians. Prince Eugene gave up to him the ground which he had defended, and crossed to the other side of the road. The enemy then began to extend himself before them, and endeavoured to break through their wings.

By the success of this first manoeuvre, the two French and Italian corps had not conquered the right to continue their retreat, but only the possibility of defending it. They were still thirty thousand strong; but in the first corps, that of Davoust, there was some disorder. The hastiness of the manoeuvre, the surprise, so much wretchedness, and, above all, the fatal example of a multitude of dismounted cavalry, without arms, and running to and fro bewildered with fear, threw it into confusion.

This sight encouraged the enemy; he took it for a rout. His artillery, superior in number, manoeuvred at a gallop: it took obliquely and in flank our lines, which it cut down, while the French cannon, already at Wiazma, and which had been ordered to return in haste, could with difficulty be brought along. However, Davoust and his generals had still their firmest troops, about them. Several of these officers, still suffering from the wounds received at the Moskwa, one with his arm in a sling, another with his head wrapped in cloths, were seen supporting the best, encouraging the most irresolute, dashing at the enemy's batteries, forcing them to retire, and even seizing three of their pieces; in short, astonishing both the enemy and their own fugitives, and combating a mischievous example by their noble behaviour.

Miloradowitch, perceiving that his prey was escaping, now applied for reinforcement; and it was again Wilson, who was sure to be present wherever he could be most injurious to France, who hastened to summon Kutusoff. He found the old marshal unconcernedly resting himself with his army within hearing of the action. The ardent Wilson, urgent as the occasion, excited him in vain: he could not induce him to stir. Transported with indignation, he called him traitor, and declared that he would instantly despatch one of his Englishmen full speed to Petersburg, to denounce his treason to his Emperor and his allies.

This threat had no effect on Kutusoff; he persisted in remaining inactive; either because to the frost of age was superadded that of winter, and that in his shattered frame his mind was depressed by the sight of so many ruins; or that, from another effect of old age, a person becomes prudent when he has scarcely any thing to risk, and a temporiser when he has no more time to lose. He seemed still to be of opinion, as at Malo-Yaroslawetz, that the Russian winter alone could overthrow Napoleon; that this genius, the conqueror of men, was not yet sufficiently conquered by Nature; that it was best to leave to the climate the honour of that victory, and to the Russian atmosphere the work of vengeance.

Miloradowitch, left to himself, then tried to break the French line of battle; but he could not penetrate it except by his fire, which made dreadful havoc in it. Eugene and Davoust were growing weak; and as they heard another action in the rear of their right, they imagined that the rest of the Russian army was approaching Wiazma by the Yuknof road, the outlet of which Ney was defending.

It was only an advanced-guard: but they were alarmed at the noise of this fight in the rear of their own, threatening their retreat. The action had lasted ever since seven in the morning; night was approaching; the baggage must by this time have got away; the French generals therefore began to retire.

This retrograde movement increased the ardour of the enemy, and but for a memorable effort of the 25th, 57th, and 85th regiments, and the protection of a ravine, Davoust's corps would have been broken, turned by its right, and destroyed. Prince Eugene, who was not so briskly attacked, was able to effect his retreat more rapidly through Wiazma; but the Russians followed him thither, and had penetrated into the town, when Davoust, pursued by twenty thousand men, and overwhelmed by eighty pieces of cannon, attempted to pass in his turn.

Morand's division first entered the town: it was marching on with confidence, under the idea that the action was over, when the Russians, who were concealed by the windings of the streets, suddenly fell upon it. The surprise was complete and the confusion great: Morand nevertheless rallied and re-encouraged his men, retrieved matters, and fought his way through.

It was Compans who put an end to the whole. He closed the march with his division. Finding himself too closely pressed by the bravest troops of Miloradowitch, he turned about, dashed in person at the most eager, overthrew them, and having thus made them fear him, he finished his retreat without further molestation. This conflict was glorious to each, and its result disastrous to all: it was without order and unity. There would have been troops enough to conquer, had there not been too many commanders. It was not till near two o'clock that the latter met to concert their manoeuvres, and these were even then executed without harmony.

When at length the river, the town of Wiazma, night, mutual fatigue, and Marshal Ney had separated them from the enemy, the danger being adjourned and the bivouacs established, the numbers were counted. Several pieces of cannon which had been broken, the baggage, and four thousand killed or wounded, were missing. Many of the soldiers had dispersed. Their honour was saved, but there were immense gaps in the ranks. It was necessary to close them up, to bring every thing within a narrower compass, to form what remained into a more compact whole. Each regiment scarcely composed a battalion, each battalion a platoon. The soldiers had no longer their accustomed places, comrades, or officers.

This sad re-organization took place by the light of the conflagration of Wiazma, and during the successive discharges of the cannon of Ney and Miloradowitch, the thunders of which were prolonged amid the double darkness of night and the forests. Several times the relics of these brave troops, conceiving that they were attacked, crawled to their arms. Next morning, when they fell into their ranks again, they were astonished at the smallness of their number.

Chapter 68
The Snow Falls

The spirits of the troops were still supported by the example of their leaders, by the hopes of finding all their wants supplied at Smolensk, and still more by the aspect of a yet brilliant sun, of that universal source of hope and life, which seemed to contradict and deny the spectacles of despair and death that already encompassed us.

But on the 6th of November, the heavens declared against us. Their azure disappeared. The army marched enveloped in cold fogs. These fogs became thicker, and presently an immense cloud descended upon it in large flakes of snow. It seemed as if the very sky was falling, and joining the earth and our enemies to complete our destruction. All objects changed their appearance, and became confounded, and not to be recognised again; we proceeded, without knowing where we were, without perceiving the point to which we were bound; every thing was transformed into an obstacle. While the soldier was struggling with the tempest of wind and snow, the flakes, driven by the storm, lodged and accumulated in every hollow; their surfaces concealed unknown abysses, which perfidiously opened beneath our feet. There the men were engulfed, and the weakest, resigning themselves to their fate, found a grave in these snow-pits.

Those who followed turned aside, but the storm drove into their faces both the snow that was descending from the sky, and that which it raised from the ground: it seemed bent on opposing their progress. The Russian winter, under this new form, attacked them on all sides: it penetrated through their light garments and their torn shoes and boots. Their wet clothes froze upon their bodies; an icy envelope encased them and stiffened all their limbs. A keen and violent wind interrupted respiration: it seized their breath at the moment when they exhaled it, and converted it into icicles, which hung from their beards all round their mouths.

The unfortunate creatures still crawled on, shivering, till the snow, gathering like balls under their feet, or the fragment of some broken article, a branch of a tree, or the body of one of their comrades, caused them to stumble and fall. There they groaned in vain; the snow soon covered them; slight hillocks marked the spot where they lay: such was their only grave! The road was studded with these undulations, like a cemetery: the most intrepid and the most indifferent were affected; they passed on quickly with averted looks. But before them, around them, there was nothing but snow: this immense and dreary uniformity extended farther than the eye could reach; the imagination was astounded; it was like a vast winding-sheet which Nature had thrown over the army. The only objects not enveloped by it, were some gloomy pines, trees of the tombs, with their funeral verdure, the motionless aspect of their gigantic black trunks and their dismal look, which completed the doleful appearance of a general mourning, and of an army dying amidst a nature already dead.

Every thing, even to their very arms, still offensive at Malo-Yaroslawetz, but since then defensive only, now turned against them. These seemed to their frozen limbs insupportably heavy, in the frequent falls which they experienced, they dropped from their hands and were broken or buried in the snow. If they rose again, it was without them; for they did not throw them away; hunger and cold wrested them from their grasp. The fingers of many others were frozen to the musket which they still held, which deprived them of the motion necessary for keeping up some degree of warmth and life.

We soon met with numbers of men belonging to all the corps, sometimes singly, at others in troops. They had not basely deserted their colours; it was cold and inanition which had separated them from their columns. In this general and individual struggle, they had parted from one another, and there they were, disarmed, vanquished, defenceless, without leaders, obeying nothing but the urgent instinct of self-preservation.

Most of them, attracted by the sight of by-paths, dispersed themselves over the country, in hopes of finding bread and shelter for the coming night: but, on their first passage, all had been laid waste to the extent of seven or eight leagues; they met with nothing but Cossacks, and an armed population, which encompassed, wounded, and stripped them naked, and then left them, with ferocious bursts of laughter, to expire on the snow. These people, who had risen at the call of Alexander and Kutusoff, and who had not then learned, as they since have, to avenge nobly a country which they were unable to defend, hovered on both flanks of the army under favour of the woods. Those whom they did not despatch with their pikes and hatchets, they brought back to the fatal and all-devouring high road.

Night then came on—a night of sixteen hours! But on that snow which covered every thing, they knew not where to halt, where to sit, where to lie down, where to find some root or other to eat, and dry wood to kindle a fire! Fatigue, darkness, and repeated orders nevertheless stopped those whom their moral and physical strength and the efforts of their officers had kept together. They strove to establish themselves; but the tempest, still active, dispersed the first preparations for bivouacs. The pines, laden with frost, obstinately resisted the flames; their snow, that from the sky which yet continued to fall fast, and that on the ground, which melted with the efforts of the soldiers, and the effect of the first fires, extinguished those fires, as well as the strength and spirits of the men.

When at length the flames gained the ascendancy, the officers and soldiers around them prepared their wretched repast; it consisted of lean and bloody pieces of flesh torn from the horses that were knocked up, and at most a few spoonfuls of rye-flour mixed with snow-water. Next morning circular ranges of soldiers extended lifeless marked the bivouacs; and the ground about them was strewed with the bodies of several thousand horses.

From that day we began to place less reliance on one another. In that lively army, susceptible of all impressions, and taught to reason by an advanced civilization, discouragement and neglect of discipline spread rapidly, the imagination knowing no bounds in evil as in good. Henceforward, at every bivouac, at every difficult passage, at every moment, some portion separated from the yet organised troops, and fell into disorder. There were some, however, who withstood this wide contagion of indiscipline and despondency. These were officers, non-commissioned officers, and steady soldiers. These were extraordinary men: they encouraged one another by repeating the name of Smolensk, which they knew they were approaching, and where they had been promised that all their wants should be supplied.

It was in this manner that, after this deluge of snow, and the increase of cold which it foreboded, each, whether officer or soldier, preserved or lost his fortitude, according to his disposition, his age, and his constitution. That one of our leaders who had hitherto been the strictest in enforcing discipline, now paid little attention to it. Thrown out of all his fixed ideas of regularity, order, and method, he was seized with despair at the sight of such universal disorder, and conceiving, before the others, that all was lost, he felt himself ready to abandon all.

From Gjatz to Mikalewska, a village between Dorogobouje and Smolensk, nothing remarkable occurred in the imperial column, unless that it was found necessary to throw the spoils of Moscow into the lake of Semlewo: cannon, gothic armour, the ornaments of the Kremlin, and the cross of Ivan the Great, were buried in its waters; trophies, glory, all those acquisitions to which we had sacrificed every thing, became a burden to us; our object was no longer to embellish, to adorn life, but to preserve it. In this vast wreck, the army, like a great ship tossed by the most tremendous of tempests, threw without hesitation into that sea of ice and snow, every thing that could slacken or impede its progress.

CHAPTER 69

Ney at Bay

During the 3rd and 4th of November Napoleon halted at Stakowo. This repose, and the shame of appearing to flee, inflamed his imagination. He dictated orders, according to which his rear-guard, by appearing to retreat in disorder, was to draw the Russians into an ambuscade, where he should be waiting for them in person; but this vain project passed off with the pre-occupation which gave it birth. On the 5th he slept at Dorogobouje. Here he found the hand-mills which were ordered for the expedition at the time the cantonments of Smolensk were projected; of these a late and totally useless distribution was made.

Next day, the 6th of November, opposite to Mikalewska, at the moment when the clouds, laden with sleet and snow, were bursting over our heads, Count Daru was seen hastening up, and a circle of vedettes forming around him and the Emperor.

An express, the first that had been able to reach us for ten days, had just brought intelligence of that strange conspiracy, hatched in Paris itself, and in the depth of a prison, by an obscure general. He had had no other accomplices than the false news of our destruction, and forged orders to some troops to apprehend the Minister, the Prefect of Police, and the Commandant of Paris. His plan had completely succeeded, from the impulsion of a first movement, from ignorance and the general astonishment; but no sooner was a rumour of the affair spread abroad, than an order was sufficient again to consign the leader, with his accomplices or his dupes, to a prison.

The Emperor was apprised at the same moment of their crime and their punishment. Those who at a distance strove to read his thoughts in his countenance could discover nothing. He repressed his feelings; his first and only words to Daru were, "How now, if we had remained at Moscow!" He then hastened into a house surrounded with a palisade, which had served for a post of correspondence.

The moment he was alone with the most devoted of his officers, all his emotions burst forth at once in exclamations of astonishment, humiliation and anger. Presently afterwards he sent for several other officers, to observe the effect which so extraordinary a piece of intelligence would produce upon them. He perceived in them a painful uneasiness and consternation, and their confidence in the stability of his government completely shaken. He had occasion to know that they accosted each other with a sigh, and the remark, that it thus appeared that the great revolution of 1789, which was thought to be finished, was not yet over. Grown old in struggles to get out of it, were they to be again plunged into it, and to be thrown once more into the dreadful career of political convulsions? Thus war was coming upon us in every quarter, and we were liable to lose every thing at once.

Some rejoiced at this intelligence, in the hope that it would hasten the return of the Emperor to France, that it would fix him there, and that he would no longer risk himself abroad, since he was not safe at home. On the following day, the sufferings of the moment put an end to these conjectures. As for Napoleon, all his thoughts again flew before him to Paris, and he was advancing mechanically towards Smolensk, when his whole attention was recalled to the present place and time, by the arrival of an aide-de-camp of Ney.

From Wiazma that Marshal had begun to protect this retreat, mortal to so many others, but immortal for himself. As far as Dorogobouje, it had been molested only by some bands of Cossacks, troublesome insects attracted by our dying and by our forsaken carriages, flying away the moment a hand was lifted, but harassing by their continual return.

They were not the subject of Ney's message. On approaching Dorogobouje he had met with the traces of the disorder which prevailed in the corps that preceded him, and which it was not in his power to efface. So far he had made up his mind to leave the baggage to the enemy; but he blushed with shame at the sight of the first pieces of cannon abandoned before Dorogobouje.

The marshal had halted there. After a dreadful night, in which snow, wind, and famine had driven most of his men from the fires, the dawn, which is always awaited with such impatience in a bivouac, had brought him a tempest, the enemy, and the spectacle of an almost general defection. In vain he had just fought in person at the head of what men and officers he had left: he had been obliged to retreat precipitately behind the Dnieper; and of this he sent to apprise the Emperor.

He wished him to know the worst. His aide-de-camp, Colonel

Dalbignac, was instructed to say, that "the first movement of retreat from Malo-Yaroslawetz, for soldiers who had never yet run away, had dispirited the army; that the affair at Wiazma had shaken its firmness; and that lastly, the deluge of snow and the increased cold which it betokened, had completed its disorganization: that a multitude of officers, having lost every thing, their platoons, battalions, regiments, and even divisions, had joined the roving masses: generals, colonels, and officers of all ranks, were seen mingled with the privates, and marching at random, sometimes with one column, sometimes with another: that as order could not exist in the presence of disorder, this example was seducing even the veteran regiments, which had served during the whole of the wars of the revolution: that in the ranks, the best soldiers were heard asking one another, why they alone were required to fight in order to secure the flight of the rest; and how any one could expect to keep up their courage, when they heard the cries of despair issuing from the neighbouring woods, in which large convoys of their wounded, who had been dragged to no purpose all the way from Moscow, had just been abandoned? Such then was the fate which awaited themselves! what had they to gain by remaining by their colours? Incessant toils and combats by day, and famine at night; no shelter, and bivouacs still more destructive than battle: famine and cold drove sleep far away from them, or if fatigue got the better of these for the moment, that repose which ought to refresh them put a period to their lives. In short, the eagles had ceased to protect—they destroyed. Why then remain around them to perish by battalions, by masses? It would be better to disperse, and since there was no other course than flight, to try who could run fastest. It would not then be the best that would fall: the cowards behind them would no longer eat up the relics of the high road." Lastly, the aide-de-camp was commissioned to explain to the Emperor all the horrors of his situation, the responsibility of which Ney absolutely declined.

But Napoleon saw enough around himself to judge of the rest. The fugitives were passing him; he was sensible that nothing could now be done but sacrifice the army successively, part by part, beginning at the extremities, in order to save the head. When, therefore, the aide-de-camp was beginning, he sharply interrupted him with these words, "Colonel, I do not ask you for these details." The Colonel was silent, aware that in this disaster, now irremediable, and in which every one had occasion for all his energies, the Emperor was afraid of complaints, which could have no other effect but to discourage both him who indulged in, and him who listened to them.

He remarked the attitude of Napoleon, the same which he retained throughout the whole of this retreat. It was grave, silent, and resigned; suffering much less in body than others, but much more in mind, and brooding over his misfortunes. At that moment General Charpentier sent him from Smolensk a convoy of provisions. Bessières wished to take possession of them, but the Emperor instantly had them forwarded to the Prince of the Moskwa, saying, "that those who were fighting must eat before the others." At the same time he sent word to Ney "to defend himself long enough to allow him some stay at Smolensk, where the army should eat, rest, and be re-organized."

But if this hope kept some to their duty, many others abandoned every thing, to hasten towards that promised term of their sufferings. As for Ney, he saw that a sacrifice was required, and that he was marked out as the victim: he resigned himself, ready to meet the whole of a danger great as his courage: thenceforward he neither attached his honour to baggage, nor to cannon, which the winter alone wrested from him. A first bend of the Borysthenes stopped and kept back part of his guns at the foot of its icy slopes; he sacrificed them without hesitation, passed that obstacle, faced about, and made the hostile river, which crossed his route, serve him as the means of defence.

The Russians, however, advanced under favour of a wood and our forsaken carriages, whence they kept up a fire of musketry on Ney's troops. Half of the latter, whose icy arms froze their stiffened fingers, got discouraged; they gave way, justifying themselves by their faintheartedness on the preceding day, fleeing because they had fled; which before they would have considered as impossible. But Ney rushed in amongst them, snatched one of their muskets, and led them back to the fire, which he was the first to renew; exposing his life like a private soldier, with a musket in his hand, the same as when he was neither husband nor father, neither possessed of wealth, nor power, nor consideration: in short, as if he had still every thing to gain, when in fact he had every thing to lose. At the same time that he again turned soldier, he ceased not to be a general; he took advantage of the ground, supported himself against a height, and covered himself with a palisaded house. His generals and his colonels, among whom he himself remarked Fezensac, strenuously seconded him; and the enemy, who expected to pursue, was obliged to retreat.

By this action, Ney gave the army a respite of twenty-four hours; it profited by it to proceed towards Smolensk. The next day, and all the succeeding days, he manifested the same heroism. Between Wiazma and Smolensk he fought ten whole days.

Chapter 70
Disaster at the Wop

On the 13th of November he was approaching that city, which he was not to enter till the ensuing day, and had faced about to keep off the enemy, when all at once the hills upon which he intended to support his left were seen covered with a multitude of fugitives. In their fright, these unfortunate wretches fell and rolled down to where he was, upon the frozen snow, which they stained with their blood. A band of Cossacks, which was soon perceived in the midst of them, sufficiently accounted for this disorder. The astonished marshal, having caused this flock of enemies to be dispersed, discovered behind it the army of Italy, returning quite stripped, without baggage, and without cannon.

Platof had kept it besieged, as it were, all the way from Dorogobouje. Near that town Prince Eugene had left the high-road, and, in order to proceed towards Witepsk, had taken that which, two months before, had brought him from Smolensk; but the Wop, which when he crossed before was a mere brook, and had scarcely been noticed, he now found swelled into a river. It ran over a bed of mud, and was bounded by two steep banks. It was found necessary to cut a way in these rough and frozen banks, and to give orders for the demolition, during the night, of the neighbouring houses, in order to build a bridge with the materials. But those who had taken shelter in them opposed their destruction. The Viceroy, more beloved than feared, was not obeyed. The pontonniers were disheartened, and when daylight appeared with the Cossacks, the bridge, after being twice broken down, was abandoned.

Five or six thousand soldiers still in order, twice the number of disbanded men, sick and wounded, upwards of a hundred pieces of cannon, ammunition wagons, and a multitude of other vehicles, lined the bank, and covered a league of ground. An attempt was made to ford through the ice carried along by the torrent. The first guns that tried to cross reached the opposite bank; but the water kept rising every moment, while at the same time the bed of the river at the ford was deepened by the wheels and the efforts of the horses. A carriage stuck fast; others did the same; and the stoppage became general.

Meanwhile the day was advancing; the men were exhausting themselves in vain efforts: hunger, cold, and the Cossacks became pressing, and the Viceroy at length found himself necessitated to order his artillery and all his baggage to be left behind. A distressing spectacle ensued. The owners had scarcely time to part from their effects; while they were selecting from them the articles which they most needed, and loading horses with them, a multitude of soldiers hastened up; they fell in preference upon the vehicles of luxury; they broke in pieces and rummaged every thing, revenging their destitution on this wealth, their privations on these superfluities, and snatching them from the Cossacks, who looked on at a distance.

It was provisions of which most of them were in quest. They threw aside embroidered clothes, pictures, ornaments of every kind, and gilt bronzes, for a few handfuls of flour. In the evening it was a singular sight to behold the riches of Paris and Moscow, the luxuries of two of the largest cities in the world, lying scattered and despised on the snow of the desert.

At the same time most of the artillerymen spiked their guns in despair, and scattered their powder about. Others laid a train with it as far as some ammunition wagons, which had been left at a considerable distance behind our baggage. They waited till the most eager of the Cossacks had come up to them, and when a great number, greedy of plunder, had collected about them, they threw a brand from a bivouac upon the train. The fire ran and in a moment reached its destination: the wagons were blown up, the shells exploded, and such of the Cossacks as were not killed on the spot dispersed in dismay.

A few hundred men, who were still called the 14th division, were opposed to these hordes, and sufficed to keep them at a respectful distance till the next day. All the rest, soldiers, administrators, women and children, sick and wounded, driven by the enemy's balls, crowded the bank of the torrent. But at the sight of its swollen current, of the sharp and massive sheets of ice flowing down it, and the necessity of aggravating their already intolerable sufferings from cold by plunging into its chilling waves, they all hesitated.

An Italian, Colonel Delfanti, was obliged to set the example and cross first. The soldiers then moved and the crowd followed. The weakest, the least resolute, or the most avaricious, staid behind. Such as could not make up their minds to part from their booty, and to forsake fortune which was forsaking them, were surprised in the midst of their hesitation. Next day the savage Cossacks were seen amid all this wealth, still covetous of the squalid and tattered garments of the unfortunate creatures who had become their prisoners: they stripped them, and then collecting them in troops, drove them along naked on the snow, by hard blows with the shaft of their lances.

The army of Italy, thus dismantled, thoroughly soaked in the waters of the Wop, without food, without shelter, passed the night on the snow near a village, where its officers expected to have found lodging for themselves. Their soldiers, however, beset its wooden houses. They rushed like madmen, and in swarms, on each habitation, profiting by the darkness, which prevented them from recognizing their officers or being known by them. They tore down every thing, doors, windows and even the wood-work of the roofs, feeling little compunction to compel others, be they who they might, to bivouac like themselves.

Their generals strove in vain to drive them off; they took their blows without murmur or opposition, but without desisting; and even the men of the royal and imperial guards: for, throughout the whole army, such were the scenes that occurred every night. The unfortunate fellows remained silently but actively engaged on the wooden walls, which they pulled in pieces on every side at once, and which, after vain efforts, their officers were obliged to relinquish to them, for fear they should fall upon their own heads. It was an extraordinary mixture of perseverance in their design, and respect for the anger of their generals.

Having kindled good fires they spent the night in drying themselves, amid the shouts, imprecations, and groans of those who were still crossing the torrent, or who, slipping from its banks, were precipitated into it and drowned.

It is a fact which reflects disgrace on the enemy, that during this disaster, and in sight of so rich a booty, a few hundred men, left at the distance of half a league from the Viceroy, on the other side of the Wop, were sufficient to curb, for twenty hours, not only the courage but also the cupidity of Platof's Cossacks.

It is possible, indeed, that the Hetman made sure of destroying the Viceroy on the following day. In fact, all his measures were so well planned, that at the moment when the army of Italy, after an unquiet and disorderly march, came in sight of Dukhowtchina, a town yet uninjured, and was joyfully hastening forward to shelter itself there, several thousand Cossacks sallied forth from it with cannon, and suddenly stopped its progress: at the same time Platof, with all his hordes, came up and attacked its rear-guard and both flanks.

Persons, who were eye-witnesses, assert that a complete tumult and disorder then ensued; that the disbanded men, the women, and the attendants, ran over one another, and broke quite through the ranks; that, in short, there was a moment when this unfortunate army was but a shapeless mass, a mere rabble rout whirling round and round. All seemed to be lost; but the coolness of the Prince and the efforts of the officers saved all. The best men disengaged themselves; the ranks were again formed. They advanced, firing a few volleys, and the enemy, who had every thing on his side excepting courage, the only advantage yet left us, opened and retired, confining himself to a mere demonstration.

The army took his place still warm in that town, beyond which he went to bivouac, and to prepare similar surprises to the very gates of Smolensk. For this disaster at the Wop had made the Viceroy give up the idea of separating from the Emperor; there these hordes grew bolder; they surrounded the 14th division. When Prince Eugene would have gone to its relief, the men and their officers, stiffened with a cold of twenty degrees, which the wind rendered most piercing, continued stretched on the warm ashes of their fires. To no purpose did he point out to them their comrades surrounded, the enemy approaching, the bullets and balls which were already reaching them; they refused to rise, protesting that they would rather perish than any longer have to endure such cruel hardships. The vedettes themselves had abandoned their posts. Prince Eugene nevertheless contrived to save his rear-guard.

It was in returning with it towards Smolensk that his stragglers had been driven back on Ney's troops, to whom they communicated their panic; all hurried together towards the Dnieper; here they crowded together at the entrance of the bridge, without thinking of defending themselves, when a charge made by the 4th regiment stopped the advance of the enemy.

Its colonel, young Fezenzac, contrived to infuse fresh life into these men who were half perished with cold. There, as in every thing that can be called action, was manifested the superiority of the sentiments of the soul over the sensations of the body; for every physical sensation tended to encourage despondency and flight; nature advised it with her hundred most urgent voices; and yet a few words of honour were sufficient to produce the most heroic devotedness. The soldiers of the

4th regiment rushed like furies upon the enemy, against the mountain of snow and ice of which he had taken possession, and in the teeth of the northern hurricane, for they had every thing against them. Ney himself was obliged to moderate their impetuosity.

A reproach from their colonel effected this change. These private soldiers devoted themselves, that they might not be wanting to their own characters, from that instinct which requires courage in a man, as well as from habit and the love of glory. A splendid word for so obscure a situation! For, what is the glory of a common soldier, who perishes unseen, who is neither praised, censured, nor regretted, but by his own division of a company! The circle of each, however, is sufficient for him: a small society embraces the same passions as a large one. The proportions of the bodies differ; but they are composed of the same elements; it is the same life that animates them, and the looks of a platoon stimulate a soldier, just as those of an army inflame a general.

CHAPTER 71

No Respite in Smolensk

At length the army again beheld Smolensk; it approached the term so often held forth to its sufferings. The soldiers pointed it out to each other. There was that land of promise where their famine was to find abundance, their fatigue rest; where bivouacs in a cold of nineteen degrees would be forgotten in houses warmed by good fires. There they should enjoy refreshing sleep; there they might repair their apparel; there they should be furnished with new shoes and garments adapted to the climate.

At this sight, the *corps d'elite*, some soldiers, and the veteran regiments, alone kept their ranks; the rest ran forward with all possible speed. Thousands of men, chiefly unarmed, covered the two steep banks of the Borysthenes: they crowded in masses round the lofty walls and gates of the city; but their disorderly multitude, their haggard faces, begrimed with dirt and smoke, their tattered uniforms and the grotesque habiliments which they had substituted for them, in short, their strange, hideous look, and their extreme ardour, excited alarm. It was conceived that if the irruption of this crowd, maddened with hunger, were not repelled, a general pillage would be the consequence, and the gates were closed against it.

It was also hoped that by this rigour these men would be forced to rally. A horrid struggle between order and disorder then commenced in the remnant of that unfortunate army. In vain did some entreat, weep, conjure, threaten, strive to burst the gates, and drop down dead at the feet of their comrades, who had orders to repel them; they found them inexorable: they were forced to await the arrival of the first troops, who were still officered and in order.

These were the old and young guard. It was not till afterwards that the disbanded men were allowed to enter; they and the other corps which arrived in succession, from the 8th to the 14th, believed that their entry had been delayed merely to give more rest and more provisions to this guard. Their sufferings rendered them unjust; they execrated it. "Were they then to be for ever sacrificed to this privileged class, fellows kept for mere parade, who were never foremost but at reviews, festivities, and distributions? Was the army always to put up with their leavings; and in order to obtain them, was it always to wait till they had glutted themselves?" It was impossible to tell them in reply, that to attempt to save all was the way to lose all; that it was necessary to keep at least one corps entire, and to give the preference to that which in the last extremity would be capable of making the most powerful effort.

At last, however, these poor creatures were admitted into that Smolensk for which they had so ardently wished; they had left the banks of the Borysthenes strewed with the dying bodies of the weakest of their number; impatience and several hours' waiting had finished them. They left others on the icy steep which they had to climb to reach the upper town. The rest ran to the magazines, and there more of them expired while they beset the doors; for they were again repulsed. "Who were they? to what corps did they belong? what had they to show for it? The persons who had to distribute the provisions were responsible for them; they had orders to deliver them only to authorized officers, bringing receipts, for which they could exchange the rations committed to their care." Those who applied had no officers; nor could they tell where their regiments were. Two thirds of the army were in this predicament.

These unfortunate men then dispersed through the streets, having no longer any other hope than pillage. But horses dissected to the very bones every where denoted a famine; the doors and windows of the houses had been all broken and torn away to feed the bivouac-fires: they found no shelter in them, no winter-quarters prepared, no wood. The sick and wounded were left in the streets, in the carts which had brought them. It was again, it was still the fatal high-road, passing through an empty name; it was a new bivouac among deceitful ruins; colder even than the forests which they had just quitted.

Then only did these disorganized troops seek their colours; they rejoined them for a moment in order to obtain food; but all the bread that could be baked had been distributed: there was no more biscuit, no butcher's meat, rye-flour, dry vegetables, and spirits were delivered out to them. It required the most strenuous efforts to prevent the detachments of the different corps from murdering one another at the doors of the magazines: and when, after long formalities, their wretched fare was delivered to them, the soldiers refused to carry it to their regiments; they fell upon their sacks, snatched out of them a few pounds of flour, and ran to hide themselves till they had devoured it. The same was the case with the spirits. Next day the houses were found full of the bodies of these unfortunate wretches.

In short, that fatal Smolensk, which the army had looked forward to as the term of its sufferings, marked only their commencement. Inexpressible hardships awaited us: we had yet to march forty days under that yoke of iron. Some, already overloaded with present miseries, sunk under the alarming prospect of those which awaited them. Others revolted against their destiny; finding they had nothing to rely on but themselves, they resolved to live at any rate.

Henceforward, according as they found themselves the stronger or the weaker, they plundered their dying companions by violence or stealth, of their subsistence, their garments, and even the gold, with which they had filled their knapsacks instead of provisions. These wretches, whom despair had made robbers, then threw away their arms to save their infamous booty, profiting by the general condition, an obscure name, a uniform no longer distinguishable, and night, in short, by all kinds of obscurities, favourable to cowardice and guilt. If works already published had not exaggerated these horrors, I should have passed in silence details so disgusting; for these atrocities were rare, and justice was dealt to the most criminal.

The Emperor arrived on the 9th of November, amid this scene of desolation. He shut himself up in one of the houses in the new square, and never quitted it till the 14th, to continue his retreat. He had calculated upon fifteen days' provisions and forage for an army of one hundred thousand men; there was not more than half the quantity of flour, rice, and spirits, and no meat at all. Cries of rage were set up against one of the persons appointed to provide these supplies. The commissary saved his life only by crawling for a long time on his knees at the feet of Napoleon. Probably the reasons which he assigned did more for him than his supplications.

"When he arrived," he said, "bands of stragglers, whom, when advancing, the army left behind it, had, as it were, involved Smolensk in terror and destruction. The men died there of hunger as upon the road. When some degree of order had been restored, the Jews alone had at first offered to furnish the necessary provisions. More generous motives subsequently engaged the aid of some Lithuanian noblemen. At length the foremost of the long convoys of provisions collected in Germany appeared. These were the carriages called *comtoises*, and were the only ones which had traversed the sands of Lithuania; they brought no more than two hundred quintals of flour and rice; several hundred German and Italian bullocks had also arrived with them.

"Meanwhile the accumulation of dead bodies in the houses, courts, and gardens, and their unwholesome effluvia, infected the air. The dead were killing the living. The civil officers as well as many of the military were attacked: some had become to all appearance idiots, weeping or fixing their hollow eyes steadfastly on the ground. There were others whose hair had become stiff, erect, and ropy, and who, amidst a torrent of blasphemies, a horrid convulsion, or a still more frightful laugh, had dropped down dead.

"At the same time it had been found necessary to kill without delay the greatest part of the cattle brought from Germany and Italy. These animals would neither walk any farther, nor eat. Their eyes, sunk in their sockets, were dull and motionless. They were killed without seeking to avoid the fatal blow. Other misfortunes followed: several convoys were intercepted, magazines taken, and a drove of eight hundred oxen had just been carried off from Krasnoë."

This man added, that "regard ought also to be had to the great quantity of detachments which had passed through Smolensk; to the stay which Marshal Victor, twenty-eight thousand men, and about fifteen thousand sick, had made there; to the multitude of posts and marauders whom the insurrection and the approach of the enemy had driven back into the city. All had subsisted upon the magazines; it had been necessary to deliver out nearly sixty thousand rations per day; and lastly, provisions and cattle had been sent forward towards Moscow as far as Mojaisk and towards Kalouga as far as Yelnia."

Many of these allegations were well founded. A chain of other magazines had been formed from Smolensk to Minsk and Wilna. These two towns were in a still greater degree than Smolensk, centres of provisioning, of which the fortresses of the Vistula formed the first line. The total quantity of provisions distributed over this space was incalculable; the efforts for transporting them thither gigantic, and the result little better than nothing. They were insufficient in that immensity.

Thus great expeditions are crushed by their own weight. Human limits had been surpassed; the genius of Napoleon, in attempting to soar above time, climate, and distances, had, as it were, lost itself in space: great as was its measure, it had been beyond it.

For the rest, he was passionate, from necessity. He had not deceived himself in regard to the inadequacy of his supplies. Alexander alone had deceived him. Accustomed to triumph over every thing by the terror of his name, and the astonishment produced by his audacity, he had ventured his army, himself, his fortune, his all, on a first movement of Alexander's. He was still the same man as in Egypt, at Marengo, Ulm, and Esslingen; it was Ferdinand Cortes; it was the Macedonian burning his ships, and above all solicitous, in spite of his troops, to penetrate still farther into unknown Asia; finally, it was Caesar risking his whole fortune in a fragile bark.

Chapter 72
Saint Cyr

The surprise of Vinkowo, however, that unexpected attack of Kutusoff in front of Moscow, was only the spark of a great conflagration. On the same day, at the same hour, the whole of Russia had resumed the offensive. The general plan of the Russians was at once developed. The inspection of the map became truly alarming.

On the 18th of October, at the very moment that the cannon of Kutusoff were destroying Napoleon's illusions of glory and of peace, Wittgenstein, at one hundred leagues in the rear of his left wing, had thrown himself upon Polotsk; Tchitchakof, behind his right, and two hundred leagues farther off, had taken advantage of his superiority over Schwartzenberg; and both of them, one descending from the north, and the other ascending from the south, were endeavouring to unite their forces at Borizof.

This was the most difficult passage in our retreat, and both these hostile armies were already close to it, at the time that Napoleon was at the distance of twelve days' journey, with the winter, famine, and the grand Russian army between them.

At Smolensk it was only suspected that Minsk was in danger; the officers who were present at the loss of Polotsk gave the following details respecting it:—

Ever since the battle of the 18th of August, which raised him to the dignity of marshal, Saint Cyr had remained on the Russian bank of the Düna, in possession of Polotsk, and of an entrenched camp in front of its walls. This camp showed how easy it would have been for the whole army to have taken up its winter quarters on the frontiers of Lithuania. Its barracks, constructed by our soldiers, were more spacious than the houses of the Russian peasantry, and equally warm: they were beautiful military villages, properly entrenched, and equally protected from the winter and from the enemy.

For two months the two armies carried on merely a war of partisans. With the French its object was to extend themselves through the country in search of provisions; on the part of the Russians, to strip them of what they found. A war of this sort was entirely in favour of the Russians, as our people, being ignorant of the country as well as of the language, even of the names of the places where they attempted to enter, were incessantly betrayed by the inhabitants, and even by their guides.

In consequence of these checks, and of hunger, and disease, the strength of Saint Cyr's army was diminished one half, while that of Wittgenstein had been more than doubled by the arrival of recruits. By the middle of October, the Russian army at that point amounted to fifty-two thousand men, while ours was only seventeen thousand. In this number must be included the 6th corps, or the Bavarians, reduced from twenty-two thousand to eighteen hundred men, and two thousand cavalry. The latter were then absent; Saint Cyr being without forage, and uneasy respecting the attempts of the enemy upon his flanks, had sent them to a considerable distance up the river, with orders to return by the left bank, in order to procure subsistence and to gain intelligence.

For this marshal was afraid of having his right turned by Wittgenstein and his left by Steingell, who was advancing at the head of two divisions of the army of Finland, which had recently arrived at Riga. Saint Cyr had sent a very pressing letter to Macdonald, requesting him to use his efforts to stop the march of these Russians, who would have to pass his army, and to send him a reinforcement of fifteen thousand men; or if he would not do that, to come himself with succours to that amount, and take the command. In the same letter he also submitted to Macdonald all his plans of attack and defence. But Macdonald did not feel himself authorized to operate so important a movement without orders. He distrusted Yorck, whom he perhaps suspected of an intention of allowing the Russians to get possession of his park of besieging artillery. His reply was that he must first of all think of defending that, and he remained stationary.

In this state of affairs, the Russians became daily more and more emboldened; and finally, on the 17th of October, the out-posts of Saint Cyr were driven into his camp, and Wittgenstein possessed himself of all the outlets of the woods which surround Polotsk. He threatened us with a battle, which he did not believe we would venture to accept.

The French marshal, without orders from his Emperor, had been too late in his determination to entrench himself. His works were only marked out as much as was necessary, (not to cover their defenders), but to point out the place where their efforts would be principally required. Their left, resting on the Düna, and defended by batteries placed on the left bank of the river, was the strongest. Their right was weak. The Polota, a stream which flows into the Düna, separated them.

Wittgenstein sent Yatchwil to threaten the least accessible side, and on the 18th he himself advanced against the other; at first with some rashness, for two French squadrons, the only ones which Saint Cyr had retained, overthrew his column in advance, took its artillery, and made himself prisoner, it is said, without being aware of it; so that they abandoned this general-in-chief, as an insignificant prize, when they were forced by numbers to retreat.

Rushing from their woods, the Russians then exhibited their whole force, and attacked Saint Cyr in the most furious manner. In one of the first discharges of their musketry, the marshal was wounded by a ball. He remained, however, in the midst of the troops, but being unable to support himself, was obliged to be carried about. Wittgenstein's determination to carry this point lasted as long as it was daylight. The redoubts, which were defended by Maison, were taken and retaken seven times. Seven times did Wittgenstein believe himself the conqueror; Saint Cyr finally wore him out. Legrand and Maison remained in possession of their entrenchments, which were bathed with the blood of the Russians.

But while on the right the victory appeared completely gained, on the left every thing seemed to be lost: the eagerness of the Swiss and the Croats was the cause of this reverse. Their rivalry had up to that period wanted an opportunity of showing itself. From a too great anxiety to show themselves worthy of belonging to the grand army, they acted rashly. Having been placed carelessly in front of their position, in order to draw on Yacthwil, they had, instead of abandoning the ground which had been prepared for his destruction, rushed forward to meet his masses, and were overwhelmed by numbers. The French artillery, being prevented from firing on this medley, became useless, and our allies were driven back into Polotsk.

It was then that the batteries on the left bank of the Düna discovered, and were able to commence firing on the enemy, but instead of arresting, they only quickened his march. The Russians under Yacthwil, in order to avoid that fire, threw themselves with great rapidity into the ravine of the Polota, by which they were about to penetrate into the town, when at last three cannon, which were hastily directed against the head of their column, and a last effort of the Swiss, succeeded in driving them back. At five o'clock the battle terminated; the

Russians retreated on all sides into their woods, and fourteen thousand men had beat fifty thousand.

The night which followed was perfectly tranquil, even to Saint Cyr. His cavalry were deceived, and brought him wrong intelligence; they assured him that no enemy had passed the Düna either above or below his position: this was incorrect, as Steingell and thirteen thousand Russians had crossed the river at Drissa, and gone up the left bank, with the object of taking the marshal in the rear, and shutting him up in Polotsk, between them, the Düna, and Wittgenstein.

The morning of the 19th exhibited the latter under arms, and making every disposition for an attack, the signal for which he appeared to be afraid of giving. Saint Cyr, however, was not to be deceived by these appearances; he was satisfied that it was not his feeble entrenchments which kept back an enterprising and numerous enemy, but that he was doubtless waiting the effect of some manoeuvre, the signal of an important co-operation, which could only be effected in his rear.

In fact, about ten o'clock in the morning, an aide-de-camp came in full gallop from the other side of the river, with the intelligence, that another hostile army, that of Steingell, was marching rapidly along the Lithuanian side of the river, and that it had defeated the French cavalry. He required immediate assistance, without which this fresh army would speedily get in the rear of the camp and surround it. The news of this engagement soon reached the army of Wittgenstein, where it excited the greatest joy, while it carried dismay into the French camp. Their position became dreadfully critical. Let any one figure to himself these brave fellows, hemmed in, against a wooden town, by a force treble their number, with a great river behind them, and no other means of retreat but a bridge, the passage from which was threatened by another army.

It was in vain that Saint Cyr then weakened his force by three regiments, which he dispatched to the other side to meet Steingell, and whose march he contrived to conceal from Wittgenstein's observation. Every moment the noise of the former's artillery was approaching nearer and nearer to Polotsk. The batteries, which from the left side protected the French camp, were now turned round, ready to fire upon this new enemy. At sight of this, loud shouts of joy burst out from the whole of Wittgenstein's line; but that officer still remained immoveable. To make him begin it was not merely necessary that he should *hear* Steingell; he seemed absolutely determined to *see* him make his appearance.

Meanwhile, all Saint Cyr's generals, in consternation, were surrounding him, and urging him to order a retreat, which would soon become impossible. Saint Cyr refused; convinced that the 50,000 Russians before him under arms, and on the tiptoe of expectation, only waited for his first retrograde movement to dart upon him, he remained immoveable, availing himself of their unaccountable inaction, and still flattering himself that night would cover Polotsk with its shades before Steingell could make his appearance.

He has since confessed, that never in his life was his mind in such a state of agitation. A thousand times, in the course of these three hours of suspense, he was seen looking at his watch and at the sun; as if he could hasten his setting.

At last, when Steingell was within half an hour's march of Polotsk, when he had only to make a few efforts to appear in the plain, to reach the bridge of the town, and shut out Saint Cyr from the only outlet by which he could escape from Wittgenstein, he halted. Soon after, a thick fog, which the French looked upon as an interposition from heaven, preceded the approach of night, and shut out the three armies from the sight of each other.

Saint Cyr only waited for that moment. His numerous artillery was already silently crossing the river, his divisions were about to follow it and conceal their retreat, when the soldiers of Legrand, either from habit, or regret at abandoning their camp entire to the enemy, set fire to it; the other two divisions, fancying that this was a signal agreed upon, followed their example, and in an instant the whole line was in a blaze.

This fire disclosed their movement; the whole of Wittgenstein's batteries immediately began their fire; his columns rushed forward, his shells set fire to the town; the French troops were obliged to contend every inch of ground with the flames, the fire throwing light on the engagement the same as broad daylight. The retreat, however, was effected in good order; on both sides the loss was great; but it was not until three o'clock in the morning of the 20th of October that the Russian eagle regained possession of Polotsk.

As good luck would have it, Steingell slept soundly at the noise of this battle, although he might have heard even the shouts of the Russian militia. He seconded the attack of Wittgenstein during that night as little as Wittgenstein had seconded his the day before. It was not until Wittgenstein had finished on the right side, that the bridge of Polotsk was broken down, and Saint Cyr, with all his force on the left bank, and then fully able to cope with Steingell, that the latter began to put himself in motion. But De Wrede, with 6,000 French, surprised him in his first movement, beat him back several leagues into the woods which he had quitted, and took or killed 2,000 of his men.

CHAPTER 73

Winter

Those three days were days of glory. Wittgenstein was repulsed, Steingell defeated, and ten thousand Russians, with six generals, killed or put *hors du combat*. But Saint Cyr was wounded, the offensive was lost, confidence, joy, and plenty reigned in the enemy's corps, despondency and scarcity in ours; it was necessary to fall back. The army required a commander: De Wrede aspired to be so, but the French generals refused even to enter into concert with that officer, from a knowledge of his character, and a belief that it was impossible to go on harmoniously with him. Amidst their jarring pretensions Saint Cyr, although wounded, was obliged to retain the command of these two corps.

Immediately after, he gave orders to retreat on Smoliantzy by all the roads leading to that place. He himself kept in the centre, regulating the march of the different columns by that of each other. This was a mode of retreat completely contrary to that which Napoleon had just followed.

Saint Cyr's object was to find more provisions, to march with greater freedom, and more concert; in short, to avoid that confusion which is so common in the march of numerous columns, when troops, artillery, and baggage are crowded together on one road. He completely succeeded. Ten thousand French, Swiss, and Croats, with fifty thousand Russians at their heels, retired slowly in four columns, without allowing themselves to be broken, and kept Wittgenstein and Steingell from advancing more than three marches in eight days.

By retreating in this manner towards the south, they covered the right flank of the road from Orcha to Borizof, by which the Emperor was returning from Moscow. One column only, that of the left, met with a check. It was that of De Wrede and his fifteen hundred Bavarians, augmented with a brigade of French cavalry, which he retained with him in spite of Saint Cyr's orders. He marched at his own pleasure; his wounded pride would no longer suffer him to yield obedience to others; but it cost him the whole of his baggage. Afterwards, under pretence of better serving the common cause by covering the line of operations from Wilna to Witepsk, which the Emperor had abandoned, he separated himself from the second corps, retreated by Klubokoe on Vileika, and made himself useless.

The discontent of De Wrede had existed ever since the 19th of August. He fancied that he had contributed so great a part to the victory of the 18th, that he thought it was made too little of in the report of the following day. This feeling had rankled in his mind, and was increased by repeated complaints, and by the instigation of a brother, who it was said was serving in the Austrian army. Added to this, it was believed, that at the last period of the retreat, the Saxon general, Thielmann, had drawn him into his plans for the liberation of Germany.

This defection was scarcely felt at the time. The Duke of Belluno, with twenty-five thousand men, hastened from Smolensk, and on the 31st of October effected a junction with Saint Cyr in front of Smoliantzy, at the very moment that Wittgenstein, ignorant of this junction, and relying on his superior strength, had crossed the Lukolmlia, imprudently engaged himself in defiles at his rear, and attacked our out-posts. It only required a simultaneous effort of the two French corps to have destroyed his army completely. The generals and soldiers of the second corps were burning with ardour. But at the moment that victory was in their hearts, and when, believing it before their eyes, they were waiting for the signal to engage, Victor gave orders to retreat.

Whether this prudence, which was then considered unseasonable, arose from his unacquaintance with a country, which he then saw for the first time, or from his distrust of soldiers whom he had not yet tried, we know not. It is possible that he did not feel himself justified in risking a battle, the loss of which would certainly have involved that of the grand army and its leader.

After falling back behind the Lukolmlia, and keeping on the defensive the whole of the day, he took advantage of the night to gain Sienno. The Russian general then became sensible of the peril of his position; it was so critical, that he only took advantage of our retrograde movement, and the discouragement which it occasioned, to effect his retreat.

The officers who gave us these details added, that ever since that time Wittgenstein seemed to think of nothing but retaking Witepsk, and keeping on the defensive. He probably thought it too rash to turn the Berezina at its sources, in order to join Tchitchakof; for a vague rumour had already reached us of the march of this army from the south upon Minsk and Borizof, and of the defection of Schwartzenberg.

It was at Mikalewska, on the 6th of November, that unfortunate day when he had just received information of Mallet's conspiracy, that Napoleon was informed of the junction of the second and the ninth corps, and of the unfortunate engagement at Czazniki. Irritated at the intelligence, he sent orders to the Duke of Belluno immediately to drive Wittgenstein behind the Düna, as the safety of the army depended upon it. He did not conceal from the marshal that he had arrived at Smolensk with an army harassed to death and his cavalry entirely dismounted.

Thus, therefore, the days of good fortune were passed, and from all quarters nothing but disastrous intelligence arrived. On one side Polotsk, the Düna, and Witepsk lost, and Wittgenstein already within four days march of Borizof; on the other, towards Elnia, Baraguay d'Hilliers defeated. That general had allowed the enemy to cut off the brigade of Augereau, and to take the magazines, and the Elnia road, by the possession of which Kutusoff was now enabled to anticipate us at Krasnoë, as he had done at Wiazma.

At the same time, at one hundred leagues in advance of us, Schwartzenberg informed the Emperor, that he was covering Warsaw; in other words, that he had uncovered Minsk and Borizof, the magazine, and the retreat of the grand army, and that probably, the Emperor of Austria would deliver up his son-in-law to Russia.

At the same moment, in our rear and our centre, Prince Eugene was conquered by the Wop; the draught-horses which had been waiting for us at Smolensk were devoured by the soldiers; those of Mortier carried off in a forage; the cattle at Krasnoë captured; the army exhibiting frightful symptoms of disease; and at Paris the period of conspiracies appeared to have returned; in short, every thing seemed to combine to overwhelm Napoleon.

The daily reports which he received of the state of each corps of the army were like so many bills of mortality; in these he saw his army, which had conquered Moscow, reduced from an hundred and eighty thousand, to thirty thousand men, still capable of fighting. To this mass of calamities, he could only oppose an inert resistance, an impassable firmness, and an unshaken attitude. His countenance remained the same; he changed none of his habits, nothing in the form of his orders; in reading them, you would have supposed that he had still several armies under his command. He did not even expedite his march. Irritated only at the prudence of Marshal Victor, he repeated his orders to him to attack Wittgenstein, and thereby remove the danger which menaced his retreat. As to Baraguay d'Hilliers, whom an officer had just accused, he had him brought before him, and sent him off to Berlin, where that general, overwhelmed by the fatigues of the retreat, and sinking under the weight of chagrin, died before he was able to make his defence.

The unshaken firmness which the Emperor preserved was the only attitude which became so great a spirit, and so irreparable a misfortune. But what appears surprising, is, that he allowed fortune to strip him of every thing, rather than sacrifice a part to save the rest. It was at first without his orders that the commanders of corps burnt the baggage and destroyed their artillery; he only allowed it to be done. If he afterwards gave similar instructions, they were absolutely extorted from him; he seemed as if he was tenacious, above every thing, that no action of his should confess his defeat; either from a feeling that he thus respected his misfortunes, and by his inflexibility set the example of inflexible courage to those around him, or from that proud feeling of men who have been long fortunate, which precipitates their downfall.

Smolensk, however, which was twice fatal to the army, was a place of rest for some. During the respite which this afforded to their sufferings, these were asking each other, "how it happened, that at Moscow every thing had been forgotten; why there was so much useless baggage; why so many soldiers had already died of hunger and cold under the weight of their knapsacks, which were loaded with gold, instead of food and raiment; and, above all, if three and thirty days rest had not allowed sufficient time to make snow shoes for the artillery, cavalry, and draught-horses, which would have made their march more sure and rapid?

"If that had been done, we should not have lost our best men at Wiazma, at the Wop, at the Dnieper, and along the whole road; in short, even now, Kutusoff, Wittgenstein, and perhaps Tchitchakof would not have had time to prepare more fatal days for us.

"But why, in the absence of orders from Napoleon, had not that precaution been taken by the commanders, all of them kings, princes, and marshals? Had not the winter in Russia been foreseen? Was it that Napoleon, accustomed to the active intelligence of his soldiers, had reckoned too much upon their foresight? Had the recollection of the campaign in Poland, during a winter as mild as that of our own climate, deceived him, as well as an unclouded sun, whose continuance, during the whole of the month of October, had astonished even the Russians themselves? What spirit of infatuation is it that has seized the whole army as well as its leader? What has every one been reckoning upon? as even supposing that at Moscow the hope of peace had dazzled us all, it was always necessary to return, and nothing had been prepared, even for a pacific journey homeward!"

The greater number could not account for this general infatuation, otherwise than by their own carelessness, and because in armies, as well as in despotic governments, it is the office of one to think for all; in this case that *one* was alone regarded as responsible, and misfortune, which authorizes distrust, led every one to condemn him. It had been already remarked, that in this important fault, this forgetfulness, so improbable in an active genius during so long and unoccupied a residence, there was something of that spirit of error, "the fatal forerunner of the fall of kings!"

Napoleon had been at Smolensk for five days. It was known that Ney had received orders to arrive there as late as possible, and Eugene to halt for two days at Doukhowtchina. "Then it was not the necessity of waiting for the army of Italy which detained him! To what then must we attribute this delay, when famine, disease and the winter, and three hostile armies were gradually surrounding us?

"While we had been penetrating to the heart of the Russian Colossus, had not his arms remained advanced and extended towards the Baltic and the Black Sea? was he likely to leave them motionless now, when, instead of striking him mortal blows, we had been struck ourselves? Was not the fatal moment arrived when this Colossus was about to surround us with his threatening arms? Could we imagine that we had either tied them up, or paralysed them, by opposing to them the Austrians in the south, and the Prussians in the north? Was it not rather a method of rendering the Poles and the French, who were mixed with these dangerous allies, entirely useless?

"But without going far in search of causes of uneasiness, was the Emperor ignorant of the joy of the Russians, when three months before he stopped to attack Smolensk, instead of marching to the right to Elnia, where he would have cut off the enemy's army from a retreat upon their capital? Now that the war has returned back to the same spots, will the Russians, whose movements are much more free than ours were then, imitate our error? Will they keep in our rear when they can so easily place themselves before us, on the line of our retreat?

"Is Napoleon unwilling to allow that Kutusoff's attack may be bolder and more skilful than his own had been? Are the circumstances still the same? Was not every thing favourable to the Russians during their retreat, and, on the contrary, has not every thing been unfavourable to us, in our retreat? Will not the cutting off Augereau and his brigade upon that road open his eyes? What business had we in the burnt and ravaged Smolensk, but to take a supply of provisions and proceed rapidly onwards?

"But the Emperor no doubt fancied that by dating his despatches five days from that city, he would give to his disorderly flight the appearance of a slow and glorious retreat! This was the reason of his ordering the destruction of the towers which surround Smolensk, from the wish, as he expressed it, of not being again stopped short by its walls! as if there was any idea of our returning to a place, which we did not even know whether we should ever get out of.

"Will any one believe that he wished to give time to the artillerymen to shoe their horses against the ice? as if he could expect any labour from workmen emaciated with hunger and long marches; from poor wretches who hardly found, the day long enough to procure provisions and dress them, whose forges were thrown away or damaged, and who besides wanted the indispensable materials for a labour so considerable.

"But perhaps he wished to allow himself time to drive on before him, out of danger and clear of the ranks, the troublesome crowd of soldiers, who had become useless, to rally the better sort, and to re-organize the army? as if it were possible to convey any orders whatever to men so scattered about, or to rally them, without lodgings, or distribution of provisions, to bivouacs; in short, to think of re-organization for corps of dying soldiers, all of whom had no longer any thing to adhere to, and whom the least touch would dissolve."

Such, around Napoleon, were the conversations of his officers; or rather their secret reflections: for their devotion to him remained entire for two whole years longer, in the midst of the greatest calamities, and of the general revolt of nations.

The Emperor, however, made an effort which was not altogether fruitless; namely, to rally, under one commander, all that remained of the cavalry: of thirty-seven thousand cavalry which were present at the passage of the Niemen, there were now only eighteen hundred left on horseback. He gave the command of them to Latour-Maubourg; whether from the esteem felt for him, or from fatigue, no one objected to it.

As to Latour-Maubourg, he received the honour or the charge without expressing either pleasure or regret. He was a character of peculiar stamp; always ready without forwardness, calm and active, remarkable for his extreme purity of morals, simple and unostentatious; in other respects, unaffected and sincere in his relations with others, and attaching the idea of glory only to actions, and not to words. He always marched with the same order and moderation in the midst of the most immoderate disorder; and yet, what does honour to the age, he attained to the highest distinctions as quickly and as rapidly as any who could be named.

This feeble re-organization, the distribution of a part of the provisions, the plunder of the rest, the repose which the Emperor and his guard were enabled to take, the destruction of part of the artillery and baggage, and finally, the expedition of a number of orders, were nearly all the benefits which were derived from that fatal delay. In other respects, all the misfortunes happened which had been foreseen. A few hundred men were only rallied for a moment. The explosion of the mines scarcely blew up the outside of some of the walls, and was only of use on the last day, in driving out of the town the stragglers whom we had been unable to set in motion.

The soldiers who had totally lost heart, the women, and several thousand sick and wounded, were here abandoned. This was when Augereau's disaster near Elnia made it but too evident that Kutusoff, now become the pursuer, did not confine himself to the high road; that he was marching from Wiazma by Elnia, direct upon Krasnoë; finally, when we ought to have foreseen that we should be obliged to cut our way through the Russian army, it was only on the 14th of November that the grand army (or rather thirty-six thousand troops) commenced its march.

The old and young guard had not then more than from nine to ten thousand infantry, and two thousand cavalry; Davoust and the first corps, from eight to nine thousand; Ney and the third corps, five to six thousand; Prince Eugene and the army of Italy, five thousand; Poniatowski, eight hundred; Junot and the Westphalians, seven hundred; Latour-Maubourg and the rest of the cavalry, fifteen hundred; there might also be about one thousand light horse, and five hundred dismounted cavalry, whom we had succeeded in collecting together.

This army had left Moscow one hundred thousand strong; in five-and-twenty days it had been reduced to thirty-six thousand men. The artillery had already lost three hundred and fifty of their cannon, and yet these feeble remains were always divided into eight armies, which were encumbered with sixty thousand unarmed stragglers, and a long train of cannon and baggage.

Whether it was this encumbrance of so many men and carriages, or a mistaken sense of security, which led the Emperor to order a day's interval between the departure of each marshal, is uncertain; most probably it was the latter. Be that as it may, he, Eugene, Davoust, and Ney only quitted Smolensk in succession; Ney was not to leave it till the 16th or 17th. He had orders to make the artillery saw the trunnions of the cannon left behind, and bury them; to destroy the ammunition, to drive all the stragglers before him, and to blow up the towers which surrounded the city.

Kutusoff, meanwhile, was waiting for us at some leagues distance from thence, and preparing to cut in pieces successively those remnants of corps thus extended and parcelled out.

Chapter 74

The Road to Europe Closed

It was on the 14th of November, about five in the morning, that the imperial column at last quitted Smolensk. Its march was still firm, but gloomy and silent as night, and mute and discoloured as the aspect of the country through which it was advancing.

This silence was only interrupted by the cracking of the whips applied to the poor horses, and by short and violent imprecations when they met with ravines; and when upon these icy declivities, men, horses, and artillery were rolling in obscurity, one over the other. The first day they advanced five leagues. The artillery of the guard took twenty-two hours to get over that ground.

Nevertheless, this first column arrived, without any great loss of men, at Korythinia, which Junot had passed with his Westphalian corps, now reduced to seven hundred men. A vanguard had pushed on as far as Krasnoë. The wounded and disbanded men were on the point of reaching Liady. Korythinia is five leagues from Smolensk; Krasnoë five leagues from Korythinia; Liady four leagues from Krasnoë. The Boristhenes flows at two leagues on the right of the high road from Korythinia to Krasnoë.

Near Korythinia another road, that from Elnia to Krasnoë, runs close to the great road. That very day Kutusoff advanced upon that road with ninety thousand men, which completely covered it; his march was parallel with that of Napoleon, whom he soon outstripped; on the crossroads he sent forward several vanguards to intercept our retreat.

One of these, said to be commanded by Ostermann, made its appearance at Korythinia at the same time with Napoleon, and was driven back.

A second, consisting of twenty thousand men, and commanded by Miloradowitch, took a position three leagues in advance of us, towards Merlino and Nikoulina, behind a ravine which skirts the left side of the great road; and there, lying in ambush on the flank of our retreat, it awaited our passage.

At the same time a third reached Krasnoë, which it surprised during the night, but was driven out by Sebastiani, who had just arrived there.

Finally, a fourth, pushed still more in advance, got between Krasnoë and Liady, and carried off, upon the high road, several generals and other officers who were marching singly.

Kutusoff, at the same time, with the bulk of his army, advanced, and took a position in the rear of these vanguards, and within reach of them all, and felicitated himself on the success of his manoeuvres, which would have inevitably failed, owing to his tardiness, had it not been for our want of foresight; for this was a contest of errors, in which ours being the greatest, we could have no thought of escaping total destruction. Having made these dispositions, the Russian commander must have believed that the French army was entirely in his power; but this belief saved us. Kutusoff was wanting to himself at the moment of action; his old age executed only half and badly the plans which it had combined wisely.

During the time that all these masses were arranging themselves round Napoleon, he remained perfectly tranquil in a miserable hut, the only one left standing in Korythinia, apparently quite unconscious of all these movements of troops, artillery, and cavalry, which were surrounding him in all directions; at least he sent no orders to the three corps which had halted at Smolensk to expedite their march, and he himself waited for daylight to proceed.

His column was advancing, without precaution, preceded by a crowd of stragglers, all eager to reach Krasnoë, when at two leagues from that place, a row of Cossacks, placed from the heights on our left all across the great road, appeared before them. Seized with astonishment, these stragglers halted; they had looked for nothing of the kind, and at first were inclined to believe that relentless fate had traced upon the snow between them and Europe, that long, black, and motionless line as the fatal term assigned to their hopes.

Some of them, stupefied and rendered insensible by the misery of their situation, with their eyes mentally fixed on home, and pursuing mechanically and obstinately that direction, would listen to no warning, and were about to surrender; the others collected together, and on both sides there was a pause, in order to consider each other's force. Several officers, who then came up, put these disbanded soldiers in some degree of order; seven or eight riflemen, whom they sent forward, were sufficient to break through that threatening curtain.

The French were smiling at the audacity of this idle demonstration, when all at once, from the heights on their left, an enemy's battery began firing. Its bullets crossed the road; at the same time thirty squadrons showed themselves on the same side, threatening the Westphalian corps which was advancing, the commander of which was so confused, that he made no disposition to meet their attack.

A wounded officer, unknown to these Germans, and who was there by mere chance, called out to them with an indignant voice, and immediately assumed their command. The men obeyed him as they would their own leader. In this case of pressing danger the differences of convention disappeared. The man really superior having shown himself, acted as a rallying point to the crowd, who grouped themselves around him, while the general-in-chief remained mute and confounded, receiving with docility the impulse the other had given, and acknowledging his superiority, which, after the danger was over, he disputed, but of which he did not, as too often happens, seek to revenge himself.

This wounded officer was Excelmans! In this action he was every thing, general, officer, soldier, even an artilleryman, for he actually laid hold of a cannon that had been abandoned, loaded and pointed it, and made it once more be of use against our enemies. As to the commander of the Westphalians, after this campaign, his premature and melancholy end makes us presume that excessive fatigue and the consequences of some severe wounds had already affected him mortally.

On seeing this leading column marching in such good order, the enemy confined itself to attacking it with their bullets, which it despised, and soon left behind it. When it came to the turn of the grenadiers of the old guard to pass through this fire, they closed their ranks around Napoleon like a moveable fortress, proud of having to protect him. Their band of music expressed this pride. When the danger was greatest, they played the well-known air, *"Où peut-on être mieux qu'au sein de sa famille!"* (Where can we be happier than in the bosom of our family!) But the Emperor, whom nothing escaped, stopped them with an exclamation, "Rather play, *Veillons au salut de l'Empire!"* (Let us watch for the safety of the empire!) words much better suited to his pre-occupation, and to the general situation.

At the same time, the enemy's fire becoming troublesome, he gave orders to silence it, and in two hours after he reached Krasnoë. The sight of Sebastiani, and of the first grenadiers who preceded him, had been sufficient to drive away the enemy's infantry. Napoleon entered in a state of great anxiety, from not knowing what corps had been attacking him, and his cavalry being too weak to enable them to get him information, out of reach of the high road. He left Mortier and the young guard a league behind him, in this way stretching out from too great a distance a hand too feeble to assist his army, and determined to wait for it.

The passage of his column had not been sanguinary, but it could not conquer the ground as it did the enemy; the road was hilly; at every eminence cannon were obliged to be left behind without being spiked, and baggage, which was plundered before it was abandoned. The Russians from their heights saw the whole interior of the army, its weaknesses, its deformities, its most shameful parts: in short, all that is generally concealed with the greatest care.

Notwithstanding, it appeared as if Miloradowitch, from his elevated position, was satisfied with merely insulting the passage of the Emperor, and of that old guard which had been so long the terror of Europe. He did not dare to gather up its fragments until it had passed on; but then he became bold, concentrated his forces, and descending from the heights, took up a strong position with twenty thousand men, quite across the high road; by this movement he separated Eugene, Davoust, and Ney from the Emperor, and closed the road to Europe against these three leaders.

Chapter 75

Deception

While he was making these preparations, Eugene was using all his efforts at Smolensk to collect his scattered troops; with great difficulty he tore them from the plunder of the magazines, and he did not succeed in rallying eight thousand men until late on the 15th of November. He was obliged to promise them supplies of provisions, and to show them the road to Lithuania, in order to induce them to renew their march. Night compelled him to halt at three leagues distance from Smolensk; the half of his soldiers had already left their ranks. Next morning he continued his march, with all that the cold of the night and of death had not fastened round their bivouacs.

The noise of the cannon which they had heard the day before had ceased; the royal column was advancing with difficulty, adding its own fragments to those which it encountered. At its head, the viceroy and the chief of his staff, buried in their own melancholy reflections, gave the reins to their horses. Insensibly they left their troop behind them, without being sensible of it; for the road was strewed with stragglers and men marching at their pleasure, the idea of keeping whom in order had been abandoned.

In this way they advanced to within two leagues of Krasnoë, but then a singular movement which was passing before them attracted their absent looks. Several of the disbanded soldiers had suddenly halted; those who followed as they came up, formed a group with them; others who had advanced farther fell back upon the first; they crowded together; a mass was soon formed. The viceroy surprised, then looked about him; he perceived that he had got the start of the main body of his army by an hour's march: that he had about him only fifteen hundred men of all ranks, of all nations, without organization, without leaders, without order, without arms ready or fit for an engagement, and that he was summoned to surrender.

This summons was answered by a general cry of indignation! But the Russian flag of truce, who presented himself singly, insisted: "Napoleon and his guard," said he to them, "have been beaten; you are surrounded by twenty thousand Russians: you have no means of safety but in accepting honourable conditions, and these Miloradowitch proposes to you."

At these words, Guyon, one of the generals whose soldiers were either all dead or dispersed, rushed from the crowd, and with a loud voice called out, "Return immediately to whence you came, and tell him who sent you, that if he has twenty thousand men, we have eighty thousand!" The Russian, confounded, immediately retired.

All this happened in the twinkling of an eye; in a moment after the hills on the left of the road were spouting out lightning and whirlwinds of smoke; showers of shells and grape-shot swept the high road, and threatening advancing columns showed their bayonets.

The viceroy hesitated for a moment; it grieved him to leave that unfortunate troop, but at last, leaving his chief of the staff with them, he returned back to his divisions, in order to bring them forward to the combat, to make them get beyond the obstacle before it became insurmountable, or to perish; for with the pride derived from a crown and so many victories, it was not to be expected that he could ever admit the thought of surrender.

Meanwhile, Guilleminot summoned about him the officers who, in this crowd, had mingled with the soldiers. Several generals, colonels, and a great number of officers immediately started forth and surrounded him; they concerted together, and accepting him for their leader, they distributed into platoons all the men who had hitherto formed but one mass, and whom in that state they had found it impossible to excite.

This organization was made under a sharp fire. Several superior officers went and placed themselves proudly in the ranks, and became once more common soldiers. From a different species of pride, some marines of the guard insisted on being commanded by one of their own officers, while each of the other platoons was commanded by a general. Hitherto the Emperor himself had been their colonel; now they were on the point of perishing they maintained their privilege, which nothing could make them forget, and which was respected accordingly.

These brave men, in this order, proceeded on their march to Krasnoë: and they had already got beyond the batteries of Miloradowitch, when the latter, rushing with his columns upon their flanks, hemmed them in so closely, as to compel them to turn about, and seek a position in which they could defend themselves. To the eternal glory of these warriors it should be told, that these fifteen hundred French and Italians, one to ten, with nothing in their favour but a determined countenance and very few fire-arms in a state fit for use, kept their enemies at a respectful distance upwards of an hour.

But as there was still no appearance of the viceroy and the rest of his divisions, a longer resistance was evidently impossible. They were again and again summoned to lay down their arms. During these short pauses they heard the cannon rolling at a distance in their front and in their rear. Thus, therefore, "the whole army was attacked at once, and from Smolensk to Krasnoë it was but one engagement! If we wanted assistance, there could be none expected by waiting for it; we must go and look for it; but on which side? At Krasnoë it was impossible; we were too far from it; there was every reason to believe that our troops were beaten there. It would besides become matter of necessity for us to retreat; and we were too near the Russians under Miloradowitch, who were calling to us from their ranks to lay down our arms, to venture to turn our backs upon them. It would therefore be a much better plan, as our faces were now turned towards Smolensk, and as Prince Eugene was on that side, to form ourselves into one compact mass, keep all its movements well connected, and rushing headlong, to re-enter Russia by cutting our way through these Russians, and rejoin the viceroy; then to return together, to overthrow Miloradowitch, and at last reach Krasnoë."

To this proposition of their leader, there was a loud and unanimous cry of assent. Instantly the column formed into a mass, and rushed into the midst of ten thousand hostile muskets and cannon. The Russians, at first seized with astonishment, opened their ranks and allowed this handful of warriors, almost disarmed, to advance into the middle of them. Then, when they comprehended their purpose, either from pity or admiration, the enemy's battalions, which lined both sides of the road, called out to our men to halt; they entreated and conjured them to surrender; but the only answer they received was a more determined march, a stern silence, and the point of the bayonet. The whole of the enemy's fire was then poured upon them at once, at the distance of a few yards, and the half of this heroic column was stretched wounded or lifeless on the ground.

The remainder proceeded without a single man quitting the body of his troop, which no Russian was bold enough to venture near. Few of these unfortunate men again saw the viceroy and their advancing divisions. Then only they separated; they ran and threw themselves into these feeble ranks, which were opened to receive and protect them.

For more than an hour the Russian cannon had been thinning them. While one half of their forces had pursued Guilleminot and compelled him to retreat, Miloradowitch, with the other half, had stopped Prince Eugene. His right rested on a wood which was protected by heights entirely covered with cannon; his left touched the great road, but more in the rear. This disposition dictated that of Eugene. The royal column, by degrees, as it came up, deployed on the right of the road, its right more forward than its left. The viceroy thus placed obliquely between him and the enemy the great road, the possession of which was the subject of contest. Each of the two armies occupied it by its left.

The Russians, placed in a position so offensive, kept entirely on the defensive; their bullets alone attacked Eugene. A cannonade was kept up on both sides, on theirs most destructive, on ours almost totally ineffective. Tired out with this firing, Eugene formed his resolution; he called the 14th French division, drew it up on the left of the great road, pointed out to it the woody height on which the enemy rested, and which formed his principal strength; *that* was the decisive point, the centre of the action, and to make the rest fall, *that* must be carried. He did not expect it would; but that effort would draw the attention and the strength of the enemy on that side, the right of the great road would remain free, and he would endeavour to take proper advantage of it.

Three hundred soldiers, formed into three troops, were all that could be found willing to mount to this assault. These devoted men advanced resolutely against hostile thousands in a formidable position. A battery of the Italian guard advanced to protect them, but the Russian batteries immediately demolished it, and their cavalry took possession of it.

In spite of the grape-shot which was mowing them rapidly down, the three hundred French kept moving on, and they had actually reached the enemy's position, when, suddenly from two sides of the wood two masses of cavalry rushed forth, bore down upon, overwhelmed and massacred them. Not one escaped; and with them perished all remains of discipline and courage in their division.

It was then that General Guilleminot again made his appearance. That in a position so critical, Prince Eugene, with four thousand enfeebled troops, the remnant of forty-two thousand and upwards, should not have despaired, that he should still have exhibited a bold countenance, may be conceived, from the known character of that commander; but that the sight of our disaster and the ardour of victory should not have urged the Russians to more than indecisive efforts, and that they should have allowed the night to put an end to the battle, is with us, to this day, matter of complete astonishment. Victory was so new to them, that even when they held it in their hands, they knew not how to profit by it; they delayed its completion until the next day.

The viceroy saw that the greater part of the Russians, attracted by his demonstrations, had collected on the left of the road, and he only waited until night, the sure ally of the weakest, had chained all their movements. Then it was, that leaving his fires burning on that side, to deceive the enemy, he quitted it, and marching entirely across the fields, he turned, and silently got beyond the left of Miloradowitch's position, while that general, too certain of his victory, was dreaming of the glory of receiving, next morning, the sword of the son of Napoleon.

In the midst of this perilous march, there was an awful moment. At the most critical instant, when these soldiers, the survivors of so many battles, were stealing along the side of the Russian army, holding their breath and the noise of their steps; when their all depended on a look or a cry of alarm; the moon all at once coming out of a thick cloud appeared to light their movements. At the same moment a Russian sentinel called out to them to halt, and demanded who they were? They gave themselves up for lost! but Klisky, a Pole, ran up to this Russian, and speaking to him in his own language, said to him with the greatest composure, in a low tone of voice, "Be silent, fellow! don't you see that we belong to the corps of Ouwarof, and that we are going on a secret expedition?" The Russian, outwitted, held his tongue.

But the Cossacks were galloping up every moment to the flanks of the column, as if to reconnoitre it, and then returned to the body of their troop. Their squadrons advanced several times as if they were about to charge; but they did no more, either from doubt as to what they saw, for they were still deceived, or from prudence, as it frequently halted, and presented a determined front to them.

At last, after two hours most anxious march, they again reached the high road, and the viceroy was actually in Krasnoë on the 17th of November, when Miloradowitch, descending from his heights in order to seize him, found the field of battle occupied only by a few stragglers, whom no effort could induce the night before to quit their fires.

Chapter 76
Stachowa

The Emperor on his side had waited for the viceroy during the whole of the preceding day. The noise of his engagement had irritated him. An effort to break through the enemy, in order to join him, had been ineffectually attempted; and when night came on without his making his appearance, the uneasiness of his adopted father was at the height. "Eugene and the army of Italy, and this long day of baffled expectation, had they then terminated together?" Only one hope remained to Napoleon; and that was, that the viceroy, driven back towards Smolensk, had there joined Davoust and Ney, and that the following day they would, with united forces, attempt a decisive effort.

In his anxiety, the Emperor assembled the marshals who remained with him. These were Berthier, Bessières, Mortier, and Lefebvre; these were saved; they had cleared the obstacle; they had only to continue their retreat through Lithuania, which was open to them; but would they abandon their companions in the midst of the Russian army? No, certainly; and they determined once more to enter Russia, either to deliver, or to perish with them.

When this resolution was taken, Napoleon coolly prepared the dispositions to carry it into effect. He was not at all shaken by the great movements which the enemy were evidently making around him. He saw that Kutusoff was advancing in order to surround and take him prisoner in Krasnoë. The very night before, he had learned that Ojarowski, with a vanguard of Russian infantry, had got beyond him, and taken a position at Maliewo, in a village in the rear of his left. Irritated, instead of depressed, by misfortune, he called his aide-de-camp, Rapp, and exclaimed, "that he must set out immediately, and proceed during the night and the darkness to attack that body of infantry with the bayonet; that this was the first time of its exhibiting so much audacity, and that he was determined to make it repent it, in such a way, that it should never again dare to approach so near to his head-quarters." Then instantly recalling him, he continued, "But, no! let Roguet and his division go alone! As for thee, remain where thou art, I don't wish thee to be killed here, I shall have occasion for thee at Dantzic."

Rapp, while he was carrying this order to Roguet, could not help feeling astonished, that his leader, surrounded by eighty thousand enemies, whom he was going to attack next day with nine thousand, should have so little doubt about his safety, as to be thinking of what he should have to do at Dantzic, a city from which he was separated by the winter, two other hostile armies, famine, and a hundred and eighty leagues.

The nocturnal attack on Chirkowa and Maliewo was successful. Roguet formed his idea of the enemy's position by the direction of their fires; they occupied two villages, connected by a causeway, which was defended by a ravine. He disposed his troop into three columns of attack; those on the right and left were to advance silently, as close as possible to the enemy; then at the signal to charge, which he himself would give them from the centre, they were to rush into the midst of the enemy without firing a shot, and making use only of their bayonets.

Immediately the two wings of the young guard commenced the action. While the Russians, taken by surprise, and not knowing on which side to defend themselves, were wavering from their right to their left, Roguet, with his column, rushed suddenly upon their centre and into the midst of their camp, into which he entered pell-mell with them. Thus divided and thrown into confusion, they had barely time to throw the best part of their great and small arms into a neighbouring lake, and to set fire to their tents, the flames arising from which, instead of saving them, only gave light to their destruction.

This check stopped the movement of the Russian army for four-and-twenty hours, put it in the Emperor's power to remain at Krasnoë, and enabled Eugene to rejoin him during the following night. He was received by Napoleon with the greatest joy; but the Emperor's uneasiness respecting Davoust and Ney became shortly after proportionally greater.

Around us the camp of the Russians presented a spectacle similar to what it had done at Vinkowo, Malo-Yaroslawetz, and Wiazma. Every evening, close to the general's tent, the relics of the Russian saints, surrounded by an immense number of wax tapers, were exposed to the adoration of the soldiers. While each of these was, according to custom, giving proofs of his devotion by an endless repetition of crossings and genuflections, the priests were addressing them with fanatical exhortations, which would appear barbarous and absurd to every civilized nation.

In spite, however, of the great power of such means, of the number of the Russians, and of our weakness, Kutusoff, who was only at two leagues' distance from Miloradowitch, while the latter was beating Prince Eugene, remained immoveable. During the following night, Beningsen, urged on by the ardent Wilson, in vain attempted to animate the old Russian. Elevating the faults of his age into virtues, he applied the names of wisdom, humanity, and prudence, to his dilatoriness and strange circumspection; he was resolved to finish as he had begun. For if we may be allowed to compare small things with great, his renown had been established on a principle directly contrary to that of Napoleon, fortune having made the one, and the other having created his fortune.

He made a boast of "advancing only by short marches; of allowing his soldiers to rest every third day; he would blush, and halt immediately, if they wanted bread or spirits for a single moment." Then, with great self-gratulation, he pretended that "all the way from Wiazma, he had been escorting the French army as his prisoners; chastising them whenever they wished to halt, or strike out of the high road; that it was useless to run any risks with captives; that the Cossacks, a vanguard, and an army of artillery, were quite sufficient to finish them, and make them pass successively under the yoke; and that in this plan, he was admirably seconded by Napoleon himself. Why should he seek to *purchase* of Fortune what she was so generously giving him? Was not the term of Napoleon's destiny already irrevocably marked? It was in the marshes of the Berezina that this meteor would be extinguished, this colossus overthrown, in the midst of Wittgenstein, Tchitchakof, and himself, and in the presence of the assembled Russian armies. As for himself, he would have the glory of delivering him up to them, enfeebled, disarmed, and dying; and to him that glory was sufficient."

To this discourse the English officer, still more active and eager, replied only by entreating the field-marshal "to leave his head-quarters only for a few moments, and advance upon the heights; there he would see that the last moment of Napoleon was already come. Would he allow him even to get beyond the frontiers of Russia proper, which loudly called for the sacrifice of this great victim? Nothing remained but to strike; let him only give the order, one charge would be sufficient, and in two hours the face of Europe would be entirely changed!"

Then, gradually getting warmer at the coolness with which Kutusoff listened to him, Wilson, for the third time, threatened him with the general indignation. "Already, in his army, at the sight of the straggling, mutilated, and dying column, which was about to escape from him, he might hear the Cossacks exclaiming, what a shame it was to allow these skeletons to escape in this manner out of their tomb!" But Kutusoff, whom old age, that misfortune without hope, rendered indifferent, became angry at the attempts made to rouse him, and by a short and violent answer, shut the indignant Englishman's mouth.

It is asserted that the report of a spy had represented to him Krasnoë as filled with an enormous mass of the imperial guard, and that the old marshal was afraid of compromising his reputation by attacking it. But the sight of our distress emboldened Beningsen; this chief of the staff prevailed upon Strogonof, Gallitzin, and Miloradowitch, with a force of more than fifty thousand Russians, and one hundred pieces of cannon, to venture to attack at daylight, in spite of Kutusoff, fourteen thousand famished, enfeebled, and half-frozen French and Italians.

This was a danger, the imminence of which Napoleon fully comprehended. He might escape from it; daylight had not yet appeared. He was at liberty to avoid this fatal engagement; to gain Orcha and Borizof by rapid marches along with Eugene and his guard; there he could rally his forces with thirty thousand French under Victor and Oudinôt, with Dombrowski, with Regnier, with Schwartzenberg, and with all his depots, and be might again, the following year, make his appearance as formidable as ever.

On the 17th, before daylight, he issued his orders, armed himself, and going out on foot, at the head of his old guard, began his march. But it was not towards Poland, his ally, that it was directed, nor towards France, where he would be still received as the head of a rising dynasty, and the Emperor of the West. His words on taking up his sword on this occasion, were "I have sufficiently acted the emperor; it is time that I should become the general." He turned back into the midst of eighty thousand enemies, plunged into the thickest of them, in order to draw all their efforts against himself, to make a diversion in favour of Davoust and Ney, and to tear them from a country, the gates of which had been closed upon them.

Daylight at last appeared, exhibiting on one side the Russian battalions and batteries, which on three sides, in front, on our right, and in our rear, bounded the horizon, and on the other, Napoleon with his six thousand guards advancing with a firm step, and proceeding to take his place in the middle of that terrible circle. At the same time Mortier, a few yards in front of his Emperor, displayed in the face of the whole Russian army, the five thousand men which still remained to him.

Their object was to defend the right flank of the great road from Krasnoë to the great ravine in the direction of Stachowa. A battalion of *chasseurs* of the old guard, formed in a square like a fortress, was planted close to the high road, and acted as a support to the left wing of our young soldiers. On their right, in the snowy plains which surrounded Krasnoë, the remains of the cavalry of the guard, a few cannon, and the four hundred cavalry of Latour-Maubourg (as, since they left Smolensk, the cold had killed or dispersed fourteen hundred of them) occupied the place of the battalions and batteries which the French army no longer possessed.

The artillery of the Duke of Treviso was reinforced by a battery commanded by Drouot; one of those men who are endowed with the whole strength of virtue, who think that duty embraces every thing, and are capable of making the noblest sacrifices simply and without the least effort.

Claparede remained at Krasnoë, where, with a few soldiers, he protected the wounded, the baggage, and the retreat. Prince Eugene continued his retreat towards Liady. His engagement of the preceding day and his night march had entirely broken up his corps; his divisions only retained sufficient unity to drag themselves along, and to perish, but not to fight.

Meantime Roguet had been recalled to the field of battle from Maliewo. The enemy kept pushing columns across that village, and was extending more and more beyond our right in order to surround us. The battle then commenced. But what kind of battle? The Emperor had here no sudden illumination to trust to, no flashes of momentary inspiration, none of these great strokes so unforeseen from their boldness, which ravish fortune, extort a victory, and by which he had so often disconcerted, stunned, and crushed his enemies. All *their* movements were now free, all *ours* enchained, and this genius of attack was reduced to defend himself.

Here therefore it became perfectly evident that renown is not a vain shadow, that she is real strength, and doubly powerful by the inflexible pride which she imparts to her favourites, and the timid precautions which she suggests to them who venture to attack her. The Russians had only to march forward without manoeuvring, even without firing: their mass was sufficient, they might have crushed Napoleon and his feeble troop: but they did not dare to come to close quarters with him. They were awed by the presence of the conqueror of Egypt and of Europe. The Pyramids, Marengo, Austerlitz, Friedland, an army of victories, seemed to rise between him and the whole of the Russians. We might almost fancy that, in the eyes of that submissive and superstitious people, a renown so extraordinary appeared like some thing supernatural; that they regarded it as beyond their reach; that they believed they could only attack and demolish it from a distance; and in short, that against that old guard, that living fortress, that column of granite, as it had been styled by its leader, human efforts were impotent, and that cannon alone could demolish it.

These made wide and deep breaches in the ranks of Roguet and the young guard, but they killed without vanquishing. These young soldiers, one half of whom had never before been in an engagement, received the shock of death during three hours without retreating one step, without making a single movement to escape it, and without being able to return it, their artillery having been broken, and the Russians keeping beyond the reach of their musketry.

But every instant strengthened the enemy and weakened Napoleon. The noise of the cannon as well as Claparede apprised him, that in the rear of Krasnoë and his army, Beningsen was proceeding to take possession of the road to Liady, and cut off his retreat. The east, the west, and the south were sparkling with the enemy's fires; one side only remained open, that of the north and the Dnieper, towards an eminence, at the foot of which were the high road and the Emperor. We fancied we saw the enemy covering this eminence with his cannon: in that situation they were just over Napoleon's head, and might have crushed him at a few yards' distance. He was apprised of his danger, cast his eyes for an instant upon it, and uttered merely these words, "Very well, let a battalion of my *chasseurs* take possession of it!" Immediately afterwards, without paying farther attention to it, his whole looks and attention reverted to the perilous situation of Mortier.

Then at last Davoust made his appearance, forcing his way through a swarm of Cossacks, whom he drove away by a precipitate march. At the sight of Krasnoë, this marshal's troops disbanded themselves, and ran across the fields to get beyond the right of the enemy's line, in the rear of which they had come up. Davoust and his generals could only rally them at Krasnoë.

The first corps was thus preserved, but we learned at the same time, that our rear-guard could no longer defend itself at Krasnoë; that Ney was probably still at Smolensk, and that we must give up waiting for him any longer. Napoleon, however, still hesitated; he could not determine on making this great sacrifice.

But at last, as all were likely to perish, his resolution was fixed. He called Mortier, and squeezing his hand sorrowfully, told him, "that he had not a moment to lose; that the enemy were overwhelming him in all directions; that Kutusoff might already reach Liady, perhaps Orcha, and the last winding of the Borísthenes before him; that he would therefore proceed thither rapidly with his old guard, in order to occupy that passage. Davoust would relieve Mortier; but both of them must endeavour to hold out in Krasnoë until night, after which they must come and rejoin him." Then with his heart full of Ney's misfortune, and of despair at abandoning him, he withdrew slowly from the field of battle, traversed Krasnoë, where he again halted, and then cleared his way to Liady.

Mortier was anxious to obey, but at that moment the Dutch troops of the guard had lost, along with a third part of their number, an important post which they were defending, which the enemy immediately after covered with his artillery. Roguet, feeling the destructive effects of its fire, fancied he was able to extinguish it. A regiment which he sent against the Russian battery was repulsed; a second (the 1st of the *voltigeurs*) got into the middle of the Russians, and stood firm against two charges of their cavalry. It continued to advance, torn to pieces by their grape-shot, when a third charge overwhelmed it. Fifty soldiers and eleven officers were all of it that Roguet was able to preserve.

That general had lost the half of his men. It was now two o'clock, and his unshaken fortitude still kept the Russians in astonishment, when at last, emboldened by the Emperor's departure, they began to press upon him so closely, that the young guard was nearly hemmed in, and very soon in a situation in which it could neither hold out, nor retreat.

Fortunately, some platoons which Davoust had rallied, and the appearance of another troop of his stragglers, attracted the enemy's attention. Mortier availed himself of it. He gave orders to the three thousand men he had still remaining to retreat slowly in the face of their fifty thousand enemies. "Do you hear, soldiers?" cried General Laborde, "the marshal orders ordinary time! Ordinary time, soldiers!" And this brave and unfortunate troop, dragging with them some of their wounded, under a shower of balls and grape-shot, retired as slowly from this field of carnage, as they would have done from a field of manoeuvre.

Chapter 77

Minsk Falls

As soon as Mortier had succeeded in placing Krasnoë between him and Beningsen, he was in safety. The communication between that town and Liady was only interrupted by the fire of the enemy's batteries, which flanked the left side of the great road. Colbert and Latour-Maubourg kept them in check upon their heights. In the course of this march a most singular accident occurred. A howitzer shell entered the body of a horse, burst there, and blew him to pieces without wounding his rider, who fell upon his legs, and went on.

The Emperor, meanwhile, halted at Liady, four leagues from the field of battle. When night came on, he learned that Mortier, who he thought was in his rear, had got before him. Melancholy and uneasy, he sent for him, and with an agitated voice, said to him, "that he had certainly fought gloriously, and suffered greatly. But why had he placed his Emperor between him and the enemy? why had he exposed himself to be cut off?"

The marshal had got the start of Napoleon without being aware of it. He exclaimed, "that he had at first left Davoust in Krasnoë, again endeavouring to rally his troops, and that he himself had halted, not far from that: but that the first corps, having been driven back upon him, had obliged him to retrograde. That besides, Kutusoff did not follow up his victory with vigour, and appeared to hang upon our flank with all his army with no other view than to feast his eyes with our distress, and gather up our fragments."

Next day the march was continued with hesitation. The impatient stragglers took the lead, and all of them got the start of Napoleon; he was on foot, with a stick in his hand, walking with difficulty and repugnance, and halting every quarter of an hour, as if unwilling to tear himself from that old Russia, whose frontier he was then passing, and in which he had left his unfortunate companions in arms.

In the evening he reached Dombrowna, a wooden town, with a population like Liady; a novel sight for an army, which had for three months seen nothing but ruins. We had at last emerged from old Russia and her deserts of snow and ashes, and entered into a friendly and inhabited country, whose language we understood. The weather just then became milder, a thaw had begun, and we received some provisions.

Thus the winter, the enemy, solitude, and with some famine and bivouacs, all ceased at once; but it was too late. The Emperor saw that his army was destroyed; every moment the name of Ney escaped from his lips, with exclamations of grief. That night particularly he was heard groaning and exclaiming, "That the misery of his poor soldiers cut him to the heart, and yet that he could not succour them without fixing himself in some place: but where was it possible for him to rest, without ammunition, provisions, or artillery? He was no longer strong enough to halt; he must reach Minsk as quickly as possible."

He had hardly spoken the words, when a Polish officer arrived with the news, that Minsk itself, his magazine, his retreat, his only hope, had just fallen into the hands of the Russians, Tchitchakof having entered it on the 16th. Napoleon, at first, was mute and overpowered at this last blow; but immediately afterwards, elevating himself in proportion to his danger, he coolly replied, "Very well! we have now nothing to do, but to clear ourselves a passage with our bayonets."

But in order to reach this new enemy, who had escaped from Schwartzenberg, or whom Schwartzenberg had perhaps allowed to pass, (for we knew nothing of the circumstances,) and to escape from Kutusoff and Wittgenstein, we must cross the Berezina at Borizof. With that view Napoleon (on the 19th of November, from Dombrowna) sent orders to Dombrowski to give up all idea of fighting Hoertel, and proceed with all haste to occupy that passage. He wrote to the Duke of Reggio, to march rapidly to the same point, and to hasten to recover Minsk; the Duke of Belluno would cover his march. After giving these orders, his agitation was appeased, and his mind, worn out with suffering, sunk into depression. It was still far from daylight, when a singular noise drew him out of his lethargy. Some say that shots were at first heard, which had been fired by our own people, in order to draw out of the houses such as had taken shelter in them, that they might take their places; others assert, that from a disorderly practice, too common in our bivouacs, of vociferating to each other, the name of *Hausanne*, a grenadier, being suddenly called out loudly, in the midst of a profound silence, was mistaken for the alert cry of *aux armes*, which announced a surprise by the enemy.

Whatever might be the cause, every one immediately saw, or fancied he saw, the Cossacks, and a great noise of war and of alarm surrounded Napoleon. Without disturbing himself, he said to Rapp, "Go and see, it is no doubt some rascally Cossacks, determined to disturb our rest!" But it became very soon a complete tumult of men running to fight or to flee, and who, meeting in the dark, mistook each other for enemies.

Napoleon for a moment imagined that a serious attack had been made. As an embanked stream of water ran through the town, he inquired if the remaining artillery had been placed behind that ravine, and being informed that the precaution had been neglected, he himself immediately ran to the bridge, and caused his cannon to be hurried over to the other side.

He then returned to his old guard, and stopping in front of each battalion: "Grenadiers!" said he to them, "we are retreating without being conquered by the enemy, let us not be vanquished by ourselves! Set an example to the army! Several of you have already deserted their eagles, and even thrown away their arms. I have no wish to have recourse to military laws to put a stop to this disorder, but appeal entirely to yourselves! Do justice among yourselves. To your own honour I commit the support of your discipline!"

The other troops he harangued in a similar style. These few words were quite sufficient to the old grenadiers, who probably had no occasion for them. The others received them with acclamation, but an hour afterwards, when the march was resumed, they were quite forgotten. As to his rear-guard, throwing the greatest part of the blame of this hot alarm upon it, he sent an angry message to Davoust on the subject.

At Orcha we found rather an abundant supply of provisions, a bridge equipage of sixty boats, with all its appurtenances, which were entirely burnt, and thirty-six pieces of cannon, with their horses, which were distributed between Davoust, Eugene, and Latour-Maubourg.

Here for the first time we again met with the officers and gendarmes, who had been sent for the purpose of stopping on the two bridges of the Dnieper the crowd of stragglers, and making them rejoin their columns. But those eagles, which formerly promised every thing, were now looked upon as of fatal omen, and deserted accordingly.

Disorder was already regularly organized, and had enlisted in its ranks men who showed their ability in its service. When an immense crowd had been collected, these wretches called out "the Cossacks!" with a view to quicken the march of those who preceded them and to increase the tumult. They then took advantage of it, to carry off the provisions and cloaks of those whom they had thrown off their guard.

The gendarmes, who again saw this army for the first time since its disaster, were astonished at the sight of such misery, terrified at the great confusion, and became discouraged. This friendly frontier was entered tumultuously; it would have been given up to pillage, had it not been for the guard, and a few hundred men who remained, with Prince Eugene.

Napoleon entered Orcha with six thousand guards, the remains of thirty-five thousand! Eugene, with eighteen hundred soldiers, the remains of forty-two thousand! Davoust, with four thousand, the remains of seventy thousand!

This marshal had lost every thing, was actually without linen, and emaciated with hunger. He seized upon a loaf which was offered him by one of his comrades, and, voraciously devoured it. A handkerchief was given him to wipe his face, which was covered with rime. He exclaimed, "that none but men of iron constitutions could support such trials, that it was physically impossible to resist them; that there were limits to human strength, the utmost of which had been exceeded."

He it was who at first supported the retreat as far as Wiazma. He was still, according to his custom, halting at all the defiles, and remaining there the very last, sending every one to his ranks, and constantly struggling with the disorder. He urged his soldiers to insult and strip of their booty such of their comrades as threw away their arms; the only means of retaining the first and punishing the last. Nevertheless, his methodical and severe genius, so much out of its element in that scene of universal confusion, has been accused of being too much intimidated at it.

The Emperor made fruitless attempts to check this discouragement. When alone, he was heard compassionating the sufferings of his soldiers; but in their presence, even upon that point, he wished to appear inflexible. He issued a proclamation, "ordering every one to return to their ranks; if they did not, he would strip the officers of their grades, and put the soldiers to death."

A threat like this produced neither good nor bad impression upon men who had become insensible, or were reduced to despair, fleeing not from danger, but from suffering, and less apprehensive of the *death* with which they were threatened than of the *life* that was offered to them.

But Napoleon's confidence increased with his peril; in his eyes, and in the midst of these deserts of mud and ice, this handful of men was still the grand army! and himself the conqueror of Europe! and there was no infatuation in this firmness; we were certain of it, when, in this very town, we saw him burning with his own hands every thing belonging to him, which might serve as trophies to the enemy, in the event of his fall. There also were unfortunately consumed all the papers which he had collected in order to write the history of his life, for such was his intention when he set out for this fatal war. He had then determined to halt as a threatening conqueror on the borders of the Düna and the Borysthenes, to which he now returned as a disarmed fugitive. At that time he regarded the *ennui* of six winter months, which he would have been detained on these rivers, as his greatest enemy, and to overcome it, this second Caesar intended there to have dictated his Commentaries.

Chapter 78
The Berezina

Every thing, however, was now changed; two hostile armies were cutting off his retreat. The question to decide was, through which of them he must attempt to force his way: and as he knew nothing of the Lithuanian forests into which he was about to penetrate, he summoned such of his officers as had passed through them in order to reach him.

The Emperor began by telling them, that "Too much familiarity with great victories was frequently the precursor of great disasters, but that recrimination was now out of the question." He then mentioned the capture of Minsk, and after admitting the skilfulness of Kutusoff's persevering manoeuvres on his right flank, declared "that he meant to abandon his line of operations on the Minsk, unite with the Dukes of Belluno and Reggio, cut his way through Wittgenstein's army, and regain Wilna by turning the sources of the Berezina."

Jomini combated this plan. That Swiss general described the position of Wittgenstein as a series of long defiles, in which his resistance might be either obstinate or flexible, but in either way sufficiently long to consummate our destruction. He added, that in this season, and in such a state of disorder, a change of route would complete the destruction of the army; that it would lose itself in the cross-roads of these barren and marshy forests; he maintained that the high road alone could keep it in any degree of union. Borizof, and its bridge over the Berezina, were still open; and it would be sufficient to reach it.

He then stated that he knew of a road to the right of that town, constructed on wooden bridges, and passing across the marshes of Lithuania. This was the only road, by his account, by which the army could reach Wilna by Zembin and Malodeczno, leaving Minsk on the left, its road a day's journey longer, its fifty broken bridges rendering a passage impracticable, and Tchitchakof in possession of it. In this manner we should pass between the two hostile armies, avoiding them both.

The Emperor was staggered; but as his pride revolted at the appearance of avoiding an engagement, and he was anxious to signalize his departure from Russia by a victory, he sent for General Dodde, of the engineers. As soon as he saw him he called out to him, "Whether shall we retreat by Zembin, or go and beat Wittgenstein at Smoliantzy?" and knowing that Dodde had just come from the latter position, he asked him if it was approachable?

His reply was, that Wittgenstein occupied a height which entirely commanded that miry country; that it would be necessary for us to tack about, within his sight and within his reach, by following the windings and turnings of the road, in order to ascend to the Russian camp; that thus our column of attack would be long exposed to their fire, first its left and then its right flank; that this position was therefore unapproachable in front, and that to turn it, it would be necessary to retrograde towards Witepsk, and take too long a circuit.

Disappointed in this last hope of glory, Napoleon then decided for Borizof. He ordered General Eblé to proceed with eight companies of sappers and pontonniers to secure the passage of the Berezina, and General Jomini to act as his guide. But he said at the same time, "that it was cruel to retreat without fighting, to have the appearance of flight. If he had any magazine, any point of support, which would allow him to halt, he would still prove to Europe that he always knew how to fight and to conquer."

All these illusions were now destroyed. At Smolensk, where he arrived first, and from which he was the first to depart, he had rather been informed of, than witnessed his disaster. At Krasnoë, where our miseries had successively been unrolled before his eyes, the peril had distracted his attention; but at Orcha he could contemplate, at once and leisurely, the full extent of his misfortunes.

At Smolensk, thirty-six thousand combatants, one hundred and fifty cannon, the army-chest, and the hope of life and breathing at liberty on the other side of the Berezina, still remained; here, there were scarcely ten thousand soldiers, almost without clothing or shoes, entangled amidst a crowd of dying men, with a few cannon, and a pillaged army-chest.

In five days, every evil had been aggravated; destruction and disorganization had made frightful progress; Minsk had been taken. He had no longer to look for rest and abundance on the other side of the Berezina, but fresh contests with a new enemy. Finally, the defection of Austria from his alliance seemed to be declared, and perhaps it was a signal given to all Europe.

Napoleon was even uncertain whether he should reach Borizof in time to meet the new peril, which Schwartzenberg's hesitation seemed to have prepared for him. We have seen that a third Russian army, that of Wittgenstein, menaced, on his right, the interval which separated him from that town; that he had sent the Duke of Belluno against him, and had ordered that marshal to retrieve the opportunity he had lost on the 1st of November, and to resume the offensive.

In obedience to these orders, on the 14th of November, the very day Napoleon quitted Smolensk, the Dukes of Belluno and of Reggio had attacked and driven back the out-posts of Wittgenstein towards Smoliantzy, preparing, by this engagement, for a battle which they agreed should take place on the following day.

The French were thirty thousand against forty thousand; there, as well as at Wiazma, the soldiers were sufficiently numerous, if they had not had too many leaders.

The two Marshals disagreed. Victor wished to manoeuvre on the enemy's left wing, to overthrow Wittgenstein with the two French corps, and march by Botscheikowo on Kamen, and from Kamen by Pouichna on Berezina. Oudinôt warmly disapproved of this plan, saying that it would separate them from the grand army, which required their assistance.

Thus, one of the leaders wishing to manoeuvre, and the other to attack in front, they did neither the one nor the other. Oudinôt retired during the night to Czereïa, and Victor, discovering this retreat at daybreak, was compelled to follow him.

He halted within a day's march of the Lukolmlia, near Sienno, where Wittgenstein did not much disturb him; but the Duke of Reggio having at last received the order dated from Dombrowna, which directed him to recover Minsk, Victor was about to be left alone before the Russian general. It was possible that the latter would then become aware of his superiority: and the Emperor, who at Orcha, on the 20th of November, saw his rear-guard, lost, his left flank menaced by Kutusoff, and his advance column stopped at the Berezina by the army of Volhynia, learned that Wittgenstein and forty thousand more enemies, far from being beaten and repulsed, were ready to fall upon his right, and that he had no time to lose.

But Napoleon was long before he could determine to quit the Boristhenes. It appeared to him that this was like a second abandonment of the unfortunate Ney, and casting off for ever his intrepid companion in arms. There, as he had done at Liady and Dombrowna, he was calling every hour of the day and night, and sending to inquire if no tidings had been heard of that marshal; but not a trace of his existence had transpired through the Russian army; four days this mortal silence had lasted, and yet the Emperor still continued to hope.

At last, being compelled, on the 20th of November, to quit Orcha, he still left there Eugene, Mortier, and Davoust, and halted at two leagues from thence, inquiring for Ney, and still expecting him. The same feeling of grief pervaded the whole army, of which Orcha then contained the remains. As soon as the most pressing wants allowed a moment's rest, the thoughts and looks of every one were directed towards the Russian bank. They listened for any warlike noise which might announce the arrival of Ney, or rather his last sighs; but nothing was to be seen but enemies who were already menacing the bridges of the Borysthenes! One of the three leaders then wished to destroy them, but the others refused their consent, on the ground, that this would be again separating them from their companion in arms, and a confession that they despaired of saving him, an idea to which, from their dread of so great a misfortune, they could not reconcile themselves.

But with the fourth day all hope at last vanished. Night only brought with it a wearisome repose. They blamed themselves for Ney's misfortune, forgetting that it was utterly impossible to wait longer for the third corps in the plains of Krasnoë, where they must have fought for another twenty-eight hours, when they had merely strength and ammunition left for one.

Already, as is the case in all cruel losses, they began to treasure up recollections. Davoust was the last who had quitted the unfortunate marshal, and Mortier and the viceroy were inquiring of him what were his last words! At the first reports of the cannonade opened on the 15th on Napoleon, Ney was anxious immediately to evacuate Smolensk in the suite of the viceroy; Davoust refused, pleading the orders of the Emperor, and the obligation to destroy the ramparts of the town. The two chiefs became warm, and Davoust persisting to remain until the following day, Ney, who had been appointed to bring up the rear, was compelled to wait for him.

It is true, that on the 16th, Davoust sent to warn him of his danger; but Ney, either from a change of opinion, or from an angry feeling against Davoust, then returned him for answer, "That all the Cossacks in the universe should not prevent him from executing his instructions."

After exhausting these recollections and all their conjectures, they again relapsed into a more gloomy silence, when suddenly they heard the steps of several horses, and then the joyful cry, "Marshal Ney is safe! here are some Polish cavalry come to announce his approach!"

One of his officers then galloped in, and informed them that the marshal was advancing on the right bank of the Boristhenes, and had sent him to ask for assistance.

Night had just set in; Davoust, Eugene, and Mortier had only its short duration to revive and animate the soldiers, who had hitherto always bivouacked. For the first time since they left Moscow, these poor fellows had received a sufficient quantum of provisions; they were about to prepare them and to take their rest, warm and under cover: how was it possible to make them resume their arms, and turn them from their asylums during that night of rest, whose inexpressible sweets they had just begun to taste? Who could persuade them to interrupt it, to retrace their steps, and return once more into the darkness and frozen deserts of Russia?

Eugene and Mortier disputed the honour of this sacrifice, and the first only carried it in right of his superior rank. Shelter and the distribution of provisions had effected that which threats had failed to do. The stragglers were rallied, the viceroy again found himself at the head of four thousand men; all were ready to march at the news of Ney's danger; but it was their last effort.

They proceeded in the darkness, by unknown roads, and had marched two leagues at random, halting every few minutes to listen. Their anxiety was already increased. Had they lost their way? were they too late? had their unfortunate comrades fallen? was it the victorious Russian army they were about to meet? In this uncertainty, Prince Eugene directed some cannon shot to be fired. Immediately after they fancied they heard signals of distress on that sea of snow; they proceeded from the third corps, which, having lost all its artillery, answered the cannon of the fourth by some volleys of platoon firing.

The two corps were thus directed towards their meeting. Ney and Eugene were the first to recognize each other; they ran up, Eugene more precipitately, and threw themselves into each other's arms. Eugene wept, Ney let some angry words escape him. The first was delighted, melted, and elevated by the warlike heroism which his chivalrous heroism had just saved! The latter, still heated from the combat, irritated at the dangers which the honour of the army had run in his person, and blaming Davoust, whom he wrongfully accused of having deserted him.

Some hours afterwards, when the latter wished to excuse himself, he could draw nothing from Ney but a severe look, and these words, "Monsieur le Maréchal, I have no reproaches to make to you; God is our witness and your judge!"

When the two corps had fairly recognized each other, they no longer kept their ranks. Soldiers, officers, generals, all ran towards each other. Those of Eugene shook hands with those of Ney; they touched them with a joyful mixture of astonishment and curiosity, and pressed them to their bosoms with the tenderest compassion. The refreshments and brandy which they had just received they lavished upon them; they overwhelmed them with questions. They then all proceeded together in company, towards Orcha, all impatient, Eugene's soldiers to hear, and Ney's to tell their story.

Chapter 79

The Bravest of the Brave

They stated, that on the 17th of November they had quitted Smolensk with twelve cannon, six thousand infantry, and three hundred cavalry, leaving there five thousand sick at the mercy of the enemy; and that had it not been for the noise of Platof's cannon, and the explosion of the mines, their marshal would never have been able to bring away from the ruins of that city seven thousand unarmed stragglers who had taken shelter in them. They dwelt upon the attentions which their leader had shown to the wounded, and to the women and their children, proving upon this occasion that the bravest was again the most humane.

At the gates of the city an unnatural action struck them with a degree of horror which was still undiminished. A mother had abandoned her little son, only five years old; in spite of his cries and tears she had driven him away from her sledge which was too heavily laden. She herself cried out with a distracted air, "that *he* had never seen France! that *he* would not regret it! as for *her*, *she* knew France! *she* was resolved to see France once more!" Twice did Ney himself replace the unfortunate child in the arms of his mother, twice did she cast him off on the frozen snow.

This solitary crime, amidst a thousand instances of the most devoted and sublime tenderness, they did not leave unpunished. The unnatural mother was herself abandoned to the same snow from which her infant was snatched, and entrusted to another mother; this little orphan was exhibited in their ranks; he was afterwards seen at the Berezina, then at Wilna, even at Kowno, and finally escaped from all the horrors of the retreat.

The officers of Ney continued, in answer to the pressing questions of those of Eugene; they depicted themselves advancing towards Krasnoë, with their marshal at their head, completely across our immense wrecks, dragging after them one afflicted multitude, and preceded by another, whose steps were quickened by hunger.

They described how they found the bottom of each ravine filled with helmets, hussar-caps, trunks broken open, scattered garments, carriages and cannon, some overturned, others with the horses still harnessed, and the poor animals worn out, expiring and half devoured.

How, near Korythinia, at the end of their first day's march, a violent cannonading and the whistling of several bullets over their heads, had led them to imagine that a battle had just commenced. This discharge appeared to proceed from before and quite close to them even upon the road, and yet they could not get sight of a single enemy. Ricard and his division advanced with a view to discover them, but they only found, in a turn of the road, two French batteries abandoned, with their ammunition, and in the neighbouring field a horde of wretched Cossacks, who immediately fled, terrified at their audacity in setting fire to them, and at the noise they had made.

Ney's officers here interrupted their narrative to inquire in their turn what had passed? What was the cause of the general discouragement? why had the cannon been abandoned to the enemy untouched? Had they not had time to spike them, or at least to spoil their ammunition?

In continuation, they said they had hitherto only discovered the traces of a disastrous march. But next morning there was a complete change, and they confessed their unlucky presentiments when they arrived at that field of snow reddened with blood, sprinkled with broken cannon and mutilated corpses. The dead bodies still marked the ranks and places of battle; they pointed them out to each other. *There* had been the 14th division; *there* were still to be seen, on the broken plates of their caps, the numbers of its regiments. *There* had been the Italian guard; there were its dead, whose uniforms were still distinguishable! But where were its living remnants? Vainly did they interrogate that field of blood, these lifeless forms, the motionless and frozen silence of the desert and the grave! they could neither penetrate into the fate of their companions, nor into that which awaited themselves.

Ney hurried them rapidly over all these ruins, and they had advanced without impediment to a part of the road, where it descends into a deep ravine, from which it rises into a broad and level height. It was that of Katova, and the same field of battle, where, three months before, in their triumphant march, they had beat Newerowskoi, and saluted Napoleon with the cannon which they had taken the day before from his enemies. They said they recollected the situation, notwithstanding the different appearance given to it by the snow.

Mortier's officers here exclaimed, "that it was in that very position that the Emperor and they had waited for them on the 17th, fighting all the time." Very well, replied those of Ney, Kutusoff, or rather Miloradowitch, occupied Napoleon's place, for the old Russian general had not yet quitted Dobroé.

Their disbanded men were already retrograding, pointing to the snowy plains completely black with the enemy's troops, when a Russian, detaching himself from their army, descended the hill; he presented himself alone to their marshal, and either from an affectation of extreme politeness, respect for the misfortune of their leader, or dread of the effects of his despair, covered with honeyed words the summons to surrender.

It was Kutusoff who had sent him. "That field-marshal would not have presumed to make so cruel a proposal to so great a general, to a warrior so renowned, if there remained a single chance of safety for him. But there were eighty thousand Russians before and around him, and if he had any doubt of it, Kutusoff offered to let him send a person to go through his ranks, and count his forces."

The Russian had not finished his speech, when suddenly forty discharges of grape shot, proceeding from the right of his army, and cutting our ranks to pieces, struck him with amazement, and interrupted what he had to say. At the same moment a French officer darted forward, seized, and was about to kill him as a traitor, when Ney, checking this fury, called to him angrily, "A marshal never surrenders; there is no parleying under an enemy's fire; you are my prisoner." The unfortunate officer was disarmed, and placed in a situation of exposure to the fire of his own army. He was not released until we reached Kowno, after twenty-six days captivity, sharing all our miseries, at liberty to escape, but restrained by his parole.

At the same time the enemy's fire became still hotter, and, as they said, all the hills, which but an instant before looked cold and silent, became like so many volcanoes in eruption, but that Ney became still more elevated at it: then with a burst of enthusiasm that seemed to return every time they had occasion to mention his name in their narrative, they added, that in the midst of all this fire that ardent man seemed to breathe an element exclusively his own.

Kutusoff had not deceived him. On the one side, there were eighty thousand men in complete ranks, full, deep, well-fed, and in double lines, a numerous cavalry, an immense artillery occupying a formidable position, in short, every thing, and fortune to boot, which alone is equal to all the rest. On the other side, five thousand soldiers, a straggling and dismembered column, a wavering and languishing march, arms defective and dirty, the greatest part mute and tottering in enfeebled hands.

And yet the French leader had no thought of yielding, nor even of dying, but of penetrating and cutting his way through the enemy; and that without the least idea that he was attempting a sublime effort. Alone, and looking no where for support, while all were supported by him, he followed the impulse of a strong natural temperament, and the pride of a conqueror, whom the habit of gaining improbable victories had impressed with the belief that every thing was possible.

But what most astonished them, was, that they had been all so docile; for all had shown themselves worthy of him, and they added, that it was there they clearly saw that it is not merely great obstinacy, great designs, or great temerity which constitute the great man, but principally the power of influencing and supporting others.

Ricard and his fifteen hundred soldiers were in front. Ney impelled them against the enemy, and prepared the rest of his army to follow them. That division descended with the road into the ravine, but in ascending, was driven back into it, overwhelmed by the first Russian line.

The marshal, without being intimidated, or allowing others to be so, collected the survivors, placed them in reserve, and proceeded forward in their place; Ledru, Razont, and Marchand seconded him. He ordered four hundred Illyrians to take the enemy on their left flank, and with three thousand men, he himself mounted in front to the assault. He made no harangue; he marched at their head, setting the example, which, in a hero, is the most eloquent of all oratorical movements, and the most imperious of all orders. All followed him. They attacked, penetrated, and overturned the first Russian line, and without halting were precipitating themselves upon the second; but before they could reach it, a volley of artillery and grape shot poured down upon them. In an instant Ney saw all his generals wounded, the greatest part of his soldiers killed; their ranks were empty, their shapeless column whirled round, tottered, fell back, and drew him along with it.

Ney found that he had attempted an impossibility, and he waited until the flight of his men had once more placed the ravine between them and the enemy, that ravine which was now his sole resource; there, equally hopeless and fearless, he halted and rallied them. He drew up two thousand men against eighty thousand; he returned the fire of two hundred cannon with six pieces, and made fortune blush that she should ever betray such courage.

She it was, doubtless, who then struck Kutusoff with the palsy of inertness. To their infinite surprise, they saw this Russian Fabius running into extremes like all imitators, persisting in what he called his humanity and prudence, remaining upon his heights with his pompous virtues, without allowing himself, or daring to conquer, as if he was astonished at his own superiority. Seeing that Napoleon had been conquered by his rashness, he pushed his horror of that fault to the very extreme of the opposite vice.

It required, however, but a transport of indignation in any one of the Russian corps to have completely extinguished them; but all were afraid to make a decisive movement; they remained clinging to their soil with the immobility of slaves, as if they had no boldness but in their watchword, or energy but in their obedience. This discipline, which formed their glory in *their* retreat, was their disgrace in *ours*.

They were for a long time uncertain, not knowing which enemy they were fighting with; for they had imagined that Ney had retreated from Smolensk by the right bank of the Dnieper; they were mistaken, as is frequently the case, from supposing that their enemy had done what he ought to have done.

At the same time, the Illyrians had returned completely in disorder; they had had a most singular adventure. In their advance to the left flank of the enemy's position, these four hundred men had met with five thousand Russians returning from a partial engagement, with a French eagle, and several of our soldiers prisoners.

These two hostile troops, the one returning to its position, the other going to attack it, advanced in the same direction, side by side, measuring each other with their eyes, but neither of them venturing to commence the engagement. They marched so close to each other, that from the middle of the Russian ranks the French prisoners stretched out their arms towards their friends, conjuring them to come and deliver them. The latter called out to them to come to them, and they would receive and defend them; but no one moved on either side. Just then Ney was overthrown, and they retreated along with him.

Kutusoff, however, relying more on his artillery than his soldiers, sought only to conquer at a distance. His fire so completely commanded all the ground occupied by the French, that the same bullet which prostrated a man in the first rank proceeded to deal destruction in the last of the train of carriages, among the women who had fled from Moscow.

Under this murderous hail, Ney's soldiers remained astonished, motionless, looking at their chief, waiting his decision to be satisfied that they were lost, hoping they knew not why, or rather, according to the remark of one of their officers, because in the midst of this extreme peril they saw his spirit calm and tranquil, like any thing in its place. His countenance became silent and devout; he was watching the enemy's army, which, becoming more suspicious since the successful artifice of Prince Eugene, extended itself to a great distance on his flanks, in order to shut him out from all means of preservation.

The approach of night began to render objects indistinct; winter, which in that sole point was favourable to our retreat, brought it on quickly. Ney had been waiting for it, but the advantage he took of the respite was to order his men to return to Smolensk. They all said that at these words they remained frozen with astonishment. Even his aide-de-camp could not believe his ears; he remained silent like one who did not understand what he heard, and looked at his general with amazement. But the marshal repeated the same order; in his brief and imperious tone, they recognized a resolution taken, a resource discovered, that self-confidence which inspires others with the same quality, and a spirit which commands his position, however strong that may be. They immediately obeyed, and without hesitation turned their backs on their own army, on Napoleon, and on France! They returned once more into that fatal Russia. Their retrograde march lasted an hour; they passed again over the field of battle marked by the remains of the army of Italy; there they halted, and their marshal, who had remained alone in the rear-guard, then rejoined them.

Their eyes followed his every movement. What was he going to do; and whatever might be his plan, whither would he direct his steps, without a guide, in an unknown country? But he, with his warlike instinct, halted on the edge of a ravine of such depth, as to make it probable that a rivulet ran through it. He made them clear away the snow and break the ice; then consulting his map, he exclaimed "That this was one of the streams which flowed into the Dnieper! this must be our guide, and we must follow it; that it would lead us to that river, which we must cross, and that on the other side we should be safe!" He immediately proceeded in that direction.

However at a little distance from the high road which he had abandoned, he again halted in a village, the name of which they knew not, but believed that it was either Fomina, or Danikowa. There he rallied his troops, and made them light their fires, as if he intended to take up his quarters in it for the night. Some Cossacks who followed him took it for granted, and no doubt sent immediately to apprise Kutusoff of the spot where, next day, a French marshal would surrender his arms to him; for shortly after the noise of their cannon was heard.

Ney listened: "Is this Davoust at last," he exclaimed, "who has recollected me?" and he listened a second time. But there were regular intervals between the firing; it was a salvo. Being then fully satisfied that the Russian army was triumphing by anticipation over his captivity, he swore he would give the lie to their joy, and immediately resumed his march.

At the same time his Poles ransacked the country. A lame peasant was the only inhabitant they had discovered; this was an unlooked-for piece of good fortune. He informed them that they were within the distance of a league from the Dnieper, but that it was not fordable there, and could not yet be frozen over. "It will be so," was the marshal's remark; but when it was observed to him that the thaw had just commenced, he added "that it did not signify, we must pass, as there was no other resource."

At last, about eight o'clock, after passing through a village, the ravine terminated, and the lame Russian, who walked first, halted and pointed to the river. They imagined that this must have been between Syrokorenia and Gusinoé. Ney, and those immediately behind him, ran up to it. They found the river sufficiently frozen to bear their weight, the course of the flakes which it bore along to that point, being counteracted by a sudden turn in its banks, was there suspended; the winter had completely frozen it over only in that single spot; both above and below it, its surface was still moveable.

This observation was sufficient to make their first sensation of joy give way to uneasiness. This hostile river might only offer them a treacherous appearance. One officer devoted himself for the rest; he crossed to the other side with great difficulty. He returned and reported, that the men, and perhaps some of the horses might pass over, but that the rest must be abandoned, and there was no time to lose, as the ice was beginning to give way in consequence of the thaw.

But in this nocturnal and silent march across fields, of a column composed of weakened and wounded men, and women with their children, they had been unable to keep close enough, to prevent their extending, separating, and losing the traces of each other in the darkness. Ney perceived that only a part of his people had come up; nevertheless, he might have always surmounted the obstacle, thereby secured his own safety, and waited on the other side. The idea never once entered his mind; some one proposed it to him, but he rejected it instantly. He allowed three hours for the rallying; and without suffering himself to be agitated by impatience, or the danger of waiting so long, he wrapped himself up in his cloak, and passed these three dangerous hours in a profound sleep on the bank of the river. So much did he possess of the temperament of great men, a strong mind in a robust body, and that vigorous health, without which no man can ever expect to be a hero.

CHAPTER 80

'I Have Saved My Eagles'

At last, about midnight, the passage began; but the first persons who ventured on the ice, called out that the ice was bending under them, that it was sinking, that they were up to their knees in water; immediately after which that frail support was heard splitting with frightful cracks, which were prolonged in the distance, as in the breaking up of a frost. All halted in consternation.

Ney ordered them to pass only one at a time; they proceeded with caution, not knowing sometimes in the darkness if they were putting their feet on the flakes or into a chasm; for there were places where they were obliged to clear large crevices, and jump from one piece of ice to another, at the risk of falling between them and disappearing for ever. The first hesitated, but those who were behind kept calling to them to make haste.

When at last, after several of these dreadful panics, they reached the opposite bank and fancied themselves saved, a perpendicular steep, entirely covered with rime, again opposed their landing. Many were thrown back upon the ice which they broke in their fall, or which bruised them. By their account, this Russian river and its banks appeared only to have contributed with regret, by surprise, and as it were by compulsion, to their escape.

But what seemed to affect them with the greatest horror in their relation, was the trouble and distraction of the females and the sick, when it became necessary to abandon, along with the baggage, the remains of their fortune, their provisions, and in short, their whole resources against the present and the future. They saw them stripping themselves, selecting, throwing away, taking up again, and falling with exhaustion and grief upon the frozen bank of the river. They seemed to shudder again at the recollection of the horrible sight of so many men scattered over that abyss, the continual noise of persons falling, the cries of such as sunk in, and, above all, of the wailing and despair of the wounded, who, from their carts, which durst not venture on this weak support, stretched out their hands to their companions, and entreated not to be left behind.

Their leader then determined to attempt the passage of several wagons, loaded with these poor creatures; but in the middle of the river, the ice sunk down and separated. Then were heard, on the opposite bank, proceeding from the gulf, first, cries of anguish long and piercing, then stifled and feeble groans, and last of all an awful silence. All had disappeared!

Ney was looking steadfastly at the abyss with an air of consternation, when through the darkness, he imagined he saw an object still moving; it turned out to be one of those unfortunate persons, an officer, named Briqueville, whom a deep wound in the groin had disabled from standing upright. A large piece of ice had borne him up. He was soon distinctly seen, dragging himself from one piece to another on his knees and hands, and on his getting near enough to the side, the marshal himself caught hold of, and saved him.

The losses since the preceding day amounted to four thousand stragglers and three thousand soldiers, either killed, dead, or missing; the cannon and the whole of the baggage were lost; there remained to Ney scarcely three thousand soldiers, and about as many disbanded men. Finally, when all these sacrifices were consummated, and all that had been able to cross the river were collected, they resumed their march, and the vanquished river became once more their friend and their guide.

They proceeded at random and uncertain, when one of them happening to fall, recognised a beaten road; it was but too much so, for those who were marching first, stooping and using their hands, as well as their eyes, halted in alarm, exclaiming, "that they saw the marks quite fresh of a great quantity of cannon and horses." They had, therefore, only avoided one hostile army to fall into the midst of another; at a time when they could scarcely walk, they must be again obliged to fight! The war was therefore everywhere! But Ney made them push on, and without disturbing himself, continued to follow these menacing traces.

They brought them to a village called Gusinoé, into which they entered suddenly, and seized every thing; they found in it all that they had been in want of since they left Moscow, inhabitants, provisions, repose, warm dwellings, and a hundred Cossacks, who awoke to find themselves prisoners. Their reports, and the necessity of taking some refreshment to enable him to proceed, detained the marshal there a few minutes.

About ten o'clock, they reached two other villages, and were resting themselves there, when suddenly they saw the surrounding forests filled with movements. They had scarcely time to call to each other, to look about, and to concentrate themselves in the village which was nearest to the Boristhenes, when thousands of Cossacks came pouring out from between the trees, and surrounded the unfortunate troop with their lances and their cannon.

These were Platof, and his hordes, who were following the right bank of the Dnieper. They might have burnt the village, discovered the weakness of Ney's force, and exterminated it; but for three hours they remained motionless, without even firing; for what reason, is not known. The account since given by themselves is, that they had no orders; that at that moment their leader was not in a state to give any: and that in Russia no one dares to take upon himself a responsibility that does not belong to him.

The bold countenance of Ney kept them in check. He himself and a few soldiers were sufficient; he even ordered the rest of his people to continue their repast till night came on. He then caused the order to be circulated to decamp in silence, to give notice to each other in a low tone of voice, and to march as compact as possible. Afterwards, they all began their march together; but their very first step was like a signal given to the enemy, who immediately discharged the whole of his artillery at them: all his squadrons also put themselves in movement at once.

At the noise occasioned by this, the disarmed stragglers, of whom there were yet between three and four thousand, took the alarm. This flock of men wandered here and there; the great mass of them kept reeling about in uncertainty, sometimes attempting to throw themselves into the ranks of the soldiers, who drove them back. Ney contrived to keep them between him and the Russians, whose fire was principally absorbed by these useless beings. The most timid, therefore, in this instance, served as a covering to the bravest.

At the same time that the marshal made a rampart of these poor wretches to cover his right flank, he regained the banks of the Dnieper, and by that covered his left flank; he marched on thus between the two, proceeding from wood to wood, from one turning to another, taking advantage of all the windings, and of the least accidents of the soil. Whenever he ventured to any distance from the river, which he was frequently obliged to do, Platof then surrounded him on all sides.

In this manner, for two days and a distance of twenty leagues, did six thousand Cossacks keep constantly buzzing about the flanks of their column, now reduced to fifteen hundred men in arms, keeping it in a state of siege, disappearing before its sallies, and returning again instantly, like their Scythian ancestors; but with this fatal difference, that they managed their cannon mounted on sledges, and discharged their bullets in their flight, with the same agility which their forefathers exhibited in the management of their bows and the discharge of their arrows.

The night brought some relief, and at first they plunged into the darkness with a degree of joy; but then, if any one halted for a moment to bid a last adieu to some worn out or wounded comrade, who sunk to rise no more, he ran the risk of losing the traces of his column. Under such circumstances there were many cruel moments, and not a few instances of despair. At last, however, the enemy slackened his pursuit.

This unfortunate column was proceeding more tranquilly, groping its way through a thick wood, when all at once, a few paces before it, a brilliant light and several discharges of cannon flashed in the faces of the men in the first rank. Seized with terror, they fancied that there was an end of them, that they were cut off, that their end was now come, and they fell down terrified; those who were behind, got entangled among them, and were brought to the ground. Ney, who saw that all was lost, rushed forward, ordered the charge to be beat, and, as if he had foreseen the attack, called out, "Comrades, now is your time: forward! They are our prisoners!" At these words, his soldiers, who but a minute before were in consternation, and fancied themselves surprised, believed they were about to surprise their foes; from being vanquished, they rose up conquerors; they rushed upon the enemy, who had already disappeared, and whose precipitate flight through the forest they heard at a distance.

They passed quickly through this wood; but about ten o'clock at night, they met with a small river embanked in a deep ravine, which they were obliged to cross one by one, as they had done the Dnieper. Intent on the pursuit of these poor fellows, the Cossacks again got sight of them, and tried to take advantage of that moment: but Ney, by a few discharges of his musketry, again repulsed them. They surmounted this obstacle with difficulty, and in an hour after reached a large village, where hunger and exhaustion compelled them to halt for two hours longer.

The next day, the 19th of Nov., from midnight till ten o'clock in the morning, they kept marching on, without meeting any other enemy than a hilly country; about that time Platof's columns again made their appearance, and Ney halted and faced them, under the protection of the skirts of a wood. As long as the day lasted, his soldiers were obliged to resign themselves to see the enemy's bullets overturning the trees which served to shelter them, and furrowing their bivouacs; for they had now nothing but small arms, which could not keep the Cossack artillery at a sufficient distance.

On the return of night, the marshal gave the usual signal, and they proceeded on their march to Orcha. During the preceding day, he had already despatched thither Pchébendowski with fifty horse, to require assistance; they must already have arrived there, unless the enemy had already gained possession of that town.

Ney's officers concluded their narrative by saying, that during the rest of their march, they had met with several formidable obstacles, but that they did not think them worth relating. They continued, however, speaking enthusiastically of their marshal, and making us sharers of their admiration of him; for even his equals had no idea of being jealous of him. He had been too much regretted, and his preservation had excited too agreeable emotions, to allow envy to have any part in them; besides, Ney had placed himself completely beyond its reach. As to himself, in all this heroism, he had gone so little beyond his natural disposition, that had it not been for the éclat of his glory in the eyes, the gestures, and the acclamations of every one, he would never have imagined that he had done a sublime action.

And this was not an enthusiasm of surprise. Each of the latter days had had its remarkable men; amongst others, that of the 16th had Eugene, that of the 17th Mortier; but from this time, Ney was universally proclaimed the hero of the retreat.

The distance between Smolensk and Orcha is hardly five days' march. In that short passage, what a harvest of glory had been reaped! how little space and time are required to establish an immortal renown! Of what nature then are these great inspirations, that invisible and impalpable germ of great devotion, produced in a few moments, issuing from a single heart, and which must fill time and eternity?

When Napoleon, who was two leagues farther on, heard that Ney had just re-appeared, he leaped and shouted for joy, and exclaimed, "I have then saved my eagles! I would have given three hundred millions from my treasury, sooner than have lost such a man."

Chapter 81
The Dnieper

The army had thus for the third and last time repassed the Dnieper, a river half Russian and half Polish, but of Russian origin. It runs from east to west as far as Orcha, where it appears as if it would penetrate into Poland; but there the heights of Lithuania oppose its farther progress, and compel it to turn towards the south, and to become the frontier of the two countries.

Kutusoff and his eighty thousand Russians halted before this feeble obstacle. Hitherto they had been rather the spectators than the authors of our calamities; we saw them no more; our army was released from the punishment of their joy.

In this war, and as always happens, the character of Kutusoff availed him more than his talents. So long as it was necessary to deceive and temporize, his crafty spirit, his indolence, and his great age, acted of themselves; he was the creature of circumstances, which he ceased to be as soon as it became necessary to march rapidly, to pursue, to anticipate, and to attack.

But after passing Smolensk, Platof passed over to the right flank of the road, in order to join Wittgenstein. The war was then entirely transferred to that side.

On the 22nd of November, the army had a disagreeable march from Orcha to Borizof, on a wide road, (skirted by a double row of large birch trees,) in which the snow had melted, and through a deep and liquid mud. The weakest were drowned in it; it detained and delivered to the Cossacks such of our wounded, as, under the idea of a continuance of the frost, had exchanged their wagons for sledges.

In the midst of this gradual decay, an action was witnessed exhibiting something of antique energy. Two marines of the guard were cut off from their column by a band of Cossacks, who seemed determined to take them. One became discouraged, and wished to surrender; the other continued to fight, and called out to him, that if he was coward enough to do so, he would certainly shoot him. In fact, seeing his companion throw away his musket, and stretching out his arms to the enemy, he brought him to the ground just as he fell into the hands of the Cossacks; then profiting by their surprise, he quickly reloaded his musket, with which he threatened the most forward. He kept them thus at bay, retreated from tree to tree, gained ground upon them, and succeeded in rejoining his troop.

It was during the first days of the march to Borizof, that the news of the fall of Minsk became generally known in the army. The leaders themselves began then to look around them with consternation; their imagination, tormented with such a long continuance of frightful spectacles, gave them glimpses of a still more fatal futurity. In their private conversations, several exclaimed, that, "like Charles XII. in the Ukraine, Napoleon had carried his army to Moscow only to destroy it."

Others would not agree in attributing the calamities we at present suffered to that incursion. Without wishing to excuse the sacrifices to which we had submitted, by the hope of terminating the war in a single campaign, they asserted, "that that hope had been well founded; that in pushing his line of operation as far as Moscow, Napoleon had given to that lengthened column a base sufficiently broad and solid."

They showed "the trace of this base marked out by the Düna, the Dnieper, the Ula, and the Berezina, from Riga to Bobruisk; they said that Macdonald, Saint Cyr and De Wrede, Victor and Dombrowski were there waiting for them; there were thus, including Schwartzenberg, and even Augereau, (who protected the interval between the Elbe and the Niemen with fifty thousand men,) nearly two hundred and eighty thousand soldiers on the defensive, who, from the north to the south, supported the attack of one hundred and fifty thousand men upon the east; and from thence they argued, that this *point* upon Moscow, however hazardous it might appear, had been both sufficiently prepared, and was worthy of the genius of Napoleon, and that its success was possible; in fact, its failure had been entirely occasioned by errors of detail."

They then brought to mind our useless waste of lives before Smolensk, Junot's inaction at Valoutina, and they maintained, "that in spite of all these losses, Russia would have been completely conquered on the field of battle of the Moskwa, if Marshal Ney's first successes had been followed up.

"Even at the last, although the expedition had failed in a military point of view, by the indecision of that day, and politically by the burning of Moscow, the army might still have returned from it safe and sound. From the time of our entrance into that capital, had not the Russian general and the Russian winter allowed us, the one forty, and the other fifty days, to recover ourselves, and to make our retreat?"

Deploring afterwards the rash obstinacy of losing so much time at Moscow, and the fatal hesitation at Malo-Yaroslawetz, they proceeded to reckon up their losses. Since their leaving Moscow, they had lost all their baggage, five hundred cannon, thirty-one eagles, twenty-seven generals, forty thousand prisoners, sixty thousand dead: all that remained were forty thousand stragglers, unarmed, and eight thousand effective soldiers.

Last of all, when their column of attack had been destroyed, they asked, "by what fatality it had happened, that the remains of this column, when collected at its base, which had been vigorously supported, were left without knowing where to halt, or to take breath? Why could they not even concentrate themselves at Minsk and at Wilna, behind the marshes of the Berezina, and there keep back the enemy, at least for some time, take advantage of the winter and recruit themselves?

"But no, all is lost by another side, by the fault of entrusting an Austrian to guard the magazines, and cover the retreat of all these brave armies, and not placing a military leader at Wilna or Minsk, with a force sufficient either to supply the insufficiency of the Austrian army to meet the combined armies of Moldavia and Volhynia, or to prevent its betraying us."

Those who made such complaints were not unaware of the presence of the Duke of Bassano at Wilna; but notwithstanding the talents of that minister, and the great confidence the Emperor placed in him, they considered that being a stranger to the art of war, and overloaded with the cares of a great administration, and of every thing political, the direction of military affairs should not have been left to him. Such were the complaints of those, whose sufferings left them the leisure necessary for observation. That a fault had been committed, it was impossible to deny; but to say how it might have been avoided, to weigh the value of the motives which had occasioned it, in so great a crisis, and in the presence of so great a man, is more than one would venture to undertake. Who is there besides that does not know, that in these hazardous and gigantic enterprises, every thing becomes a fault, when the object of them has failed?

Although the treachery of Schwartzenberg was by no means so evident, it is certain, that, with the exception of the three French generals who were with him, the whole of the grand army considered it as beyond a doubt. They said, "that Walpole's only object at Vienna was to act as a secret agent of England; that he and Metternich composed between them the perfidious instructions which were sent to Schwartzenberg. Hence it was that ever since the 20th of September, the day when the arrival of Tchitchakof and the battle of Lutsk closed the victorious career of Schwartzenberg, that marshal had repassed the Bug, and covered Warsaw by uncovering Minsk; hence his perseverance in that false manoeuvre: hence, after a feeble effort towards Bresklitowsky on the 10th of October, his neglect to avail himself of Tchitchakof's inaction by getting between him and Minsk, and hence his losing his time in military promenades, and insignificant marches towards Briansk, Bialystok, and Volkowitz.

"He had thus allowed the admiral to take rest, and rally his sixty thousand men, to divide them into two, to leave one half with Sacken to oppose him, and to set out on the 27th of October with the other half to take possession of Minsk, of Borizof, of the magazine, of the passage of Napoleon, and of his winter quarters. Then only did Schwartzenberg put himself in the rear of this hostile movement, instead of anticipating it, as he had orders to do, leaving Regnier in the presence of Sacken, and marching so slowly, that from the very first the admiral had got five marches the start of him.

"On the 14th of November, at Volkowitz, Sacken attacked Regnier, separated him from the Austrians, and pressed him so closely, that he was obliged to call Schwartzenberg to his aid. Immediately, the latter, as if he had been expecting the summons, retrograded, leaving Minsk to its fate. It is true that he released Regnier, that he beat Sacken and destroyed half his army, pursuing him as far as the Bug; but on the 16th of November, the very day of his victory, Minsk was taken by Tchitchakof: this was a double victory for Austria. Thus all appearances were preserved; the new field-marshal satisfied the wishes of his government, which was equally the enemy of the Russians whom he had just weakened on one side, and of Napoleon, whom on the other he had betrayed to them."

Such was the language of almost the whole of the grand army; its leader was silent, either because he expected no more zeal on the part of an ally, or from policy, or because he believed that Schwartzenberg had acted with sufficient honour, in sending him the sort of notice which he did six weeks before, when he was at Moscow.

However, he did address some reproaches to the field-marshal. To these the latter replied, by complaining bitterly, first, of the double and contradictory instructions which he had received, to cover Warsaw and Minsk at the same time; and second, of the false news which had been transmitted to him by the Duke of Bassano.

He said, "that minister had constantly represented to him that the grand army was retreating safe and sound, in good order, and always formidable. Why had he been trifled with, by sending him bulletins made to deceive the idlers of the capital? His only reason for not making greater efforts to join the grand army was, because he believed that it was fully able to protect itself."

He also alleged his own weakness. "How could it be expected that with twenty-eight thousand men he could so long keep sixty thousand in check? In that situation, if Tchitchakof stole a few marches on him, was it at all wonderful? Had he then hesitated to follow him, to leave Gallicia, his point of departure, his magazines, and his depot? If he ceased his pursuit, it was only because Regnier and Durutte, the two French generals, summoned him in the most urgent manner to come to their assistance. Both they and he had reason to expect that Maret, Oudinôt, or Victor, would provide for the safety of Minsk."

CHAPTER 82

Towards the Berezina

In fact, no one had any right to accuse another of treachery, when we had betrayed ourselves, for all had been wanting in the time of need.

At Wilna, they appeared to have had no suspicion of the real state of affairs; and at a time when the garrisons, the depots, the marching battalions, and the divisions of Durutte, Loison, and Dombrowski, between the Berezina and the Vistula, might have formed at Minsk an army of thirty thousand men, three thousand men, headed by a general of no reputation, were the only forces which Tchitchakof found there to oppose him. It was a known fact that this handful of young soldiers was exposed in front of a river, into which they were precipitated by the admiral, whereas, if they had been placed on the other side, that obstacle would have protected them for some time.

For thus, as frequently happens, the faults of the general plan had led to faults of detail. The governor of Minsk had been negligently chosen. He was, it was said, one of those men who undertake every thing, who promise every thing, and who do nothing. On the 16th of November, he lost that capital, and with it four thousand seven hundred sick, the warlike ammunition, and two million rations of provisions. It was five days since the news of this loss had reached Dombrowna, and the news of a still greater calamity came on the heels of it.

This same governor had retreated towards Borizof. There he neglected to inform Oudinôt, who was only at the distance of two marches, to come to his assistance; and failed to support Dombrowski, who made a hasty march thither from Bobruisk and Igumen. The latter did not arrive, however, in the night of the 20th and 21st, at the *tête-du-pont*, until after the enemy had taken possession of it; notwithstanding, he expelled Tchitchakof's vanguard, took possession of it, and defended himself gallantly there until the evening of the 21st; but being then overwhelmed by the fire of the Russian artillery, which took him in flank, and attacked by a force more than double his own, he was driven across the river, and out of the town, as far as the road to Moscow.

Napoleon was wholly unprepared for this disaster; he fancied that he had completely prevented it by the instructions he had sent to Victor from Moscow, on the 6th of October. These instructions "anticipated a warm attack from Wittgenstein or Tchitchakof; they recommended Victor to keep within reach of Polotsk and of Minsk; to have a prudent, discreet, and intelligent officer about Schwartzenberg; to keep up a regular correspondence with Minsk, and to send other agents in different directions."

But Wittgenstein having made his attack before Tchitchakof, the nearer and more pressing danger had attracted every one's attention; the wise instructions of the 6th of October had not been repeated by Napoleon, and they appeared to have been entirely forgotten by his lieutenant. Finally, when the Emperor learned at Dombrowna the loss of Minsk, he had no idea that Borizof was in such imminent danger, as when he passed the next day through Orcha, he had the whole of his bridge-equipage burnt.

His correspondence also of the 20th of November with Victor proved his security; it supposed that Oudinôt would have nearly arrived on the 25th at Borizof, while that place had been taken possession of by Tchitchakof on the 21st.

It was on the day immediately subsequent to that fatal catastrophe, at the distance of three marches from Borizof, and upon the high road, that an officer arrived and announced to Napoleon this fresh disaster. The Emperor, striking the ground with his stick, and darting a furious look to heaven, pronounced these words, "It is then written above that we shall now commit nothing but faults!"

Meanwhile Marshal Oudinôt, who was already marching towards Minsk, totally ignorant of what had happened, halted on the 21st between Bobr and Kroupki, when in the middle of the night General Brownikowski arrived to announce to him his own defeat, as well as that of General Dombrowski; that Borizof was taken, and that the Russians were following hard at his heels.

On the 22nd the marshal marched to meet them, and rallied the remains of Dombrowski's force.

On the 23rd, at three leagues on the other side of Borizof, he came in contact with the Russian vanguard, which he overthrew, taking from it nine hundred men and fifteen hundred carriages, and drove back by the united force of his artillery, infantry, and cavalry, as far as the Berezina; but the remains of Lambert's force, on repassing Borizof and that river, destroyed the bridge.

Napoleon was then at Toloczina: he made them describe to him the position of Borizof. They assured him that at that point the Berezina was not merely a river but a lake of moving ice; that the bridge was three hundred fathoms in length; that it had been irreparably destroyed, and the passage by it rendered completely impracticable.

At that moment arrived a general of engineers, who had just returned from the Duke of Belluno's corps. Napoleon interrogated him; the general declared "that he saw no means of escape but through the middle of Wittgenstein's army." The Emperor replied, "that he must find a direction in which he could turn his back to all the enemy's generals, to Kutusoff, to Wittgenstein, to Tchitchakof;" and he pointed with his finger on the map to the course of the Berezina below Borizof; it was there he wished to cross the river. But the general objected to him the presence of Tchitchakof on the right bank; the Emperor then pointed to another passage below the first, and then to a third, still nearer to the Dnieper. Recollecting, however, that he was then approaching the country of the Cossacks, he stopped short, and exclaimed, "Oh yes! Pultawa! that is like Charles XII.!"

In fact, every disaster which Napoleon could anticipate had occurred; the melancholy conformity, therefore, of his situation with that of the Swedish conqueror, threw his mind into such a state of agitation, that his health became still more seriously affected than it had been at Malo-Yaroslawetz. Among the expressions he made use of, loud enough to be overheard, was this: "See what happens when we heap faults on faults!" Nevertheless, these first movements were the only ones that had escaped him, and the *valet-de-chambre* who assisted him, was the only person that witnessed his agitation. Duroc, Daru, and Berthier have all said, that they knew nothing of it, that they saw him unshaken; this was very true, humanly speaking, as he retained sufficient command over himself to avoid betraying his anxiety, and as the strength of man most frequently consists in concealing his weakness.

A remarkable conversation, which was overheard the same night, will show better than any thing else, how critical was his position, and how well he bore it. It was getting late; Napoleon had gone to bed. Duroc and Daru, who remained in his chamber, fancying that he was asleep, were giving way, in whispers, to the most gloomy conjectures; he overheard them, however, and the word "prisoner of state," coming to his ear, "How!" exclaimed he, "do you believe they would dare?" Daru, after his first surprise, immediately answered, "that if we were compelled to surrender, we must be prepared for every thing; that he had no reliance on an enemy's generosity; that we knew too well that great state-policy considered itself identified with morality, and was regulated by no law." "But France," said the Emperor, "what would France say?" "Oh, as to France," continued Daru, "we are at liberty to make a thousand conjectures more or less disagreeable, but none of us can know what will take place there." And he then added, "that for the sake of the Emperor's chief officers, as well as the Emperor himself, the most fortunate thing would be, if by the air or otherwise, as the earth was closed upon us, the Emperor could reach France, from whence he could much more certainly provide for their safety, than by remaining among them!" "Then I suppose I am in your way?" replied the Emperor, smiling. "Yes, Sire." "And you have no wish to be a prisoner of state?" Daru replied in the same tone, "that it was enough for him to be a prisoner of war." On which the Emperor remained for some time in a profound silence; then with a more serious air: "Are all the reports of my ministers burnt?" "Sire, hitherto you would not allow that to be done." "Very well, go and destroy them; for it must be confessed, we are in a most melancholy position." This was the sole avowal which it wrested from him, and on that idea he went to sleep, knowing, when it was necessary, how to postpone every thing to the next day.

His orders displayed equal firmness. Oudinôt had just sent to inform him of his determination to overthrow Lambert; this he approved of, and he also urged him to make himself master of a passage, either above or below Borizof. He expressed his anxiety, that by the 24th this passage should be fixed on, and the preparations begun, and that he should be apprised of it, in order to make his march correspond. Far from thinking of making his escape through the midst of these three hostile armies, his only idea now was, that of beating Tchitchakof, and retaking Minsk.

It is true, that eight hours afterwards, in a second letter to the Duke of Reggio, he resigned himself to cross the Berezina near Veselowo, and to retreat directly upon Wilna by Vileika, avoiding the Russian admiral.

But on the 24th he learned that the passage could only be attempted near Studzianka; that at that spot the river was only fifty-four fathoms wide, and six feet deep; that they would land on the other side, in a marsh, under the fire of a commanding position strongly occupied by the enemy.

CHAPTER 83

The Crossing Opposed

All hope of passing between the Russian armies was thus lost; driven by the armies of Kutusoff and Wittgenstein upon the Berezina, there was no alternative but to cross that river in the teeth of the army of Tchitchakof, which lined its banks.

Ever since the 23rd, Napoleon had been preparing for it, as for a desperate action. And first he had the eagles of all the corps brought to him, and burnt. He formed into two battalions, eighteen hundred dismounted cavalry of his guard, of whom only eleven hundred and fifty-four were armed with muskets and carbines.

The cavalry of the army of Moscow was so completely destroyed, that Latour-Maubourg had not now remaining under his command more than one hundred and fifty men on horseback. The Emperor collected around his person all the officers of that arm who were still mounted; he styled this troop, of about five hundred officers, his *sacred squadron*. Grouchy and Sebastiani had the command of them; generals of division served in it as captains.

Napoleon ordered further that all the useless carriages should be burnt; that no officer should keep more than one; that half the wagons and carriages of all the corps should also be burnt, and that the horses should be given to the artillery of the guard. The officers of that arm had orders to take all the draught-cattle within their reach, even the horses of the Emperor himself, sooner than abandon a single cannon, or ammunition wagon.

After giving these orders, he plunged into the gloomy and immense forest of Minsk, in which a few hamlets and wretched habitations have scarcely cleared a few open spots. The noise of Wittgenstein's artillery filled it with its echo. That Russian general came rushing from the north upon the right flank of our expiring column; he brought back with him the winter which had quitted us at the same time with Kutusoff; the news of his threatening march quickened our steps. From forty to fifty thousand men, women, and children, glided through this forest as precipitately as their weakness and the slipperiness of the ground, from the frost beginning again to set in, would allow.

These forced marches, commenced before daylight, and which did not finish at its close, dispersed all that had remained together. They lost themselves in the darkness of these great forests and long nights. They halted at night and resumed their march in the morning, in darkness, at random, and without hearing the signal; the dissolution of the remains of the corps was then completed; all were mixed and confounded together.

In this last stage of weakness and confusion, as we were approaching Borizof, we heard loud cries before us. Some ran forward fancying it was an attack. It was Victor's army, which had been feebly driven back by Wittgenstein to the right side of our road, where it remained waiting for the Emperor to pass by. Still quite complete and full of animation, it received the Emperor, as soon as he made his appearance, with the customary but now long forgotten acclamations.

Of our disasters it knew nothing; they had been carefully concealed even from its leaders. When therefore, instead of that grand column which had conquered Moscow, its soldiers perceived behind Napoleon only a train of spectres covered with rags, with female pelisses, pieces of carpet, or dirty cloaks, half burnt and holed by the fires, and with nothing on their feet but rags of all sorts, their consternation was extreme. They looked terrified at the sight of those unfortunate soldiers, as they defiled before them, with lean carcasses, faces black with dirt, and hideous bristly beards, unarmed, shameless, marching confusedly, with their heads bent, their eyes fixed on the ground and silent, like a troop of captives.

But what astonished them more than all, was to see the number of colonels and generals scattered about and isolated, who seemed only occupied about themselves, and to think of nothing but saving the wrecks of their property or their persons; they were marching pell-mell with the soldiers, who did not notice them, to whom they had no longer any commands to give, and of whom they had nothing to expect, all ties between them being broken, and all ranks effaced by the common misery.

The soldiers of Victor and Oudinôt could not believe their eyes. Moved with compassion, their officers, with tears in their eyes, detained such of their companions as they recognised in the crowd. They first supplied them with clothes and provisions, and then asked them where were their *corps d'armée*? And when the others pointed them out, seeing, instead of so many thousand men, only a weak platoon of officers and non-commissioned officers round a commanding officer, their eyes still kept on the look out.

The sight of so great a disaster struck the second and the ninth corps with discouragement, from the very first day. Disorder, the most contagious of all evils, attacked them; for it would seem as if order was an effort against nature. And yet the disarmed, and even the dying, although they were now fully aware that they had to fight their way across a river, and through a fresh enemy, never doubted of their being victorious.

It was now merely the shadow of an army, but it was the shadow of the grand army. It felt conscious that nature alone had vanquished it. The sight of its Emperor revived it. It had been long accustomed not to look to him for its means of support, but solely to lead it to victory. This was its first unfortunate campaign, and it had had so many fortunate ones! it only required to be able to follow him. He alone, who had elevated his soldiers so high, and now sunk them so low, was yet able to save them. He was still, therefore, cherished in the heart of his army, like hope in the heart of man.

Thus, amid so many beings who might have reproached him with their misfortunes, he marched on without the least fear, speaking to one and all without affectation, certain of being respected as long as glory could command our respect. Knowing perfectly that he belonged to us, as much as we to him, his renown being a species of national property, we should have sooner turned our arms against ourselves, (which was the case with many,) than against him, and it was a minor suicide.

Some of them fell and died at his feet, and though in the most frightful delirium, their sufferings never gave its wanderings the turn of reproach, but of entreaty. And in fact did not he share the common danger? Which of them all risked so much as he? Who suffered the greatest loss, in this disaster?

If any imprecations were uttered, it was not in his presence; it seemed, that of all misfortunes, that of incurring his displeasure was still the greatest; so rooted were their confidence in, and submission to that man who had subjected the world to them; whose genius, hitherto uniformly victorious and infallible, had assumed the place of their free-will, and who having so long in his hands the book of pensions, of rank, and of history, had found wherewithal to satisfy not only covetous spirits, but also every generous heart.

Chapter 84
The Bridge

We were now approaching the most critical moment; Victor was in the rear with 15,000 men; Oudinôt in front with 5,000, and already on the Berezina; the Emperor, between them, with 7,000 men, 40,000 stragglers, and an enormous quantity of baggage and artillery, the greatest part of which belonged to the second and the ninth corps.

On the 25th, as he was about to reach the Berezina, he appeared to linger on his march. He halted every instant on the high road, waiting for night to conceal his arrival from the enemy, and to allow the Duke of Reggio time to evacuate Borizof.

This marshal, when he entered that town upon the 23rd, found the bridge, which was 300 fathoms in length, destroyed at three different points, and that the vicinity of the enemy rendered it impossible to repair it. He had ascertained, that on his left, two miles lower down the river, there was, near Oukoholda, a deep and unsafe ford; that at the distance of a mile above Borizof, namely, at Stadhof, there was another, but of difficult approach. Finally, he had learned within the last two days, that at Studzianka, two leagues above Stadhof, there was a third passage;—for the knowledge of this he was indebted to Corbineau's brigade.

This was the same brigade which the Bavarian general, De Wrede, had taken from the second corps, in his march to Smoliantzy. He had retained it until he reached Dokszitzi, from whence he sent it back to the second corps by way of Borizof. When Corbineau arrived there, he found Tchitchakof already in possession of it, and was compelled to make his retreat by ascending the Berezina, and concealing his force in the forests which border that river. Not knowing at what point to cross it, he accidentally saw a Lithuanian peasant, whose horse seemed to be quite wet, as if he had just come through it. He laid hold of this man, and made him his guide; he got up behind him, and crossed the river at a ford opposite to Studzianka. He immediately rejoined Oudinôt, and informed him of the discovery he had made.

As Napoleon's intention was to retreat directly upon Wilna, the marshal saw at once that this passage was the most direct, as well as the least dangerous. It was also observed, that even if our infantry and artillery should be too closely pressed by Wittgenstein and Kutusoff, and prevented from crossing the river on bridges, there was at least a certainty, from the ford having been tried, that the Emperor and the cavalry would be able to pass; that all would not then be lost, both peace and war, as if Napoleon himself remained in the enemy's hands. The marshal therefore did not hesitate. In the night of the 23rd, the general of artillery, a company of pontonniers, a regiment of infantry, and the brigade Corbineau, took possession of Studzianka.

At the same time the other two passages were reconnoitred, and both found to be strongly observed. The object therefore was to deceive and displace the enemy. As force could do nothing, recourse was had to stratagem; in furtherance of which, on the 24th, three hundred men and several hundred stragglers were sent towards Oukoholda, with instructions to collect there, with as much noise as possible, all the necessary materials for the construction of a bridge; the whole division of the cuirassiers was also made to promenade on that side within view of the enemy.

In addition to this, Major General Lorencé had several Jews sought out and brought to him; he interrogated them with great apparent minuteness relative to that ford, and the roads leading from it to Minsk. Then, affecting to be mightily pleased with their answers, and to be satisfied that there was no better passage to be found, he retained some of these rascals as guides, and had the others conveyed beyond our out-posts. But to make still more sure of the latter *not* keeping their word with him, he made them swear that they would return to meet us, in the direction of lower Berezina, in order to inform us of the enemy's movements.

While these attempts were making to draw Tchitchakof's attention entirely to the left, the means of effecting a passage were secretly preparing at Studzianka. It was only on the 25th, at five in the evening, that Eblé arrived there, followed only by two field forges, two wagons of coal, six covered wagons of utensils and nails, and some companies of pontonniers. At Smolensk he had made each workman provide himself with a tool and some cramp-irons.

But the trestles, which had been made the day before, out of the beams of the Polish cabins, were found to be too weak. The work was all to do over again. It was found to be quite impossible to finish the bridge during the night; it could only be fixed during the following day, the 26th, in full daylight, and under the enemy's fire; but there was no room for hesitation.

On the first approach of that decisive night, Oudinôt ceded to Napoleon the occupation of Borizof, and went to take position with the rest of his corps at Studzianka. They marched in the most profound obscurity, without making the least noise, and mutually recommending to each other the deepest silence.

By eight o'clock at night Oudinôt and Dombrowski had taken possession of the heights commanding the passage, while General Eblé descended from them. That general placed himself on the borders of the river, with his pontonniers and a wagon-load of the irons of abandoned wheels, which at all hazards he had made into cramp-irons. He had sacrificed every thing to preserve that feeble resource, and it saved the army.

At the close of the night of the 25th he made them sink the first trestle in the muddy bed of the river. But to crown our misfortunes, the rising of the waters had made the traces of the ford entirely disappear. It required the most incredible efforts on the part of our unfortunate sappers, who were plunged in the water up to their mouths, and had to contend with the floating pieces of ice which were carried along by the stream. Many of them perished from the cold, or were drowned by the ice flakes, which a violent wind drove against them.

They had every thing to conquer but the enemy. The rigour of the atmosphere was just at the degree necessary to render the passage of the river more difficult, without suspending its course, or sufficiently consolidating the moving ground upon which we were about to venture. On this occasion the winter showed itself more Russian than even the Russians themselves. The latter were wanting to their season, which never failed them.

The French laboured during the whole night by the light of the enemy's fires, which shone on the heights of the opposite bank, and within reach of the artillery and musketry of the division Tchaplitz. The latter, having no longer any doubt of our intentions, sent to apprise his commander-in-chief.

CHAPTER 85

The Emperor Crosses the River

The presence of a hostile division deprived us of all hope of deceiving the Russian admiral. We were expecting every instant to hear the whole fire of his artillery directed upon our workmen; and even if he did not discover them until daylight, their labours would not then be sufficiently advanced; and the opposite bank, being low and marshy, was too much commanded by Tchaplitz's positions to make it at all possible for us to force a passage.

When he quitted Borizof, therefore, at ten o'clock at night, Napoleon imagined that he was setting out for a most desperate contest. He settled himself for the night, with the 6,400 guards which still remained to him, at Staroi-Borizof, a chateau belonging to Prince Radzivil, situated on the right of the road from Borizof to Studzianka, and equidistant from these two points.

He passed the remainder of that night on his feet, going out every moment, either to listen, or to repair to the passage where his destiny was accomplishing; for the magnitude of his anxieties so completely filled his hours, that as each revolved, he fancied that it was morning. Several times he was reminded of his mistake by his attendants.

Darkness had scarcely disappeared when he joined Oudinôt. The sight of danger tranquillized him, as it always did; but on seeing the Russian fires and their position, his most determined generals, such as Rapp, Mortier, and Ney, exclaimed, "that if the Emperor escaped this danger, they must absolutely believe in the influence of his star!" Murat himself thought it was now time to think of nothing but saving Napoleon. Some of the Poles proposed it to him.

The Emperor was waiting for the approach of daylight in one of the houses on the borders of the river, on a steep bank which was crowned with Oudinôt's artillery. Murat obtained access to him; he declared to his brother-in-law, "that he looked upon the passage as impracticable; he urged him to save his person while it was yet time. He informed him that he might, without any danger, cross the Berezina a few leagues above Studzianka; that in five days he would reach Wilna; that some brave and determined Poles, perfectly acquainted with all the roads, had offered themselves for his guards, and to be responsible for his safety."

But Napoleon rejected this proposition as an infamous plan, as a cowardly flight, and was indignant that any one should dare to think for a moment that he would abandon his army, so long as it was in danger. He was not, however, at all displeased with Murat, probably because that prince had afforded him an opportunity of showing his firmness, or rather because he saw nothing in his proposal but a mark of devotion, and because the first quality in the eyes of sovereigns is attachment to their persons.

At that moment the appearance of daylight made the Russian fires grow pale and disappear. Our troops stood to their arms, the artillerymen placed themselves by their pieces, the generals were observing, and the looks of all were steadily directed to the opposite bank, preserving that silence which betokens great expectation, and is the forerunner of great danger.

Since the day before, every blow struck by our pontonniers, echoing among the woody heights, must, we concluded, have attracted the whole attention of the enemy. The first dawn of the 26th was therefore expected to display to us his battalions and artillery, drawn up, in front of the weak scaffolding, to the construction of which Eblé had yet to devote eight hours more. Doubtless they were only waiting for daylight to enable them to point their cannon with better aim. When day appeared, we saw their fires abandoned, the bank deserted, and upon the heights, thirty pieces of artillery in full retreat. A single bullet of theirs would have been sufficient to annihilate the only plank of safety, which we were about to fix, in order to unite the two banks; but that artillery retreated exactly as ours was placed in battery.

Farther off, we perceived the rear of a long column, which was moving off towards Borizof without ever looking behind it; one regiment of infantry, however, and twelve cannon remained, but without taking up any position; we also saw a horde of Cossacks wandering about the skirts of the wood: they formed the rear-guard of Tchaplitz's division, six thousand strong, which was thus retiring, as if for the purpose of delivering up the passage to us.

The French, at first could hardly venture to believe their eyes. At last, transported with joy, they clapped their hands, and uttered loud shouts. Rapp and Oudinôt rushed precipitately into the house where the Emperor was. "Sire," they said to him, "the enemy has just raised his camp, and quitted his position!"—"It is not possible!" he replied; but Ney and Murat just then entered and confirmed this report. Napoleon immediately darted out; he looked, and could just see the last files of Tchaplitz's column getting farther off and disappearing in the woods. Transported with joy, he exclaimed, "I have outwitted the admiral!"

During this first movement, two of the enemy's pieces re-appeared, and fired. An order was given to remove them by a discharge of our artillery.

One salvo was enough; it was an act of imprudence which was not repeated, for fear of its recalling Tchaplitz. The bridge was as yet scarcely begun; it was eight o'clock, and the first trestles were only then fixing.

The Emperor, however, impatient to get possession of the opposite bank, pointed it out to the bravest. Jacqueminot, aide-de-camp to the Duke of Reggio, and the Lithuanian count Predziecski, were the first who threw themselves into the river, and in spite of the pieces of ice, which cut and bled the chests and sides of their horses, succeeded in reaching the other side. Sourd, chief of the squadron, and fifty chasseurs of the 7th, each carrying a voltigeur *en croupe,* followed them, as well as two frail rafts which transported four hundred men in twenty trips. The Emperor having expressed a wish to have a prisoner to interrogate, Jacqueminot, who overheard him, had scarcely crossed the river, when he saw one of Tchaplitz's soldiers; he rushed after, attacked, and disarmed him; then seizing and placing him on the bow of his saddle, he brought him through the river and the ice to Napoleon.

About one o'clock the bank was entirely cleared of the Cossacks, and the bridge for the infantry finished. The division Legrand crossed it rapidly with its cannon, the men shouting "Vive l'Empereur!" in the presence of their sovereign, who was himself actively pressing the passage of the artillery, and encouraged his brave soldiers by his voice and example.

He exclaimed, when he saw them fairly in possession of the opposite bank, "Behold my star again appear!" for he was a believer in fatality, like all conquerors, those men, who, having the largest accounts with Fortune, are fully aware how much they are indebted to her, and who, moreover, having no intermediate power between themselves and heaven, feel themselves more immediately under its protection.

Chapter 86
Errors!

At that moment, a Lithuanian nobleman, disguised as a peasant, arrived from Wilna with the news of Schwartzenberg's victory over Sacken. Napoleon appeared pleased in proclaiming it aloud, with the addition, that "Schwartzenberg had immediately returned upon the heels of Tchitchakof, and that he was coming to our assistance." A conjecture, to which the disappearance of Tchaplitz gave considerable probability.

Meantime, as the first bridge which was just finished had only been made for the infantry, a second was begun immediately after, a hundred fathoms higher up, for the artillery and baggage, which was not finished until four o'clock in the afternoon. During that interval, the Duke of Reggio, with the rest of the second corps, and Dombrowski's division, followed General Legrand to the other side; they formed about seven thousand men.

The marshal's first care was to secure the road to Zembin, by a detachment which chased some Cossacks from it; to push the enemy towards Borizof, and to keep him as far back as possible from the passage of Studzianka.

Tchaplitz, in obedience to the admiral's orders, proceeded as far as Stakhowa, a village close to Borizof, he then turned back, and encountered the first troops of Oudinôt commanded by Albert. Both sides halted. The French, finding themselves rather too far off from their main body, only wanted to gain time, and the Russian general waited for orders.

Tchitchakof had found himself in one of those difficult situations, in which prepossession, being compelled to fluctuate in uncertainty between several points at once, has no sooner determined and fixed upon one side, than it removes and gets overturned upon another.

His march from Minsk to Borizof in three columns, not only by the high road, but by the roads of Antonopolia, Logoïsk, and Zembin, showed that his whole attention was at first directed to that part of the Berezina, above Borizof. Feeling himself then so strong upon his left, he felt only that his right was weakened, and in consequence, his anxiety was entirely transferred to that side.

The error which led him into that false direction had other and stronger foundations. Kutusoff's instructions directed his responsibility to that point. Ertell, who commanded twelve thousand men near Bobruisk, refused to quit his cantonments, to follow Dombrowski, and to come and defend that part of the river. He alleged, as his justification for refusal, the danger of a distemper among the cattle, a pretext unheard of and improbable, but perfectly true, as Tchitchakof himself has admitted.

The admiral adds further, that information sent to him by Wittgenstein directed his anxiety towards Lower Berezino, as well as the supposition, natural enough, that the presence of that general on the right flank of the grand army and above Borizof, would push Napoleon below that town.

The recollection of the passages of Charles XII. and of Davoust at Berezino, might also be another of his motives. By taking that direction, Napoleon would not only escape Wittgenstein, but he might retake Minsk, and form a junction with Schwartzenberg. This last was a serious consideration with Tchitchakof, Minsk being his conquest, and Schwartzenberg his first adversary. Lastly, and principally, Oudinôt's demonstration near Ucholoda, and probably the report of the Jews, determined him.

The admiral, completely deceived, had therefore resolved, on the evening of the 25th, to descend the Berezina, at the very moment that Napoleon had determined to re-ascend it. It might almost be said that the French Emperor dictated the Russian general's resolution, the time for adopting it, the precise moment, and every detail of its execution. Both started at the same time from Borizof, Napoleon for Studzianka, Tchitchakof for Szabaszawiczy, turning their backs to each other as if by mutual agreement, and the admiral recalling all the troops which he had above Borizof, with the exception of a small body of light troops, and without even taking the precaution of breaking up the roads.

Notwithstanding, at Szabaszawiczy, he was not more than five or six leagues from the passage which was effectuating. On the morning of the 26th he must have been informed of it. The bridge of Borizof was only three hours' march from the point of attack. He had left fifteen thousand men before that bridge; he might therefore have returned in person to that point, rejoined Tchaplitz at Stakhowa, on the same day made an attack, or at least made preparations for it, and on the following day, the 27th, overthrown with eighteen thousand men the seven thousand soldiers of Oudinôt and Dombrowski; and finally resumed, in front of the Emperor and of Studzianka, the position which Tchaplitz had quitted the day before.

But great errors are seldom repaired with the same readiness with which they are committed; either because it is in our nature to be at first doubtful of them, and that no one is disposed to admit them until they are completely certain; or because they confuse, and in the distrust of our own judgment, we hesitate, and require the support of other opinions.

Thus it was, that the admiral lost the remainder of the 26th and the whole of the 27th in consultations, in feeling his way, and in preparations. The presence of Napoleon and his grand army, of the weakness of which it was impossible for him to have any idea, dazzled him. He saw the Emperor every where; before his right, in the simulated preparations for a passage; opposite his centre at Borizof, because in fact the arrival of the successive portions of our army filled that place with movements; and finally, at Studzianka before his left, where the Emperor really was.

On the 27th, so little had he recovered from his error that he made his chasseurs reconnoitre and attack Borizof; they crossed over upon the beams of the burnt bridge, but were repulsed by the soldiers of Partouneaux's division.

On the same day, while he was thus irresolute, Napoleon, with about five thousand guards, and Ney's corps, now reduced to six hundred men, crossed the Berezina about two o'clock in the afternoon; he posted himself in reserve to Oudinôt, and secured the outlet from the bridges against Tchitchakof's future efforts.

He had been preceded by a crowd of baggage and stragglers. Numbers of them continued to cross the river after him as long as daylight lasted. The army of Victor, at the same time, succeeded the guard in its position on the heights of Studzianka.

Chapter 87
A Division Surrenders

Hitherto all had gone on well. But Victor, in passing through Borizof, had left there Partouneaux with his division. That general had orders to stop the enemy in the rear of that town, to drive before him the numerous stragglers who had taken shelter there, and to rejoin Victor before the close of the day. It was the first time that Partouneaux had seen the disorder of the grand army. He was anxious, like Davoust at the beginning of the retreat, to hide the traces of it from the Cossacks of Kutusoff, who were at his heels. This fruitless attempt, the attacks of Platof by the high road of Orcha, and those of Tchitchakof by the burnt bridge of Borizof, detained him in that place until the close of the day.

He was preparing to quit it, when an order reached him from the Emperor himself, to remain there all night. Napoleon's idea, no doubt, was, in that manner to direct the whole attention of the three Russian generals upon Borizof, and that Partouneaux's keeping them back upon that point, would allow him sufficient time to operate the passage of his whole army.

But Wittgenstein left Platof to pursue the French army along the high road, and directed his own march more to the right. He debouched the same evening on the heights which border the Berezina, between Borizof and Studzianka, intercepted the road between these two points, and captured all that was found there. A crowd of stragglers, who were driven back on Partouneaux, apprised him that he was separated from the rest of the army.

Partouneaux did not hesitate: although he had no more than three cannon with him, and three thousand five hundred soldiers, he determined to cut his way through, made his dispositions accordingly, and began his march. He had at first to march along a slippery road, crowded with baggage and runaways; with a violent wind blowing directly in his face, and in a dark and icy-cold night. To these obstacles were shortly added the fire of several thousand enemies, who lined the heights upon his right. As long as he was only attacked in flank, he proceeded; but shortly after, he had to meet it in front from numberless troops well posted, whose bullets traversed his column through and through.

This unfortunate division then got entangled in a shallow; a long file of five or six hundred carriages embarrassed all its movements; seven thousand terrified stragglers, howling with terror and despair, rushed into the midst of its feeble lines. They broke through them, caused its platoons to waver, and were every moment involving in their disorder fresh soldiers who got disheartened. It became necessary to retreat, in order to rally, and take a better position, but in falling back, they encountered Platof's cavalry.

Half of our combatants had already perished, and the fifteen hundred soldiers who remained found themselves surrounded by three armies and by a river.

In this situation, a flag of truce came, in the name of Wittgenstein and fifty thousand men, to order the French to surrender. Partouneaux rejected the summons. He recalled into his ranks such of his stragglers as yet retained their arms; he wanted to make a last effort, and clear a sanguinary passage to the bridge of Studzianka; but these men, who were formerly so brave, were now so degraded by their miseries, that they would no longer make use of their arms.

At the same time, the general of his vanguard apprised him that the bridges of Studzianka were burnt; an aide-de-camp, named Rochex, who had just brought the report, pretended that he had seen them burning. Partouneaux believed this false intelligence, for, in regard to calamities, misfortune is credulous.

He concluded that he was abandoned and sacrificed; and as the night, the encumbrances, and the necessity of facing the enemy on three sides, separated his weak brigades, he desired each of them to be told to try and steal off, under favour of the darkness, along the flanks of the enemy. He himself, with one of these brigades, reduced to four hundred men, ascended the steep and woody heights on his right, with the hope of passing through Wittgenstein's army in the darkness, of escaping him, and rejoining Victor; or, at all events, of getting round by the sources of the Berezina.

But at every point where he attempted to pass, he encountered the enemy's fires, and he turned again; he wandered about for several hours quite at random, in plains of snow, in the midst of a violent hurricane. At every step he saw his soldiers transfixed by the cold, emaciated with hunger and fatigue, falling half dead into the hands of the Russian cavalry, who pursued him without intermission.

This unfortunate general was still struggling with the heavens, with men, and with his own despair, when he felt even the earth give way under his feet. In fact, being deceived by the snow, he had fallen into a lake, which was not frozen sufficiently hard to bear him, and in which he would have been drowned. Then only he yielded and gave up his arms.

While this catastrophe was accomplishing, his other three brigades, being more and more hemmed in upon the road, lost all power of movement. They delayed their surrender till the next morning, first by fighting, and then by parleying; they then all fell in their turn; a common misfortune again united them with their general.

Of the whole division, a single battalion only escaped: it had been left the last in Borizof. It quitted it in the midst of the Russians of Platof and of Tchitchakof, who were effecting in that town, and at that very moment, the junction of the armies of Moscow and of Moldavia. This battalion, being alone and separated from its division, might have been expected to be the first to fall, but that very circumstance saved it. Several long trains of equipages and disbanded soldiers were flying towards Studzianka in different directions; drawn aside by one of these crowds, mistaking his road, and leaving on his right that which had been taken by the army, the leader of this battalion glided to the borders of the river, followed all its windings and turnings, and protected by the combat of his less fortunate comrades, by the darkness, and the very difficulties of the ground, moved off in silence, escaped from the enemy, and brought to Victor the confirmation of Partouneaux's surrender.

When Napoleon heard the news, he was struck with grief, and exclaimed, "How unfortunate it was, that when all appeared to be saved, as if miraculously, this *defection* had happened, to spoil all!" The expression was improper, but grief extorted it from him, either because he anticipated that Victor, being thus weakened, would be unable to hold out long enough next day; or because he had made it a point of honour to have left nothing during the whole of his retreat in the hands of the enemy, but stragglers, and no armed and organised corps. In fact, this division was the first and the only one which laid down its arms.

Chapter 88
Russia Attacks

This success encouraged Wittgenstein. At the same time, after two days feeling his way, the report of a prisoner, and the recapture of Borizof by Platof had opened Tchitchakof's eyes. From that moment the three Russian armies of the north, east, and south, felt themselves united; their commanders had mutual communications. Wittgenstein and Tchitchakof were jealous of each other, but they detested us still more; hatred, and not friendship, was their bond of union. These generals were therefore prepared to attack in conjunction the bridges of Studzianka, on both sides of the river.

This was on the 28th of November. The grand army had had two days and two nights to effect its passage; it ought to have been too late for the Russians. But the French were in a state of complete disorder, and materials were deficient for two bridges. Twice during the night of the 26th, the one for the carriages had broke down, and the passage had been retarded by it for seven hours: it broke a third time on the 27th, about four in the afternoon. On the other hand, the stragglers, who had been dispersed in the woods and surrounding villages, had not taken advantage of the first night, and on the 27th, when daylight appeared, they all presented themselves at once in order to cross the bridges.

This was particularly the case when the guard, by whose movements they regulated themselves, began its march. Its departure was like a signal; they rushed in from all parts, and crowded upon the bank. Instantly there was seen a deep, broad, and confused mass of men, horses, and chariots, besieging the narrow entrance of the bridge, and overwhelming it. The first, pushed forward by those behind them, and driven back by the guards and pontonniers, or stopped by the river, were crushed, trod underfoot, or precipitated among the floating ices of the Berezina. From this immense and horrible rabble-rout there arose at times a confused buzzing noise, at others a loud clamour, mingled with groans and fearful imprecations.

The efforts of Napoleon and his lieutenants to save these desperate men by restoring order among them, were for a long time completely fruitless. The disorder was so great, that, about two o'clock, when the Emperor presented himself in his turn, it was necessary to employ force to open a passage for him. A corps of grenadiers of the guard, and Latour-Maubourg, out of pure compassion, declined clearing themselves a way through these poor wretches.

The imperial head-quarters were established at the hamlet of Zaniwki, which is situated in the midst of the woods, within a league of Studzianka. Eblé had just then made a survey of the baggage with which the bank was covered; he apprised the Emperor that six days would not be sufficient to enable so many carriages to pass over. Ney, who was present, immediately called out, "that in that case they had better be burnt immediately." But Berthier, instigated by the demon of courts, opposed this; he assured the Emperor that the army was far from being reduced to that extremity, and the Emperor was led to believe him, from a preference for the opinion which flattered him the most, and from a wish to spare so many men, whose misfortunes he reproached himself as the cause of, and whose provisions and little all these carriages contained.

In the night of the 27th the disorder ceased by the effect of an opposite disorder. The bridges were abandoned, and the village of Studzianka attracted all these stragglers; in an instant, it was pulled to pieces, disappeared, and was converted into an infinite number of bivouacs. Cold and hunger kept these wretched people fixed around them; it was found impossible to tear them from them. The whole of that night was again lost for their passage.

Meantime Victor, with six thousand men, was defending them against Wittgenstein. But with the first dawn of the 28th, when they saw that marshal preparing for a battle, when they heard the cannon of Wittgenstein thundering over their heads, and that of Tchitchakof at the same time on the opposite bank, they rose all at once, they descended, precipitated themselves tumultuously, and returned to besiege the bridges.

Their terror was not without foundation; the last day of numbers of these unfortunate persons was come. Wittgenstein and Platof, with forty thousand Russians of the armies of the north and east, attacked the heights on the left bank, which Victor, with his small force, defended. On the right bank, Tchitchakof, with his twenty-seven thousand

Russians of the army of the south, debouched from Stachowa against Oudinôt, Ney, and Dombrowski. These three could hardly reckon eight thousand men in their ranks, which were supported by the sacred squadron, as well as by the old and young guard, who then consisted of three thousand eight hundred infantry and nine hundred cavalry.

The two Russian armies attempted to possess themselves at once of the two outlets from the bridges, and of all who had been unable to push forward beyond the marshes of Zembin. More than sixty thousand men, well clothed, well fed, and completely armed, attacked eighteen thousand half-naked, badly armed, dying of hunger, separated by a river, surrounded by morasses, and additionally encumbered with more than fifty thousand stragglers, sick or wounded, and by an enormous mass of baggage. During the last two days, the cold and misery had been such that the old guard had lost two-thirds, and the young guard one-half of their effective men.

This fact, and the calamity which had fallen upon Partouneaux's division, sufficiently explain the frightful diminution of Victor's corps, and yet that marshal kept Wittgenstein in check during the whole of that day, the 28th. As to Tchitchakof, he was beaten. Marshal Ney, with his eight thousand French, Swiss, and Poles, was a match for twenty-seven thousand Russians.

The admiral's attack was tardy and feeble. His cannon cleared the road, but he durst not venture to follow his bullets, and penetrate by the chasm which they made in our ranks. Opposite to his right, however, the legion of the Vistula gave way to the attack of a strong column. Oudinôt, Albert, Dombrowski, Claparede, and Kosikowski were then wounded; some uneasiness began to be felt. But Ney hastened forward; he made Doumerc and his cavalry dash quite across the woods upon the flank of that Russian column; they broke through it, took two thousand prisoners, cut the rest to pieces, and by this vigorous charge decided the fate of the battle, which was dragging on in uncertainty. Tchitchakof, thus defeated, was driven back into Stachowa.

On our side, most of the generals of the second corps were wounded; for the less troops they had, the more they were obliged to expose their persons. Many officers on this occasion took the muskets and the places of their wounded men. Among the losses of the day, that of young Noailles, Berthier's aide-de-camp, was remarkable. He was struck dead by a ball. He was one of those meritorious but too ardent officers, who are incessantly exposing themselves, and are considered sufficiently rewarded by being employed.

During this combat, Napoleon, at the head of his guard, remained in reserve at Brilowa, covering the outlet of the bridges, between the two armies, but nearer to that of Victor. That marshal, although attacked in a very dangerous position, and by a force quadruple his own, lost very little ground. The right of his *corps d'armée*, mutilated by the capture of Partouneaux's division, was protected by the river, and supported by a battery which the Emperor had erected on the opposite bank. His front was defended by a ravine, but his left was in the air, without support, and in a manner lost, in the elevated plain of Studzianka.

Wittgenstein's first attack was not made until ten o'clock in the morning of the 28th, across the road of Borizof, and along the Berezina, which he endeavoured to ascend as far as the passage, but the French right wing stopped him, and kept him back for a considerable time, out of reach of the bridges. He then deployed, and extended the engagement with the whole front of Victor, but without effect. One of his attacking columns attempted to cross the ravine, but it was attacked and destroyed.

At last, about the middle of the day, the Russian discovered the point where his superiority lay: he overwhelmed the French left wing. Every thing would then have been lost had it not been for an effort of Fournier, and the devotion of Latour-Maubourg. That general was passing the bridges with his cavalry; he perceived the danger, retraced his steps, and the enemy was again stopped by a most sanguinary charge. Night came on before Wittgenstein's forty thousand men had made any impression on the six thousand of the Duke of Belluno. That marshal remained in possession of the heights of Studzianka, and still preserved the bridges from the attacks of the Russian infantry, but he was unable to conceal them from the artillery of their left wing.

Chapter 89
Carnage in the River

During the whole of that day, the situation of the ninth corps was so much more critical, as a weak and narrow bridge was its only means of retreat; in addition to which its avenues were obstructed by the baggage and the stragglers. By degrees, as the action got warmer, the terror of these poor wretches increased their disorder. First of all they were alarmed by the rumours of a serious engagement, then by seeing the wounded returning from it, and last of all by the batteries of the Russian left wing, some bullets from which began to fall among their confused mass.

They had all been already crowding one upon the other, and the immense multitude heaped upon the bank pell-mell with the horses and carriages, there formed a most alarming encumbrance. It was about the middle of the day that the first Russian bullets fell in the midst of this chaos; they were the signal of universal despair.

Then it was, as in all cases of extremity, that dispositions exhibited themselves without disguise, and actions were witnessed, most base, and others most sublime. According to their different characters, some furious and determined, with sword in hand, cleared for themselves a horrible passage. Others, still more cruel, opened a way for their carriages by driving them without mercy over the crowd of unfortunate persons who stood in the way, whom they crushed to death. Their detestable avarice made them sacrifice their companions in misfortune to the preservation of their baggage. Others, seized with a disgusting terror, wept, supplicated, and sunk under the influence of that passion, which completed the exhaustion of their strength. Some were observed, (and these were principally the sick and wounded,) who, renouncing life, went aside and sat down resigned, looking with a fixed eye on the snow which was shortly to be their tomb.

Numbers of those who started first among this crowd of desperadoes missed the bridge, and attempted to scale it by the sides, but the greater part were pushed into the river. There were seen women in the midst of the ice, with their children in their arms, raising them as they felt themselves sinking, and even when completely immerged, their stiffened arms still held them above them.

In the midst of this horrible disorder, the artillery bridge burst and broke down. The column, entangled in this narrow passage, in vain attempted to retrograde. The crowds of men who came behind, unaware of the calamity, and not hearing the cries of those before them, pushed them on, and threw them into the gulf, into which they were precipitated in their turn.

Every one then attempted to pass by the other bridge. A number of large ammunition wagons, heavy carriages, and cannon crowded to it from all parts. Directed by their drivers, and carried along rapidly over a rough and unequal declivity, in the midst of heaps of men, they ground to powder the poor wretches who were unlucky enough to get between them; after which, the greater part, driving violently against each other and getting overturned, killed in their fall those who surrounded them. Whole rows of these desperate creatures being pushed against these obstacles, got entangled among them, were thrown down and crushed to pieces by masses of other unfortunates who succeeded each other uninterruptedly.

Crowds of them were rolling in this way, one over the other, nothing was heard but cries of rage and suffering. In this frightful medley, those who were trod under and stifled, struggled under the feet of their companions, whom they laid hold of with their nails and teeth, and by whom they were repelled without mercy, as if they had been enemies.

Among them were wives and mothers, calling in vain, and in tones of distraction, for their husbands and their children, from whom they had been separated but a moment before, never more to be united: they stretched out their arms and entreated to be allowed to pass in order to rejoin them; but being carried backwards and forwards by the crowd, and overcome by the pressure, they sunk under without being even remarked. Amidst the tremendous noise of a furious hurricane, the firing of cannon, the whistling of the storm and of the bullets, the explosion of shells, vociferations, groans, and the most frightful oaths, this infuriated and disorderly crowd heard not the complaints of the victims whom it was swallowing up.

The more fortunate gained the bridge by scrambling over heaps of wounded, of women and children thrown down and half suffocated, and whom they again trod down in their attempts to reach it. When at last they got to the narrow defile, they fancied they were safe, but the fall of a horse, or the breaking or displacing of a plank again stopped all.

There was also, at the outlet of the bridge, on the other side, a morass, into which many horses and carriages had sunk, a circumstance which again embarrassed and retarded the clearance. Then it was, that in that column of desperadoes, crowded together on that single plank of safety, there arose an internal struggle, in which the weakest and worst situated were thrown into the river by the strongest. The latter, without turning their heads, and carried away by the instinct of self-preservation, pushed on toward the goal with fury, regardless of the imprecations of rage and despair, uttered by their companions or their officers, whom they had thus sacrificed.

But on the other hand, how many noble instances of devotion! and why are time and space denied me to relate them? There were seen soldiers, and even officers, harnessing themselves to sledges, to snatch from that fatal bank their sick or wounded comrades. Farther off, and out of reach of the crowd, were seen soldiers motionless, watching over their dying officers, who had entrusted themselves to their care; the latter in vain conjured them to think of nothing but their own preservation, they refused, and, sooner than abandon their leaders, were contented to wait the approach of slavery or death.

Above the first passage, while the young Lauriston threw himself into the river, in order to execute the orders of his sovereign more promptly, a little boat, carrying a mother and her two children, was overset and sunk under the ice; an artilleryman, who was struggling like the others on the bridge to open a passage for himself, saw the accident; all at once, forgetting himself, he threw himself into the river, and by great exertion, succeeded in saving one of the three victims. It was the youngest of the two children; the poor little thing kept calling for its mother with cries of despair, and the brave artilleryman was heard telling it, "not to cry; that he had not preserved it from the water merely to desert it on the bank; that it should want for nothing; that he would be its father, and its family."

The night of the 28th added to all these calamities. Its darkness was insufficient to conceal its victims from the artillery of the Russians. Amidst the snow, which covered every thing, the course of the river, the thorough black mass of men, horses, carriages, and the noise proceeding from them, were sufficient to enable the enemy's artillerymen, to direct their fire.

About nine o'clock at night there was a still farther increase of desolation, when Victor began his retreat, and his divisions came and opened themselves a horrible breach through these unhappy wretches, whom they had till then been protecting. A rear-guard, however, having been left at Studzianka, the multitude, benumbed with cold, or too anxious to preserve their baggage, refused to avail themselves of the last night for passing to the opposite side. In vain were the carriages set fire to, in order to tear them from them. It was only the appearance of daylight, which brought them all at once, but too late, to the entrance of the bridge, which they again besieged. It was half-past eight in the morning, when Eblé, seeing the Russians approaching, at last set fire to it.

The disaster had reached its utmost bounds. A multitude of carriages, three cannon, several thousand men and women, and some children, were abandoned on the hostile bank. They were seen wandering in desolate troops on the borders of the river. Some threw themselves into it in order to swim across; others ventured themselves on the pieces of ice which were floating along: some there were also who threw themselves headlong into the flames of the burning bridge, which sunk under them; burnt and frozen at one and the same time, they perished under two opposite punishments. Shortly after, the bodies of all sorts were perceived collecting together and the ice against the trestles of the bridge. The rest awaited the Russians. Wittgenstein did not show himself upon the heights until an hour after Eblé's departure, and, without having gained a victory, reaped all the fruits of one.

Chapter 90
Brilowa

While this catastrophe was accomplishing, the remains of the grand army on the opposite bank formed nothing but a shapeless mass, which unravelled itself confusedly, as it took the road to Zembin. The whole of this country is a high and woody plain of great extent, where the waters, flowing in uncertainty between different inclinations of the ground, form one vast morass. Three consecutive bridges, of three hundred fathoms in length, are thrown over it; along these the army passed, with a mingled feeling of astonishment, fear, and delight.

These magnificent bridges, made of resinous fir, began at the distance of a few *wersts* from the passage. Tchaplitz had occupied them for several days. An abatis and heaps of *bavins* of combustible wood, already dry, were laid at their entrance, as if to remind him of the use he had to make of them. It would not have required more than the fire from one of the Cossacks' pipes to set these bridges on fire. In that case all our efforts and the passage of the Berezina would have been entirely useless. Caught between the morass and the river, in a narrow space, without provisions, without shelter, in the midst of a tremendous hurricane, the grand army and its Emperor must have been compelled to surrender without striking a blow.

In this desperate situation, in which all France seemed destined to be taken prisoner in Russia, where every thing was against us and in favour of the Russians, the latter did nothing but by halves. Kutusoff did not reach the Dnieper, at Kopis, until the very day that Napoleon approached the Berezina. Wittgenstein allowed himself to be kept in check during the time that the former required for his passage. Tchitchakof was defeated; and of eighty thousand men, Napoleon succeeded in saving sixty thousand.

He remained till the last moment on these melancholy banks, near the ruins of Brilowa, unsheltered, and at the head of his guards, one-third of whom were destroyed by the storm. During the day they stood to arms, and were drawn up in order of battle; at night, they bivouacked in a square round their leader; there the old grenadiers incessantly kept feeding their fires. They sat upon their knapsacks, with their elbows planted on their knees, and their hands supporting their head; slumbering in this manner doubled upon themselves, in order that one limb might warm the other, and that they should feel less the emptiness of their stomachs.

During these three days and three nights, spent in the midst of them, Napoleon, with his looks and his thoughts wandering on three sides at once, supported the second corps by his orders and his presence, protected the ninth corps and the passage with his artillery, and united his efforts with those of Eblé in saving as many fragments as possible from the wreck. He at last directed the remains to Zembin, where Prince Eugene had preceded him.

It was remarked that he still gave orders to his marshals, who had no soldiers to command, to take up positions on that road, as if they had still armies at their beck. One of them made the observation to him with some degree of asperity, and was beginning an enumeration of his losses; but Napoleon, determined to reject all reports, lest they should degenerate into complaints, warmly interrupted him with these words: "why then do you wish to deprive me of my tranquillity?" and as the other was persisting, he shut his mouth at once, by repeating, in a reproachful manner, "I ask you, sir, why do you wish to deprive me of my tranquillity?" An expression, which in his adversity, explained the attitude which he imposed upon himself, and that which he exacted of others.

Around him during these mortal days, every bivouac was marked by a heap of dead bodies. There were collected men of all classes, of all ranks, of all ages; ministers, generals, administrators. Among them was remarked an elderly nobleman of the times long passed, when light and brilliant graces held sovereign sway. This general officer of sixty was seen sitting on the snow-covered trunk of a tree, occupying himself with unruffled gaiety every morning with the details of his toilette; in the midst of the hurricane, he had his hair elegantly dressed, and powdered with the greatest care, amusing himself in this manner with all the calamities, and with the fury of the combined elements which assailed him.

Near him were officers of the scientific corps still finding subjects of discussion. Imbued with the spirit of an age, which a few discoveries have encouraged to find explanations for every thing, the latter, amidst the acute sufferings which were inflicted upon them by the north wind, were endeavouring to ascertain the cause of its constant direction. According to them, since his departure for the Antarctic pole, the sun, by warming the southern hemisphere, converted all its emanations into vapour, elevated them, and left on the surface of that zone a vacuum, into which the vapours of our hemisphere, which were lower, on account of being less rarefied, rushed with violence. From one to another, and from a similar cause, the Russian pole, completely surcharged with vapours which it had emanated, received, and cooled since the last spring, greedily followed that direction. It discharged itself from it by an impetuous and icy current, which swept the Russian territory quite bare, and stiffened or destroyed every thing which it encountered in its passage.

Several others of these officers remarked with curious attention the regular hexagonal crystallization of each of the flakes of snow which covered their garments.

The phenomenon of *parhelias*, or simultaneous appearances of several images of the sun, reflected to their eyes by means of icicles suspended in the atmosphere, was also the subject of their observations, and occurred several times to divert them from their sufferings.

CHAPTER 91

Napoleon Leaves the Army

On the 29th the Emperor quitted the banks of the Berezina, pushing on before him the crowd of disbanded soldiers, and marching with the ninth corps, which was already disorganized. The day before, the second and the ninth corps, and Dombrowski's division presented a total of fourteen thousand men; and now, with the exception of about six thousand, the rest had no longer any form of division, brigade, or regiment.

Night, hunger, cold, the fall of a number of officers, the loss of the baggage on the other side of the river, the example of so many runaways, and the much more forbidding one of the wounded, who had been abandoned on both sides of the river, and were left rolling in despair on the snow, which was covered with their blood—every thing; in short, had contributed to discourage them; they were confounded in the mass of disbanded men who had come from Moscow.

The whole still formed sixty thousand men, but without the least order or unity. All marched pell-mell, cavalry, infantry, artillery, French and Germans; there was no longer either wing or centre. The artillery and carriages drove on through this disorderly crowd, with no other instructions than to proceed as quickly as possible.

On this narrow and hilly causeway, many were crushed to death in crowding together through the defiles, after which there was a general dispersion to every point where either shelter or provisions were likely to be found. In this manner did Napoleon reach Kamen, where he slept, along with the prisoners made on the preceding day, who were put into a fold like sheep. These poor wretches, after devouring even the dead bodies of their fellows, almost all perished of cold and hunger.

On the 30th he reached Pleszezenitzy. Thither the Duke of Reggio, after being wounded, had retired the day before, with about forty officers and soldiers. He fancied himself in safety, when all at once the

Russian partisan, Landskoy, with one hundred and fifty hussars, four hundred Cossacks, and two cannon, penetrated, into the village, and filled all the streets of it.

Oudinôt's feeble escort was dispersed. The marshal saw himself reduced to defend himself with only seventeen others, in a wooden house, but he did so with such audacity and success, that the enemy was astonished, quitted the village, and took position on a height, from which he attacked it with his cannon. The relentless destiny of this brave marshal so ordered it, that in this skirmish he was again wounded by a splinter of wood.

Two Westphalian battalions, which preceded the Emperor, at last made their appearance and disengaged him, but not till late, and not until these Germans and the marshal's escort (who at first did not recognize each other as friends) had taken a long and anxious survey of each other.

On the 3rd of December, Napoleon arrived in the morning at Malodeczno, which was the last point where Tchitchakof was likely to have got the start of him. Some provisions were found there, the forage was abundant, the day beautiful, the sun shining, and the cold bearable. There also the couriers, who had been so long in arrears arrived all at once. The Poles were immediately directed forward to Warsaw through Olita, and the dismounted cavalry by Merecz to the Niemen; the rest of the army was to follow the high road, which they had again regained.

Up to that time, Napoleon seemed to have entertained no idea of quitting his army. But about the middle of that day, he suddenly informed Daru and Duroc of his determination to set off immediately for Paris.

Daru did not see the necessity of it. He objected, "that the communication with France was again opened, and the most dangerous crisis passed; that at every retrograde step he would now be meeting the reinforcements sent him from Paris and from Germany." The Emperor's reply was, "that he no longer felt himself sufficiently strong to leave Prussia between him and France. What necessity was there for his remaining at the head of a routed army? Murat and Eugene would be sufficient to direct it, and Ney to cover its retreat.

"That his return to France was become indispensable, in order to secure her tranquillity, and to summon her to arms; to take measures there for keeping the Germans steady in their fidelity to him; and finally, to return with new and sufficient forces to the assistance of his grand army.

"But, in order to attain that object, it was necessary that he should travel alone over four hundred leagues of the territories of his allies; and to do so without danger, that his resolution should be there unforeseen, his passage unknown, and the rumour of his disastrous retreat still uncertain; that he should precede the news of it, and anticipate the effect which it might produce on them, and all the defections to which it might give rise. He had, therefore, no time to lose, and the moment of his departure was now arrived."

He only hesitated in the choice of the leader whom he should leave in command of the army; he wavered between Murat and Eugene. He liked the prudence and devotedness of the latter; but Murat had greater celebrity, which would give him more weight. Eugene would remain with that monarch; his youth and his inferior rank would be a security for his obedience, and his character for his zeal. He would set an example of it to the other marshals.

Finally, Berthier, the channel, to which they had been so long accustomed, of all the imperial orders and rewards, would remain with them; there would consequently be no change in the form or the organization of the army; and this arrangement, at the same time that it would be a proof of the certainty of his speedy return, would serve both to keep the most impatient of his own officers in their duty, and the most ardent of his enemies in a salutary dread.

Such were the motives assigned by Napoleon. Caulaincourt immediately received orders to make secret preparations for their departure. The rendezvous was fixed at Smorgoni, and the time, the night of the 5th of December.

Although Daru was not to accompany Napoleon, who left him the heavy charge of the administration of the army, he listened in silence, having nothing to urge in reply to motives of such weight; but it was quite otherwise with Berthier. This enfeebled old man, who had for sixteen years never quitted the side of Napoleon, revolted at the idea of this separation.

The private scene which took place was most violent. The Emperor was indignant at his resistance. In his rage he reproached him with all the favours with which he had loaded him; the army, he told him, stood in need of the reputation which he had made for him, and which was only a reflection of his own; but to cut the matter short, he allowed him four-and-twenty hours to decide; and if he then persisted in his disobedience, he might depart for his estates, where he should order him to remain, forbidding him ever again to enter Paris or his presence. Next day, the 4th of December, Berthier, excusing himself for his previous refusal by his advanced age and impaired health, resigned himself sorrowfully to his sovereign's pleasure.

Chapter 92
The Weather Worsens

But at the very moment that Napoleon determined on his departure, the winter became terrible, as if the Russian atmosphere, seeing him about to escape from it, had redoubled its severity in order to overwhelm him and destroy us. On the 4th of December, when we reached Bienitza, the thermometer was at 26 degrees.

The Emperor had left Count Lobau and several hundred men of his old guard at Malodeczno, at which place the road to Zembin rejoins the high-road from Minsk to Wilna. It was necessary to guard this point until the arrival of Victor, who in his turn would defend it until that of Ney.

For it was still to this marshal, and to the second corps commanded by Maison, that the rear-guard was entrusted. On the night of the 29th of November, when Napoleon quitted the banks of the Berezina, Ney, and the second and third corps, now reduced to three thousand soldiers, passed the long bridges leading to Zembin, leaving at their entrance Maison, and a few hundred men to defend and to burn them.

Tchitchakof made a late but warm attack, and not only with musketry, but with the bayonet: but he was repulsed. Maison at the same time caused these long bridges to be loaded with the bavins, of which Tchaplitz, some days before, had neglected to make use. When every thing was ready, the enemy completely sickened of fighting, and night and the bivouacs well advanced, he rapidly passed the defile, and set fire to them. In a few minutes these long causeways were burnt to ashes, and fell into the morasses, which the frost had not yet rendered passable.

These quagmires stopped the enemy and compelled him to make a detour. During the following day, therefore, the march of Ney and of Maison was unmolested. But on the day after, the 1st of December, as they came in sight of Pleszezenitzy, lo and behold! the whole of the

Russian cavalry were seen rushing forward impetuously, and pushing Doumerc and his cuirassiers on their right. In an instant they were attacked and overwhelmed on all sides.

At the same time, Maison saw that the village through which he had to retreat, was entirely filled with stragglers. He sent to warn them to flee directly; but these unfortunate and famished wretches, not seeing the enemy, refused to leave their meals which they had just begun; Maison was driven back upon them into the village. Then only, at the sight of the enemy, and the noise of the shells, the whole of them started up at once, rushed out, and crowded and encumbered every part of the principal street.

Maison and his troop found themselves all at once in a manner lost in the midst of this terrified crowd, which pressed upon them, almost stifled them, and deprived them of the use of their arms. This general had no other remedy than to desire his men to remain close together and immoveable, and wait till the crowd had dispersed. The enemy's cavalry then came up with this mass, and got entangled with it, but it could only penetrate slowly and by cutting down. The crowd having at last dispersed, discovered to the Russians, Maison and his soldiers waiting for them with a determined countenance. But in its flight, the crowd had drawn along with it a portion of our combatants. Maison, in an open plain, and with seven or eight hundred men against thousands of enemies, lost all hope of safety; he was already seeking only to gain a wood not far off, in order to sell their lives more dearly, when he saw coming out of it eighteen hundred Poles, a troop quite fresh, which Ney had met with and brought to his assistance. This reinforcement stopped the enemy, and secured the retreat as far as Malodeczno.

On the 4th of December, about four o'clock in the afternoon, Ney and Maison got within sight of that village, which Napoleon had quitted in the morning. Tchaplitz followed them close. Ney had now only six hundred men remaining with him. The weakness of this rear-guard, the approach of night, and the prospect of a place of shelter, excited the ardour of the Russian general; he made a warm attack. Ney and Maison, perfectly certain that they would die of cold on the high-road, if they allowed themselves to be driven beyond that cantonment, preferred perishing in defending it.

They halted at its entrance, and as their artillery horses were dying, they gave up all idea of saving their cannon; determined however that it should do its duty for the last time in crushing the enemy, they formed every piece they possessed into a battery, and made a tremendous fire. Tchaplitz's attacking column was entirely broken by it, and halted. But that general, availing himself of his superior forces, diverted a part of them to another entrance, and his first troops had already crossed the enclosures of Malodeczno, when all at once, they there encountered a fresh enemy.

As good luck would have it, Victor, with about four thousand men, the remains of the ninth corps, still occupied this village. The fury on both sides was extreme; the first houses were several times taken and retaken. The combat on both sides was much less for glory than to keep or acquire a refuge against the destructive cold. It was not until half-past eleven at night that the Russians gave up the contest, and went from it half frozen, to seek for another in the surrounding villages.

The following day, December 5th, Ney and Maison had expected that the Duke of Belluno would replace them at the rear-guard; but they found that that marshal had retired, according to his instructions, and that they were left alone in Malodeczno with only sixty men. All the rest had fled; the rigour of the climate had completely knocked up their soldiers, whom the Russians to the very last moment were unable to conquer; their arms fell from their hands, and they themselves fell at a few paces distance from their arms.

Maison, who united great vigour of mind with a very strong constitution, was not intimidated; he continued his retreat to Bienitza, rallying at every step men who were incessantly escaping from him, but still continuing to give proofs of the existence of a rear-guard, with a few foot-soldiers. This was all that was required; for the Russians themselves were frozen, and obliged to disperse before night into the neighbouring habitations, which they durst not quit until it was completely daylight. They then recommenced their pursuit of us, but without making any attack; for with the exception of some numb efforts, the violence of the temperature was such as not to allow either party to halt with the view of making an attack, or of defending themselves.

In the mean time, Ney, being surprised at Victor's departure, went after him, overtook him, and tried to prevail upon him to halt; but the Duke of Belluno, having orders to retreat, refused. Ney then wanted him to give him up his soldiers, offering to take the command of them; but Victor would neither consent to do that, nor to take the rear-guard without express orders. In the altercation which arose in consequence between these two, the Prince of the Moskwa gave way to his passion in a most violent manner, without producing any effect on the coolness of Victor. At last an order of the Emperor arrived; Victor was instructed to support the retreat, and Ney was summoned to Smorgoni.

CHAPTER 93

Murat Takes Command

Napoleon had just arrived there amidst a crowd of dying men, devoured with chagrin, but not allowing the least emotion to exhibit itself in his countenance, at the sight of these unhappy men's sufferings, who, on the other hand, had allowed no murmurs to escape them in his presence. It is true that a seditious movement was impossible; it would have required an additional effort, as the strength of every man was fully occupied in struggling with hunger, cold, and fatigue; it would have required union, agreement, and mutual understanding, while famine and so many evils separated and isolated them, by concentrating every man's feelings completely in himself. Far from exhausting themselves in provocations or complaints, they marched along silently, exerting all their efforts against a hostile atmosphere, and diverted from every other idea by a state of continual action and suffering. Their physical wants absorbed their whole moral strength; they thus lived mechanically in their sensations, continuing in their duty from recollection, from the impressions which they had received in better times, and in no slight degree from that sense of honour and love of glory which had been inspired by twenty years of victory, and the warmth of which still survived and struggled within them.

The authority of the commanders also remained complete and respected, because it had always been eminently paternal, and because the dangers, the triumphs, and the calamities had always been shared in common. It was an unhappy family, the head of which was perhaps the most to be pitied. The Emperor and the grand army, therefore, preserved towards each other a melancholy and noble silence; they were both too proud to utter complaints, and too experienced not to feel the futility of them.

Meantime, however, Napoleon had entered precipitately into his last imperial head-quarters; he there finished his final instructions, as well as the 29th and last bulletin of his expiring army. Precautions were taken in his inner apartment, that nothing of what was about to take place there should transpire until the following day.

But the presentiment of a last misfortune seized his officers; all of them would have wished to follow him. Their hearts yearned after France, to be once more in the bosom of their families, and to flee from this horrible climate; but not one of them ventured to express a wish of the kind; duty and honour restrained them.

While they affected a tranquillity which they were far from tasting, the night and the moment which the Emperor had fixed for declaring his resolution to the commanders of the army arrived. All the marshals were summoned. As they successively entered, he took each of them aside in private, and first of all gained their approbation of his plan, of some by his arguments, and of others by confidential effusions.

Thus it was, that on perceiving Davoust, he ran forward to meet him, and asked him why it was that he never saw him, and if he had entirely deserted him? And upon Davoust's reply that he fancied he had incurred his displeasure, the Emperor explained himself mildly, received his answers favourably, confided to him the road he meant to travel, and took his advice, respecting its details.

His manner was kind and flattering to them all; afterwards, having assembled them at his table, he complimented them for their noble actions during the campaign. As to himself, the only confession he made of his temerity was couched in these words: "If I had been born to the throne, if I had been a Bourbon, it would have been easy for me not to have committed any faults."

When their entertainment was over, he made Prince Eugene read to them his twenty-ninth bulletin; after which, declaring aloud what he had already confided to each of them, he told them, "that he was about to depart that very night with Duroc, Caulaincourt, and Lobau, for Paris. That his presence there was indispensable for France as well as for the remains of his unfortunate army. It was there only he could take measures for keeping the Austrians and Prussians in check. These nations would certainly pause before they declared war against him, when they saw him at the head of the French nation, and a fresh army of twelve hundred thousand men."

He added, that "he had ordered Ney to proceed to Wilna, there to reorganise the army. That Rapp would second him, and afterwards go to Dantzic, Lauriston to Warsaw, and Narbonne to Berlin; that his household would remain with the army; but that it would be necessary to strike a blow at Wilna, and stop the enemy there. There they would find Loison, De Wrede, reinforcements, provisions, and ammunition of all sorts; afterwards they would go into winter-quarters on the other side of the Niemen; that he hoped the Russians would not pass the Vistula before his return."

In conclusion, "I leave the King of Naples to command the army. I hope that you will yield him the same obedience as you would to myself, and that the greatest harmony will prevail among you."

As it was now ten o'clock at night, he then rose, squeezed their hands affectionately, embraced them, and departed.

Chapter 94
Every Man for Himself

Comrades! I must confess that my spirit, discouraged, refused to penetrate farther into the recollection of so many horrors. Having arrived at the departure of Napoleon, I had flattered myself that my task was completed. I had announced myself as the historian of that great epoch, when we were precipitated from the highest summit of glory to the deepest abyss of misfortune; but now that nothing remains for me to retrace but the most frightful miseries, why should we not spare ourselves, you the pain of reading them, and myself that of tasking a memory which has now only to rake up embers, nothing but disasters to reckon, and which can no longer write but upon tombs?

But as it was our fate to push bad as well as good fortune to the utmost verge of improbability, I will endeavour to keep the promise I have made you to the conclusion. Moreover, when the history of great men relates even their last moments, how can I conceal the last sighs of the grand army when it was expiring? Every thing connected with it appertains to renown, its dying groans as well as its cries of victory. Every thing in it was grand; it will be our lot to astonish future ages with our glory and our sorrow. Melancholy consolation! but the only one that remains to us; for doubt it not, comrades, the noise of so great a fall will echo in that futurity, in which great misfortunes immortalize as much as great glory.

Napoleon passed through the crowd of his officers, who were drawn up in an avenue as he passed, bidding them adieu merely by forced and melancholy smiles; their good wishes, equally silent, and expressed only by respectful gestures, he carried with him. He and Caulaincourt shut themselves up in a carriage; his Mameluke, and Wonsowitch, captain of his guard, occupied the box; Duroc and Lobau followed in a sledge.

His escort at first consisted only of Poles; afterwards of the Neapolitans of the royal guard. This corps consisted of between six and seven hundred men, when it left Wilna to meet the Emperor; it perished entirely in that short passage; the winter was its only adversary. That very night the Russians surprised and afterwards abandoned Youpranoui, (or, as others say, Osmiana,) a town through which the escort had to pass. Napoleon was within an hour of falling into that affray.

He met the Duke of Bassano at Miedniki. His first words to him were, "that he had no longer an army; that for several days past he had been marching in the midst of a troop of disbanded men wandering to and fro in search of subsistence; that they might still be rallied by giving them bread, shoes, clothing, and arms; but that the Duke's military administration had anticipated nothing, and his orders had not been executed." But upon Maret replying, by showing him a statement of the immense magazines collected at Wilna, he exclaimed, "that he gave him fresh life! that he would give him an order to transmit to Murat and Berthier to halt for eight days in that capital, there to rally the army, and infuse into it sufficient heart and strength to continue the retreat less deplorably."

The subsequent part of Napoleon's journey was effected without molestation. He went round Wilna by its suburbs, crossed Wilkowiski, where he exchanged his carriage for a sledge, stopped during the 10th at Warsaw, to ask the Poles for a levy of ten thousand Cossacks, to grant them some subsidies, and to promise them he would speedily return at the head of three hundred thousand men. From thence he rapidly crossed Silesia, visited Dresden, and its monarch, passed through Hanau, Mentz, and finally got to Paris, where he suddenly made his appearance on the 19th of December, two days after the appearance of his twenty-ninth bulletin.

From Malo-Yaroslawetz to Smorgoni, this master of Europe had been no more than the general of a dying and disbanded army. From Smorgoni to the Rhine, he was an unknown fugitive, travelling through a hostile country; beyond the Rhine he again found himself the master and the conqueror of Europe. A last breeze of the wind of prosperity once more swelled his sails.

Meanwhile, his generals, whom he left at Smorgoni, approved of his departure, and, far from being discouraged, placed all their hopes in it. The army had now only to flee, the road was open, and the Russian frontier at a very short distance. They were getting within reach of a reinforcement of eighteen thousand men, all fresh troops, of a great city, and immense magazines. Murat and Berthier, left to themselves, fancied themselves able to regulate the flight. But in the midst of the extreme disorder, it required a colossus for a rallying point, and he had just disappeared. In the great chasm which he left, Murat was scarcely perceptible.

It was then too clearly seen that a great man is not replaced, either because the pride of his followers can no longer stoop to obey another, or that having always thought of, foreseen, and ordered every thing himself, he had only formed good instruments, skilful lieutenants, but no commanders.

The very first night, a general refused to obey. The marshal who commanded the rear-guard was almost the only one who returned to the royal head-quarters. Three thousand men of the old and young guard were still there. This was the whole of the grand army, and of that gigantic body there remained nothing but the head. But at the news of Napoleon's departure, these veterans, spoiled by the habit of being commanded only by the conqueror of Europe, being no longer supported by the honour of serving him, and scorning to act as guards to another, gave way in their turn, and voluntarily fell into disorder.

Most of the colonels of the army, who had hitherto been such subjects of admiration, and had marched on, with only four or five officers or soldiers around their eagle, preserving their place of battle, now followed no orders but their own; each of them fancied himself entrusted with his own safety, and looked only to himself for it. Men there were who marched two hundred leagues without even looking round. It was an almost general *sauve-qui-peut*.

The Emperor's disappearance and Murat's incapacity were not, however, the only causes of this dispersion; the principal certainly was the severity of the winter, which at that moment became extreme. It aggravated every thing, and seemed to have planted itself completely between Wilna and the army.

Till we arrived at Malodeczno, and up to the 4th of December, the day when it set in upon us with such violence, the march, although painful, had been marked by a smaller number of deaths than before we reached the Berezina. This respite was partly owing to the vigorous efforts of Ney and Maison, which had kept the enemy in check, to the then milder temperature, to the supplies which were obtained from a less ravaged country, and, finally, to the circumstance that they were the strongest men who had escaped from the passage of the Berezina.

The partial organization which had been introduced into the disorder was kept up. The mass of runaways kept on their way, divided into a number of petty associations of eight or ten men. Many of these bands still possessed a horse, which carried their provisions, and was himself finally destined to be converted to that purpose. A covering of rags, some utensils, a knapsack, and a stick, formed the accoutrements and the armour of these poor fellows. They no longer possessed either the arms or the uniform of a soldier, nor the desire of combating any other enemies than hunger and cold; but they still retained perseverance, firmness, the habit of danger and suffering, and a spirit always ready, pliant, and quick in making the most of their situation. Finally, among the soldiers still under arms, the dread of a nickname, by which they themselves ridiculed their comrades who had fallen into disorder, retained some influence.

But after leaving Malodeczno, and the departure of Napoleon, when winter with all its force, and doubled in severity, attacked each of us, there was a complete dissolution of all those associations against misfortune. It was no longer any thing but a multitude of isolated and individual struggles. The best no longer respected themselves; nothing stopped them; no speaking looks detained them; misfortune was hopeless of assistance, and even of regret; discouragement had no longer judges to condemn, or witnesses to prove it; all were its victims.

Henceforward there was no longer fraternity in arms, there was an end to all society, to all ties; the excess of evils had brutified them. Hunger, devouring hunger, had reduced these unfortunate men to the brutal instinct of self-preservation, all which constitutes the understanding of the most ferocious animals, and which is ready to sacrifice every thing to itself; a rough and barbarous nature seemed to have communicated to them all its fury. Like savages, the strongest despoiled the weakest; they rushed round the dying, and frequently waited not for their last breath. When a horse fell, you might have fancied you saw a famished pack of hounds; they surrounded him, they tore him to pieces, for which they quarrelled among themselves like ravenous dogs.

The greater number, however, preserved sufficient moral strength to consult their own safety without injuring others; but this was the last effort of their virtue. If either leader or comrade fell by their side, or under the wheels of the cannon, in vain did they call for assistance, in vain did they invoke the names of a common country, religion, and cause; they could not even obtain a passing look. The cold inflexibility of the climate had completely passed into their hearts; its rigour had contracted their feelings equally with their countenances. With the exception of a few of the commanders, all were absorbed by their sufferings, and terror left no room for compassion.

Thus it was that the same egotism with which excessive prosperity has been reproached, was produced by the excess of misfortune, but much more excusable in the latter; the first being voluntary, and the last compulsive; the first a crime of the heart, and the other an impulse of instinct entirely physical; and certainly it was hazarding one's life to stop for an instant. In this universal shipwreck, the stretching forth one's hand to a dying leader or comrade was a wonderful act of generosity. The least movement of humanity became a sublime action.

There were a few, however, who stood firm against both heaven and earth; these protected and assisted the weakest; but these were indeed rare.

Chapter 95

The Last Days of the Grand Army

On the 6th of December, the very day after Napoleon's departure, the sky exhibited a still more dreadful appearance. You might see icy particles floating in the air; the birds fell from it quite stiff and frozen. The atmosphere was motionless and silent; it seemed as if every thing which possessed life and movement in nature, the wind itself, had been seized, chained, and as it were frozen by an universal death. Not the least word or murmur was then heard: nothing but the gloomy silence of despair and the tears which proclaimed it.

We flitted along in this empire of death like unhappy spirits. The dull and monotonous sound of our steps, the cracking of the snow, and the feeble groans of the dying, were the only interruptions to this vast and doleful silence. Anger and imprecations there were none, nor any thing which indicated a remnant of heat; scarcely did strength enough remain to utter a prayer; most of them even fell without complaining, either from weakness or resignation, or because people only complain when they look for kindness, and fancy they are pitied.

Such of our soldiers as had hitherto been the most persevering, here lost heart entirely. Sometimes the snow opened under their feet, but more frequently its glassy surface affording them no support, they slipped at every step, and marched from one fall to another. It seemed as if this hostile soil refused to carry them, that it escaped under their efforts, that it led them into snares, as if to embarrass and slacken their march, and deliver them to the Russians who were in pursuit of them, or to their terrible climate.

And really, whenever they halted for a moment from exhaustion, the winter, laying his heavy and icy hand upon them, was ready to seize upon his prey. In vain did these poor unfortunates, feeling themselves benumbed, raise themselves, and already deprived of the power of speech and plunged into a stupor, proceed a few steps like automatons; their blood freezing in their veins, like water in the current of rivulets, congealed their heart, and then flew back to their head; these dying men then staggered as if they had been intoxicated. From their eyes, which were reddened and inflamed by the continual aspect of the snow, by the want of sleep, and the smoke of bivouacs, there flowed real tears of blood; their bosom heaved heavy sighs; they looked at heaven, at us, and at the earth, with an eye dismayed, fixed and wild; it expressed their farewell, and perhaps their reproaches to the barbarous nature which tortured them. They were not long before they fell upon their knees, and then upon their hands; their heads still wavered for a few minutes alternately to the right and left, and from their open mouth some agonizing sounds escaped; at last it fell in its turn upon the snow, which it reddened immediately with livid blood; and their sufferings were at an end.

Their comrades passed by them without moving a step out of their way, for fear of prolonging their journey, or even turning their head, for their beards and their hair were stiffened with the ice, and every moment was a pain. They did not even pity them; for, in short, what had they lost by dying? what had they left behind them? They suffered so much; they were still so far from France; so much divested of feelings of country by the surrounding aspect, and by misery; that every dear illusion was broken, and hope almost destroyed. The greater number, therefore, were become careless of dying, from necessity, from the habit of seeing it, and from fashion, sometimes even treating it contemptuously; but more frequently, on seeing these unfortunates stretched out, and immediately stiffened, contenting themselves with the thought that they had no more wishes, that they were at rest, that their sufferings were terminated! And, in fact, death, in a situation quiet, certain, and uniform, may be always a strange event, a frightful contrast, a terrible revolution; but in this tumult and violent and continual movement of a life of constant action, danger, and suffering, it appeared nothing more than a transition, a slight change, an additional removal, and which excited little alarm.

Such, were the last *days* of the grand army. Its last *nights* were still more frightful; those whom they surprised marching together, far from every habitation, halted on the borders of the woods; there they lighted their fires, before which they remained the whole night, erect and motionless like spectres. They seemed as if they could never have enough of the heat; they kept so close to it as to burn their clothes, as well as the frozen parts of their body, which the fire decomposed. The most dreadful pain then compelled them to stretch themselves, and the next day they attempted in vain to rise.

In the mean time, such as the winter had almost wholly spared, and who still retained some portion of courage, prepared their melancholy meal. It consisted, ever since they had left Smolensk, of some slices of horse-flesh broiled, and some rye-meal diluted into a *bouillie* with snow water, or kneaded into muffins, which they seasoned, for want of salt, with the powder of their cartridges.

The sight of these fires was constantly attracting fresh spectres, who were driven back by the first comers. These poor wretches wandered about from one bivouac to another, until they were struck by the frost and despair together, and gave themselves up for lost. They then laid themselves down upon the snow, behind their more fortunate comrades, and there expired. Many of them, devoid of the means and the strength necessary to cut down the lofty fir trees, made vain attempts to set fire to them at the trunk; but death speedily surprised them around these trees in every sort of attitude.

Under the vast pent-houses which are erected by the sides of the high road in some parts of the way, scenes of still greater horror were witnessed. Officers and soldiers all rushed precipitately into them, and crowded together in heaps. There, like so many cattle, they squeezed against each other round the fires, and as the living could not remove the dead from the circle, they laid themselves down upon them, there to expire in their turn, and serve as a bed of death to some fresh victims. In a short time additional crowds of stragglers presented themselves, and being unable to penetrate into these asylums of suffering, they completely besieged them.

It frequently happened that they demolished their walls, which were formed of dry wood, in order to feed their fires; at other times, repulsed and disheartened, they were contented to use them as shelters to their bivouacs, the flames of which very soon communicated to these habitations, and the soldiers whom they contained, already half dead with the cold, were completely killed by the fire. Such of us as these places of shelter preserved, found next day our comrades lying frozen and in heaps around their extinguished fires. To escape from these catacombs, a horrible effort was required to enable them to climb over the heaps of these poor wretches, many of whom were still breathing.

At Youpranoui, the same village where the Emperor only missed by an hour being taken by the Russian partisan Seslawin, the soldiers burnt the houses completely as they stood, merely to warm themselves for a few minutes. The light of these fires attracted some of these miserable wretches, whom the excessive severity of the cold and their sufferings had rendered delirious; they ran to them like madmen, and gnashing their teeth and laughing like demons, they threw themselves into these furnaces, where they perished in the most horrible convulsions. Their famished companions regarded them undismayed; there were even some who drew out these bodies, disfigured and broiled by the flames, and it is but too true, that they ventured to pollute their mouths with this loathsome food!

This was the same army which had been formed from the most civilized nation in Europe; that army, formerly so brilliant, which was victorious over men to its last moment, and whose name still reigned in so many conquered capitals. Its strongest and bravest warriors, who had recently been proudly traversing so many scenes of their victories, had lost their noble countenance; covered with rags, their feet naked and torn, supporting themselves on branches of fir tree, they dragged themselves along; all the strength and perseverance which they had hitherto put forth in order to conquer, they now made use of to flee.

Then it was, that, like superstitious nations, we also had our prognostications, and heard talk of prophecies. Some pretended that a comet had enlightened our passage across the Berezina with its ill-omened fire; it is true that they added, "that doubtless these stars did not foretell the great events of this world, but that they might certainly contribute to modify them; at least, if we admitted their material influence upon our globe, and all the consequences which that influence may exercise upon the human mind, so far as it is dependant on the matter which it animates."

There were others who quoted ancient predictions, which, they said, "had announced for that period, an invasion of the Tartars as far as the banks of the Seine. And, behold! they were already at liberty to pass over the overthrown French army, and in a fair way to accomplish that prediction."

Some again there were, who were reminding each other of the awful and destructive storm which had signalized our entrance on the Russian territory. "Then it was heaven itself that spoke! Behold the calamity which it predicted! Nature had made an effort to prevent this catastrophe! Why had we been obstinately deaf to her voice?" So much did this simultaneous fall of four hundred thousand men (an event which was not in fact more extraordinary than the host of epidemical disorders and of revolutions which are constantly ravaging the globe) appear to them an extraordinary and unique event, which must have occupied all the powers of heaven and earth; so much is our understanding led to bring home every thing to itself; as if Providence, in compassion to our weakness, and from the fear of its annihilating itself at the prospect of eternity, had so ordered it, that every man, a mere point in space, should act and feel as if he himself was the centre of immensity.

Chapter 96
Wilna!

The army was in this last state of physical and moral distress, when its first fugitives reached Wilna. Wilna! their magazine, their depot, the first rich and inhabited city which they had met with since their entrance into Russia. Its name alone, and its proximity, still supported the courage of a few.

On the 9th of December, the greatest part of these poor soldiers at last arrived within sight of that capital. Instantly, some dragging themselves along, others rushing forward, they all precipitated themselves headlong into its suburbs, pushing obstinately before them, and crowding together so fast, that they formed but one mass of men, horses, and chariots, motionless, and deprived of the power of movement.

The clearing away of this crowd by a narrow passage became almost impossible. Those who came behind, guided by a stupid instinct, added to the encumbrance, without the least idea of entering the city by its other entrances, of which there were several. But there was such complete disorganization, that during the whole of that fatal day, not a single staff-officer made his appearance to direct these men to them.

For the space of ten hours, with the cold at 27 and even at 28 degrees, thousands of soldiers who fancied themselves in safety, died either from cold or suffocation, just as had happened at the gates of Smolensk, and at the bridges across the Berezina. Sixty thousand men had crossed that river, and twenty thousand recruits had since joined them; of these eighty thousand, half had already perished, the greater part within the last four days, between Malodeczno and Wilna.

The capital of Lithuania was still ignorant of our disasters, when, all at once, forty thousand famished soldiers filled it with groans and lamentations. At this unexpected sight, its inhabitants became alarmed, and shut their doors. Deplorable then was it to see these troops of wretched wanderers in the streets, some furious and others desperate, threatening or entreating, endeavouring to break open the doors of the houses and the magazines, or dragging themselves to the hospitals. Everywhere they were repulsed; at the magazines, from most unseasonable formalities, as, from the dissolution of the corps and the mixture of the soldiers, all regular distribution had become impossible.

There had been collected there sufficient flour and bread to last for forty days, and butcher's meat for thirty-six days, for one hundred thousand men. Not a single commander ventured to step forward and give orders for distributing these provisions to all that came for them. The administrators who had them in charge were afraid of being made responsible for them; and the others dreaded the excesses to which the famished soldiers would give themselves up, when every thing was at their discretion. These administrators besides were ignorant of our desperate situation, and when there was scarcely time for pillage, had they been so inclined, our unfortunate comrades were left for several hours to die of hunger at the very doors of these immense magazines of provisions, all of which fell into the enemy's hands the following day.

At the barracks and the hospitals they were equally repulsed, but not by the living, for there death held sway supreme. The few who still breathed complained that for a long time they had been without beds, even without straw, and almost deserted. The courts, the passages, and even the apartments were filled with heaps of dead bodies; they were so many charnel houses of infection.

At last, the exertions of several of the commanders, such as Eugene and Davoust, the compassion of the Lithuanians, and the avarice of the Jews, opened some places of refuge. Nothing could be more remarkable than the astonishment which these unfortunate men displayed at finding themselves once more in inhabited houses. How delicious did a loaf of leavened bread appear to them, and how inexpressible the pleasure of eating it seated! and afterwards, with what admiration were they struck at seeing a scanty battalion still under arms, in regular order, and uniformly dressed! They seemed to have returned from the very extremities of the earth; so much had the violence and continuity of their sufferings torn and cast them from all their habits, so deep had been the abyss from which they had escaped!

But scarcely had they begun to taste these sweets, when the cannon of the Russians commenced thundering over their heads and upon the city. These threatening sounds, the shouts of the officers, the drums beating to arms, and the wailings and clamour of an additional multitude of unfortunates, which had just arrived, filled Wilna with fresh confusion. It was the vanguard of Kutusoff and Tchaplitz, commanded by O'Rourke, Landskoy, and Seslawin, which had attacked Loison's division, which was protecting the city, as well as the retreat of a column of dismounted cavalry, on its way to Olita, by way of Novoï-Troky.

At first an attempt was made to resist. De Wrede and his Bavarians had also just rejoined the army by Naroc-Zwiransky and Niamentchin. They were pursued by Wittgenstein, who from Kamen and Vileika hung upon our right flank, at the same time that Kutusoff and Tchitchakof pursued us. De Wrede had not two thousand men left under his command. As to Loison's division and the garrison of Wilna, which had come to meet us as far as Smorgoni, and render us assistance, the cold had reduced them from fifteen thousand men to three thousand in the space of three days.

De Wrede defended Wilna on the side of Rukoni; he was obliged to fall back after a gallant resistance. Loison and his division, on his side, which was nearer to Wilna, kept the enemy in check. They had succeeded in making a Neapolitan division take arms, and even to go out of the city, but the muskets actually slipped from the hands of these "children of the sun" transplanted to a region of ice. In less than an hour they all returned disarmed, and the best part of them maimed.

At the same time, the *générale* was ineffectually beat in the streets; the old guard itself, now reduced to a few platoons, remained dispersed. Every one thought much more of disputing his life with famine and the cold than with the enemy. But when the cry of "Here are the Cossacks" was heard, (which for a long time had been the only signal which the greater number obeyed,) it echoed immediately throughout the whole city, and the rout again began.

De Wrede presented himself unexpectedly before the king of Naples. He said, "the enemy were close at his heels! the Bavarians had been driven back into Wilna, which they could no longer defend." At the same time, the noise of the tumult reached the king's ears. Murat was astonished; fancying himself no longer master of the army, he lost all command of himself. He instantly quitted his palace on foot, and was seen forcing his way through the crowd. He seemed to be afraid of a skirmish, in the midst of a crowd similar to that of the day before. He halted, however, at the last house in the suburbs, from whence he despatched his orders, and where he waited for daylight and the army, leaving Ney in charge of the rest.

Wilna might have been defended for twenty-four hours longer, and many men might have been saved. This fatal city retained nearly twenty thousand, including three hundred officers and seven generals. Most of them had been wounded by the winter more than by the enemy, who had the merit of the triumph. Several others were still in good health, to all appearance at least, but their moral strength was completely exhausted. After courageously battling with so many difficulties, they lost heart when they were near the port, at the prospect of four more days' march. They had at last found themselves once more in a civilized city, and sooner than make up their minds to return to the desert, they placed themselves at the mercy of Fortune; she treated them cruelly.

It is true that the Lithuanians, although we had compromised them so much, and were now abandoning them, received into their houses and succoured several; but the Jews, whom we had protected, repelled the others. They did even more; the sight of so many sufferers excited their cupidity. Had their detestable avarice been contented with speculating upon our miseries, and selling us some feeble succours for their weight in gold, history would scorn to sully her pages with the disgusting detail; but they enticed our unhappy wounded men into their houses, stripped them, and afterwards, on seeing the Russians, threw the naked bodies of these dying victims from the doors and windows of their houses into the streets, and there unmercifully left them to perish of cold; these vile barbarians even made a merit in the eyes of the Russians of torturing them there; such horrible crimes as these must be denounced to the present and to future ages. Now that our hands are become impotent, it is probable that our indignation against these monsters may be their sole punishment in this world; but a day will come, when the assassins will again meet their victims, and there certainly, divine justice will avenge us!

On the 10th of December, Ney, who had again voluntarily taken upon himself the command of the rear-guard, left that city, which was immediately after inundated by the Cossacks of Platof, who massacred all the poor wretches whom the Jews threw in their way. In the midst of this butchery, there suddenly appeared a piquet of thirty French, coming from the bridge of the Vilia, where they had been left and forgotten. At sight of this fresh prey, thousands of Russian horsemen came hurrying up, besetting them with loud cries, and assailing them on all sides.

But the officer commanding this piquet had already drawn up his soldiers in a circle. Without hesitation, he ordered them to fire, and then, making them present bayonets, proceeded at the *pas de charge*. In an instant all fled before him; he remained in possession of the city; but without feeling more surprise about the cowardice of the Cossacks, than he had done at their attack, he took advantage of the moment, turned sharply round, and succeeded in rejoining the rear-guard without any loss.

The latter was engaged with Kutusoff's vanguard, which it was endeavouring to drive back; for another catastrophe, which it vainly attempted to cover, detained it at a short distance from Wilna.

There, as well as at Moscow, Napoleon had given no regular order for retreat; he was anxious that our defeat should have no forerunner, but that it should proclaim itself, and take our allies and their ministers by surprise, and that, taking advantage of their first astonishment, it might be able to pass through those nations before they were prepared to join the Russians and overpower us.

This was the reason why the Lithuanians, foreigners, and every one at Wilna, even to the minister himself, had been deceived. They did not believe our disaster until they saw it; and in that, the almost superstitious belief of Europe in the infallibility of the genius of Napoleon was of use to him against his allies. But the same confidence had buried his own officers in a profound security; at Wilna, as well as at Moscow, not one of them was prepared for a movement of any description.

This city contained a large proportion of the baggage of the army, and of its treasures, its provisions, a crowd of enormous wagons, loaded with the Emperor's equipage, a large quantity of artillery, and a great number of wounded men. Our retreat had come upon them like an unexpected storm, almost like a thunderbolt. Some were terrified and thrown into confusion, while consternation kept others motionless. Orders, men, horses, and carriages, were running about in all directions, crossing and overturning each other.

In the midst of this tumult, several of the commanders pushed forward out of the city, towards Kowno, with every thing they could contrive to carry with them; but at the distance of a league from the latter place this heavy and frightened column had encountered the height and the defile of Ponari.

During our conquering march, this woody hillock had only appeared to our hussars a fortunate accident of the ground, from which they could discover the whole plain of Wilna, and take a survey of their enemies. Besides, its rough but short declination had scarcely been remarked. During a regular retreat it would have presented an excellent position for turning round and stopping the enemy: but in a disorderly flight, where every thing that might be of service became injurious, where in our precipitation and disorder, every thing was turned against ourselves, this hill and its defile became an insurmountable obstacle, a wall of ice, against which all our efforts were powerless. It detained every thing, baggage, treasure, and wounded. The evil was sufficiently great in this long series of disasters to form an epoch.

Here, in fact, it was, that money, honour, and every remains of discipline and strength were completely lost. After fifteen hours of fruitless efforts, when the drivers and the soldiers of the escort saw the King of Naples and the whole column of fugitives passing them by the sides of the hill, when turning their eyes at the noise of the cannon and musketry which was coming nearer them every instant they saw Ney himself retreating with three thousand men (the remains of De Wrede's corps and Loison's division); when at last turning their eyes back to themselves, they saw the hill completely covered with cannon and carriages, broken or overturned, men and horses fallen to the ground, and expiring one upon the other,—then it was, that they gave up all idea of saving any thing, and determined only to anticipate the enemy by plundering themselves.

One of the covered wagons of treasure, which burst open of itself, served as a signal; every one rushed to the others; they were immediately broken, and the most valuable effects taken from them. The soldiers of the rear-guard, who were passing at the time of this disorder, threw away their arms to join in the plunder; they were so eagerly engaged in it as neither to hear nor to pay attention to the whistling of the balls and the howling of the Cossacks in pursuit of them.

It is even said that the Cossacks got mixed among them without being observed. For some minutes, French and Tartars, friends and foes, were confounded in the same greediness. French and Russians, forgetting they were at war, were seen pillaging together the same treasure-wagons. Ten millions of gold and silver then disappeared.

But amidst all these horrors, there were noble acts of devotion. Some there were, who abandoned every thing to save some unfortunate wounded by carrying them on their shoulders; several others, being unable to extricate their half-frozen comrades from this medley, lost their lives in defending them from the attacks of their countrymen, and the blows of their enemies.

On the most exposed part of the hill, an officer of the Emperor, Colonel the Count de Turenne, repulsed the Cossacks, and in defiance of their cries of rage and their fire, he distributed before their eyes the private treasure of Napoleon to the guards whom he found within his reach. These brave men, fighting with one hand and collecting the spoils of their leader with the other, succeeded in saving them. Long afterwards, when they were out of all danger, each man faithfully restored the depot which had been entrusted to him. Not a single piece of money was lost.

Chapter 97

The Rear Guard

This catastrophe at Ponari was the more disgraceful, as it was easy to foresee, and equally easy to prevent it; for the hill could have been turned by its sides. The fragments which we abandoned, however, were at least of some use in arresting the pursuit of the Cossacks. While these were busy in collecting their prey, Ney, at the head of a few hundred French and Bavarians, supported the retreat as far as Evé. As this was his last effort, we must not omit the description of his method of retreat which he had followed ever since he left Wiazma, on the 3rd of November, during thirty-seven days and thirty-seven nights.

Every day, at 5 o'clock in the evening, he took his position, stopped the Russians, allowed his soldiers to eat and take some rest, and resumed his march at 10 o'clock. During the whole of the night, he pushed the mass of the stragglers before him, by dint of cries, of entreaties, and of blows. At daybreak, which was about 7 o'clock, he halted, again took position, and rested under arms and on guard until 10 o'clock; the enemy then made his appearance, and he was compelled to fight until the evening, gaining as much or as little ground in the rear as possible. That depended at first on the general order of march, and at a later period upon circumstances.

For a long time this rear-guard did not consist of more than two thousand, then of one thousand, afterwards about five hundred, and finally of sixty men; and yet Berthier, either designedly or from mere routine, made no change in his instructions. These were always addressed to the commander of a corps of thirty-five thousand men; in them he coolly detailed all the different positions, which were to be taken up and guarded until the next day, by divisions and regiments which no longer existed. And every night, when, in consequence of Ney's urgent warnings, he was obliged to go and awake the King of Naples, and compel him to resume his march, he testified the same astonishment.

In this manner did Ney support the retreat from Wiazma to Evé, and a few *wersts* beyond it. There, according to his usual custom, he had stopped the Russians, and was giving the first hours of the night to rest, when, about ten o'clock, he and De Wrede perceived that they had been left alone. Their soldiers had deserted them, as well as their arms, which they saw shining and piled together close to their abandoned fires.

Fortunately the intensity of the cold, which had just completed the discouragement of our people, had also benumbed their enemies. Ney overtook his column with some difficulty; it was now only a band of fugitives; a few Cossacks chased it before them; without attempting either to take or to kill them; either from compassion, for one gets tired of every thing in time, or that the enormity of our misery had terrified even the Russians themselves, and they believed themselves sufficiently revenged, and many of them behaved generously; or, finally, that they were satiated and overloaded with booty. It might be also, that in the darkness, they did not perceive that they had only to do with unarmed men.

Winter, that terrible ally of the Muscovites, had sold them his assistance dearly. Their disorder pursued our disorder. We often saw prisoners who had escaped several times from their frozen hands and looks. They had at first marched in the middle of their straggling column without being noticed by it. There were some of them, who, taking advantage of a favourable moment, ventured to attack the Russian soldiers when isolated, and strip them of their provisions, their uniforms, and even their arms, with which they covered themselves. Under this disguise, they mingled with their conquerors; and such was the disorganization, the stupid carelessness; and the numbness into which their army had fallen, that these prisoners marched for a whole month in the midst of them without being recognised. The hundred and twenty thousand men of Kutusoff's army were then reduced to thirty-five thousand. Of Wittgenstein's fifty thousand, scarcely fifteen thousand remained. Wilson asserts, that of a reinforcement of ten thousand men, sent from the interior of Russia with all the precautions which they know how to take against the winter, not more than seventeen hundred arrived at Wilna. But a head of a column was quite sufficient against our disarmed soldiers. They attempted in vain to tally a few of them, and he who had hitherto been almost the only one whose commands had been obeyed in the rout, was now compelled to follow it.

He arrived along with it at Kowno, which was the last town of the Russian empire. Finally, on the 13th of December, after marching forty-six days under a terrible yoke, they once more came in sight of a friendly country. Instantly, without halting or looking behind them, the greater part plunged into, and dispersed themselves, in the forests of Prussian Poland. Some there were, however, who, on their arrival on the allied bank of the Niemen, turned round. There, when they cast a last look on that land of suffering from which they were escaping, when they found themselves on the same spot, whence five months previously their countless eagles had taken their victorious flight, it is said that tears flowed from their eyes, and that they uttered exclamations of grief.

"This then was the bank which they had studded with their bayonets! this the allied country which had disappeared only five months before, under the steps of their immense united army, and seemed to them then to be metamorphosed into moving hills and valleys of men and horses! These were the same valleys, from which, under the rays of a burning sun, poured forth the three long columns of dragoons and cuirassiers, resembling three rivers of glittering iron and brass. And now men, arms, eagles, horses, the sun itself, and even this frontier river, which they had crossed replete with ardour and hope, all have disappeared. The Niemen is now only a long mass of flakes of ice, caught and chained to each other by the increasing severity of the winter. Instead of the three French bridges, brought from a distance of five hundred leagues, and thrown across it with such audacious promptitude, a Russian bridge is alone standing. Finally, in the room of these innumerable warriors, of their four hundred thousand comrades, who had been so often their partners in victory, and who had dashed forward with such joy and pride into the territory of Russia, they saw issuing from these pale and frozen deserts, only a thousand infantry and horsemen still under arms, nine cannon, and twenty thousand miserable wretches covered with rags, with downcast looks, hollow eyes, earthy and livid complexions, long beards matted with the frost; some disputing in silence the narrow passage of the bridge, which, in spite of their small number was not sufficient to the eagerness of their flight; others fleeing dispersed over the asperities of the river, labouring and dragging themselves from one point of ice to another; and this was the whole grand army! Besides, many of these fugitives were recruits who had just joined it."

Two kings, one prince, eight marshals followed by a few officers, generals on foot, dispersed, and without any attendants; finally, a few hundred men of the old guard, still armed, were its remains; they alone represented it.

Or rather, I should say, it still breathed completely and entirely in Marshal Ney. Comrades! allies! enemies! here I invoke your testimony; let us pay the homage which is due to the memory of an unfortunate hero: the facts will be sufficient.

All were flying, and Murat himself, traversing Kowno as he had done Wilna, first gave, and then withdrew the order to rally at Tilsit, and subsequently fixed upon Gumbinnen. Ney then entered Kowno, accompanied only by his aides-de-camp, for all besides had given way, or fallen around him. From the time of his leaving Wiazma, this was the fourth rear-guard which had been worn out and melted in his hands. But winter and famine, still more than the Russians, had destroyed them. For the fourth time, he remained alone before the enemy, and still unshaken, he sought for a fifth rear-guard.

At Kowno the marshal found a company of artillery, three hundred German soldiers who formed its garrison, and General Marchand with four hundred men; of these he took the command. He first walked over the town to reconnoitre its position, and to rally some additional forces, but he found only some sick and wounded, who were endeavouring, in tears, to follow our retreat. For the eighth time since we left Moscow, we were obliged to abandon these *en masse* in their hospitals, as they had been abandoned singly along the whole march, on all our fields of battle, and at all our bivouacs.

Several thousand soldiers covered the marketplace and the neighbouring streets; but they were laid out stiff before the magazines of spirits which they had broken open, and where they drank the cup of death, from which they fancied they were to inhale fresh life. These were the only succours which Murat had left him; Ney found himself left alone in Russia, with seven hundred foreign recruits. At Kowno, as it had been after the disasters of Wiazma, of Smolensk, of the Berezina, and of Wilna, it was to him that the honour of our arms and all the peril of the last steps of our retreat were again confided.

On the 14th, at daybreak, the Russians commenced their attack. One of their columns made a hasty advance from the Wilna road, while another crossed the Niemen on the ice above the town, landed on the Prussian territory, and, proud of being the first to cross its frontier, marched to the bridge of Kowno, to close that outlet upon Ney, and completely cut off his retreat.

The first firing was heard at the Wilna gate; Ney ran thither, with a view to drive away Platof's artillery with his own; but he found his cannon had been already spiked, and that his artillerymen had fled! Enraged, he darted forward, and elevating his sword, would have killed the officer who commanded them, had it not been for his aide-de-camp, who warded off the blow, and enabled this miserable fellow to make his escape.

Ney then summoned his infantry, but only one of the two feeble battalions of which it was composed had taken up arms; it consisted of the three hundred Germans of the garrison. He drew them up, encouraged them, and as the enemy was approaching, was just about to give them the order to fire, when a Russian cannon ball, grazing the palisade, came and broke the thigh of their commanding officer. He fell, and without the least hesitation, finding that his wound was mortal, he coolly drew out his pistols and blew out his brains before his troop. Terrified at this act of despair, his soldiers were completely scared, all of them at once threw down their arms, and fled in disorder.

Ney, abandoned by all, neither deserted himself nor his post. After vain efforts to detain these fugitives, he collected their muskets, which were still loaded, became once more a common soldier, and with only four others, kept facing thousands of the Russians. His audacity stopped them; it made some of his artillerymen ashamed, who imitated their marshal; it gave time to his aide-de-camp Heymès, and to General Gérard to embody thirty soldiers, bring forward two or three light pieces, and to Generals Ledru and Marchand to collect the only battalion which remained.

But at that moment the second attack of the Russians commenced on the other side of the Niemen, and near the bridge of Kowno; it was then half-past two o'clock. Ney sent Ludru, Marchand, and their four hundred men forward to retake and secure that passage. As to himself, without giving way, or disquieting himself farther as to what was passing in his rear, he kept on fighting at the head of his thirty men, and maintained himself until night at the Wilna gate. He then traversed the town and crossed the Niemen, constantly fighting, retreating but never flying, marching after all the others, supporting to the last moment the honour of our arms, and for the hundredth time during the last forty days and forty nights, putting his life and liberty in jeopardy to save a few more Frenchmen. Finally, he was the last of the grand army who quitted that fatal Russia, exhibiting to the world the impotence of fortune against great courage, and proving that with heroes every thing turns to glory, even the greatest disasters.

It was eight o'clock at night when he reached the allied bank. Then it was, that seeing the completion of the catastrophe, Marchand repulsed to the entrance of the bridge, and the road of Wilkowiski which Murat had taken, completely covered with the enemy's troops, he darted off to the right, plunged into the woods, and disappeared.

Chapter 98
Konigsberg

When Murat reached Gumbinnen, he was exceedingly surprised to find Ney already there, and to find, that since it had left Kowno, the army was marching without a rear-guard. Fortunately, the pursuit of the Russians, after they had reconquered their own territory, became slackened. They seemed to hesitate on the Prussian frontier, not knowing whether they should enter it as allies or as enemies. Murat took advantage of their uncertainty to halt a few days at Gumbinnen, and to direct the remains of the different corps to the towns on the borders of the Vistula.

Previous to this dislocation of the army, he assembled the commanders of it. I know not what evil genius it was that inspired him at this council. One would fain believe that it was the embarrassment he felt before these warriors for his precipitate flight, and spite against the Emperor, who had left him with the responsibility of it; or it might be shame at appearing again, vanquished, in the midst of the nations whom our victories had most oppressed; but as his language bore a much more mischievous character, which his subsequent actions did not belie, and as they were the first symptoms of his defection, history must not pass over them in silence.

This warrior, who had been elevated to the throne solely by the right of victory, now returned discomfited. From the first step he took upon vanquished territory, he fancied he felt it everywhere trembling under his feet, and that his crown was tottering on his head. A thousand times during the campaign, he had exposed himself to the greatest dangers; but he, who, as a king, had shown as little fear of death as the meanest soldier of the vanguard, could not bear the apprehension of living without a crown. Behold him then, in the midst of the commanders, whom his brother had placed under his direction, accusing that brother's ambition, which he had shared, in order to free himself from the responsibility which its gratification had involved.

He exclaimed, "that it was no longer possible to serve such a madman! that there was no safety in supporting his cause; that no monarch in Europe could now place any reliance on his word, or in treaties concluded with him. He himself was in despair for having rejected the propositions of the English; had it not been for that, he would still be a great monarch, such as the Emperor of Austria, and the King of Prussia."

Davoust abruptly cut him short. "The King of Prussia, the Emperor of Austria," said he to him, "are monarchs by the grace of God, of time, and the custom of nations. But as to you, you are only a king by the grace of Napoleon, and of the blood of Frenchmen; you cannot remain so but through Napoleon, and by continuing united to France. You are led away by the blackest ingratitude!" And he declared to him that he would immediately denounce his treachery to his Emperor; the other marshals remained silent. They made allowance for the violence of the king's grief, and attributed solely to his inconsiderate heat, the expressions which the hatred and suspicious character of Davoust had but too clearly comprehended.

Murat was put entirely out of countenance; he felt himself guilty. Thus was stifled the first spark of treachery, which at a later period was destined to ruin France. It is with regret that history commemorates it, as repentance and misfortune have atoned for the crime.

We were soon obliged to carry our humiliation to Königsberg. The grand army, which, during the last twenty years, had shown itself successively triumphant in all the capitals of Europe, now, for the first time, re-appeared mutilated, disarmed, and fugitive, in one of those which had been most humiliated by its glory. Its population crowded on our passage to count our wounds, and to estimate, by the extent of our disasters, that of the hopes they might venture to entertain; we were compelled to feast their greedy looks with our miseries, to pass under the yoke of their hope, and while dragging our misfortunes through the midst of their odious joy, to march under the insupportable weight of hated calamity.

The feeble remnant of the grand army did not bend under this burden. Its shadow, already almost dethroned, still exhibited itself imposing; it preserved its royal air; although vanquished by the elements, it kept up, in the presence of men, its victorious and commanding attitude.

On their side, the Germans, either from slowness or fear, received us docilely; their hatred restrained itself under an appearance of coolness; and as they scarcely ever act from themselves, they were obliged to relieve our miseries, during the time that they were looking for a signal. Königsberg was soon unable to contain them. Winter, which had followed us thither, deserted us there all at once; in one night the thermometer fell twenty degrees.

This sudden change was fatal to us. A great number of soldiers and generals, whom the tension of the atmosphere had hitherto supported by a continued irritation, sunk and fell into decomposition. Lariboissière, general-in-chief of the artillery, fell a sacrifice; Eblé, the pride of the army, followed him. Every day and every hour, our consternation was increased by fresh deaths.

In the midst of this general mourning, a sudden insurrection, and a letter from Macdonald, contributed to convert all these sorrows into despair. The sick could no longer cherish the expectation of dying free; the friend was either compelled to desert his expiring friend, the brother his brother, or to drag them in that state to Elbing. The insurrection was only alarming as a symptom; it was put down; but the intelligence transmitted by Macdonald was decisive.

Chapter 99
Riga

On the side where that marshal commanded, the whole of the war had been only a rapid march from Tilsit to Mittau, a display of force from the mouth of the Aa to Dünaburg, and finally, a long defensive position in front of Riga; the composition of that army being almost entirely Prussian, its position and Napoleon's orders so willed it.

It was a piece of great audacity in the Emperor to entrust his left wing, as well as his right and his retreat, to Prussians and Austrians. It was observed, that at the same time he had dispersed the Poles throughout the whole army; many persons thought that it would have been preferable to collect in one point the zeal of the latter, and to have divided the hatred of the former. But we everywhere required natives as interpreters, scouts, or guides, and felt the value of their audacious ardour on the true points of attack. As to the Prussians and Austrians, it is probable that they would not have allowed themselves to be dispersed. On the left, Macdonald, with seven thousand Bavarians, Westphalians, and Poles, mixed with twenty-two thousand Prussians, appeared sufficient to answer for the latter, as well as for the Russians.

In the advance march, there had been at first nothing to do, but to drive the Russian posts before them, and to carry off some magazines. Afterwards there were a few skirmishes between the Aa and Riga. The Prussians, after a rather warm affair, took Eckau from the Russian General Lewis; after which both sides remained quiet for twenty days. Macdonald employed that time in taking possession of Dünaburg, and in getting the heavy artillery brought to Mittau, which was necessary for the siege of Riga.

On the intelligence of his approach, on the 23rd of August, the commander-in-chief at Riga made all his troops march out of the place in three columns. The two weakest were to make two false attacks; the first by proceeding along the coast of the Baltic sea, and the second directly on Mittau; the third, which was the strongest, and commanded by Lewis, was at the same time to retake Eckau, drive back the Prussians as far as the Aa, cross that river, and either capture or destroy the park of artillery.

The plan succeeded as far as beyond the Aa, when Grawert, supported latterly by Kleist, repulsed Lewis, and following the Russians closely as far as Eckau, defeated them there entirely, Lewis fled in disorder as far as the Düna, which he recrossed by fording it, leaving behind a great number of prisoners.

Thus far Macdonald was satisfied. It is even said, that at Smolensk, Napoleon thought of elevating Yorck to the dignity of a marshal of the empire, at the same time that at Vienna he caused Schwartzenberg to be named field-marshal. The claims of these two commanders to the honour were by no means equal.

In both wings, disagreeable symptoms were manifested; with the Austrians, it was among the officers that they were fermenting; their general kept them firm in their alliance with us; he even apprised us of their bad disposition, and pointed out the means of preventing the contagion from spreading among the other allied troops which were mixed with his.

The case was quite the contrary with our left wing; the Prussian army marched without the least after-thought, at the very time that its general was conspiring against us. On the right wing, therefore, during the time of combat, it was the leader who drew his troops after him in spite of themselves, while, on the left wing, the troops pushed forward their commander, almost in spite of himself.

Among the latter, the officers, the soldiers, and Grawert himself, a loyal old warrior, who had no political feelings, entered frankly into the war. They fought like lions on all occasions when their commander left them at liberty to do so; they expressed themselves anxious to wash out, in the eyes of the French, the shame of their defeat in 1806, to reconquer our esteem, to vanquish in the presence of their conquerors, to prove that their defeat was only attributable to their government, and that they were worthy of a better fate.

Yorck had higher views. He belonged to the society of the *Friends of Virtue*, whose principle was hatred of the French, and whose object was their complete expulsion from Germany. But Napoleon was still victorious, and the Prussian afraid to commit himself. Besides, the justice, the mildness, and the military reputation of Macdonald had completely gained the affection of his troops. They said "they had never been so happy as when under the command of a Frenchman."

In fact, as they were united with the conquerors, and shared the rights of conquest with them, they had allowed themselves to be seduced by the all-powerful attraction of being on the side of the victor.

Every thing contributed to it. Their administration was directed by an intendant and agents taken from their own army. They lived in abundance. It was on that very point, however, that the quarrel between Macdonald and Yorck began, and that the hatred of the latter found an opening to diffuse itself.

First of all, some complaints were made in the country against their administration. Shortly after, a French administrator arrived, and either from rivalry or a spirit of justice, he accused the Prussian intendant of exhausting the country by enormous requisitions of cattle. "He sent them," it was said, "into Prussia, which had been exhausted by our passage; the army was deprived of them, and a dearth would very soon be felt in it." By his account, Yorck was perfectly aware of the manoeuvre. Macdonald believed the accusation, dismissed the accused person, and confided the administration to the accuser; Yorck, filled with spite, thought henceforward of nothing but revenge.

Napoleon was then at Moscow. The Prussian was on the watch; he joyfully foresaw the consequences of that rash enterprise, and it appears as if he yielded to the temptation of taking advantage of it, and of getting the start of fortune. On the 29th of September, the Russian general learned that Yorck had uncovered Mittau; and either from having received reinforcements, (two divisions had actually just arrived from Finland,) or from confidence of another kind, he adventured himself as far as that city, which he retook, and was preparing to push his advantage. The grand park of the besiegers' artillery was about to be carried off; Yorck, if we are to believe those who were witnesses, had exposed it, he remained motionless, he betrayed it.

It is said that the chief of his staff felt indignant at this treachery; we are assured that he represented to his general in the warmest terms, that he would ruin himself, and destroy the honour of the Prussian arms; and that, finally, Yorck, moved by his representations, allowed Kleist to put himself in movement. His approach was quite sufficient. But on this occasion, although there was a regular battle, there were scarcely four hundred men put *hors du combat* on both sides. As soon as this petty warfare was over, each army tranquilly resumed its former quarters.

Chapter 100
Macdonald

On the receipt of this intelligence, Macdonald became uneasy, and very much incensed; he hurried from his right wing, where perhaps he had remained too long at a distance from the Prussians. The surprise of Mittau, the danger which his park of artillery had run of being captured, Yorck's obstinacy in refusing to pursue the enemy, and the secret details which reached him from the interior of Yorck's headquarters, were all sufficiently alarming. But the more ground there was of suspicion, the more it was necessary to dissemble; for as the Prussian army was entirely guiltless of the designs of its leader, and had fought readily, and as the enemy had given way, appearances had been preserved, and it would have been wise policy in Macdonald if he had appeared satisfied.

He did quite the contrary. His quick disposition, or his loyalty, were unable to dissemble; he burst out into reproaches against the Prussian general, at the very moment when his troops, satisfied with their victory, were only looking for praise and rewards. Yorck artfully contrived to make his soldiers, whose expectations had been frustrated, participators in the disgust of a humiliation which had been reserved solely for himself.

We find in Macdonald's letters the real causes of his dissatisfaction. He wrote to Yorck, "that it was shameful that his posts were continually attacked, and that in return he had never once harassed the enemy; that ever since he had been in sight of them, he had done no more than repel attacks, and in no one instance had ever acted on the offensive, although his officers and troops were filled with the best dispositions." This last remark was very true, for in general it was remarkable to see the ardour of all these Germans for a cause completely foreign to them, and which might to them even appear hostile.

They all rivalled each other in eagerness to rush into the midst of danger, in order to acquire the esteem of the grand army, and an eulogium from Napoleon. Their princes preferred the plain silver star of French honour to their richest orders. At that time the genius of Napoleon still appeared to have dazzled or subdued every one. Equally munificent to reward as prompt and terrible to punish, he appeared like one of those great centres of nature, the dispenser of all good. In many of the Germans, there was united with this feeling that of a respectful admiration for a life which was so completely stamped with the marvellous, which so much affects them.

But their admiration was a consequence of victory, and our fatal retreat had already commenced; already, from the north to the south of Europe, the Russian cries of vengeance replied to those of Spain. They crossed and echoed each other in the countries of Germany, which still remained under the yoke; these two great fires, lighted up at the two extremities of Europe, were gradually extending towards its centre, where they were like the dawn of a new day; they covered sparks which were fanned by hearts burning with patriotic hatred, and exalted to fanaticism by mystic rites. Gradually, as our disaster approached to Germany, there was heard rising from her bosom an indistinct rumour, a general, but still trembling, uncertain and confused murmur.

The students of the universities, bred up with ideas of independence, inspired by their ancient constitutions, which secure them so many privileges, full of exalted recollections of the ancient and chivalrous glory of Germany, and for her sake jealous of all foreign glory, had always been our enemies. Total strangers to all political calculations, they had never bent themselves under our victory. Since it had become pale, a similar spirit had caught the politicians and even the military. The association of the *Friends of Virtue* gave this insurrection the appearance of an extensive plot; some chiefs did certainly conspire, but there was no conspiracy; it was a spontaneous movement, a common and universal sensation.

Alexander skilfully increased this disposition by his proclamations, by his addresses to the Germans, and by the distinction which he made in the treatment of their prisoners. As to the monarchs of Europe, he and Bernadotte were as yet the only ones who marched at the head of their people. All the others, restrained by policy or feelings of honour, allowed themselves to be anticipated by their subjects.

This infection even penetrated to the grand army; after the passage of the Berezina, Napoleon had been informed of it. Communications had been observed to be going on between the Bavarian, Saxon, and

Austrian generals. On the left, Yorck's bad disposition increased, and communicated itself to a part of his troops; all the enemies of France had united, and Macdonald was astonished at having to repel the perfidious insinuations of an aide-de-camp of Moreau. The impression made by our victories was still however so deep in all the Germans, they had been so powerfully kept under, that they required a considerable time to raise themselves.

On the 15th of November, Macdonald, seeing that the left of the Russian line had extended itself too far from Riga, between him and the Düna, made some feigned attacks on their whole front, and pushed a real one against their centre, which he broke through rapidly as far as the river, near Dahlenkirchen. The whole left of the Russians, Lewis, and five thousand men, found themselves cut off from their retreat, and thrown back on the Düna. Lewis vainly sought for an outlet; he found his enemy every where, and lost at first two battalions and a squadron. He would have infallibly been taken with his whole force, had he been pressed closer, but he was allowed sufficient space and time to take breath; as the cold increased, and the country offered no means of escape, he ventured to trust himself to the weak ice which had begun to cover the river. He made his troops lay a bed of straw and boards over it, in that manner crossed the Düna at two points between Friedrichstadt and Lindau, and re-entered Riga, at the very moment his comrades had begun to despair of his preservation.

The day after this engagement, Macdonald was informed of the retreat of Napoleon on Smolensk, but not of the disorganization of the army. A few days after, some sinister reports brought him the news of the capture of Minsk. He began to be alarmed, when, on the 4th of December, a letter from Maret, magnifying the victory of the Berezina, announced to him the capture of nine thousand Russians, nine standards, and twelve cannon. The admiral, according to this letter, was reduced to thirteen thousand men.

On the third of December the Russians were again repulsed in one of their sallies from Riga, by the Prussians. Yorck, either from prudence or conscience, restrained himself. Macdonald had become reconciled to him. On the 19th of December, fourteen days after the departure of Napoleon, eight days after the capture of Wilna by Kutusoff, in short when Macdonald commenced his retreat, the Prussian army was still faithful.

CHAPTER 101

The Russian Desert

It was from Wilna, on the 9th of December, that orders were transmitted to Macdonald, of which a Prussian officer was the bearer, directing him to retreat slowly upon Tilsit. No care was taken to send these instructions by different channels. They did not even think of employing Lithuanians to carry a message of that importance. In this manner the last army, the only one which remained unbroken, was exposed to the risk of destruction. An order, which was written at the distance of only four days' journey from Macdonald, lingered so long on the road, that it was nine days in reaching him.

The marshal directed his retreat on Tilsit, by passing between Telzs and Szawlia. Yorck, with the greatest part of the Prussians, forming his rear-guard, marched at a day's distance from him, in contact with the Russians, and left entirely to themselves. By some this was regarded as a great error on the part of Macdonald; but the majority did not venture to decide, alleging that in a situation so delicate, confidence and suspicion were alike dangerous.

The latter also said that the French marshal did every thing which prudence required of him, by retaining with him one of Yorck's divisions; the other, which was commanded by Massenbach, was under the direction of the French general Bachelu, and formed the vanguard. The Prussian army was thus separated into two corps, Macdonald in the middle, and the one seemed to be a guarantee to him for the other.

At first every thing went on well, although the danger was every where, in the front, in the rear, and on the flanks; for the grand army of Kutusoff had already pushed forward three vanguards, on the retreat of the Duke of Tarentum. Macdonald encountered the first at Kelm, the second at Piklupenen, and the third at Tilsit. The zeal of the black hussars and the Prussian dragoons appeared to increase. The Russian hussars of Ysum were sabred and overthrown at Kelm. On the 27th of December, at the close of a ten hours' march, these Prussians came in sight of Piklupenen, and the Russian brigade of Laskow; without stopping to take breath, they charged, threw it into disorder, and cut off two of its battalions; next day they retook Tilsit from the Russian commander Tettenborn.

A letter from Berthier, dated at Antonowo, on the 14th of December, had reached Macdonald several days before, in which he was informed that the army no longer existed, and that it was necessary that he should arrive speedily on the Pregel, in order to cover Königsberg, and to be able to retreat upon Elbing and Marienburg. This news the marshal concealed from the Prussians. Hitherto the cold and the forced marches had produced no complaints from them; there was no symptom of discontent exhibited by these allies; brandy and provisions were not deficient.

But on the 28th, when General Bachelu extended to the right, towards Regnitz, in order to drive away the Russians, who had taken refuge there after their expulsion from Tilsit, the Prussian officers began to complain that their troops were fatigued; their vanguard marched unwillingly and carelessly, allowed itself to be surprised, and was thrown into disorder. Bachelu, however, restored the fortune of the day, and entered Regnitz.

During this time, Macdonald, who had arrived at Tilsit, was waiting for Yorck and the rest of the Prussian army, which did not make its appearance. On the 29th, the officers, and the orders which he sent them, were vainly multiplied; no news of Yorck transpired. On the 30th, Macdonald's anxiety was redoubled; it was fully exhibited in one of his letters of that day's date, in which, however, he did not yet venture to appear suspicious of a defection. He wrote "that he could not understand the reason of this delay; that he had sent a number of officers and emissaries with orders to Yorck to rejoin him, but that he had received no answer. In consequence, when the enemy was advancing against him, he was compelled to suspend his retreat; for he could not make up his mind to desert this corps, to retreat without Yorck; and yet this delay was ruinous." This letter concluded thus:—"I am lost in conjectures. If I retreat, what would the Emperor say? what would be said by France, by the army, by Europe? Would it not be an indelible stain on the tenth corps, voluntarily to abandon a part of its troops, and without being compelled to it otherwise than by prudence? Oh, no; whatever may be the result, I am resigned, and willingly devote myself as a victim, provided I am the only one:" and he concluded by wishing the French general "that sleep which his melancholy situation had long denied him."

On the same day, he recalled Bachelu and the Prussian cavalry, which was still at Regnitz, to Tilsit. It was night when Bachelu received the order; he wished to execute it, but the Prussian colonels refused; and they covered their refusal under different pretexts. "The roads," they said, "were not passable. They were not accustomed to make their men march in such dreadful weather, and at so late an hour! They were responsible to their king for their regiments." The French general was astonished, commanded them to be silent, and ordered them to obey; his firmness subdued them, they obeyed, but slowly. A Russian general had glided into their ranks, and pressed them to deliver up this Frenchman, who was alone in the midst of those who commanded them; but the Prussians, although fully prepared to abandon Bachelu, could not resolve to betray him: at last they began their march.

At Regnitz, at eight o'clock at night, they had refused to mount their horses; at Tilsit, where they arrived at two in the morning, they refused to alight from them. At five o'clock in the morning, however, they had all gone to their quarters, and as order appeared to be restored among them, the general went to take some rest. But the obedience had been entirely feigned, for no sooner did the Prussians find themselves unobserved, than they resumed their arms, went out with Massenbach at their head, and escaped from Tilsit in silence, and by favour of the night. The first dawn of the last day of the year 1812, informed Macdonald that the Prussian army had deserted him.

It was Yorck, who, instead of rejoining him, deprived him of Massenbach, whom he had just recalled. His own defection, which had commenced on the 26th of December, was just consummated. On the 30th of December, a convention between Yorck and the Russian general Dibitch was concluded at Taurogen. "The Prussian troops were to be cantoned on their own frontiers, and remain neutral during two months, even in the event of this armistice being disapproved of by their own government. At the end of that time, the roads should be open to them to rejoin the French troops, should their sovereign persist in ordering them to do so."

Yorck, but more particularly Massenbach, either from fear of the Polish division to which they were united, or from respect for Macdonald, showed some delicacy in their defection. They wrote to the marshal. Yorck announced to him the convention he had just concluded, which he coloured with specious pretexts. "He had been reduced to it by fatigue and necessity; but," he added, "that whatever judgment the world might form of his conduct, he was not at all uneasy about; that his duty to his troops, and the most mature reflection, had dictated it to him; that, finally, whatever might be the appearances, he was actuated by the purest motives."

Massenbach excused himself for his clandestine departure. "He had wished to spare himself a sensation which his heart felt too painfully. He had dreaded, lest the sentiments of respect and esteem which he should preserve to the end of his life for Macdonald, should have prevented him from doing his duty."

Macdonald saw all at once his force reduced from twenty-nine thousand to nine thousand, but in the state of anxiety in which he had been living for the last two days, any termination to it was a relief.

Chapter 102

The Defection of Allies

Thus commenced the defection of our allies. I shall not venture to set myself up as a judge of the morality of this event; posterity will decide upon it. As a contemporaneous historian, however, I conceive myself bound not only to state the facts, but also the impression they have left, and such as it still remains, in the minds of the principal leaders of the two corps of the allied army, either as actors or sufferers.

The Prussians only waited for an opportunity to break our alliance, which was forced upon them; when the moment arrived, they embraced it. Not only, however, did they refuse to betray Macdonald, but they did not even wish to quit him, until they had, as it may be said, drawn him out of Russia and placed him in safety. On his side, when Macdonald became sensible that he was abandoned, but without having positive proofs of it, he obstinately remained at Tilsit, at the mercy of the Prussians, sooner than give them a motive of defection, by too speedy a retreat.

The Prussians did not abuse this noble conduct. There was defection on their part, but no treachery; which, in this age, and after the evils they had endured, may still appear meritorious; they did not join themselves with the Russians. When they arrived on their own frontier, they could not resign themselves to aid their conqueror in defending their native soil against those who came in the character of their deliverers, and who were so; they became neutral, and this was not, I must repeat, until Macdonald, disengaged from Russia and the Russians, had his retreat free.

This marshal continued it from Königsberg, by Labiau and Tente. His rear was protected by Mortier, and Heudelet's division, whose troops, newly arrived, still occupied Insterburg, and kept Tchitchakof in check. On the 3rd of January he effected his junction with Mortier and covered Königsberg.

It was, however, a happy circumstance for Yorck's reputation, that Macdonald, thus weakened, and whose retreat his defection had interrupted, was enabled to rejoin the grand army. The inconceivable slowness of Wittgenstein's march saved that marshal; the Russian general, however, overtook him at Labiau and Tente; and there, but for the efforts of Bachelu and his brigade, the valour of the Polish Colonel Kameski, and Captain Ostrowski, and the Bavarian Major Mayer, the corps of Macdonald, thus deserted, would have been broken or destroyed; in that case Yorck would appear to have betrayed him, and history would, with justice, have stigmatized him with the name of traitor. Six hundred French, Bavarians, and Poles, remained dead on these two fields of battle; their blood accuses the Prussians for not having provided, by an additional article, for the safe retreat of the leader whom they had deserted.

The King of Prussia disavowed Yorck's conduct. He dismissed him, appointed Kleist to succeed him in the command, ordered the latter to arrest his late commander, and send him, as well as Massenbach, to Berlin, there to undergo their trial. But these generals preserved their command in spite of him; the Prussian army did not consider their monarch at liberty; this opinion was founded on the presence of Augereau and some French troops at Berlin.

Frederick, however, was perfectly aware of the annihilation of our army. At Smorgoni, Narbonne refused to accept the mission to that monarch, until Napoleon gave him authority to make the most unreserved communication. He, Augereau, and several others have declared that Frederick was not merely restrained by his position in the midst of the remains of the grand army, and by the dread of Napoleon's re-appearance at the head of a fresh one, but also by his plighted faith; for every thing is of a mixed character in the moral as well as the physical world, and even in the most trifling of our actions there is a variety of different motives. But, finally, his good faith yielded to necessity, and his dread to a greater dread. He saw himself, it was said, threatened with a species of forfeiture by his people and by our enemies.

It should be remarked that the Prussian nation, which drew its sovereign toward Yorck, only ventured to rise successively, as the Russians came in sight, and by degrees, as our feeble remains quitted their territory. A single fact, which took place during the retreat, will paint the dispositions of the people, and show how much, notwithstanding the hatred they bore us, they were curbed under the ascendancy of our victories.

When Davoust was recalled to France, he passed, with only two attendants, through the town of ———. The Russians were daily expected there; its population were incensed at the sight of these last Frenchmen. Murmurs, mutual excitations, and finally, outcries, rapidly succeeded each other; the most violent speedily surrounded the carriage of the marshal, and were already about to unharness the horses, when Davoust made his appearance, rushed upon the most insolent of these insurgents, dragged him behind his carriage, and made his servants fasten him to it. Frightened at this action, the people stopped short, seized with motionless consternation, and then quietly and silently opened a passage for the marshal, who passed through the midst of them, carrying off his prisoner.

CHAPTER 103

The Austrians

In this sudden manner did our left wing fall. On our right wing, on the side of the Austrians, whom a well-cemented alliance retained, a phlegmatic people, governed despotically by an united aristocracy, there was no sudden explosion to be apprehended. This wing detached itself from us insensibly, and with the formalities required by its political position.

On the 10th of December, Schwartzenberg was at Slonim, presenting successively vanguards towards Minsk, Nowogrodeck, and Bienitza. He was still persuaded that the Russians were beaten and fleeing before Napoleon, when he was informed at the same moment of the Emperor's departure, and of the destruction of the grand army, but in so vague a manner that he was for some time without any direction.

In his embarrassment he addressed himself to the French ambassador at Warsaw. The answer of that minister authorized him "not to sacrifice another man." In consequence, he retreated on the 14th of December from Slonim towards Bialystok. The instructions which reached him from Murat in the middle of this movement were conformable to it.

About the 21st of December, an order from Alexander suspended hostilities on that point, and as the interest of the Russians agreed with that of the Austrians, there was very soon a mutual understanding. A moveable armistice, which was approved by Murat, was immediately concluded. The Russian general and Schwartzenberg were to manoeuvre on each other, the Russian on the offensive, and the Austrian on the defensive, but without coming to blows.

Regnier's corps, now reduced to ten thousand men, was not included in the arrangement; but Schwartzenberg, while he yielded to circumstances, persevered in his loyalty. He regularly gave an account of every thing to the commander of the army; he covered the whole front of the French line with his Austrian troops, and preserved it. This prince was not at all complaisant towards the enemy; he believed him not upon his bare word; at every position he was about to yield, he would actually satisfy himself with his own eyes, that he only yielded it to a superior force, ready to combat him. In this manner he arrived upon the Bug and the Narew, from Nur to Ostrolenka, where the war terminated.

He was in this manner covering Warsaw, when, on the 22nd of January, he received instructions from his government to abandon the Grand-duchy, to separate his retreat from that of Regnier, and to re-enter Gallicia. To these instructions he only yielded a tardy obedience; he resisted the pressing solicitations and threatening manoeuvres of Miloradowitch until the 25th of January; even then, he effected his retreat upon Warsaw so slowly, that the hospitals and a great part of the magazines were enabled to be evacuated. Finally, he obtained a more favourable capitulation for the Warsavians than they could venture to expect. He did more; although that city was to have been delivered up on the 5th, he only yielded it on the 8th, and thus gave Regnier the start of three days upon the Russians.

Regnier was afterwards, it is true, overtaken and surprised at Kalisch, but that was in consequence of halting too long to protect the flight of some Polish depots. In the first disorder occasioned by this unexpected attack, a Saxon brigade was separated from the French corps, retreated on Schwartzenberg, and was well received by him; Austria allowed it to pass through her territory, and restored it to the grand army, when it was assembled near Dresden.

On the 1st of January, 1813, however, at Königsberg, where Murat then was, the desertion of the Prussians and the intrigues forming by Austria were not known, when suddenly Macdonald's despatch, and an insurrection of the people of Königsberg, gave information of the beginning of a defection, of which it was impossible to foresee the consequences. The consternation was excessive. The seditious movement was at first only kept down by representations, which Ney very soon changed into threats. Murat hastened his departure for Elbing. Königsberg was encumbered with ten thousand sick and wounded, most of whom were abandoned to the generosity of their enemies. Some of them had no reason to complain of it; but prisoners who escaped declared that many of their unfortunate companions were massacred and thrown out of the windows into the streets; that an hospital which contained several hundred sick was set fire to; and they accused the inhabitants of committing these horrid deeds.

On another side, at Wilna, more than sixteen thousand of our prisoners had already perished. The convent of St. Basil contained the greatest number; from the 10th to the 23rd of December they had only received some biscuits; but not a piece of wood nor a drop of water had been given them. The snow collected in the courts, which were covered with dead bodies, quenched the burning thirst of the survivors. They threw out of the windows such of the dead bodies as could not be kept in the passages, on the staircases, or among the heaps of corpses which were collected in all the apartments. The additional prisoners that were every moment discovering were thrown into this horrible place.

The arrival of the Emperor Alexander and his brother was the only thing that put a stop to these abominations. They had lasted for thirteen days, and if a few escaped out of the twenty thousand of our unfortunate comrades who were made prisoners, it was to these two princes they owed their preservation. But a most violent epidemic had already arisen from the poisonous exhalations of so many corpses; it passed from the vanquished to the victors, and fully avenged us. The Russians, however, were living in plenty; our magazines at Smorgoni and Wilna had not been destroyed, and they must have found besides immense quantities of provisions in the pursuit of our routed army.

But Wittgenstein, who had been detached to attack Macdonald, descended the Niemen; Tchitchakof and Platof had pursued Murat towards Kowno, Wilkowiski, and Insterburg; shortly after, the admiral was sent towards Thorn. Finally, on the 9th of January, Alexander and Kutusoff arrived on the Niemen at Merecz. There, as he was about to cross his own frontier, the Russian emperor addressed a proclamation to his troops, completely filled with images, comparisons, and eulogiums, which the winter had much better deserved than his army.

Chapter 104
The Vistula

It was not until the 22nd of January, and the following days, that the Russians reached the Vistula. During this tardy march, from the 3rd to the 11th of January, Murat had remained at Elbing. In this situation of extremity, that monarch was wavering from one plan to another, at the mercy of the elements which were fermenting around him; sometimes they raised his hopes to the highest pitch, at others they sunk him into an abyss of disquietude.

He had taken flight from Königsberg in a complete state of discouragement, when the suspension in the march of the Russians, and the junction of Macdonald with Heudelet and Cavaignac, which doubled his forces, suddenly inflamed him with vain hopes. He, who had the day before believed that all was lost, wished to resume the offensive, and began immediately; for he was one of those dispositions who are making fresh resolutions every instant. On that day he determined to push forward, and the next to flee as far as Posen.

This last determination, however, was not taken without reason. The rallying of the army on the Vistula had been completely illusory; the old guard had not altogether more than five hundred effective men; the young guard scarcely any; the first corps, eighteen hundred; the second, one thousand; the third, sixteen hundred; the fourth, seventeen hundred; added to which, most of these soldiers, the remains of six hundred thousand men, could scarcely handle their arms.

In this state of impotence, with the two wings of the army already detached from us, Austria and Prussia failing us together, Poland became a snare which might close around us. On the other hand, Napoleon, who never consented to any cession, was anxious that Dantzic should be defended; it became necessary, therefore, to throw into it all that could keep the field.

Besides, if the truth must be told, when Murat, when at Elbing, talked of reconstituting the army, and was even dreaming of victories, he found that most of the commanders were themselves worn out and disgusted. Misfortune, which leads to fear every thing, and to believe readily all that one fears, had penetrated into their hearts. Several of them were already uneasy about their rank and their grades, about the estates which they had acquired in the conquered countries, and the greater part only sighed to recross the Rhine.

As to the recruits who arrived, they were a mixture of men from several of the German nations. In order to join us they had passed through the Prussian states, from whence arose the exhalation of so much hatred. As they approached, they encountered our discouragement and our long train of disorder; when they entered into line, far from being put into companies with, and supported by old soldiers, they found themselves left alone, to fight with every kind of scourge, to support a cause which was abandoned by those who were most interested in its success; the consequence was, that at the very first bivouac, most of these Germans disbanded themselves. At sight of the disasters of the army returning from Moscow, the tried soldiers of Macdonald were themselves shaken. Notwithstanding this *corps d'armée*, and the completely fresh division of Heudelet preserved their unity. All these remains were speedily collected into Dantzic; thirty-five thousand soldiers from seventeen different nations, were shut up in it. The remainder, in small numbers, did not begin rallying until they got to Posen and upon the Oder.

Hitherto it was hardly possible for the King of Naples to regulate our flight any better; but at the moment he passed through Marienwerder on his way to Posen, a letter from Naples again unsettled all his resolutions. The impression which it made upon him was so violent, that by degrees as he read it, the bile mixed itself with his blood so rapidly, that he was found a few minutes after with a complete jaundice.

It appeared that an act of government which the queen had taken upon herself had wounded him in one of his strongest passions. He was not at all jealous of that princess, notwithstanding her charms, but furiously so of his royal authority; and it was particularly of the queen, as sister of the Emperor, that he was suspicious.

Persons were astonished at seeing this prince, who had hitherto appeared to sacrifice every thing to glory in arms, suffering himself to be mastered all at once by a less noble passion; but they forgot that, with certain characters, there must be always a ruling passion.

Besides, it was still the same ambition under different forms, and always entering completely into each of them; for such are passionate characters. At that moment his jealousy of his authority triumphed over his love of glory; it made him proceed rapidly to Posen, where, shortly after his arrival, he disappeared, and abandoned us.

This defection took place on the 16th of January, twenty-three days before Schwartzenberg detached himself from the French army, of which Prince Eugene took the command.

Alexander arrested the march of his troops at Kalisch. There, the violent and continued war, which had followed us all the way from Moscow, slackened: it became only, until the spring, a war of fits, slow and intermittent. The strength of the evil appeared to be exhausted; but it was merely that of the combatants; a still greater struggle was preparing, and this halt was not a time allowed to make peace, but merely given to the premeditation of slaughter.

CHAPTER 105
Conclusion

Thus did the star of the North triumph over that of Napoleon. Is it then the fate of the South to be vanquished by the North? Cannot that subdue it in its turn? Is it against nature that that aggression should be successful? and is the frightful result of our invasion a fresh proof of it?

Certainly the human race does not march in that direction; its inclination is towards the south, it turns its back to the north; the sun attracts its regards, its wishes, and its steps. We cannot with impunity turn back this great current of men; the attempt to make them return, to repel them, and confine them within their frozen regions, is a gigantic enterprise. The Romans exhausted themselves by it. Charlemagne, although he rose when one of these great invasions was drawing to a termination, could only check it for a short time; the rest of the torrent, driven back to the east of the empire, penetrated it through the north, and completed the inundation.

A thousand years have since elapsed; the nations of the north have required that time to recover from that great migration, and to acquire the knowledge which is now indispensable to a conquering nation. During that interval, it was not without reason that the Hanse Towns opposed the introduction of the warlike arts into the immense camp of the Scandinavians. The event has justified their fears. Scarcely had the science of modern war penetrated among them, when Russian armies were seen on the Elbe, and shortly after in Italy; they came to reconnoitre these countries, some day they will come and settle there.

During the last century, either from philanthropy or vanity, Europe was eager in contributing to civilize these men of the north, of whom Peter had already made formidable warriors. She acted wisely, in so far as she diminished for herself the danger of falling back into fresh barbarism; if we allow that a second relapse into the darkness of the middle ages is possible, war having become so scientific, that mind predominates in it, so that to succeed in it, a degree of instruction is required, which nations that still remain barbarous can only acquire by civilization.

But, in hastening the civilization of these Normans, Europe has probably hastened the epoch of their next invasion. For let no one believe that their pompous cities, their exotic and forced luxury, will be able to retain them; that by softening them, they will be kept stationary, or rendered less formidable. The luxury and effeminacy which are enjoyed in spite of a barbarous climate, can only be the privilege of a few. The masses, which are incessantly increasing by an administration which is gradually becoming more enlightened, will continue sufferers by their climate, barbarous like that, and always more and more envious; and the invasion of the south by the north, recommenced by Catherine II. will continue.

Who is there that can fancy that the great struggle between the North and the South is at an end? Is it not, in its full grandeur, the war of privation against enjoyment, the eternal war of the poor against the rich, that which devours the interior of every empire?

Comrades, whatever was the motive of our expedition, this was the point which made it of importance to Europe. Its object was to wrest Poland from Russia, its result would have been to throw the danger of a fresh invasion of the men of the north, at a greater distance, to weaken the torrent, and oppose a new barrier to it; and was there ever a man, or a combination of circumstances, so well calculated to ensure the success of so great an enterprise?

After fifteen hundred years of victories, the revolution of the fourth century, that of the kings and nobles against the people, was, in its turn, vanquished by the revolution of the nineteenth century, that of the people against the nobles and kings. Napoleon was born of this conflagration; he obtained such complete power over it, that it seemed as if that great convulsion had only been that of the bringing into the world one man. He commanded the Revolution as if he had been the genius of that terrible element. At his voice she became tranquil. Ashamed of her excesses, she admired herself in him, and precipitating herself into his glory, she had united Europe under his sceptre, and obedient Europe rose at his call to drive back Russia within her ancient limits. It seemed as if the North was in his turn about to be vanquished, even among his own ices.

And yet this great man, with these great circumstances in his favour, could not subdue nature! In this powerful effort to re-ascend that rapid declivity, so many forces failed him! After reaching these icy regions of Europe, he was precipitated from their very summit. The North, victorious over the South in her defensive war, as she had been in the middle ages in her offensive one, now believes herself invulnerable and irresistible.

Comrades, believe it not! Ye might have triumphed over that soil and these spaces, that climate, and that rough and gigantic nature, as ye had conquered its soldiers.

But some errors were punished by great calamities! I have related both the one and the other. On that ocean of evils I have erected a melancholy beacon of gloomy and blood-red light; and if my feeble hand has been insufficient for the painful task, at least I have exhibited the floating wrecks, in order that those who come after us may see the peril and avoid it.

Comrades, my task is finished; it is now for you to bear your testimony to the truth of the picture. Its colours will no doubt appear pale to your eyes and to your hearts, which are still full of these great recollections. But which of you is ignorant that an action is always more eloquent than its description; and that if great historians are produced by great men, the first are still more rare than the last?

ALSO FROM LEONAUR

AVAILABLE IN SOFTCOVER OR HARDCOVER WITH DUST JACKET

SEPOYS, SIEGE & STORM *by Charles John Griffiths*—The Experiences of a young officer of H.M.'s 61st Regiment at Ferozepore, Delhi ridge and at the fall of Delhi during the Indian mutiny 1857.

CAMPAIGNING IN ZULULAND *by W. E. Montague*—Experiences on campaign during the Zulu war of 1879 with the 94th Regiment.

THE STORY OF THE GUIDES *by G. J. Younghusband*—The Exploits of the Soldiers of the famous Indian Army Regiment from the northwest frontier 1847 - 1900..

ZULU: 1879 *by D.C.F. Moodie & the Leonaur Editors*—The Anglo-Zulu War of 1879 from contemporary sources: First Hand Accounts, Interviews, Dispatches, Official Documents & Newspaper Reports.

THE RECOLLECTIONS OF SKINNER OF SKINNER'S HORSE *by James Skinner*—James Skinner and his 'Yellow Boys' Irregular cavalry in the wars of India between the British, Mahratta, Rajput, Mogul, Sikh & Pindarree Forces.

TOMMY ATKINS' WAR STORIES 14 FIRST HAND ACCOUNTS—Fourteen first hand accounts from the ranks of the British Army during Queen Victoria's Empire Original & True Battle Stories Recollections of the Indian Mutiny With the 49th in the Crimea With the Guards in Egypt The Charge of the Six Hundred With Wolseley in Ashanti Alma, Inkermann and Magdala With the Gunners at Tel-el-Kebir Russian Guns and Indian Rebels Rough Work in the Crimea In the Maori Rising Facing the Zulus From Sebastopol to Lucknow Sent to Save Gordon On the March to Chitral Tommy by Rudyard Kipling

CHASSEUR OF 1914 *by Marcel Dupont*—Experiences of the twilight of the French Light Cavalry by a young officer during the early battles of the great war in Europe.

TROOP HORSE & TRENCH *by R. A. Lloyd*—The experiences of a British Lifeguardsman of the household cavalry fighting on the western front during the First World War 1914-18.

THE EAST AFRICAN MOUNTED RIFLES *by C. J. Wilson*—Experiences of the campaign in the East African bush during the First World War.

THE FIGHTING CAMELIERS *by Frank Reid*—The exploits of the Imperial Camel Corps in the desert and Palestine campaigns of the First World War.

AVAILABLE ONLINE AT
www.leonaur.com
AND OTHER GOOD BOOK STORES

ALSO FROM LEONAUR
AVAILABLE IN SOFTCOVER OR HARDCOVER WITH DUST JACKET

THE COMPLEAT RIFLEMAN HARRIS *by Benjamin Harris as told to & transcribed by Captain Henry Curling*—The adventures of a soldier of the 95th (Rifles) during the Peninsular Campaign of the Napoleonic Wars

WITH WELLINGTON'S LIGHT CAVALRY *by William Tomkinson*—The Experiences of an officer of the 16th Light Dragoons in the Peninsular and Waterloo campaigns of the Napoleonic Wars.

SERGEANT BOURGOGNE *by Adrien Bourgogne*—With Napoleon's Imperial Guard in the Russian Campaign and on the Retreat from Moscow 1812 - 13.

SWORDS OF HONOUR *by Henry Newbolt & Stanley L. Wood*—The Careers of Six Outstanding Officers from the Napoleonic Wars, the Wars for India and the American Civil War, with dozens of illustrations by Stanley L. Wood.

SURTEES OF THE RIFLES *by William Surtees*—A Soldier of the 95th (Rifles) in the Peninsular campaign of the Napoleonic Wars.

ENSIGN BELL IN THE PENINSULAR WAR *by George Bell*—The Experiences of a young British Soldier of the 34th Regiment 'The Cumberland Gentlemen' in the Napoleonic wars.

HUSSAR IN WINTER *by Alexander Gordon*—A British Cavalry Officer during the retreat to Corunna in the Peninsular campaign of the Napoleonic Wars.

NAPOLEONIC WAR STORIES *by Sir Arthur Quiller-Couch*—Tales of soldiers, spies, battles & sieges from the Peninsular & Waterloo campaingns.

JOURNALS OF ROBERT ROGERS OF THE RANGERS *by Robert Rogers*—The exploits of Rogers & the Rangers in his own words during 1755-1761 in the French & Indian War.

KERSHAW'S BRIGADE VOLUME 1 *by D. Augustus Dickert*—Manassas, Seven Pines, Sharpsburg (Antietam), Fredricksburg, Chancellorsville, Gettysburg, Chickamauga, Chattanooga, Fort Sanders & Bean Station..

KERSHAW'S BRIGADE VOLUME 2 *by D. Augustus Dickert*—At the wilderness, Cold Harbour, Petersburg, The Shenandoah Valley and Cedar Creek.

A TIGER ON HORSEBACK *by L. March Phillips*—The Experiences of a Trooper & Officer of Rimington's Guides - The Tigers - during the Anglo-Boer war 1899 - 1902.

ALSO FROM LEONAUR
AVAILABLE IN SOFTCOVER OR HARDCOVER WITH DUST JACKET

CAPTAIN OF THE 95th (Rifles) *by Jonathan Leach*—An officer of Wellington's Sharpshooters during the Peninsular, South of France and Waterloo Campaigns of the Napoleonic Wars.

THE KHAKEE RESSALAH *by Robert Henry Wallace Dunlop*—Service & adventure with the Meerut volunteer horse during the Indian mutiny 1857-1858

BUGLER AND OFFICER OF THE RIFLES *by William Green & Harry Smith* With the 95th (Rifles) during the Peninsular & Waterloo Campaigns of the Napoleonic Wars

BAYONETS, BUGLES AND BONNETS *by James 'Thomas' Todd*—Experiences of hard soldiering with the 71st Foot - the Highland Light Infantry - through many battles of the Napoleonic wars including the Peninsular & Waterloo Campaigns

A NORFOLK SOLDIER IN THE FIRST SIKH WAR *by J W Baldwin*—Experiences of a private of H.M. 9th Regiment of Foot in the battles for the Punjab, India 1845-46

A CAVALRY OFFICER DURING THE SEPOY REVOLT *by A.R.D. Mackenzie*—Experiences with the 3rd Bengal Light Cavalry, the Guides and Sikh Irregular Cavalry from the outbreak to Delhi and Lucknow

THE ADVENTURES OF A LIGHT DRAGOON *by George Farmer & G.R. Gleig*—A cavalryman during the Peninsular & Waterloo Campaigns, in captivity & at the siege of Bhurtpore, India

THE COMPLEAT RIFLEMAN HARRIS *by Benjamin Harris as told to & transcribed by Captain Henry Curling*—The adventures of a soldier of the 95th (Rifles) during the Peninsular Campaign of the Napoleonic Wars

THE RED DRAGOON *by W.J. Adams*—With the 7th Dragoon Guards in the Cape of Good Hope against the Boers & the Kaffir tribes during the 'war of the axe' 1843-48

THE LIFE OF THE REAL BRIGADIER GERARD - Volume 1 - THE YOUNG HUSSAR 1782 - 1807 *by Jean-Baptiste De Marbot*—A French Cavalryman Of the Napoleonic Wars at Marengo, Austerlitz, Jena, Eylau & Friedland

THE LIFE OF THE REAL BRIGADIER GERARD Volume 2 IMPERIAL AIDE-DE-CAMP 1807 - 1811 *by Jean-Baptiste De Marbot*—A French Cavalryman of the Napoleonic Wars at Saragossa, Landshut, Eckmuhl, Ratisbon, Aspern-Essling, Wagram, Busaco & Torres Vedras

AVAILABLE ONLINE AT
www.leonaur.com
AND OTHER GOOD BOOK STORES

www.ingramcontent.com/pod-product-compliance
Lightning Source LLC
Chambersburg PA
CBHW020938230426
43666CB00005B/77